WORD ORIGINS

This is not a squirrel (see p. 44).
Detail from *Allegorical "Millefleurs" Tapestry with Animals*,
c. 1530–45, Bruges, Belgium. *The Minneapolis Institute of Arts,
Gift of Mrs. C. J. Martin in Memory of Charles Jairus Martin.*

WORD ORIGINS

... *and How We Know Them*

Etymology for Everyone

ANATOLY LIBERMAN

UNIVERSITY PRESS

2005

OXFORD
UNIVERSITY PRESS

Oxford University Press, Inc., publishes works that further
Oxford University's objective of excellence
in research, scholarship, and education.

Oxford   New York
Auckland   Cape Town   Dar es Salaam   Hong Kong   Karachi
Kuala Lumpur   Madrid   Melbourne   Mexico City   Nairobi
New Delhi   Shanghai   Taipei   Toronto

With offices in
Argentina   Austria   Brazil   Chile   Czech Republic   France   Greece
Guatemala   Hungary   Italy   Japan   Poland   Portugal   Singapore
South Korea   Switzerland   Thailand   Turkey   Ukraine   Vietnam

Copyright © 2005 by Oxford University Press

Published by Oxford University Press, Inc.
198 Madison Avenue, New York, New York 10016
www.oup.com

Library of Congress Cataloging-in-Publication Data
Liberman, Anatoly.
Word origins : and how we know them :
etymology for everyone / Anatoly Liberman.
p. cm.
Includes bibliographical references.
ISBN-13: 978-0-19-516147-2
ISBN-10: 0-19-516147-5
1. English language—Etymology.
I. Title.
PE1574.L43 2005
422—dc22   2004023057

3 5 7 9 8 6 4
Printed in the United States of America
on acid free paper.

Contents

Chapter One

in which the author introduces himself, assumes a confidential tone, and suggests that etymology and entomology are different sciences, or

The Object of Etymology

Jacob Grimm's hours of leisure.—Heifers as moving forces in the progress of etymology.—Pride before the fall.—The simple-minded Nathan Bailey.—Who else if not I?—Past fame counts for nothing.— The search begins.—Words and bugs.

One evening, nearly twenty years ago, I was reading a description of a German dialect. Jacob Grimm, of fairy tale fame, the elder of the two brothers[1] and the founder of just about everything in the science of historical linguistics, used to copy Anglo-Saxon manuscripts before going to bed, but doing so would nowadays be a waste of time, because all Anglo-Saxon, or Old English, texts exist in multiple editions. German dialects have also been discussed in such detail since the Grimms' days that hardly a village remains whose vernacular is not known from a dissertation by a native speaker. It was, therefore, not my goal to copy anything. Like ancient manuscripts, though, tales of rural life told in the peculiar idiom of a remote hamlet have a soothing, even soporific, effect and are good to read after midnight.

In an anecdote recorded in Hesse (the Germans call this province Hessen) and included in the book I had in front of me, the word *Hette* (goat) occurred. Although familiar to me from my earlier studies, it suddenly set me thinking, for at that time I was trying to discover what the Old Scandinavian name *Heiðrún* means (*ð* = *th*, as in Engl. *this; ú* means "long *u*" as in Engl. *who*). According to a myth preserved in a medieval Icelandic lay, *Heiðrún* is a goat from whose udder a never-ceasing stream of mead flows. Each part of *Heiðrún* is transparent (*heið*- [brightness of the sky] or [heath], or [honor], and *rún* [rune]), but the whole makes little sense when applied to a goat. Yet a heavenly goat is a character in many myths, along with she-bears, horses, and harts, so that *Heiðrún*'s name could not be bestowed upon it by chance or by mistake.[2] "Is it possible," I asked myself, "that *Hette* is in some obscure way related to *Heiðrún?*" If this conjecture had turned out to be correct (it did not), *Heiðrún* would have emerged as meaning "goat," a most appropriate name for a goat.

While searching for the origin of *Heiðrún* and *Hette,* of which only the first interested me seriously, I remembered the English noun *heifer.* At present, it rhymes with *deafer* and *zephyr,* but judging by its spelling, at one time it must have had the vowel of *chafer–safer–wafer.* The original meaning of animal names is often "soft," "furry," "horned," "producer," and the like, and for that reason they can be transferred from one creature to another (this subject is discussed at length in Chapter 10). Perhaps "a young cow" in one language, but "goat" in two others?

I looked up *heifer* in Skeat, the *Oxford English Dictionary,*[3] and a few other easily available books. They offered conflicting solutions and gave no references to their competitors or predecessors. Some cited the Old English form *heahfore* and stopped there, others ventured to gloss (that is, translate) *heahfore* as "high-farer" (a puzzling gloss even for a frolicsome calf, let alone a cow that has not calved), but most made do with the unassailable verdict "origin unknown." I kept reading and half a year later came up with a conclusion that was at best half-correct.

It proved to be hard to find any scholarly literature on *heifer.* My adventure began before the Internet became part of everyone's life, but even today I would not have been better off than I was in the eighties, for what do you search for if you are interested in the origin of the word *heifer?* Information is hidden where you least expect to find it. For example, the eleventh edition of the *Encyclopaedia Britannica* has an entry HEIFER, all of which is devoted to the etymology of the word! Surprisingly, the Britannica etymology is different from every other one I have seen. More sources presented themselves almost by chance.

In 1721 Nathan Bailey brought out *An Universal Etymological English Dictionary,* a useful book with a misleading title, because it is not a dictionary whose sole purpose was to discuss word origins, but a dictionary in which words are supplied with concise etymological notes.[4] Since 1721 most English lexicographers felt it to be their duty to say something about the origin of every word. In most cases, they were not equal to the task. Bailey did not realize that etymology should be left to etymologists, partly because in the eighteenth century, anyone could indulge in etymological speculation and be taken seriously. Neither did his immediate followers, but the harm was done, and we are still paying the price for his naiveté and sticking to the format he invented.

Unlike the rather simple-minded Bailey, modern editors of English dictionaries are heirs to a tradition whose beginning, in England, goes back to the seventeenth century. Guesses on the origin of English words fill thousands of pages. A footnote on the derivation of *dwarf* appears in a lengthy article with the uninformative and uninspiring title "Arica XIV,"[5] and another article contains a reasonable explanation of why a certain plant is called *henbane,* though its subject is a forgotten god of death.[6] Since the titles of those excellent contributions do not mention dwarves and poisonous plants, no bibliography of English words will include them, unless someone screens every journal in the world. The authors of etymological dictionaries cannot look through the entire Library of Congress chasing its dusty rainbows; as a result, many crumbs of wisdom will remain undiscovered. It took me half a year to collect an insufficient bibliography of *heifer,* and I shuddered at the thought that the next project would be even more time consuming.

However, etymological dictionaries in which one can find a survey of at least the main ideas on the prehistory of words exist. Goths, once a powerful tribe, were converted to Christianity in the fourth century, and part of the Bible in their native language has come down to us. The best etymological dictionary of Gothic is a model of scholarship:[7] every word in it is discussed with great care, the literature is sifted, and the author's opinion concludes each entry. Similar dictionaries have been written for Sanskrit, Ancient Greek, Latin, and several living languages.[8] The multivolume etymological dictionary of French takes up three shelves.[9] Its Spanish counterpart is less expansive but equally useful.[10] Among the European languages only English stands out as an etymological orphan. The *Oxford English Dictionary* never neglects the questions of origin, but it was written to present the history rather than the undocumented prehistory of English words. The *heifer* episode filled me with great sadness. I decided that, since no one had taken the trouble to write a dictionary comparable to those used by students of Latin, French, and Spanish enjoy, it was my duty to do so.

Self-inflicted wounds hurt the most. Numerous prefaces contain a statement to the effect that if the author had known how long the work would take, he or she would never have undertaken it. But I had no illusions about the magnitude of the enterprise on which I was embarking. The most formidable task consisted in reclaiming as much as possible of what had been said about the origin of English words, from *grig* (a young eel) to *paling man* (a person who sells eels). And this was to be only the first step, for a good bibliography is not a goal but a means to an end. Those who consult an etymological dictionary expect a solution rather than an exhaustive survey.

All the obvious etymologies were discovered long ago. If after so many efforts the origin of *heifer* is still obscure, unknown, uncertain, or disputable, as dictionaries put it, how good was the chance that I would be able to break the spell? And how many such heifers are there? Will all or most of them come home? It is too early to answer this question, but the bibliography, a labor of many years, is ready. Both *grig* and *paling man* are there, among 13,000 other English words, common and rare, recent and archaic, stylistically neutral and slangy. About 17,000 articles, notes, and reviews in 20 languages have been analyzed and put to use.

Quite naturally, I have not done all the work alone. Over fifty volunteers leafed through popular and semipopular periodicals, about as many smart undergraduates examined linguistic journals, and I skimmed three centuries' worth of articles in every language I know and in a few languages I don't. No one expected that we would hit a gold mine, but we did. Thought-provoking conjectures, clever parallels, and persuasive solutions turned up by the hundred. They lay buried in stray notes and fugitives magazines with titles like *The Cheshire Sheaf* and *The Nineteenth Century,* in notes on Faroese bird names, and in observations of Dutch school slang. At all times some people believe that they can coax an etymology out of a word by looking hard at it. Amateurs do not like to be told that historical linguistics is an area for specialists, and specialists seldom agree on anything. The journals mentioned above contain tons of etymological chaff, but even erroneous ideas are useful to know, for when dealing with an inscrutable word, people tend to offer the same wrong explanation of its origin over and over again, and it will do them good to learn at the outset that they are wasting their time.

Our team worked with sustained vigor and "clenched resolve," to use Stanhope Worsley's phrase, quoted by Skeat. We spent long hours at the library reading and copying. Illegible microfilms were turned into regular books, permission to copy eighteenth-century journals was asked for and granted, and musty tomes came to my office from all over the world, the pages of many of them uncut. Rumors of a new dictionary began to circulate in the neighboring streets. At least once a month perfect strangers sent me orders for the unwritten first volume, and after I published an article on the etymology of the *F*-word, I became the recipient of e-mails I did not dare answer; but the number of volunteers increased, and each of them was exposed to a crash course on etymology.[11] It was during one such session that the idea of this book occurred to me. As an author, I had already experienced a few moments of ultimate satisfaction. A copy of my book on Scandinavian linguistics had been stolen from an exhibit at the Faculty Club (a unique case, my publisher assured me), and my other book was twice chosen by students as a Christmas gift (both times I autographed it). I could certainly hope for a larger audience with a subject like etymology.

However, there was a problem. Most people who expressed their interest in my work were unable to distinguish between etymology and entomology. Some said *etymiology,* which added philosophical or medical dimensions to the science I study. As is known, entomology is all about insects. Etymology also deals with them, but in its own way. For example, the origin of the word *bug* has bothered (one might even say bugged) researchers for decades. However, despite some overlap, etymology and entomology should be kept separate. I was surprised to discover how well everyone remembered what *entomology* meant and how they still thought that I was an entomologist. Ignorant of the causes of the confusion, I ascribed it to some twist of the Midwestern mentality, incomprehensible to an outsider. One can therefore imagine my joy when in looking through the journal *College English,* I ran into an article by James T. Barrs, who in 1962 was an Associate Professor of English at Northeastern University, Boston.[12] This is the beginning of his article.

> The title of one of my television lectures over Boston's educational station WGBH-TV back in 1958 was "Folk Etymology." But somewhere along the line the title was garbled, and it appeared on the Station's printed and circulated program as "Folk Entomology." Now, I don't propose to discuss on this occasion the place of insect-study in linguistics; but since the word *entomology* has appeared in the ointment, so to speak, let's look at it for a moment. Its main part is the Greek word *éntomos,* which means "insect" or, literally, "something cut in"—the main part, in turn, of *éntomos* is *tom,* whose root means "to cut or segment;" indeed, the *sect* of the word *insect,* from Latin, means "cut" too.

It appeared that at least on one coast, the confusion is the same as in the state of Minnesota. I realized that I was in good company. *Etymology,* like *entomology,* goes back to Ancient Greek. *Étumos* means "true," and *étumon* referred to the true, or original, meaning of a word. The noun *etumología* has also been recorded.[13] In the next chapter, it will be shown that the true, or original, meaning of a word is an ambiguous concept, but the etymological ointment contains no fly. Fortified with this knowledge, we can now turn to the history of etymology, its principles, and its methods.

Chapter Two

in which another important distinction, this time between words and things, is made, or

The Thing and the Sign

The day's eye.—Adam in Paradise.—Plato in Greece.—Socrates, Cratylus, and Hermogenes have a talk.—The knowledge of things cannot be derived from their names.—The Greeks' ignorance of foreign languages.—Language and fashion.—"People create."—St. Cecilia and her name.—*Homo* and *humus, god* and *good.*

The word *daisy* first surfaced in a manuscript going back to the year 1000, that is, to the time about two centuries after the emergence of the earliest texts in the English language.[1] It had to be coined before 1000, of course, to get into the manuscript, but probably after 450, the date given for the invasion of Britain by Germanic (or Teutonic, to use an old-fashioned term) tribes, since no word like *daisy* has been recorded on the continent. During the period to which we now refer as Old English, people called the daisy *dæges ēage* (pronounced approximately as *'day-ez éay-e,* with *ea* as in the French name *Réamur).*[2] *Dæges ēage* was a phrase that meant "day's eye," either because the daisy resembles the sun (which is indeed the eye of the day) or because it covers the yellow disk in the evening and opens it in the morning.

Who coined this remarkable word? A child discovering the world and, Adam-like, creating naïve and beautiful metaphors?[3] Or a farmer who needed a new plant name and used the resources of his mother tongue? The poetry of the Anglo-Saxons and related tribes was full of circumlocutions like *day's eye* (sun); in medieval Scandinavia they were called kennings. But the person who was the first to say *dæges ēage* need not have been a poet: long exposure to kennings and the abundance of compounds in conversational Old English would have made the task of producing such circumlocutions easy.

In other countries, people called the daisy or a plant like it "earth apple" (such as Greek *khamáimelon*),[4] from which, via Latin and French, English has *c(h)amomile,* or even "gooseflower" (such as German *Gänseblümchen*). *Dæges ēage* could not have been the first name of this flower, but it suppressed its synonyms and stayed until today. Can we imagine a golden age when all the words were young and as transparent as "day's eye"? If such an age existed, it was one of perfect harmony: things revealed their nature in words, and words captured the most salient features of things. Happy cave dwellers exchanged nosegays of day's eyes, and no one needed lessons in etymology.

The question about the first human words has occupied philosophers and linguists since antiquity. Greek scholars often discussed it, as follows from the extant documents. The most famous of them is Plato's dialogue *The Cratylus,* which has come down to us intact. Two opinions clash in it. Cratylus believes in a bond between language, thought, and reality and insists that words reflect some properties of things. We remember the history of *daisy* and tend to agree with him. Cratylus's opponent Hermogenes maintains the opposite view. According to him, the names of all things are the result of convention, and again we agree, for, if all words are natural, why are things called differently in different languages, and why do the same groups of sounds have divergent meanings in one and the same language? English, for example, has thousands of homonyms. We would also like to know how *day* and *eye* got their names and whether all words are, like *daisy,* contractions of longer units.

Hermogenes invites Socrates to resolve the dispute. All of them—Socrates, Cratylus, and Hermogenes—were Plato's teachers. Socrates sides with neither opponent but applies his dialectics to rise above both rigid formulations ("all words are natural" versus "all words are conventional") and reconciles them by offering a deeper truth. He begins by pointing out that since words are instruments with whose help we teach and separate things, they must be treated like all other instruments and tools, for example, a borer, a sail, or a loom. First of all, they must be functional or usable (a point for Cratylus). Secondly, they must be (or must have been) "made" by specialists. A smith forges swords, while a wordsmith coins words. Socrates has great respect for wordsmiths and calls them lawgivers. A lawgiver suggests names that bring out the essence of the thing named (another point for Cratylus). However, a smith need not make swords of the same iron; likewise, different legislators will use different syllables for naming the same object. Every word, if it serves its purpose, is usable, which is not the same as natural; it is not predestined to have the form we happen to know. At last Hermogenes scores a point. Moreover, smiths may be skillful or inept, and some lawgivers come up with inappropriate names. As time goes on, words deteriorate, and many of them lose their former clarity. Words, we are given to understand, are natural only insofar as they reflect the first lawgivers' vision of the world. The knowledge of things cannot be derived from names (let us remember this statement).

Socrates assumes that all names owe their existence to legislation and that lawgivers had prior knowledge of reality. Hermogenes's standing is now as good as Cratylus's. It should be borne in mind that the three men are discussing language, but they mean only Greek. Barbarians also speak, but what kind of speech is it? The very word *barbarian* means "someone who says *bar-bara,* a babbler or a stammerer producing unintelligible gibberish." The Greeks must have learned some Phrygian from their slaves, the more so because the two languages were rather similar. Aeschylos cited a few exotic words from other countries, and Aristophanes reproduced the Phrygian accent in his comedies, but their contemporaries did not value the mastery of foreign languages, nor did they think much of Latin.[5]

Hermogenes, a down-to-earth man, is not content with abstract theorizing, and Socrates (or Plato, Socrates's mouthpiece) satisfies his curiosity and explains the origin of numerous words. Today we are confident that his derivations are fanciful, for we know more about the origin of Greek than the ancients did. This is a fact, not hubris. Socrates believed that one could separate a Greek word into elements, add a sound (he said *letter*), subtract a sound, or scramble the letters a bit and arrive at a word's true, original meaning, as the lawgivers had intended us to see it. Greek words are sometimes very long. Socrates would have been puzzled by a sentence like *come and have a look at my cats and dogs.* Even centuries ago, when most native English words were di- or trisyllabic, they never had the length that would be enough for a Germanic Socrates. Nor did such a thinker ever live among the Anglo-Saxons. Although Socrates's explanations were not fully dependent on contraction and trickery, for the moment we will pass over his other methods of etymologizing.[6]

Ancient lawgivers must have been endowed with the power of articulate speech, but we are left in the dark as to who taught them to speak. Socrates did not realize the tremendous complexity of the problem he approached. We do; yet we still wonder how the first words were coined. We again turn to the child (farmer, poet, scholar?) who examined a yellow flower and called it day's eye. That person was not a lawgiver and could not make other people adopt the new name. Language is like many other human institutions—for example, fashion. The news of an invention spreads, and acceptance or rejection follows. Every novelty must be an act of an individual, despite the fact that in language, anonymous tradition reigns supreme, and inventors of the past may not have been aware of their input. In literature, the concept of individual authorship also developed late, and originality is a recent virtue.[7]

Ages of recitation could polish tales like the *Iliad* because there was something to polish. Jacob Grimm, whose name graces the first page of this book, used to say: "People create."[8] The question is how they do it. If every word is the product of an individual act of creativity, wordsmiths, it is reasonable to assume, did not use the material at their disposal haphazardly, though we notice with surprise that the origin of some words launched within the last decades, *glitch* and *nerd* among them, is no less obscure than that of *come* and *look,* which have existed from time immemorial. We could have enlightened Cratylus and Hermogenes on many things, but not on the process of original word creation. Even Rudyard Kipling fails us here. Two of his charming and edifying *Just So Stories* are entitled "How the First Letter Was Written" ("Once upon a most early time was a Neolithic man. He was not a Jute or an Angle, or even a Dravidian, which he might well have been, Best Beloved, but never mind why.

He was a Primitive, and he lived cavily in a Cave, and he wore very few clothes, and he couldn't read and he couldn't write and he didn't want to, and except when he was hungry he was quite happy") and "How the Alphabet was Made" (the characters are again the Neolithic man and the author's daughter). As ill luck would have it, no story exists about the creation of the first words.

Socrates's most important conclusions are two: (1) words are hallowed by convention, but they are not "natural," and (2) the knowledge of things cannot be derived from their names (a thesis emphasized above). Both of his conclusions were forgotten or rejected in antiquity and in the Middle Ages. Cratylus's arguments are attractive, and it is no wonder that later generations have reinvented them time and again. At a certain stage, etymology lost its cognitive value altogether and became part of the science of things rather than words. Here is the introduction to Chaucer's tale of the Second Nun, translated from the original Latin:

Cecilia is as though "lily of heaven" *[celi lilia]* or "way of the blind" *[cecis via]* or from "heaven" *[celo]* and "Leah" [lya]. Or *Cecilia* is as though "free of blindness" *[cecitate carens]*. Or she is named from heaven *[celo]* and *leos,* that is, "people." For she was a "lily of heaven" because of her virgin chastity. Or she is called "lily" because she had the white of purity, the green of conscience, the odor of good fame. She was "way of the blind" because of her teaching by example, "heaven" for her devoted contemplation, "Leah" for her constant business. Or she is called "heaven" because, as Isidore[9] says, the scientists have said that heaven is swift, round, and burning. So also she was swift through her solicitous work, round through her perspicuity, burning through her flaming love. She also was "free of blindness" because of the brilliant light of her wisdom. She was also "heaven of people" *[celum + leos]* because in her, as in a heaven, people wanting a role model might in a spiritual way gaze upon her sun, moon, and stars, that is, the far-sightedness of her wisdom, the greatness of her faith, and the variety of her virtues.

This "etymology" of Cecilia's name appears in the preface to Jacopo da Varagine's account of the life of St. Cecilia included in his mid-thirteenth-century anthology of saints' lives, *The Golden Legend.*[10]

Cecil goes back to Lat. *Caecilius,* the name of a Latin gens (patrilinear clan), in which *-il-* is a suffix, the second *-i-* a marker of the declension, and -*us* an ending. *Cecilia* is a feminine counterpart of *Cecilius*. *Ceac-*, as in *caecus,* the root of *Caecilius,* means "blind." It need not concern us how the gens got its name and whether in the beginning it had any religious significance (contained the memory of ritual mutilation or was the cognomen of a blind god) or whether a non-fictitious blind man founded the clan. Suffice it to say that the connection between *Caecilius ~ Caecilia* and *caecus* is real and speakers of Latin could not miss it. That is why after her martyrdom Cecilia became a patron saint of the blind.

Jacopo da Varagine would have been unimpressed by this information and perhaps dismissed it as ignorant nonsense. Like his predecessors, he attempted to derive the knowledge of things from words. Proper names lend themselves to quasi-etymological exercises especially well, and the characters in Plato's dialogue also paid tribute to them. For many centuries linguistics constituted part of theology and philosophy and could not have an object of its own. Nor did Jacopo pursue a linguistic goal. Any of the combinations he offered seemed equally valid to him because he looked on the name *Cecilia* as a charade, and to the extent that the whole meant something good and pure he accepted the interpretation. By chance, not all of his guesses are wrong: "way of the blind" and "free of blindness" refer to the real root of Cecilia's name, though "blind" had to be twisted into "the way of blindness" and alternately into "free from, devoid of blindness," an opposite concept.

Such etymologies are easy to propose, especially when the elements are borrowed from several languages.[11] For example, where did the word *student* come from? Perhaps it is the sum of English *stew* and Latin *dent* (tooth), since students are usually poor and cannot afford steak. But students are tough and hardened young people, wholly devoted to learning *(stud + ent[ire]);* compare the title of James T. Farrell's novel *Studs Lonigan.* Still another venue opens up if we add *stud(y)* and *ent(irely).* In similar fashion, paper may be called paper because, when we buy it, we *pay per* sheet. Etymologies of this type do not presuppose verification; they exist to justify the name rather than find out its ancient meaning.

We have nothing to learn from Jacopo. But let us not hurry. Someone called a plant with a yellow disk "day's eye." That person was a good wordsmith. There must have been others like him. About a dozen etymologies of Greek *theos*[12] and Latin *deus* (god) have come down to us from the Middle Ages (both words are familiar from Engl. *theology* and *deity*). It was taken for granted that *theós* and *deus* are different pronunciations of the same word (this idea proved to be wrong) and that the name of the Lord had something to do with His greatness, omnipotence, omniscience, and so forth—a reasonable conjecture on the face of it. Some fruits of medieval scholarship lacked juice even in their prime, as when *deus* was derived from *dans eternam uitam suis* ([the one] giving eternal life to his own.) Others were astute. For example, *theós* was compared with *théo* (to move fast), *thermós* (warm), and *áithos* (fire, flame),[13] among others, and Latin *homo* (man) was traced to *humus* (earth).

Today we believe that *theós* and *deus* meant "spirit" and "shining, glorious," respectively, though the origin of *theós* has not been fully clarified. Our solutions have the support of well-tested procedures; they are not fantasies, but our glosses do not differ in principle from "rushing," "flaming," or "aerial." *Homo* and *humus* are indeed related.[14] Unlike medieval scholars, we do not connect Engl. *god* and *good* and can prove our thesis, but even here our answers would have been acceptable to them: *god,* we think, is either "one receiving sacrifices" (the preferred derivation) or "one called upon." The etymology of *god* does not bring out the essence of the Godhead but gives a clue to why *god* is called *god.* People of the Middle Ages may not have appreciated this all-important difference but would have had no serious objections to our etymologies.

An etymologist, of necessity, shuttles between words and things. Words may be conventional, but we do not want them to be arbitrary, and for this reason the study of words is inseparable from the study of things. The question is not whether but how the two areas interact. Linguists planning to investigate the origin of *knife, sheep,* and *witch* cannot be experts in ancient weaponry, cattle breeding, and magic, but without going into prehistoric warfare, primitive economy, and superstitions they will not discover what kind of a tool a knife was (was it short or long, homemade or imported, meant for stabbing, cutting, or thrusting?), whether the animal called "sheep" got its name at the time when it served mainly as a provider of meat or wool (or both), and whether a witch offered her services as a healer or was shunned as an evildoer. Only an exact knowledge of things will allow us to reconstruct the process of name giving.

People were satisfied with the ancestor of Engl. *ewe* for thousands of years, but something made them coin *sheep* (it had a different pronunciation then), whereas Scandinavians added *fær* (approximately "wool animal"; *æ* had the phonetic value of *a* in Engl. *bag,* and *ð,* it will be remembered, sounded like *th* in *this*) and *sauðr*[15] to their vocabulary; *sauðr,* which is akin to Engl. *seethe,* must have been food. Every time the function of the domesticated animal changed, it acquired a new name. According to one theory, *sheep* has the same root as *shave;* then, like *fær,* it belongs in the epoch of wool shearing, even though shave and shear are different things. The oldest meaning of *ewe* was probably "sheep with lambs," but this is only an intelligent guess. *Knife, sheep,* and *witch* are nouns. Verbs and adjectives present the same picture. To penetrate the origin of *kiss,* we must know whether the verb denoted ceremonial greeting or had erotic connotations and when people began to kiss. By comparison, the history of *hiss* and *piss* is easier.

Languages differ dramatically in their use of color terms, and associations that conjured up such terms also differ. Engl. *white* is akin to *wheat,* but it is wheat (or more probably flour made from it) that borrowed its name from *white,* not the other way around. To learn where *white* came from, we must go further afield (so to speak). *Green* was, in all likelihood, derived from the root of *grow* and designated the color of vegetation. Words name and classify things for the speaking individual *(homo loquens).* They do not merge with things, but it would be strange if the original meaning of words could be disclosed without recourse to the properties of the objects to which they stick.

Let us admire Socrates who was fluent only in Greek but understood so much about language and repeat the watchword of etymological research: original "names" were conventional (for other sounds could have expressed the same meaning) but not arbitrary (the speakers who chose those sounds had a reason to do so). The entire science of etymology is centered on finding that reason.

Chapter Three

*which descends from philosophical heights to cooing
doves and mooing cows and explains in passing
that sauce for the goose is sauce for the gander
and that boys will be boys, or*

Sound Imitative Words

The *ku-ku* nest.—On kites and cows.—Onomatopoeic, or echoic,
words.—Geese gaggle, hens cackle.—The horror and grandeur of *gr.*—
A foster home for unrelated words.—From *clock* to *cloak.* — A few
pedestrian etymologies.—Chuchundra's dangerous example.—*Jump*—
thump—*dump.* Boys, bellboys, and devils.

If it is true that at the dawn of civilization, things were not named
pall-mall and *beriberi* because it occurred to someone to use arbitrary groups of sounds to designate things, we may hope to penetrate
the mental processes of our remote ancestors. "The namegiver," Plato
says, "is the rarest of craftsmen among men." He "must understand
how to render the naturally fitting name for each thing into letters
and syllables . . ." *Naturally* is the key word in his dictum.

It is natural to hear *ku-ku* and call the bird saying *ku-ku* a *cuckoo.*
Many words of this type must have been in circulation when the
world was young. Their origin seems to need no explanation, but
their simplicity is often misleading. About two thousand years ago, the
cuckoo was called approximately **gaukaz* (*au* as in *Audi;* an asterisk
means that such a form has not been attested but can be reconstructed).
Icelanders still say *gaukur,* and earlier the root of this word had *ū.*
From the beginning of creation, *cuckoos* have not changed their song,
and people have always heard something like *koo(k)-koo(k)* or *goo(k)-*
goo(k) in it. If Old Engl. *gēac* had survived, it would have been pronounced *yeak* today (rhyming with *beak*) and the connection between

15

the bird and its name would have all but disappeared. This may be the reason the French word supplanted the native one.

Kite is universally believed to contain an imitation of the bird's cry, though here the situation is more complicated. The oldest form of *kite* must have been **kūtja,* and the name was probably applied to the screech owl (German *Kauz,* closely related to *kite,* means "barn owl"). The sound *u* is prominent in the cry of the owl. The Old English for *owl* was *ūle.* In French, the owl is called *hibou,* in German it was once called *ūwila,* and in Modern German it is simply *Uhu.* But what is the origin of *k* and *t?* Perhaps they came from the word *cat,* because the owl is often called "cat"; for example, French *chathuant* is literally "screeching cat." However, *kūt-* resembles *ku-ku,* the English verb *caw,* French *chouette* (another word for "owl"; a diminutive of Old French *choe*), and the names of many birds with the sounds *ki, kit-* and *kiw-* in their roots. Once the name of the owl was transferred to the kite, famous for its graceful flight (compare Engl. *glede,* an archaic synonym of *kite,* that is, "glider") rather than for a shrill plaintive voice, and **ū* (as in Engl. *oo*) changed to the vowel of the modern word, the connection between the sound and the name of the kite was lost.

Moo turned up in an English text only in the sixteenth century. Surely, it is older, but no contemporary of Kind Alfred or Chaucer recorded it, for where does such a word occur outside children's stories and essays on etymology? Both genres were sadly underdeveloped in Medieval English literature. The German for "cow" is *Kuh* (pronounced *koo*); its Dutch and most of its Scandinavian cognates (that is, related forms going back to the same parent) sound like the German word (in English, *cow* goes back to *cū*), and it has been suggested that *moo* arose under the influence of *Kuh* and so forth. Indeed, we hear *mmm* rather than *moo* from cows, but since a word, however primitive, must contain at least one syllable, some vowel had to follow *m.* The consonant *m* is produced by compressing the lips, and people protruded them, in order to finish the word. Besides this, *mū* describes lowing in a number of languages in which the name of the cow bears no resemblance to *kū.* Most likely, *moo* is a true imitative word and owes nothing to the rhyme *mū ~ kū.*

The *Oxford English Dictionary* informs us that even *miaow* is possibly of French origin. The spelling *miaow* may owe its existence to French. Other than that, neither cats nor French speakers had to be imported from the continent to teach the English the sound the cat makes. Words based on the imitation of natural sounds are called onomatopoeias (from Greek *onomatopoiiā: ónoma* "name" + *poi-* [make,] as in *poet*,[1] literally "maker"). For the adjective *onomatopoeic* James A. H. Murray, the main editor of the *Oxford English Dictionary*, coined the synonym *echoic*. Onomatopoeias (echoic words) play a noticeable role in our vocabulary. It is not due to chance that the name of the bird whose cry we associate with *ga-ga* (that is, with gaggling) begins with *g-*. *Goose, gander,* and *gannet* are closely related because the earliest form of *goose* was **gansaz,* and the German for *goose* is still *Gans*. Likewise, the noun *crow* is from the verb *crow* (Old Engl. *crāwan*); *caw-caw, kar-kar,* and *kra-kra* are the usual renderings of the crow's voice. *Rook* (Old Engl. *hrōc*) has a similar history. The difference between *crā(w)-* and *hrōc* is small. Neither the crow nor the rook is a warbler; hence the raucous combinations *kr-, hr-*. *Crane, grackel,* and the verb *crack* are three more siblings of *crow* and *rook*.

The consonants and vowels of human speech cannot do justice to animal cries. People try their best but come up with different results. For *cock-a-doodle-do* German has *kikiriki,* Russian *kukareku,* and French *cocorico*. The ear of English speakers missed *r* here (as it did in *caw*). The same happened to the rendering of the dove's note. Most languages use syllables like *gir(r), gur(r),* and *kur(r)* for this purpose. English, however, resorted to *coo,* which cannot have been the first attempt at imitating the dove, for, like *miaow,* it goes back to the seventeenth century. The voices of French doves and pigeons are described by the verb *roucouler.* It is a native verb. Only English cuckoos and cats are sufficiently genteel to express themselves in a foreign language.

Geese gaggle, hens cackle, pigs, rather uncharacteristically, say *oink-oink,* and little pig Robinson, the hero of Beatrix Potter's long story, when he was kidnapped by sailors, cried in despair *wee-wee,* "like a little Frenchman."[2] The witty simile is her own, but the source of the cry is easy to guess: "This little pig said, 'Wee, wee! / I can't find my way home.'" The situations in the book and the nursery rhyme ("This Little Pig Went to Market") are similar. Usually the pig's grunt, when people attempt to reproduce it, begins with *gr-* or *khr-*. One cannot expect consistency or precision in such matters, but in naming the inhabitants of the animal world humans make the widest use of onomatopoeia. Bird names depend heavily on it.[3] The same is true of many verbs denoting our own utterances and multifarious noises. *Croak* and *creak* resemble *crow* and *rook*. *Squawk* (to give a loud harsh cry), *squeak, squeal, screech, scream* and *shriek* make up a distinct group, and so do *whine, whinny,* and *whimper.*

The origin of words that reproduce natural sounds is self-explanatory. French or English, *cockoo* and *miaow* are unquestionable onomatopoeias. If we assume that *growl* belongs with *gaggle, cackle, croak,* and *creak* and reproduces the sound it designates, we will be able to go a bit further. Quite a few words in the languages of the world begin with *gr-* and refer to things threatening or discordant. From Scandinavian, English has *grue,* the root of *gruesome* (an adjective popularized by Walter Scott), but Old Engl. *gryre* (horror) existed long before the emergence of *grue-*. The epic hero Beowulf fought Grendel, an almost invincible monster. Whatever the origin of the name, it must have been frightening even to pronounce it.

Things that are grim do not bode well, either. *Grumble* is a lighter, less menacing variant of *growl,* and *grouch* is its next of kin. *Grouch* surfaced only in the twentieth century in American English, but *grutch,* arguably from French, was recorded 700 years earlier. A doublet of *grutch* is *grudge,* originally again "to murmur, grumble." Another synonym of *grudge* (to grumble) is *grouse.* The first example of it in the *Oxford English Dictionary* has the date 1892 and is marked "army slang." The verb was known so little in the eighteen-nineties that even the extremely complete *Century Dictionary*[4] missed it. Later dictionaries call it informal. Regardless of whether *grouse* is related to *grouch, grutch,* and *grudge,* it looks like one of them. A grin is today a mischievous smile, but in older days to grin meant "to scowl, to show the teeth as a sign of anger," the way a wild beast does. Likewise, *grimace,* which did a lot of wandering from language to language before it reached English, has the same root as *grin*. Finally, there is *groan,* another loud deep sound of grief and pain, and *grief* in its definition reminds us that fright, pain, and distress go together. Therefore, coming across Old English *grorn* (sorrow) and *grētan* (to weep) causes no surprise. From *grētan* we have Scots *greet* (the same meaning) and via French *regret*. *Greet* (to salute) once meant "to call upon, cry out, assail" (so in the languages related to English), and it may ultimately be of the same origin as *greet* (to weep).

We arrive at the conclusion that *hr-* and *gr-* tend to occur in numerous words whose meaning can be understood as "(to produce) a nonsonorous sound (of discontent)." An association between *kr-, khr-,* and *gr-* with a growl or low roar is universal. French *crier,* from which English has *cry,* is, most likely, an onomatopoeic verb despite its resemblance to Latin *quirītāre* (to cry aloud, wail). It compares easily with English *grate* (as in *grating sound,* another wanderer, like *grimace,* from Germanic to Romance and back to English), Russian *krik* (shout) (noun), and Welsh *crych* (raucous); for completeness' sake, Icelandic *hrikja* (to creak) may be added. *Gr-* made people cower in the nineteenth century, as it did in the days of Grendel and the "grinning" warriors of old. When David Copperfield decided to flee from his stepfather's business (a firm called Murdstone and Grinby!) and seek the protection of his aunt, he covered the distance from London to Dover on foot. Along the way, he sold most of his clothes to ragmen. One of the shopkeepers bargained furiously, and nothing dismayed David more than the old man's repeated shout "Goroo, goroo," with which he concluded every offer.

The criteria for calling a word echoic are not clearly defined. *Grunt* is an onomatopoeia. A grumpy person may be prone to growling and grousing, though even without *gr-* in his or her name such an individual would be equally obnoxious. Consider *hump,* which rhymes with *grump* and means "a fit of ill temper," its soft sound texture notwithstanding. *The Oxford Dictionary of English Etymology* suggests that this sense of *hump* is rooted in the idea of humping the back in sulkiness.[5] Whether such a conjecture deserves credence is a matter of opinion. Kipling had a similar explanation of the origin of the giraffe's humps; his giraffe was irascible and spiteful. Another grumpy growler is the cur. Old Icelandic *kurra* means "to grumble." The chances that *cur* is an onomatopoeic word are good but not overwhelming.

Gr-gr represents not only the sound of growling and grumbling. A grinding wheel also goes *gr-gr.* The most important product of grinding is flour, and several *gr-* words denote small particles; *grit* (sand) is one of them. *Grits* is merely the plural of *grit.* Dictionaries pass by the origin of *nitty-gritty,* a word that became known some 40 years ago (the earliest citation is dated 1963), but it would be strange if the person who coined *nitty-gritty* on the analogy of such pairs as *willy-nilly* did not think of grit. *Groats* and its partial synonym *grouts* mean "hulled grain"; like *grit, groats* is traceable to Old English.

Old French *gruel,* the etymon of Engl. *gruel,* goes back to **grūt-* with a diminutive suffix. Gruel is a thin porridge made from oatmeal, chiefly used as an article of diet for invalids, as the *Oxford English Dictionary* explains. On this article of diet Oliver Twist and his cheerless companions lived for years in the workhouse. According to Mr. Bumble, the villainous beadle, liquid food prevented the boys from rebelling. Dickens must have known the idiom *to get one's gruel* (to die). (From some such phrase the verb *gruel* [exhaust, disable] was coined in the middle of the nineteenth century; hence *grueling experience.*) The most unexpected sibling of *grit* is *great.* In Old English, it meant not only "bulky" but also "thick" and "coarse," presumably, "coarsely ground," "gritty." Later the sense "big" overshadowed and ousted all others.[6]

It may seem that we wield a key to the etymology of innumerable words. However, reality is less rosy than it appears to an enthusiastic beginner. Each word mentioned above has been the object of intense research. We know when *grim, grin, grit,* and so forth were first recorded in English, what they meant at that time, and how some of the old senses yielded to new ones. A net has been cast broadly for words in other languages in the hope of finding reliable cognates. Various look-alikes have been examined and often discarded as irrelevant. For example, *coarse, crass,* and *gross,* despite their *cr-* ~ *gr-* and reference to things rough and thick, did not enter into the picture. They are borrowings from Latin, in which their traces are lost.

Gross, a close synonym of *great* (thick), seems to be an especially attractive candidate for comparison. A "thick" coin is called *groot* in Dutch (borrowed as *groat* into English), and the Dutch for *great* is also *groot.* The same coin gained currency in Germany *(Groschen).* Opinions are divided on whether *groot₁* and *groot₂* belong together. Most recent dictionaries keep them apart. *The Oxford Dictionary of English Etymology* accepted the nearly incontestable etymology of Engl. *great* from "coarsely ground" with reservations. On the other hand, some language historians connect *grue(some)* and *grate* (to rub). They gloss the Germanic root as "recoil" and derive it from the meaning "to be offended, to be grated on by."[7]

Even if ties between *great* and *grit—groats—grout* and between the three of them and *grue(some)* were more obvious, the problem of their etymology would not have been solved by classifying them with onomatopoeic words. In some general way, *growl, grumble, grin,* and *groan* belong together, but their common "echoic" part is only *gr-.* The other sounds also need an explanation. Then there is the question of chronology. *Growl* has been known from books only since the eighteenth century; its similarity with late Middle Engl. *grolle, groule,* and *gurle* may be accidental. *Grumble* turned up first in the sixteenth century. Its predecessor, without the suffix *-le,* was *grumme.* In the absence of *grumme,* we might have supposed that *grumble* is *rumble,* with *g-* added under the influence of other vaguely synonymous *gr-* words. *Grin* and *groan* were well established in Old English and have bona fide counterparts elsewhere. The late attestation of *growl* and *grumble* is no proof of their young age, but since not all words have existed forever, both may have been coined approximately when they made their way into books.

Words sharing an onomatopoeic combination of sounds are like children living in the same foster home at the same time: they form a close-knit group without being related to one another. Such words can appear at any time, because *gr-* will always evoke a mental image of a muted roar and a scraping noise. They may arise in any century and in any community, provided speakers have *g-* and *r-* in

their language. When we label *cry, crow, growl,* and *grit* onomatopoeic, we clarify the sought-for connection between words and things
but leave many questions unanswered. *Oink-oink* is an easy item for
an etymologist, *grunt* is more complicated, while the origin of *growl*
and *grumble* requires a serious investigation. Plato, about whose ideas
of word origins more will be said later, dismissed onomatopoeia as
insignificant, though he believed that the letter ρ (rho) was "a good
tool for [expressing] all kinds of movement." Our task is not to reject
the existence of onomatopoeia (this would be counterproductive) or
minimize its role (this would be incautious), but to show its place in
etymological pursuits.

The more expressive human speech is, the more "echoic" words it
contains. This is true of dialects, which give free rein to language
creativity, and of children, when, overwhelmed by emotion, they hurry
to describe a dramatic event they have witnessed. However, as the
excursus on *gr-* has shown, traces of sound imitation are plentiful
everywhere. In Standard English, we find *tap-tap-tap* alongside *rap,
clap, flap,* and *slap, pat-pat, pit-a-pat,* and *bang.* Their origin, like
that of *ding-dong* and *ping-pong,* is not in doubt. It seems that *splash,
swish,* and *buzz* also render accurately the sounds made by an object
falling into water, a whip moving forcibly through the air, and an
insect humming as it flies.

People resort to onomatopoeias when they coin words for beating, falling, breaking, jostling, thrusting, crushing, crashing, and the
like. But once such words become regular nouns and verbs, they
often develop in unpredictable directions. For example, Medieval
Latin *clocca* (bell, chime), possibly borrowed from Irish, may be an
onomatopoeia (it reproduces the sound metal gives forth when struck).
We will accept this etymology for the sake of the argument, though
other derivations of *clocca* exist. The word was known in many countries, including the Netherlands. It is usually believed that in the fourteenth century, Flemish masters introduced clocks into England, and
since bells had traditionally been used to mark time, Dutch *klocke*
acquired a new meaning on English soil. The distance between "bell"
and "clock" is not so long as to blur the picture entirely. But then we
turn to French and discover, beside *cloche* (bell), its dialectal vari-

ants *cloke* and *cloque* that designated a bell-shaped garment. English borrowed *cloke* as *cloak,* and it is now totally divorced from its "echoic" past. (*The Century Dictionary* explains: "In the sixteenth century the cloak was an article of every-day wear, and was made with large loose armholes, through which the sleeves of the undergarment were passed, as is seen in portraits of Henry VIII. and the nobles of his court.") Equally removed from that past is Irish *clog,* which means "clock" as well as "blister" and "bubble" (because both are round; no connection with Engl. *clog*).[8]

The sounds of a word may also change beyond recognition. Engl. *laugh* was pronounced *hlahhian* about two thousand years ago, with *-hh-* having the phonetic value of *ch* in Scots *loch.* It was a word like *chuck(le), cough* (earlier *cohettan* [shout]), and *cluck-cluck,* an imitation of a deep guttural sound. Later, *h* before *l* was dropped, while *-hh-* changed to *f* (as it also did in *cough*), and only the spelling *-gh-* reminds us today of how things once stood. *Laugh* has stopped being an onomatopoeia, and we are fortunate that we can retrace its history (we were also fortunate in dealing with *clock* and *cloak),* because luck does not always attend rambles through language thickets.

We recognize the imitative nature of *tap-tap* and *pat-pat.* The order of consonants and the quality of the vowel between them are of little consequence, for *tup-tup, top-top,* and *pit-a-pat* would do equally well, and a pat *(p-a-t),* if dictionaries are right, is a gentle tap *(t-a-p).* The Latin for "foot" was *pes,* its root being *ped-* (as in *pedal* and *pedicure).* The Greek cognate of *ped-* is *pod-* (as in *podagra* [gout] and *podium).* *Ped* resembles Engl. *pad* (a hairy paw). Feet exist for walking, and, sure enough, *pad (footpad)* can mean "road" (as, for instance, in *gentleman of the pad* [highwayman]); *paddle,* too, consists of the root *pad* and the suffix *-le,* and paths are for pedestrians to pad-pad them.

A daring etymology explains Greek *pod-,* Latin *ped-,* Engl. *pad,* and Engl. *path* as developments of the originally onomatopoeic complexes *pat-pat, pad-pad.*[9] It is a tempting etymology, but it passes over some chronological difficulties, already familiar to us from the discussion of *grumble, grit,* and other *gr-*words. *Pod-* and *ped-* date back to antiquity. *Pad* appeared in print in 1554, and its earliest recorded meaning was "a bundle of straw" and "a soft stuffed saddle." Perhaps wolves and foxes were known to have pads even then, but no occurrence of *pad* (paw) turned up before 1790. Northern German and Flemish have *patte* and *pad* (the sole of the foot); Engl. *pad* with reference to animals looks like a loan from the continent. *Path,* which traces back to Old English, is related to German *Pfad.* English vagabonds borrowed it in its northern guise as *pad* (road). In distant lands, a doublet of *path* occurs only in an old Iranian language. An etymology based on onomatopoeia presents its data as timeless and free from national and geographical borders, and the rather predictable character of imitating natural sounds in human speech makes the most dubious conclusions of this type look good. Perhaps *pod-, ped-, pad* (road), and *path* are imitative after all. This is the most one can say.

If an onomatopoeic word is an echo of some natural sound—from the growl of a disgruntled cur to an accelerated heartbeat—we expect it to resemble its source. *Gr-gr* satisfies that condition. *Bow-wow, yap-yap, bark-bark, hee-haw* (note the donkey Eeyore in *Winnie-the-Pooh*), and *quack-quack* are tolerable substitutes for animal cries.[10] Our consonants cannot capture the acoustic signal produced by slapping, bursting, and marching, and we make do with *pat-pat* and *tap-tap*. We follow the development of *cloak* and *laugh* and observe the well-documented changes they have undergone over time. But it is better to avoid bold steps that would make alleged echoes too distant from the original rumble.

Rudyard Kipling, our occasional guide through the jungle of word origins, wrote a story about Rikki-tikki-tavi, a mongoose, and his great war with cobras. One of the characters in his story is Chuchundra, a muskrat, a little beast that always crept by the wall and never had spirit enough to run out into the middle of the room. Not everybody is like Chuchundra. Some linguists place themselves at the center of their universe and detect onomatopoeia everywhere. Their vision is sharp, sometimes too sharp. Here is a case in point. *Bat* may be regarded as imitative of a heavy dull blow. Vowels, as usual in such syllables, vary. Beside *bat,* English has *beat,* Russian has *bit'* (the apostrophe indicates a special pronunciation of *t*), and Latin had *battāre* (compare Engl. *batter, battery,* and *battle*). *Bat* (stick, club) seems to belong here, too. Difficulties arise when *bat* (bundle) (recorded in the *Oxford English Dictionary*) and *bat* (river islet; short ridge; corner of a field) (recorded in Wright's dictionary)[11] are co-opted into the *bat-battāre* group.[12] *Pit* in *pit-a-pat* seems to be an unobjectionable onomatopoeia, and so does *pitter-patter. Patter* does not even need the support of *pitter* (compare *the patter of children's feet*). But *pit* (the stone of a fruit) and *pit* (a hole in the ground) are less clear. Did they acquire their meaning from *pit* (the sound of something small striking, as a raindrop), to quote a dictionary definition? A positive answer needs a good deal of proof.

It also happens that the sounds supposedly common to a group of "echoic" words are not understood as an echo of anything. In English, German, Dutch, and the Scandinavian languages, several dozen verbs and nouns either begin or once began with *gn-* and *kn-*. (In English, *g-* and *k-* were dropped before *n,* and only spelling occasionally hints at the earlier pronunciation.) Consider *gnaw, gnarl, gnash, knuckle,* and *knob,* among many others. They refer to various objects made of wood or bone (and a knuckle is just bone), to crushing bone with the teeth, gnawing and nibbling, and, more broadly, to knocking, notching, and nudging. The trouble is that *gn-* and *kn-* hardly convey the idea of processing a hard substance. One can imagine almost anything when hearing *gn-gn-gn* or *kn-kn-kn*.

How many onomatopoeic words exist in Modern English? The answer depends on the generosity of the teller. In any case, outside the *moo* group, reference to onomatopoeia may (and often does) clarify the connection between the world full of noises and their reflection in words, but it stops short of providing full-scale etymologies. The case of *growl* and *grumble* is typical. However secure the clue that the combination *gr-* may provide to the initial impulse behind language creativity, it fails to account for *-owl* and *-umble.*

Thud, like *bat,* perhaps suggests a dull heavy sound, but if the inconclusive data on the history of *thud* can be relied on, in Old English it had a vowel like French *u* or German *ü* (that is, it sounded much "thinner"), had two syllables, and meant "to thrust, push," possibly, "to beat." In the full light of history (in the sixteenth century), *thud* first meant "blast" or "gust," so that its onomatopoeic character begins to fade. *Thump* rhymes with *dump, bump,* and *jump.* Even if *-ump* describes throwing things or moving with great force, the origin of each member of the group remains a mystery. Dictionaries tell us that *dump* and *bump* may have come to England from Scandinavia, the first in the fourteenth, the second in the sixteenth century. *Jump* is roughly contemporaneous with *dump* and resembles several words in other languages. *Hump* and *lump* are reminiscent of *bump* in that all three denote swellings, and it is not improbable that all of them once referred to protuberances, with the later development being "obstacle; colliding with, getting over an obstacle" and as a result "jump(ing)." If this reconstruction is right, setting up the onomatopoeic group *-ump* loses most of its appeal.

We may press the matter further. In Danish, *gumpe* (to ride on a bumpy road) has a synonym *skumpe; gumpe* also means " to jump." Hans Christian Andersen knew a story of Klumpe-Dumpe, who fell off the stairs but later married a princess and supposedly lived happily ever after. Several centuries ago, a German verb *gumpen* (to jump) was current, and a few verbs of the same type with initial *ts-, dz-,* and *j-* have been recorded in modern Italian dialects. In trying to make sense of this jumble, while stumbling and tumbling at every turn, one is prone to hear noises all over the place; yet the picture comes out blurred. If *bump* and *dump* are Scandinavian loans, at least in English they were not spontaneous creations, and the onomatopoeic association may have arisen because many similar words referred to falling and jumping. We are also left wondering whether Scandinavian, German, Italian, and English verbs emerged independent of one another and why people needed *jump* if they already had *hop* and *spring.* (The sixteenth century seems to have been prime time for jumpers: the verbs *bound* and *gambol* emerged at about the same time.) These are some of the questions facing the etymologists who realize that the road they have taken cannot be covered in one elegant leap.

By way of conclusion, we will examine briefly the history of *boy*. The earliest recorded example of this word goes back to 1240, though the proper name *Boi(a)* turned up much earlier. In literary works, it first designated servants and other persons of low ranks and was a term of contempt and abuse. *Boy* (executioner) may have existed, too. At present, only compounds like *bellboy* and the colonial or derogatory use of *boy* (servant) remind us of the otherwise forgotten medieval senses. The easiest thing would be to dismiss *boy* as a baby word, for *ba-ba* and *bo-bo* are the names infants give everywhere to those who take care of them. However, the meaning of "boy" does not quite fit "daddy," "mummy," and "granny."

B-words often refer to things and actions in some way connected with fright. The most primitive of them is the English verb *boo* (to hoot). Devils and devilish creatures regularly meet us here. Apparently, evil spirits used to strike fear in people's hearts by screaming *boo!* Identical words have been recorded in Sanskrit, Classical Greek, Latin, Slavic, and Celtic. For example, Russian *buka* is almost indistinguishable from Engl. *booga,* and their kin are Dutch *bui* (gust, squall), Russian *bui* (a violent man), and all kinds of bogeymen that boggle the mind, bug us (and our computers), and make us bow to their authority. A friendly version of booing is still present in the game known as peek-a-boo in America and bo-peep in England. Several occurrences of *boy* (devil) have been found in Chaucer.[13] German *Bube* displays the same unexpected blend of the meanings "scoundrel" and "a dear child."

It seems that two words—one from baby talk ("baby, brother") and one onomatopoeic ("booer, a noisy spirit")—met in English and produced the meaning *boy* (a person of a lower rank): neither a sweet baby nor a devil, rather an imp. The change to "a male child" happened later. If *boy* developed along the lines suggested here, it shows once again how much has to be done after we have detected an "echo" behind a common word.[14]

Chapter Four

which makes sense because it is sound.
Mooing cows and cooing doves give way to sleazy
politicians, but they unite later to produce a coherent
theory of word formation, or

Sound Symbolism

Soft, hard, dark, thick, and slender sounds.—Whispering in the dark.—
One man's pimple is another man's pumple.—Ideophones.—Otto
Jespersen and Hensleigh Wedgwood.—A glimpse of a slum.—The
glamour of grammar.—*Flip-flop.*—*Nudge* and *budge.*—Abrupt movements, short vowels, and long consonants.—Max Müller, William
Dwight Whitney, *bow-vow,* and *ding-dong.*—Wilhelm Oehl and primitive creation.

The form of the word (and, consequently, its origin) may depend on
the impression the sounds of speech evoke in us. The extent of the
dependence is hard to assess, and etymologists, like all scholars, feel
uneasy in dealing with evasive data. Even in the driest phonetic descriptions, one comes across terms like *soft* and *hard, thick* and *thin*
(or *slender*), *dark* and *light.* For example, in Russian and Polish, all
consonants can be pronounced with the middle of the tongue raised
toward the roof of the mouth; such consonants are termed soft. In a
group of Swedish and Norwegian dialects, a variety of *l* exists that
outsiders usually mistake for an *r;* this is the so-called thick *l.* In
British English, *l* in *will* is closer to the *l* usually heard in America
than does *l* in *will you.* American *l* is called "dark."

In such descriptions, we are dealing with metaphors. If beginning
students of Russian or Norwegian are told to make their *l* softer or
darker or thicker, this advice will not help them to master the pro-

nunciation of a foreign language. Yet the association between the acoustic effect of a sound and light, size, and even taste (especially sweetness) is stable across language borders.[1] One looks at a string of words referring to darkness and finds Russian *tusk* (pronounced *toosk*, with the vowel of *push*, mainly known as part of the adjective *tuskly*), Engl. *dusk*, related to Latin *fuscus* (as in Engl. *obfuscate*), Engl. *mist*, Old Engl. *þēostre* (*þ* = *th* as in *thigh*), and Old Engl. *-þūhsian* (to make dark). The voice is all but absent in the pronunciation of those words. It is as though one were whispering something in the dead of night: *sk, st, th-st, th-hs.* A poet would not have chosen less audible words for conveying a verbal image of darkness.

No definite conclusions follow from such facts, because words change their shape over time. In the remote past, Old Engl. *þēostre* and *-þūhsian* began with *d* rather than *th.* Latin *tenebrae* (darkness) (compare Engl. *Tenebrae* [a church service observed during the final part of Holy Week, with the progressive extinguishing of all candles]) and German *Nebel* (mist) (compare Engl. *nebulous,* from a similar Latin word) do without *sk* or *st.* The first of them contains the group *br,* whereas Engl. *tusk,* which was at one time pronounced like Russian *tusk,* means "a long-pointed tooth" and has nothing to do with darkness. This is the reason etymologists shy away from explaining the origin of words in terms of such associations. The moment we decide that *br* is a "loud" group connected in our consciousness with brightness and brilliance, someone will remember *tenebrae* or words from entirely different fields like *bread* and *broom* or mention the zebra, which is white but has black stripes.

Yet sound and meaning are not only partners in every word; they influence each other. Outside onomatopoeia, historical linguists can rarely prove the existence of that influence, but they are aware of it as a factor in the life of language. The most comfortable position here is that of the devil's advocate, the position I will choose, though I will leave it to the readers to figure out whose side the devil is on. German *finster* means "dark." It resembles somewhat its synonym *düster,* a cognate of Old Engl. *þēostre,* mentioned above, but the resemblance is illusory. *Finstar,* an earlier form of *finster,* had two synonyms, *dinstar* and *timbar.* Both belong to a respectable stock: *dinstar* is related to Latin *tenebrae,* and *timbar* is a cognate of Engl. *dim.* Only *finster* is devoid of kin in other languages. Good ancestry plays no role in the fortunes of words, and we see that *finster* is still around, whereas its competitors have disappeared from Standard German without a trace. Was *timbar* too "bright" for its meaning? But the continuations (reflexes) of Latin *tenebrae* have survived in modern Romance languages. If *finster* is an alteration of *dinstar,* did people change the first consonant to produce a more whispery adjective? This is an adventurous hypothesis, for nothing like it has happened to German *dunkel,* another synonym of *finster,* or Engl. *dark.* No mechanism has been discovered that would allow us to register unconscious impulses of past epochs. Even the causes of the changes occurring in the contemporary language remain largely undisclosed.

We are on safer ground with vowels. Speakers everywhere associate *a,* as in *rag* or *Prague,* and *i,* as in *pin,* with a big and a small size, respectively, and *e,* as in *pen,* with an intermediate stage.[2] The fact that the words *big* and *small* (the latter once had the *a* of Modern Engl. *father,* only shorter) show "wrong" vowels, as though to tease us, should be cited as exceptions proving the rule. *Little* and *large* behave according to expectation. *Pimp* seems originally to have meant "a little boy" (as does German *Pimpf*) and "servant." *Pimple* is a tiny swelling, while *pamper,* known from texts since the fourteenth century, meant "to cram with food." Judging by the vowel, the feeding proceeded on a grand scale. In addition to *pimple,* English dialects have *pumple* (like *tusk,* it had, until approximately the seventeenth century, the vowel *u* of Modern Engl. *push*).

People of all ages, regardless of the language they speak, call the vowel *i* (chosen over *u* and *a* to name small objects) thin—that is, when they are asked some such question. Knowing only the names of the swellings, *pimple* and *pumple,* we need not doubt which contains more poison matter. One of the Latin words for "pustule" was *papula.* That both *pumple* and *papula* designate bigger swellings than *pimple* is clear. It would be interesting to draw pictures of three men, one short and thin, another of a "regular" size, and the third short and fat and ask children of kindergarten age which of them is Mr. Pimple, Mr. Pumple, and Mr. Pample. This is precisely the type of experiment linguists conduct when studying the symbolic value of sounds.[3]

Examples like *pimple–pumple–papula* are common. *Sip* presupposes drinking very little at a time. It was first attested in the seventeenth century and sounds like a "weakened" variant of *sup* (an old word), which is a partial synonym of *sip*. Alongside *sip*, *sup* has grown in stature and designates a larger quantity of liquid imbibed. (*Sop, soup,* and *supper* are related to *sup,* but not directly, and *supper* may have influenced our understanding of it.) *Grift*, which refers to all kinds of swindling, and *graft* ("bribe") are not too remote in meaning, but *grift,* from the sound of it, is "thinner," and in our linguistic intuition it denotes a more sophisticated, more subtle kind of fraud. Likewise, *bilk* seems to be a "weaker" variant of *balk*.

The feeling that certain words mean exactly what they should is widespread. *Sippet* is "a small piece of bread to be dipped in liquid." This is what a sippet should be, and note the unconscious beauty of the above definition of *sippet* (borrowed from *The Oxford Dictionary of English Etymology*), with its *i*'s going through the whole phrase like a spit. *Snippet* and *tidbit* are also apt, well-nigh perfect names. The shark's jaws snap, while a twig is snipped by a gardener. Words like *zigzag* usually progress from *i* to a more open vowel and reach the climax toward the end: *chit-chat, mishmash, fiddle-faddle, shilly-shally, pit-a-pat, tiptop,* and dozens of others.

The symbolic value of vowels and consonants has never been a secret to linguists, but, as stated above, etymologists feel uneasy when confronted with such imprecise data and are not sure what to do with them. Perhaps *sip, bilk,* and *grift* were coined as "thinner" variants of *sup, balk,* and *graft,* but perhaps we simply do not know under what circumstances those late verbs arose and so invent explanations in the belief that a shaky reconstruction is better than none. My conjecture that German *finster* acquired its *f-,* to sound more crepuscular (tenebrous, as it were), can be dismissed for lack of proof. Such proof does not exist. (Those who find *tenebrous* unbearably highbrowish may take comfort in Longfellow's translation of Dante: "Huge hail and water somber-hued, and snow / Athwart the tenebrous air pour down amain." However, Longfellow has fallen from grace among the *literati,* and reference to him carries little weight.)

Sound symbolism is a favorite subject among those who discuss language creativity as a process, but the same investigators show great reticence when it comes to the history of individual words. Although etymological dictionaries often mention onomatopoeia, and it would be strange if they did not in tracing the origin of *roar* or *twitter,* references to sound symbolism are few and far between. Yet, the examples of *sip, bilk,* and *grift* turned up in the form cited here in *The Oxford Dictionary of English Etymology,* which stays away from risky hypotheses. Onomatopoeia has an observable base (sound imitation), whereas "the thinning of *a*" is a loose concept. Echoic and sound symbolic formations thrive in dialects and in the languages that, until now, have partly escaped the dictate of the norm imposed by educational standards. Specialists in African linguistics call such formations ideophones, that is, phones (sounds) carrying their own "idea." In 1954 this term was introduced into English studies, and now it occurs regularly in scholarly works.[4]

We will follow the history of one ideophone. The example will be familiar from the previous exposition. Among other things, we will see that the line separating ideophones and onomatopoeias frequently becomes invisible. Classical Greek had the verb *pémpo*[5] (to send), from which *pompé*[6] (sending, escorting, solemn procession) was formed (whence *pompillus,* literally "a fish that follows ships"). Romans took over this word in the form *pompa.* From Latin it went to French *(pompe)* and from there to English *(pomp).* Monosyllables like *pop, pomp, bob, blob, bomb, bulb,* and *pulp,* which begin and end with *p* or *b,* tend to convey the meaning of something round and swollen.

The path from *pop, bob,* and the rest to roundness is not always straight. Greek *bómbos,* the ultimate etymon of Engl. *bomb,* meant "a humming noise" and was imitative, like Engl. *boom,* rather than symbolic. *Pump* (a machine for raising water) may go back to the same Greek noun, but some people think that its source was German *Pumpe,* from Spanish or Portuguese *bomba* (pump), a Romance onomatopoeia, unrelated to the Greek word.[7] Since onomatopoeia and sound symbolism are "panhuman" rather than language specific phenomena, the existence of *pop, bob, bomb, pomp,* and so on in several languages does not point to their kinship or borrowing. The existence of French *pompon* (a topknot; a tuft of feathers for a bonnet or hat) shows that the idea of roundness prevailed in *pomp.* In Early French, Latin *pepō(n-)* was transformed into *pompon,* a homonym of *pompon* (topknot), which reached English as *pumpion* and *pumpkin,* the latter with a pseudo-Dutch (diminutive!) suffix. The reason *pepōn* (from a Greek word meaning "ripe") turned into *pompon* is unknown. The change did no one any good, for now speakers, burdened with a new pair of homonyms, had to distinguish between *pompon₁* and *pompon₂.* A force stronger than the fear of homonyms was at play, and *pepon* may have become *pompon* to conform to the word's meaning: a pumpkin is the embodiment of pompous rotundity. We will for a moment return to pimples and pumples. *Pump-* ~ *pumper-,* with its "thick" *u* (*u* as in Engl. *push*) suggests swelling and, by implication, a full stomach. *Pumpernickel* probably got its name on account of the flatulence it causes: *pumper-* and Engl. *pamper* belong to the same class of words.

A pump, while working, makes a lot of noise: approximately *chug-chug.* Nor does the water remain silent. One hears *plash-plash* or *splash-splash.* At one time, northern Germans began to call the pump *plumpe* instead of *pumpe* (the earliest recorded example is dated 1564), and both words are extant. About 70 years earlier, Engl. *plump* turned up in texts. Whether German *Plumpe* is a loan from English is uncertain, though the coincidence is striking. Dictionaries call German *Plumpe* and *plump* an alteration of *Pumpe* and *pump* (*l* and *r* are often inserted for "reinforcement"). If they are right, the noun *plump* is vaguely imitative of the sound a heavy object makes in contact with water. The verb *plump,* known from books since the fourteenth century, already then meant "to fall or come down with a heavy and abrupt impact," and it is presumably onomatopoeic, like *jump, thump, dump,* and *hump.* On the other hand, the adjective *plump* (rounded, chubby), believed to be a sixteenth-century borrowing from Dutch or northern German *(plomp, plump)*, looks like the ideophones *pompe, poupon,* and even *pumpkin.* Are we dealing with two different groups of words? A well-formed round object *(pump, pomp)* would go into the water with a big *plop, plump,* or *plomp.* Ideophones and onomatopoeias emerge as two sides of the same phenomenon.

More and more words will claim to belong to a sound symbolic or onomatopoeic group once it has been established. Perhaps *pump* and *plump* go together. We understand why widows in British novels are often called plump and why we plump into our seats when we come to the theater at the last moment. But what does Latin *plumbum* (lead, the name of a metal) have to do with them? Its origin is debatable. People tend to borrow the names of material objects when they learn the existence of corresponding things. For instance, Engl. *iron* is of Celtic origin. *Silver* migrated to Europe from the East. The Greeks called lead *mólubdos, mólubos, mólibos, bólibos,*[8] and so forth (compare Engl. *molybdenum);* apparently, they had some trouble with this word. *Plumbum* and *mólubdos* do not resemble each other, but there is a consensus that they have a common source because both contain *m, l,* and *b.* Since the source has not been identified, the consensus should be respectfully ignored.

Otto Jespersen suggested that Latin *plumbum (-um* is an ending of the neuter) is an imitative word, which meant "at first not the metal, but the plummet that was dumped and plumped into the water and was denominated from the sound; as this was generally made of lead, the word came to be used for the metal." He compared *plumb* with *plop, plout, plunk, plounce, pop,* and *bob,* to which we can add Russian *pliukh.*[9] French *plonger,* believed to be derived from the unattested verb **plumbicāre* (to throw lead into water), furnishes indirect proof of the correctness of Jespersen' s idea. Old Provençal *plombiar* makes one think that **plumbiāre* also existed. In the fourteenth century, Old English borrowed Old French *plungier,* the ancestor of *plonger,* and it yielded *plunge.* No one supported Jespersen's guess. Yet, most likely, Romans knew *mólubdos* and replaced it with the popular, perhaps even humorous word *plumbum.*

Skeat cites with approval Hensleigh Wedgwood's idea that "language took its rise from expressive interjections" (Wedgwood was the author of an earlier English etymological dictionary; see Chapter 17), but notes the following: "Unluckily, it influenced the author far too much in his account of various words. . . . In the case of the verb *to plunge,* for example, Wedgwood's statement that its origin, 'like that of *plump,* is a representation of the noise made by the fall', is purely fanciful; for it is merely borrowed from the F[rench] *plonger,* answering to the Low Latin type **plumbicare,* a derivative of *plumbum,* lead. . . ."[10] Skeat is right: *plunge* is a borrowing from French, and the French verb can be traced to Latin *plumbum,* but if *plumbum* is of onomatopoeic origin, Wedgwood's statement finds some justification despite his unpardonable shortcut: *plunge* has retained only an echo of an ancient plop.

Sound symbolism is often the result of a secondary association. The words *glow, gleam, glimmer, glare, glisten, glitter, glacier,* and *glide* suggest that in English the combination *gl-* conveys the idea of sheen and smoothness. Against this background, *glory, glee,* and *glad* emanate brightness by their very form, *glance* and *glimpse* reinforce our conclusion (because eyesight is inseparable from light), and *glib* has no other choice than to denote specious luster, and, indeed, in the sixteenth century, when it became known in English, it meant "smooth and slippery." The intense, at times malicious, satisfaction implied in gloating is in some vague way also akin to brilliance, whereas *globe* and *gland* are round or spherical and hence slippery.

Some of the words listed above are related, for example, *glass* and *glare; gleam, glimmer,* and *glimpse.* But *glacier,* like German *Gletscher,* goes back to Latin *gelidus* (frost) (compare Engl. *congeal* and *jelly*). Neither *gelidus* nor its English cognate *cold* has anything to do with radiance. *Glory,* another Romance word (Latin *glōria*), is of unascertained origin, but whatever its etymon, the idea of brilliance hardly played any role in its creation. Nor should it be taken for granted that *gl-* carries the same connotations in other languages, though such a supposition would not necessarily be wrong. In English, the symbolic value of *gl-* cannot be called into question, and it is instructive to watch some enigmatic changes that may be connected with it.

The ultimate source of the word *grammar* is a Greek noun meaning "letter."[11] Old French had *gramaire* (grammar) (a formation without direct antecedents in Greek or Latin), and in the thirteenth century, its evil twin *grimoir* was born. Initially, it referred to Latin grammar only (an allusion to French *grimaud* [morose, sullen]?) as something unintelligible, and soon came to mean "a book of occult learning." Modern French *grimoir* has retained both senses: "gibberish" and "a wizard's book of spells." *Grimoire* reached England around the fourteenth century and had the form *gramarie*. Walter Scott revived its medieval sense "magic," and this is the reason *gramary* and *gramarye* still turn up in our thickest dictionaries. But then, in the north, alterations of *gramarie* appeared. The recorded forms are numerous: *glamer, glamor, glamour, glamerie, glammerie,* and *glaumerie.* It was again Walter Scott who revived *glamor,* but note the development of meaning: "grammar," "profound (occult) learning," "enchantment" (as in *cast a glamour over someone or something*), and "compelling beauty." Why did *gr-* change to *gl-?* Did *gr-* evoke unpleasant feelings, whereas *gl-* made people think of the allure of magic, with all its forbidden sheen?

The other seemingly promising cognates of *glamour* provide false leads. Thus Old Icelandic *glámr,* one of the names of the moon and a cognate of Engl. *gloam,* is unrelated to *glamour* despite the existence of Icelandic *glámsýni* (illusion). Early dictionaries connected *glamour* and *glámr ~ glámsýni.* They were wrong, and their mistake shows how easily look-alikes can deceive an etymologist. Not all is gold that glitters.

Sometimes we witness a puzzling change of *kl-* to *gl-.* The etymon of Engl. *glaire* (the white of an egg), from Old French *glaire,* is the Latin adjective *clārus.* It may be natural to call the white part of something "clear" (because whiteness and sheen are often associated), but why *gl-* in French? Does it owe its origin to sound symbolism (whiteness = glow)? In other cases, it is the meaning of a word that undergoes an equally puzzling change. Engl. *glaive* (sword), now archaic or poetic, is, like *glaire,* a borrowing from French. It may be akin to Latin *gladius* (sword) (memorable from *gladiator*), but *-d-* in *gladius* does not match *-v-* in *glaive,* and in Old French, *glaive* usually meant "spear," as Engl. dialectal *gleave* still does ("fish spear"). If *glaive* altered its meaning under the influence of Gaulish **gladebo* (compare Gaelic *claidheamh* and Irish *claideb*), also popularized by Walter Scott in its Scots form *claymore* (a Highlander's two-edged broadsword) (formerly *glaymore*),[12] part of the riddle will be solved, but could the meaning "spear" change somewhere along the way to "sword" because a weapon whose name began with *gl-* suggested the idea of gleaming steel?

In other cases, *gl-*words come as though from nowhere but manage to live up to their sound shape. One of them is *gloss* (superficial luster) (not to be confused with *gloss* [interpretation, marginal note]), first recorded in the sixteenth century. It may have been borrowed from the continent, for both German and Dutch had similar words at that time, and so did the Scandinavian languages. Perhaps we have here one of many *gl-*words for brilliance.[13]

More examples of sound symbolic consonant groups are easy to find. *Glide* has a near synonym *slide*. The idea of smoothness gives way in it to that of slipperiness. Consider the following list: *sleek* and its etymological doublet *slick* (from the historical point of view they are two forms of the same adjective); *slide, sled, sleet, slip, slither, slobber, slope, slant, sloppy; slough* (swamp) (as in the *Slough of Despond;* rhyming with *how*) and *slough* (the outer skin of a reptile) (rhyming with *enough*), *sludge, sluice, slur, slush,* and even *slattern* and *slut.* If we came across *glib* for the first time and looked it up in a dictionary, we might feel that its meaning fits its form. Likewise, if we were to guess the meaning of the phrase *a sleazy politician,* we would probably think of someone slippery or disgustingly sleek. The word *sleazy,* with its *sl-* at the beginning and *-zy* at the end, has a truly ominous ring.

Sleazy (cheap) dresses, and sleazy (poor) excuses were known as far back as the seventeenth century. The origin of this (slang) adjective has not been discovered. It appears to be derived from the noun *sleaze* (compare *easy, hazy,* and *crazy* from *ease, haze,* and *craze*), but in fact, *sleaze* was abstracted from *sleazy,* rather than being its etymon. (Words derived in such a way—*sleaze* from *sleazy, sculpt* from *sculptor,* and so forth—are called back formations.) However, the most interesting thing about *sleazy* is that its current senses "disreputable" and "sordid, filthy" *(a sleazy hotel)* do not antedate the twentieth century; the *Oxford English Dictionary* could find no citations for them before 1941. The adjective *sleazy* must have acquired its present-day meaning to conform to its sound shape. A word cannot exist in slums, surrounded by slatterns and sluts, and preserve its purity amid all this slime.

One can repeat the experiment made with *gl-* and *sl-* on *fl-*. Here words denoting unsteady light and quivering motion will be especially conspicuous: *flit, flirt, flicker, flutter, flip, flap, flop,* and many others. *Flap* may be onomatopoeic like *clap, slap, rap,* and *tap,* whereas *flop* expresses a duller sound than *flap,* of which it is a variant, but *fl-* does not allow it to designate an action entailing the use of force. For such purposes we have *dump,* and *thump. Flatter* (not a borrowing from French) belongs here too. Flatterers flutter around, that is, dance attendance on their victims, to get what they want. German *flattern* means "to flutter."

Although a strong case can be made for the inherent properties of sounds arousing certain associations, the symbolism of some consonants is hard to account for. Such common English names as *John, Jim,* and *Jenny* begin with *j,* a sound devoid of symbolic value. The same holds for the final *j* of *bridge* and *edge.* Yet it is amazing how often *j* (the sound, not the letter) occurs in words of obscure origin in which it contributes to the feeling that we have colloquialisms, if not exactly slang. Consider *budge, grudge, drudge; fudge* (to fake, patch up) (apparently, related to the earlier verbs *fadge* and *fodge* [to adjust, fit]), *trudge, nudge, fidget; jab, job, jam* (verb), *jerk, jib, jinks, jitter, jog, jolt,* and *jumble.* And this is not a complete list.

It may be useful to repeat that reference to sound symbolism tells us something about the soil from which a word or a group of words receives its nourishment and that it occasionally shows the direction in which a word's meaning has developed (as was perhaps the case with *sleazy*), but it is unable to provide etymologies. *Glide* and *slide* consist not only of *gl-* and *sl-; dump* and *thump* are more than *-ump. Nudge* and *job* may have obtained their aura from *j; j* may even have become part of their makeup to lend them a slangy character, but understanding those facts (assuming that we have indeed captured the truth) is only a first step toward reconstructing the early history of *-j-* words. *Nudge* and *budge, job* and *jog* are equals from the sound symbolic point of view; other than that, they are as different as *Jack* and *Jill*. We are a bit closer to a convincing etymology in *flip-flap-flop* and *flitter-(flatter)-flutter,* in which not only the consonants but also the vowels are endowed with a symbolic value.

In trying to make the next step, we encounter two noteworthy facts. First, verbs designating abrupt movements tend to have short vowels. Some such verbs are ancient, and we can observe their derivation from bases with long vowels. Others are late, but they have a similar structure. Here are a few of them: *put, push, pull, knock, kick, chop, cut, hug, tug, crack, crash, dash, smash,* and *toss.* Second, certain categories of words tend to have long consonants, or geminates, to use a technical term. Symbolic gemination (that is, consonant lengthening) is impossible to demonstrate in Modern English, because English lost its long consonants (of the type heard in Swedish, Norwegian, Italian, and Finnish) many centuries ago. Even in *illegal* and *immobile,* hardly anyone pronounces *-ll-* and *-mm-,* but long consonants are heard at word boundaries in combinations like *at table, in New York, self-focused,* and *big girl.* In Modern English, geminates always point to a word group: *red ditch* (with long *d*) is a phrase, while the place name *Redditch* (with short *d*) is one word.

In Old English, the doubling of letters usually meant gemination, and in that language, verbs designating physical effort tend to have long consonants, which is not surprising. Words are not indifferent labels. Products of human creativity, they are coined to render the speaker's attitude toward the world. It is natural to have a long vowel in a word denoting a protracted action and a short vowel in the name of a momentary act. Don't *dawdle* and *drawl, dip* and *clip* partly tell their story? We are not dealing with a law (compare what has been said about Engl. *big* and *small*); in language, we are lucky even when we can trace certain credible tendencies.[14]

A few examples from Old English, given here to illustrate geminates, will suffice: *cnyllan* (to strike, knock), *cnyssan* (to strike, to press), *roccian* (to rock a child) (that is, "to push"), *crimman* (to cram, insert), *forstoppian* (to stop up, close), *sticcian* (a variant of *stician*) (to prick, stick), *hnoppian* (to pluck), *pullian* (to pull, draw, pluck off wool), *pluccian* and *ploccian* (to pluck, tear), *hreppan* (a variant of *hrepian*) (to touch), *(for)cippan* (to cut off) (the ancestor of Modern Engl. *chip*), *liccian* (to lick, lap), and *hoppian,* with its variant *hoppetan* (to hop, leap).

In the history of English, several old animal names have been replaced with homey baby words like *kitty* and *puppy.* The presence of long consonants in them is incontestable evidence of their emphatic nature. The colloquial form of Latin *asinus* was Old Engl. *assa* (ass, donkey), a synonym for the more dignified *asa. Hog* was *hocg* or *hogg* (those are different spellings of the same form), *frog* was *frocga.* The billy goat and stag, both of them "bucks," were called *bucca.* Old Engl. *ticcen* meant "kid" (not "tyke"). The loss of geminates in Middle English resulted in the loss by such words of their expressive character.

Plato, who thought nothing of onomatopoeia, held a more sympathetic view of sound symbolism. He anticipated modern linguists by saying that ι (*iota* [ἰῶτα]: Plato always speaks of letters) represents objects that are thin, small, and refined (the Greek epithet is *leptá* [λεπτά], whereas λ (*lábda* [λά(μ)βδα]) represents smoothness. We cannot tell how he arrived at such conclusions. Perhaps he realized that the vowel designated by ι was pronounced with the mouth almost closed and therefore connoted delicate things. The letter ρ (*rho* [ῥῶ]), in Plato's opinion, imitated motion. He may have thought that *r,* a trill, renders the noise of rolling chariots or that, in producing this consonant, the tongue rolls in the mouth.[15]

Words like *cuckoo, thump,* and *sleazy* bring us to the dawn of language. Little can be said with authority about the conditions in which people began to speak. Etymology at its most successful explains how things came by their names, not how language originated. Yet it is instructive to watch some students of language history trying to bridge the gap between the likes of *cuckoo* and the inception of human speech.

According to one theory,

the earliest names of objects and actions were produced by imitation of natural sounds: animals, for instance, were denominated from their characteristic utterances, as, with us, the cuckoo is so named: the dog was called a *bow-wow,* the sheep a *baa,* the cow a *moo,* and so on; while the many noises of inanimate nature, as the whistling of the wind, the rustling of leaves, the gurgling and splashing of water, the cracking and crashing of heavy falling objects, suggested in like manner imitative utterances which were applied to designate them; and that by such means a sufficient store of radical words was originated to serve as the germs of language. This is called the onomatopoeic theory. The second is to this effect: that the natural sounds which we utter when in a state of excited feeling, the *oh's* and *ah's,* the *poo's* and *pshaw's,* are the ultimate beginnings of speech. This is styled the interjectional theory.[16]

Max Müller, at one time the most popular linguist in the world, ridiculed both such attempts to come to grips with language origins and called them mockingly the bow-wow theory and the pooh-pooh theory, respectively. He found a trenchant opponent in another eminent scholar, the American William Dwight Whitney, whose book contains the quotation above. Whitney offered an eloquent defense of the theories that Max Müller rejected. "[T]he mind pleases itself," he contended, "with bringing about a sort of agreement between the sign and the thing signified." He did not stop short of the most daring conclusion one can imagine in such a situation: "There was doubtless a period in the progress of speech when its whole structure was palpably onomatopoetic; but not a long one: the onomatopoetic stage was only a stepping-stone to something higher and better."[17] As we have seen, Wedgwood and Skeat were of the same opinion.

    In Müller's opinion, language originated according to what was, also mockingly, termed the ding-dong theory. A human being, as he put it, possessed an instinctive "faculty for giving articulate expression to the rational conceptions of his mind. . . . [T]his creative faculty, which gave to each conception, as it thrilled for the first time through the brain, a phonetic expression, became extinct when its object was fulfilled."[18] Admittedly, those are vague statements. The irate Whitney remarks scornfully that Müller's ideas "may be very summarily dismissed, as wholly unfounded and worthless."[19] "He [Müller] tells us, virtually, that man was at the outset a kind of bell; and that, when an idea struck him, he naturally rang. We wonder, it was not added that, like other bells, he naturally rang by the tongue: this would have been quite in keeping with the rest, and would merely have set more plainly before our minds the real character of the whole theory."[20]

It was perhaps the Swiss linguist Wilhelm Oehl who made the strongest attempt to connect onomatopoeia and sound symbolism with the laws of creativity. Contrary to Whitney and many other people who shared Whitney's ideas, Oehl was interested less in the beginning of language than in coining new words. In Whitney's opinion, the nascent humanity first used only onomatopoeic sound groups that in turn served as the foundation of more complex units. This may be true, as far as it goes. People hear (or think that they hear) *cock-a-doodle-doo,* call the bird singing so *coq,* use *coq-* to form the noun *coquet* (gallant) (someone strutting and showing off the way a rooster does before hens) and *coquette* (feminine) (a flirt). The development is of the same type as from *clock* to *cloak,* discussed in Chapter 3. Oehl concentrated on the eternal, never-changing impulses that lead to the creation of similar words in all languages at all times. Some of the coinages he explored are onomatopoeic, the others sound symbolic. For example, he researched the worldwide distribution of the syllable *kap* (to catch, seize, grasp; hand).[21]

The first word one recalls in this connection is Latin *capere;* we see its root in Engl. *capture, captive, captor,* and *captivate.* Its analogs are Hebrew *caph* (hand), Finnish *kappan* (to seize), Old Engl. *copian* (to plunder) (Modern Engl. *keep,* from *cēpan,* is related to *copian*), and a number of others in Austro-Asian, Altaic, and Hamitic languages. People, wherever they live, seem to exclaim *kap! khop! gop!* when they catch or seize something. German linguists call such words *Lautgebärden* (sound gestures). The same "gesture" underlies Latin *habēre* (to have) and Engl. *have.* Oehl, not unlike Whitney, observes that such primitive words, once they become part of the vocabulary, develop other meanings. For example, "seize" leads not only to "have" but also to "give." He posits phonetic variants of the initial "gesture" and cites *kam* as one of the modifications of *kap.* Dependence on arbitrary modifications is the most vulnerable part of his theory, but even if some of his etymologies are wrong, hundreds of synonymous and almost identical words from all continents make a strong impression. Throughout his work, he keeps repeating that kinship has nothing to do with the similarity of the forms he has assembled, which are products of "primitive creation" *(Urschöpfung)*.

Etymology, as it developed within the framework of nineteenth-century comparative linguistics, studies genetic ties among words. Its main objective is to perfect the mechanisms by which those ties can be reconstructed. Sound symbolic formations need none of its elaborate machinery. If Old Engl. *copian* (or *cōpian*) (to plunder), Russian *kopat'* (to dig) (stress on the second syllable) and *khapat'* (to grab) (stress on the first syllable), and Latin *capere* (to seize) are "primitive creations," nothing more can be said about them before turning to psychology. It is no wonder that Oehl's articles consist mainly of long lists of such words. Etymologists distrust look-alikes because cognates usually differ in their sounds (see Chapter 14), whereas *kop–kap–gop–khop–khap* are the same in all languages by definition. Historical linguistics is about kinship, whereas sound symbolism reveals universal "gestures." The two need not be at cross-purposes. We will return to this question in Chapter 15, and in Chapter 16 the relationship between etymology and the eternal question about the origin of language will again be raised.

Chapter Five

*in which people take the cause of
word origins in hand, or*

Folk Etymology

Squirrels have no horns and yet they do.—*Kitty-corner* and its kin.—
Wormwood without gall.—*All my eye and Betty Martin.*—*Penny Come
Quick* and *Cape Despair.*—Abhominable literati.—Old Fellow and
Thursday Morning as Shakespeare's tragic characters.—John Bellenden
Ker and A. Smythe Palmer.—Dear me!—Walter W. Skeat strikes out
a line for himself.

The oldest German name for the squirrel was *eihhurno*. The first
syllable either coincided with *eih* (oak) or is indeed *eih*. Even if the
association with *oak* is secondary, it does not militate against common sense. But *-hurn-* coincided with the word for "horn" by chance.
The result is Modern German *Eichhorn*, today usually *Eichhörnchen*
(with the diminutive suffix *-chen*). Thus did the squirrel turn into "a
little oakhorn." The absence of horned squirrels of whatever size has
never troubled German speakers. People will pick up any weapon to
defend themselves against a conventional linguistic sign: a squirrel
looking like a unicorn is more acceptable to them than an arbitrary
combination of sounds conveying an unpredictable meaning. The
Russian for "squirrel" is *belka,* and *bel* means white (as in *beluga,*
literally "white fish"). Etymological dictionaries may be right that
white squirrels were at one time hunted for their valuable fur, which
allegedly explains the animal's present-day generic name, but one
wonders when and where ermine-like squirrels populated the woods
of Russia. The common Russian squirrel is gray (only the underside
of its coat is white). Yet, as with German *Eichhörnchen,* the name
belka satisfies everybody.

44

Not only do speakers put up with absurdities like "oakhorn": they create them whenever they can. In the fifteenth century, the English danced the moreys dance; *moreys* or *mores* means "Moorish." Similar names exist in French, Spanish, German, Dutch, and Flemish (French *danse moresque,* and so forth). French *moresque,* Flemish *mooriske,* and others point to Spain as the most probable place of the origin of the dance, with "Moorish" referring to something grotesque, fantastic, bizarre. In England, the dance acquired national forms, and the connection with "Moors" was forgotten. It represented characters from the Robin Hood legend, such as Friar Tuck and Maid Marian, and was performed in fancy costumes (especially prominent were hoods and dresses tagged with bells, and the hobby horse, about which see p. 115, below). The foreign word *mores* gave way to *Morris.* It mattered little that no individual named Morris invented the dance or participated in the entertainment. If there is a piece of furniture called *Morris chair* (designed by William Morris), why shouldn't there be *Morris dance?*

The process of altering otherwise incomprehensible words, in order to give them a semblance of meaning, is called folk, or popular, etymology. A product of ignorance, it nevertheless should not be underestimated as a factor of language history, for many familiar words owe their form to it. In *kitty-corner, kitty* is a jocular substitution for *cater-. Cater-corner* is an opaque compound, while *kitty-corner* (diagonally from) suggests the movement of a prowling cat. Crows prefer straight lines, "kitties" don't; nothing more natural. Anyone perennially kept on a hot tin roof will sooner or later start cutting corners. In fact, *cater-* (across, askew) probably goes back to some Scandinavian word like Danish *kejte* (left hand) or *kejtet* (clumsy): the left hand is not "right," not "straight." (The derivation of *cater-* from French *quatre* [four] has little to recommend it.)

Forlorn hope is a nice bookish expression, and the epithet in it is, from a historical point of view, the same word as *forlorn* (pitiable, wretched), literally "lost" (compare German *verloren,* the past participle of *verlieren* [to lose]), but *hope* is not Engl. *hope.* The phrase traces to Dutch *verloren hoop* (lost troop) (*hoop* is akin to Engl. *heap*). It once meant "a picked force detailed for an attack," the same as

French *enfants perdus. Hoop* was mistaken for *hope,* and the phrase came to mean "a body of desperate men who have abandoned all hope for surviving" and "a hopeless enterprise," as in "to cherish a forlorn hope."

Since wormwood is a grass, *-wood* in its name seems to be out of place. Old English had *wormōd* from *wermōd.* German *Wermut* (earlier spelled *Wermuth,* from which English has *vermouth*) is allied to *wormwood.* The change of *-mood* to *-wood* is due to folk etymology and perhaps to the influence of initial *w.* However silly it may be to call a grass *wood, mood* is sillier still. Not improbably, even worms have no relation to wormwood, because we do not know whether the Old English word was *werm-ōd* or *wer-mōd.* Plant names are often borrowed from other languages. For example, Latin *absinthium* (wormwood) is from Greek, and the Greek word came from an unknown source. The plant was a remedy, used against worms, among other things. It upset the stomach and perhaps had the desired effect. Here is a quotation from a late-sixteenth-century herbal: "Wormwood voideth away the wormes of the guts, not onely taken inwardly, but applied outwardly: . . . it keepeth garments also from the Mothes, it driueth away gnats, the bodie being annointed [*sic*] with the oyle thereof." In Holland's once widely read translation of Pliny's *Natural History,* it is said that wormwood is "an enemy . . . to the Stomacke: howbeit the belly it looseth, and chaseth worms out of the guts, for which purpose, it is good to drink it with oile and salt."[1]

Stepmother, stepdaughter, and so forth suggest the derivation from *step.* Yet a stepchild is not one step removed from its natural parent; *-step* goes back to a word meaning "bereaved." Many people share Samuel Johnson's opinion that *bonfire* is "a good fire," from French *bon,* but it means "bonefire." Old bones were used as fuel down to the 1800s. The vowel *ō* was shortened before *-nf-* (a regular change before two consonants), and a native English word began to look half-French. (But if we recognize French *feu* in *curfew,* we won't be mistaken: the word is indeed from Old French *cuevrefeu* [coverfire]. Another time, *-few* turns up in the plant name *feverfew,* ultimately from Latin *febrifuga* [a driver away of fever]. *Feverfew* was recorded as *fewerfue* in the thirteenth century. The result is fully satisfactory because *feverfew* suggests an antidote for fever. Among the folk etymological variants of this word are *featherfew,* from the feather-like appearance of the leaves, and *fetterfoe,* a powerful compound.)

The verb *curry* means "to rub down (a horse) with a brush" and "to dress (tanned) leather." Old French *fauvel* (a fallow or chestnut horse) may have been associated with *favelle* (flattery, falsehood), and an idiom appeared that yielded Middle Engl. *to curry favel.* The French said *estriller fauvel* and later *estriller fauveau.* Currying a chestnut horse became a symbol of duplicity and toadyism in Western Europe. A character in the fourteenth-century *Roman de Fauvel* is a classic hypocrite. The Germans had a similar expression. We polish apples, they rubbed down the chestnut horse of the person with whom they wanted to ingratiate themselves. It is only the choice of the color that remains unclear, unless the probable pun (*fauvel ~ favelle*) furnishes a clue to the riddle. In English, *curry favel* was changed to *curry favor.* The horse disappeared from the idiom; *favor,* free from equestrian allusions, suggested the right meaning better than any circumlocution. The questions about how favor can be curried and what *curry* means requires no answer: in the fairyland of horned squirrels and Morris dances, anything is possible.

Some folk etymological reshapings are marvels of resourcefulness. *Furbelow* (a pleated border; in the plural, "showy trimming") is an alteration of *falbala* (French *falbala,* apparently one of many affected words for women's clothing. Russian had *tiuliurliu* "mantilla," as though from French, with stress on the last syllable, but French **turlurlu* has not been recorded: several similar-sounding onomatopoeic words refer to bagpipe music and the like). Words from other languages typically fall prey to mangling. Whatever associations people may have with *penthouse,* the form suggests a house in which one is pent up. But a penthouse is not a house, and those who live in it need not be cramped for room. Only the spelling *pentice* reflects the word's derivation accurately: *penthouse,* from *pentice,* means "appendix." *Mandragora* appears in English as *mandrake.* The root of the plant resembles a human figure and a phallus. According to a widespread superstition, mentioned in *Romeo and Juliet* IV: iii, 27, the mandrake groans so loudly, when pulled from the ground, that mortal ears cannot endure its shrieks. A powerful narcotic, it has also been regarded as an aphrodisiac for centuries. *Drake* (dragon) (not "the male of the duck"; the form *mandragon* has been attested) finds no rational explanation. Dragons dominated ancient myths and medieval heroic poetry: they guarded gold, spewed fire, crawled, flew, and swam with equal ease, and great warriors covered themselves with glory by battling them. Mandrake, that is, a dragon in human form, is a wonderful image. Once such a word enters into the vocabulary, it reinforces the myth, and more people begin to believe in the object's magical properties. Deciphering words as though they are acronyms is akin to folk etymology. It is doubtful that *posh* is an acronym for "**p**ort(side) **o**ut, **s**tarboard **h**ome," and the first letters of "**f**ornicate **u**nder **c**ommand of the **K**ing" (or any such phrase, of which several are in circulation) definitely do not provide us with the etymon of the English verb.

Every time a specious form disguises a nonsensical meaning, folk etymology may have been at large. Who is the lady celebrated in the exclamation *all my eye and Betty Martin* (humbug!) and what is *all my eye?* According to one suggestion, this gibberish goes back to the beginning of the Catholic prayer: "Oh, mihi, beate Martine" ("Ah, grant me, blessed St. Martin"). For a long time the English pronounced Latin words as though they were native (for example, *vee-nigh vie-die vie-sigh* [veni vidi vici]), so that *mihi,* the dative of *ego* (I), sounded like *my-high.* With *h* dropped, *my-(h)igh* would have yielded *'my eye.* The distance from *beate Martine* to *Betty Martin* is short. However, we cannot be sure that such is the etymon of the funny phrase.[2]

Foreign place names are hard to remember and even harder to pronounce. People change them merrily and mercilessly. Hundreds of outwardly reasonable names are the product of folk etymology. Perhaps the most often cited example is *Rotten Row* (in London) from French *route du roi* (king's way). The origin of a place name (when it is not *42nd Street* or *University Avenue*) is as difficult to discover as that of any other word. Here we are interested only in folk etymology. Gaelic *abhir-croisean* (confluence of troubles) and *bun'-a-gleanna* (the end of the glen) became *Applecross* and *Bonnyglen. Coach-and-Six Lane* in Cork comes from *Couchanex,* the family name of a Huguenot settler, whereas *Penny Come Quick* in Cornwall is an Anglicizing of *pen y cum gwic* (the head of the creek valley) (the Cornish language is now dead). In America, French *Purgatoire* (purgatory) and *Cap d'Espoir* (Cape of Hope) gave way to *Picketwire* and (!) *Cape Despair;* the last case of degradation is worse than *route du roi* turning into *Rotten Row.*[3]

Imaginative legends account for strange place names, and here linguistics (onomastics, to be precise) merges with folklore.

"Consider the plight of the captive, who, begging his Indian captor to spare his life, is told unmistakably and with the appropriate accompanying gesture— 'skin neck t'day', which curt and unrelenting judgment is said to have given us the name of the town *Schenectady* in our own New York" and "The town of *Wynot,* Nebraska, 'was started in 1907. A few citizens were trying to think up a name for the new town. One said, 'Why not name it–?, another 'Why not name it–?' This situation kept so long that an old German settler who had been taking it all in quietly finally exploded, 'Vi not! Name it Vi Not!'"[4]

It is not always necessary to change anything in the word for folk etymology to have its way. Everybody knows what a lifeguard's duties are. Yet a lifeguard is a *body*guard. The word was probably modeled on Dutch *lijfgarde*, in which *lijf* means "body." Pronounced by an English speaker, *lijf* became *life*. Latin *minium* denoted red lead, and Italian *miniatura* meant "a rubricated figure or vignette drawn with minium." Since miniatures regularly appeared in illuminated manuscripts, they were paintings on a smaller scale, and that is why we do not expect to see a large miniature and derive the word from the root of the word *minimal*. *Cushy*, as in *cushy job,* is a fairly accurate rendering of Hindi *khush* "excellent, pleasant" (with the suffix -*y*). The word originated in Anglo-Indian slang early in the twentieth century. It would hardly have become so popular, were it not for an association with *cushion* and the idea of "soft, comfortable." Life and body are connected in a natural way (compare the German alliterating phrase *Leib und Leben*), so that *lifeguard* is no worse a coinage than *bodyguard,* but the true derivation of *miniature* always surprises those who hear it for the first time, and when German *Tran* (blubber oil) yields in English *train oil,* trying to understand its meaning is a forlorn hope.

Misguided learned etymology does not differ from folk etymology. We spell *island* with *s* because it sounds like *isle,* and the literate men of the past decided that the two words are related. In fact, they are not. *Island,* from Old Engl. *īgland,* is a compound meaning "land (in the) water"; *īg-* is a cognate of Modern Engl. *ait* or *eyot* (islet). *Isle,* on the other hand, continues Old French *ile.* Its etymon is *insula.* Modern French does without *s* in *île* (only the *accent circonflexe* tells us that *s* has been lost between *i* and *l*), and English needs it even less. Adding *s* to *island* in the fourteenth century and not getting rid of it later is a product of ignorance compounded by stubbornness. The ancients explained Latin *insula* as from *in salō* (in the salt sea), but their explanation may also be folk etymology, reminiscent of the derivation of *Aphrodite* from *aphrós* (foam)[5] (the Greeks told of the birth of Aphrodite from the sea precisely because they detected "foam" in her name). Engl. *foreign* and *sovereign* got *g,* which has never been pronounced, under the influence of *reign.* Latin *regnum* did have *g,* but the etymon of *foreign* (Old French *forein*) is akin to Latin *forēs* (door), while *sovereign* goes back to Old French *soverain,* ultimately from Latin *super. Liquorice* has *qu* (so mainly in British English), in order for it to look like *liquor, rhyme* is spelled with an *h* because *rhythm* was supposed to be its cognate, and *delight* acquired its shape to resemble *light. Abominable,* which has the same root as *omen,* was derived from Latin *ab + homo* (away from man, inhuman). For over three centuries, beginning in the fourteenth, the word was spelled *abhominable* in Medieval Latin, French, and English.

Chance produced ties between the unrelated *buttery* (of unclear origin) and *butter; pantry* (its root is the same as in Latin *pānis* [bread]), and *pan; cesspool* (a Romance word) and *pool; belfry* (whose original meaning was "siege tower") and *bell; standard* (cognate with *extend*) and *stand; cutlass* (related to *colter*), *cutlet* (French *côtelette*), and *cut; teetotal* and *tea; hawk* (going back to Old English) and *hawker* (a borrowing from German); *hag* and *haggard* (both of obscure origin but unrelated); *raven* (a word of Germanic descent) and *ravenous* (a French word). Their closeness does not affect the nature of things. Chestnuts are still not kept in chests, walnuts do not grow on walls, and walleyes do not spawn near walls; however, those who look for butter in a buttery may occasionally find it there.

We smile condescendingly at hearing an anecdote about a coachman who called his master's horses Othello and Desdemona *Old Fellow* and *Thursday Morning*. Students of English have been taught not to derive *coward* from *cowherd* or *sirloin* from *Sir Loin*, but the creators and shapers of language are not university professors. For millennia people have spoken as they saw fit and did not bother about the disapproval of the literate (who, as we remember, introduced the spelling *foreign, rhyme,* and *island*). They changed Old French *primerole* (primula) (from *primus* [first]) to *primrose; *samblind* (half-blind) to *sandblind;* and *shamefast* to *shamefaced*. Now we all say those words as they did. The inner parts of an animal as used for food are called *numbles* or *umbles*. The umble pie, made of the entrails of a deer, was formerly given to dependents after the chase. *Umble* experienced the attraction of *humble,* especially in the speech of those who dropped their *h*'s. This is how the idiom *to eat humble pie* (to submit to humiliation, make abject apology) came into being. Now only the likes of Dickens's Uriah Heep, who constantly repeated that he was very 'umble, would use the historically correct form; the only acceptable variant is *humble pie.*

Experience puts us on our guard, and we begin to suspect that even *leap* in *leap year* and *leap* (to jump) are different words. Our caution partly pays off. Only a few dictionaries supply *leap year* with an etymology, and this is what we find in them. *The Century Dictionary:* "The exact reason of [*sic*] the name is unknown; but it probably arose from the fact that any date in such a year after the added day (February 29th) 'leaps over' the day of the week on which it would fall in ordinary years; thus if March 1st falls on Monday in one year, it will fall on Tuesday in the next if that is an ordinary year of 365 days, but on Wednesday if it is a leap-year." *The Oxford Dictionary of English Etymology:* "The term prob[ably] refers to the fact that in the bissextile year any fixed festival falls on the next weekday but one to that on which it fell in the preceding year." It is good to know that, after all, some leaping is involved in leap years.

Bowing to the power of folk etymology (eating humble pie, as it were) does not mean that we should look for its traces everywhere. John Bellenden Ker published one of the most amusing books ever written about English words.[6] He explained the commonest idioms, children's verses, and many words, as "corruption" of Dutch phrases, most of which do not exist—a veritable feast of folk etymology allegedly put right. The Reverend A. Smythe Palmer was, unlike Ker, a learned man, and his book (see note 1) is far from useless. But he mistook every change for "corruption" and lumped together the most dissimilar cases under the title "folk etymology." A modern student will easily see through his weaknesses. However, a mild warning is in order. I will quote parts of three entries from his work:

"DEAR ME! a vulgar exclamation of mild surprise, is supposed to be a corruption of It[alian] *Dio mio!* It is rather from Fr[ench] *(aide) Dieu me . . .*" "FOX-GLOVE. It might be argued with some plausibility that this is a corruption of *folk's-glove,* just as Foxhall in Pepys's Diary (May 29, 1662), now Vauxhall, is a corruption of Fulke's Hall. The *Digitalis,* with its fingerlike flowers suggesting a *glove,* is considered sacred to the 'good people' or fairy *folks* in most parts of the British Isles and Ireland. . . ." "CAT'S CRADLE . . . is a corruption of *cratch-cradle,* the word *cratch* being the usual term formerly for a manger rack, or crib (Fr[ench] *crèche*), of interlaced wickerwork. Latin *craticus, crates.* If, as Nares affirms, the game was also called *scratch-cradle,* this account may be received without hesitation, and an allusion may be traced to the manger-cradle of the Sacred History. . . ."

Nothing is more damaging to an argument than the words *without hesitation, without doubt, undoubtedly, certainly,* and the like. They are used only when proof is wanting. Smythe Palmer was close to the truth when he compared *dear me* and *Dieu me aide* because *dear* in that phrase stands for *Lord (Lord help me!),* but the similarity between *dear* and *Dio ~ Dieu* is accidental. Allusions to animals' names are often unclear in words like *foxglove* and *cat's cradle,* but no evidence points to the derivation of those words from *folk's glove* and *cratch cradle.* Unless we can reconstruct the change step by step in texts (as is the case with *forlorn hope* and *curry favor,* for example), it is better not to use folk etymology as the master key to words of unknown origin. Ker did not write his book in vain: he provided us with an experience we would prefer to avoid.

In 1896 Walter W. Skeat collected some of the approximately 500 short notes that had appeared in *Notes and Queries* and brought them out in book form.[7] The book opens with a long introduction. This is what he writes about "corruption":

> One of the queerest crazes in English etymology is the love of paradox, which is often carried to such an extent that it is considered mean if not despicable, to accept an etymology that is obvious. It is of no use to prove, to some people, by the clearest evidence, that *beef-eater* is derived from *beef* and *eater;* or *fox-glove* from *fox* and *glove;* or *offal* from *off* and *fall;* or *garret* from the French *garite;* or the A[nglo]-S[axon] *hlāfmæsse* (Lammas) from *hlāf*, a loaf; or *marigold* from *Mary* and *gold;* or *Whitsunday* from *white* and *Sunday;* all this is to them but food for babes, and they crave for strong meat, such as only themselves can digest. Most of these questions are here touched upon; but I only attempt to convince such as are more humble-minded.
>
> Against this desire of seeing "corruption" in almost every word, I have always waged war. . . . if etymology is to be scientific, the appeal lies to the facts; and the facts, in this case, are accurate quotations, with exact references, from all available authors. To attempt to etymologize without the help of quotations, is like learning geology without inspecting specimens.[8]

Skeat forgot to mention that quotations should be not only accurate but to the point. Smythe Palmer is a generous quoter, but the passages he gives, interesting in themselves, do not prove the validity of his solutions. On the whole, etymologists should be aware of two dangerous impulses: the first is to believe one's eyes (and ears), the other not to believe them. The rest is plain (plane) sailing.[9]

Chapter Six

*in which words dilly-dally, shilly-shally,
and play tick-tack-toe in disregard of the
hubbub they produce, or*

Words Based on Reduplication

Mrs. Tittlemouse and Mr. Jackson—Heebie-jeebies, yes; namby-
pamby, no.—The coxy-loxy Roister Doister.—*Hugger-mugger* from
Iceland to the Netherlands.—Hobnobbing with fuddy-duddies.—*Flip-
flop* again.—A questionable zigzag.—"When the hurly-burly's done."

Language is always at play. Creating words may be the most delightful game of all. To come up with something really new is hard, but it
requires a minimal effort to change one sound in a word that already
exists, and this is how we get the likes of *roley-poley* and *harum-
scarum.* Mr. Jackson, one of the unwelcome visitors in Beatrix Potter's
The Tale of Mrs. Tittlemouse, "sat such a while that he had to be
asked if he would take some dinner," but he wanted "a little dish of
honey." On being informed that there was none in the house, he said
with a smile: "Tiddly, widdly, widdly, Mrs. Tittlemouse. I can *smell*
it; that is why I came to call." He searched the house thoroughly,
found no honey, but commented a good deal, and never failed to
begin his pronouncements with: "Tiddly, widdly, widdly, Mrs. Tittlemouse." I suspect that Mr. Jackson (who was a frog) got his inspiration for *tiddly* from *tittle-* and added *widdly* for emphasis, without
trying to analyze his linguistic intuition. Dictionaries call such formations rhyming jingles. Children of a certain age rhyme joyously,
almost instinctively; some of their coinages remain in the language
of grownups. *Fuddy-duddy* must be one such coinage: *duddy* resembles *daddy,* with *fuddy,* like *widdly,* added for reinforcement.

Pokey-hokey is the name of a bugbear with which to frighten babies, but *hokey-pokey* means (or used to mean) "a cheap kind of ice cream, sold by street vendors." A snail can be called *haddy-daddy, hoddy-mandoddy, hudmandud,* and *horny-dorney,* whereas a caterpillar is a *marly-scarly.*[1]

Let no one say that only tiny tots and professional jesters use such words, for they are as real as our most learned creations. What would the English language be without *Georgie-Porgie, tootsy-wootsy, razzle-dazzle, heebie-jeebies, walkie-talkie, nitty-gritty,* and *polly-wolly-doodle?* True, such words are often "exotic," for example, *cagmag* (an old tough goose unfit for the table; decayed meat offal) (exotic to most of us but not in the north and east of England), *frigpig* (a finicking trifler), *hauvey-gauvey* (an awkward simpleton), and *tozy-mozy* (tipsy), but others are understood and used by most native speakers of English: *hoity-toity, fuzzy-wuzzy, higgledy-piggledy, mumbo-jumbo,* and, not to forget, *itsy-bitsy.* We barely notice the presence of rhyme in *picnic, humdrum, humbug, hobnob,* and *tidbit:* the humor of their inner form has worn off.

Admittedly, we cannot know too much about the origin of such words. Someone said *la-di-da* and *lardy-dardy* (they are defined as "an affectionate 'swell'"), someone repeated them, and they became part of the language. A local wit called punch (the beverage) *glimgrim,* and the word stayed in the dialect for some time. As always, we are fortunate to have the record of the "perpetrator" only in exceptional cases. Ambrose Phillips was the author of feeble pastorals that Henry Carey and Alexander Pope loved to ridicule. Carey seems to be the man to whom we owe the adjective *namby-pamby* (weakly sentimental, childishly simple): *namby-* is *Ambrose,* with *n* added (as in *Ned ~ Ed*), and *-pamby* echos *namby. Namby-pamby* surfaced in 1726; its authorship is almost certain. *Niminy-piminy* first appeared in print later. In the 1801 citation, it is spelled *nimeny-pimeny* and is given in quotes: the word must have been a recent neologism, and whoever coined it used *namby-pamby* as a model. In 1815, *miminy-piminy* turned up with the same meaning (ridiculously delicate or over-refined).

An ancient Roman invented *lardum* (lard), and a nineteenth-century Englishman thought of *lardy-dardy.* A word history need not be full of breathtaking adventures. One of Oscar Wilde's stories is called "The Sphinx without a Secret." It may not be his best story, but the title is excellent. Although the *lardy-dardy* group conceals few secrets, even in their origin not everything is "food for babes," as Skeat put it. We may assume that *roly-* refers to something rolling, while *-poly* is a riddle-less sphinx: *roly* with *p* substituted for *r* for the sake of a rhyming variation. The next episode is a trifle more exciting. *Roister* (a swaggering or blustering fellow) (now usually *roisterer*) has been known since 1551 (this is the date of the earliest recording in a book) and is believed to be an Anglicized form of French *rustre* (bumpkin) (from Latin *rusticus* [rustic]). When Nicholas Udall (1505–1556) was writing the first English comedy, he came up with the name *Ralph Roister Doister.* The play is about the courtship of Dame Christian Custance by the titular hero, whose name has become proverbial.

Coxy-loxy (good-tempered; drunk) was at one time Norfolk slang; its synonym in East Anglia was *coxy-roxy.* Both words may still be current in dialects. *Coxy* is apparently *cocksy* (compare the spelling of *coxcomb*), whereas the second part seems to be arbitrary: *loxy* is as good as *roxy. Moxy* would also have been perfect if one can judge by *crawley-mawley* (in a weakly and ailing state), another East Anglian word, and *frobly-mobly* (the same meaning, according to an old provincial dictionary). Variation is rife in such coinages. *Hanky-panky* (mystery; jugglery, legerdemain, later "mischievous activity"), competes with *hanky-spanky* (dashing). A 1865 tailor's circular advertised "pair of Moleskins, built hanky-spanky, with a double fakement down the sides, and artful buttons at bottom half a monarch" (*fakement* means "decoration," *monarch* is the coin called a sovereign—thus "a pair of richly decorated fur trousers for ten shillings"). If *-panky* is a mere rhyme for *hanky, spanky* must have been coined with reference to *spanky* (showy) and *spanking* (exceptionally good in some respect, frequently with an implication of showiness or smartness). *Cawdy-mawdy* and *coddy-moddy* are words from Northampton. Both are the names of birds (of the hooded crow, or curlew, and the common gull, respectively). The cawdy-mawdy probably says *caw-caw,* but why *coddy-moddy?* As we will see in Chapter 10 (pp. 115–17), the syllables *cub, cob, lub, rob, mock,* and so forth recur over and over again in animal names. In Yorkshire, *moddy calf* is a young calf and *coddy* is a young foal, but *coddy-moddy* is a gull, not a foal or a calf, or anyone's pet.

Hanky-spanky is an example of a word made from two existing words, cleverly combined to produce a third, and in this respect it differs from *hanky-panky*. Such formations are not uncommon. For example, in *arsey-varsy* (upside down; topsy-turvy), *arse* is the British counterpart of American Engl. *ass* (that is, "behind, buttocks," not "donkey"), and *varsey* reflects the popular pronunciation of *vers-* (as in *versus* and *vice versa*), the pronunciation that, several centuries ago, changed *person* to *parson,* '*versity* to '*varsity, clerk* to *clark* (now spelled so only in the family name *Clark*), *Derby* to *Darby,* and possibly *dern* (dark) to the imprecation *darn,* among others. The spellings *arsie-versie, arsey-versey,* and *arsey-warsey* have also been recorded. Unlike *hanky-panky* and *fuddy-duddy, arsey-varsey* has a vulgar but solid etymology.

In contrast, the origin of *hugger-mugger* remains a puzzle. Word lovers who open a dictionary and find a few dry lines telling them where anything from *aardwolf* to *zymosis* has come from, or are dismissed with the curt statement "origin unknown," seldom realize how much work precedes the writing of those lines. Even when no acceptable hypothesis on the derivation of a word exists, it does not follow that no one tried to solve the riddle. As a rule, the opposite is true. Specialists and amateurs are forever offering conjectures, buttressed by clever or fanciful arguments. Unless a dictionary maker's aim is to survey and sift reams of scholarly papers and heaps of pretentious rubbish and summarize the findings, we learn nothing about the unsuccessful reconstructions by philologists or the failed efforts of many a country squire to trace the word to its source. Published entries contain only pieces of presumably unshakable truth. But what is truth to one is falsehood to another. The origin of *hugger-mugger* (an unforgotten word, partly because it occurs in *Hamlet* IV. v. 84: the king rues that Polonius was buried in hugger-mugger) is a case in point.

The Oxford Dictionary of English Etymology repeats the *Oxford English Dictionary* in saying that *hugger-mugger* was preceded by similar rhyming jingles (*hucker mucker* or *moker,* and *hoder-moder*) and is probably based on dialectal *mucker* (from Middle Engl. *mokere* [to hoard]) and Middle Engl. *hoder* (to huddle up, wrap up). It concludes that the word's ultimate origin is unknown. *The Universal Dictionary of the English Language,* which pays great attention to etymology, is unusually reticent: "Origin unknown" is all we find in it. Finally, *The Century Dictionary* has the following to say:

> Also *hucker-mucker, hugger-mucker, hocker-mocker, hoker-moker, huker-moker, hudder-mudder* (Ascham has *huddermother* (Toxophilus, 1545), Skelton *hoder-moder),* etc.; in similar uses are found *huggrie-muggrie, hudge-mudge,* M[iddle] E[ngl.] *mokeren, mukren,* hoard up, conceal, but, as in many other riming compounds, the parts seem to have lost their specific meaning, and the word took on a vague general sense, not capable of etymological analysis.

The etymon of *hugger-mugger* has been sought in Spanish (*hogar* [hearth, fireplace] and *mujer* [woman]), Dutch (*Hogen Mogen* [The States General of Holland], used derisively from *Hoog en Mogend* [high and mighty]), Old Engl. *hogian* (think, intend) and Engl. *murk* (*hugger-mugger* emerged as "observation in the dark"), Engl. *hug* and *murk* (as though *hugger-mugger* were "a hug in the dark"), and even in the names of the Scandinavian god Odin's ravens *Hugin* (thought) and *Munin* (memory) (every day they flew over the earth and reported what they had seen; Odin worried about their safety, but the ravens' flight was not clandestine).[2] This array of wild guesses is typical.

Neither hugs nor observation in the dark will result in the discovery of how *hugger-mugger* came about, but those seem to have been on the right track who noted that many words with the root *mug-* (its vowel and final consonant may vary) refer to secret dealings and illegal actions. The verbs *mug* (to waylay and rob), *mooch* (to obtain by begging; filch) (and its doublet *miche,* as in Hamlet's *miching malecho* [sneaking mischief]), German *meucheln* (to assassinate), and Latin *muger* (a cheat at dice) belong here. They have been part of thieves' and criminals' international slang ("cant") for millennia. Some of them begin with *s-;* therefore, *smuggle* is possibly akin to *mug.* If this explanation is correct, *-mugger* need not be connected with *moder* or *mucker,* the words the *Oxford English Dictionary* cites.

But what about *hugger-?* The index to Nils Thun's book *Redupli-cative Words in English* (see note 1) contains close to 26 pages; *h*-words take up four-and-a-half of them. No other letter in the index is represented even approximately so well. Here we find *hanky-panky, harum-scarum, higgledy-piggledy, hoity-toity* (all of them mentioned above), *hullabaloo, hob-job* (offhand, without deliberation) (dialec-tal), *histy-fisty* (using the fists, with the fists), *hurly-burly, howdy-dowdy* (untidy, unkempt), and dozens of others. We observe how natural it is to take a common word, for example, *fist(y), job,* or *dowdy,* substitute *h* for the first sound, and end up with a rhyming jingle. Whatever the origin of *harum-scarum* and *higgledy-piggledy,* their history must have begun with *-scarum* (from *scare*) and *piggledy* (from *pig*). In some compounds, *h-* appears to have been chosen al-most by default. *Hugger-* may not be an etymological sphinx: it is more likely *mugger* (in secret), with *m* replaced by *h.* Once *hugger-mugger* (gibberish to most people, though they knew its meaning) had been coined, it began to change, whence the variants recorded in sixteenth- and seventeenth-century books. *Hucker-mucker* (as though from *muck*) and *hudder-mudder* (as though from *mud*) were the best finds. Another alteration of *hugger-mugger* is Irish Engl. *cugger-mugger* (secret conversation), from *cugger* (to hold a confidential conversation, talk in private). *Hugger-mugger* is a funny street word, but its etymology is as worthy of attention as that of the most digni-fied verbs, nouns, and adjectives of remote epochs.

A few compounds like *fuddy-duddy* probably go back to fused phrases. For instance, the predecessor of *hurly-burly* in texts was *hurling and burling.* However, in the past, such conversational words found their way into print by chance, and we should not look on the dates of the first recordings as their dates of birth. *Hurly-burly* may have existed before *hurling and burling* and later developed into a compound. Thus, *harum-scarum* is sometimes understood as *hare 'em, scare 'em* (*hare* [to worry, harass, frighten]). Since slang, and especially the cant of itinerant actors, hawkers, mercenaries, and pros-titutes, was to a certain extent international, it is no wonder that some jingles (which are not only easy to coin but also easy to remember) came to English from abroad. French has *hurluberli,* taken to mean "a hasty harum-scarum person" (Rabelais's word), and German has *hurliburli* (headlong). We are not certain in which language those compounds originated, but all three words could not have been coined independent of one another. *Hubbub* is believed to be of Gaelic origin: *abú* was an Old Irish war cry. *Charivari, picnic,* and *pall-mall* are French, and so is, of course, *cancan* (the dance). Most often, the origin of such words in the lending language is said to be unknown.

If Old English favored rhyming compounds, they are lost, though rhyming binomials like *hond and rond,* literally "(the) hand and (the) shield," were widely used in poetry.[3] Some examples have been gleaned from Middle English books, but most such words are late. A few compounds have been around for a long time: *hodge-podge* (1426), *hugger-mugger* (1526), *hurly-burly* (1539), *hubbub* (1555), *helter-skelter* (1593), *higgledy-piggledy* (1598), *hobnob* (1601; *hob or nob* was recorded in 1756 and *hob and nob* in 1762; see what has been said above about the dating of *hurling and burling* versus *hurly-burly*), and *humpty-dumpty* (the name of a drink, 1700).[4] Other compounds are more recent. *Fuzzy-Wuzzy* surfaced first in Kipling, and *nitwit* was a new word in 1928. Words like *hugger-mugger* and *higgledy-piggledy* have their limitations. They are expressive and refer mainly to tumult and confusion, foolishness, and trickery. It is dangerous to overuse them, for they are like condiments and should be consumed in moderation.

The title of this chapter suggests that words can play tick-tack-toe (*trictrac,* too, would be appropriate). In the examples discussed above, a change of the first consonant produced the other part of the compound: from *mugger* to *hugger,* from *horny* to *dorney,* and so on. But it is possible to change a vowel in a word and come up with *tick-tock* or *ding-dong.* (Only *sc-* ~ *sk-*, as in *harum-scarum* and *helter-skelter,* is an indivisible unit; it has been such throughout the history of English.) Words like *tick-tock, flip-flop,* and *pitter-patter,* though they are of onomatopoeic origin, have a wide sphere of application. A bow-wow is an animal name only in a little child's language, but *yiff-yaff* (a small person who talks a great deal and little to the purpose) has been recorded in Scots, and in British dialects we find *yip-yap* and *yip-yop* (an upstart, a young, scatterbrained person), alongside *yap* (an impudent, forward child or youth; a fool). *Yiff-yaff* and *yip-yap* are words of the same order as *bow-wow, arf-arf,* and *yap-yap.* (Against the background of *yip-yap, yuppie* looks natural, and that may be the reason it has struck root.)

A vowel alternation in a word consisting of two parts produces a swinging effect; hence *see-saw* and its synonyms. The base of *see-saw,* first recorded in 1704, is probably the verb *to saw. Teeter* is an alteration of *titter* (to totter) (note how close *totter* is to *titter,* though they are supposedly unrelated), not of *titter* (to giggle), and numerous compounds like *titter-totter* and *titter-tatter* (or with *teeter-* as their first part) meaning "to swing" exist. Here are a few non-onomatopoeic words of the *flip-flap* and *see-saw* type that entered the Standard with the dates of their first recordings as they appear in the *Oxford English Dictionary: mishmash* (ca. 1450), *riffraff* (1470), *gewgaw* (1529), *flim-flam* (1538), *fiddle-faddle* (1577), *whim-wham* (1580), *dilly-dally* (ca. 1610), *knick-knack* (1682), *wishy-washy* (1693), *zig-zag* (1712), *criss-cross* (1818), *tip-top* (1860), *shilly-shally* (1865), and *ping-pong* (the game, 1900). The construction of *ship-shape* is especially elegant: two words have been combined, and the whole resembles other compounds with alternating vowels. Of so-called suggestive words perhaps only *hootchy-kootchy* (1899) has spread far and wide. Among myriad slang names for male and female genitals, compounds are in the minority. I will not comment on which of the following are men's and which are women's organs: *placket-racket, roly-poly, tirly-whirly, tuzzy-muzzy,* and *dingle-dangle.*

Words of the *drib-drab* type (with different vowels) and rhyming jingles enter the language and behave in a similar way. (I have coined *drib-drab* from *dribs and drabs:* "The meager information reaches me drib-drab," and now at least one database will probably register my neologism.) Some of them are native, while others are borrowings. At first sight, *zigzag* poses no problems. If we discover how *zig-* arose, we will assume that *-zag* is its alteration. On the other hand, if *-zag* is primary, we will conclude that *zig-* was coined to match it. The *Oxford English Dictionary* quotes Robert Burns: "Zig here, zag there" (1793, prose). The laws of sound symbolism teach us that zag-ging entails more work than zigging. Inasmuch as *zig* and *zag* resemble onomatopoeias, the etymology of *zigzag* seems to be self-explanatory (for comparison, *zip* as in *zipper* imitates the sharp sound of contact). However, *zigzag* exists not only in English. French has *zigzag,* and the German for *zigzag* is *Zickzack* (*z* in German is pronounced approximately as *ts* in Engl. *cats*). In French books, *zigzag* appeared in 1680; in German it was presumably known but not attested before 1680, and in English the earliest citation goes back to 1712.

Perhaps German -*zack* is the same as *Zacke* (point; tooth, prong); Germ. *Zackenlinie* means "jagged line." The origin of *Zacke* and its English cognate *tack* (clasp, fastening) (both words are old) is of no consequence for the history of *zigzag*. If that history began with German *Zacke,* then, according to an earlier agreement, we should treat *zick* as a "thinning" of *zack* and suppose that *Zickzack* existed long before it turned up in print, early enough for French to borrow it from books. Somebody must have *read* the German word in the French way, for otherwise *tsicktsack* (the form one hears) would not have become *zigzag*. The English word would then be a loan from French. And this is what most etymologists say. Their argument is clear: only the German word can be explained ("etymologized") from the resources of the language in which it is current. Consequently, its place of origin is Germany. This reasoning is good but not flawless (what if *zigzag* appeared in French as a rootless onomatopoeia, became known in German, and was there associated with the noun *Zacke,* which accidentally looks like the etymon of *zigzag?*). However, the principle invoked in the reasoning is sound, and we will return to it in dealing with the word *hackney* in Chapter 10.

French *hurluberlu* and Engl. *hurly-burly* may have different origins, though such a coincidence is improbable. It has been suggested that *hurly-* is Engl. *hurl* or French *hurler* (to howl) + *y*. Northern German *hurreln* means "to toss, throw; push," and all three—*hurl, hurler,* and *hurreln*—may at one time have meant "to do something with a lot of noise" (later "to howl" and "to dash"). The -*burly* of *hurly-burly* reminds one of Italian *burla* (ridicule, joke, fun), from which, via French, English has *burlesque.* There was once an English verb *birl* (to pierce, stab) (perhaps also in figurative use *"to make sniding remarks"?), but the connection between it and -*burly* cannot be made out.

In all probability, Engl. *hurr-y* has the same root as *hur-l:* whenever a *hur-* word occurs, the reference is to tumult and commotion. The same holds for *whirl* and partly for *twirl. Hurly-burly* is an onomatopoeic formation like *hurdy-gurdy,* that is, a rhyming jingle. Without *r, hurly-burly* turns into a variant of *hullabaloo.* Perhaps *hullabaloo* is nothing more than *hullo!* + *ba* + *loo* (on -*ba*-, see the next chapter). Yet people looked for its origin in the Irish place name *Ballaholy,* French hunting or warning cries with *loup* "wolf" at the end, Gaelic nursery phrases, and Swedish *kalabalic* (or its Turkish source).[5] "When the hurlyburly's done," if one is allowed to quote a witch from *Macbeth,* we are left with admiration for scholarly ingenuity and the suspicion that it sometimes takes researchers too far.

Attempts to trace the origin of *hugger-mugger, zigzag, hurly-burly,* and *hullabaloo* go a long way toward showing how much we can find when studying such simple words. Only compounds that lack variation, from *beriberi* to *goodie-goodie* and *pooh-pooh,* are transparent, because where there is no resistance, no force is needed.[6]

Chapter Seven

which extols swelling from within, or

Infixation

The benefits of edumacation.—Take your pick: figmajig or fashizzle my nizzle.—From *Ragman's Roll* to *rigmarole* and *rigamarole.*—Daffy-down-dilly comes to town.—Heinrich Schröder's fandamnastic book.—On finagling and skedaddling.—The habitual grinner grizzle-de-mundy, the sexually repressed hobbledehoy, and sundry types of gobbledegook.—Hush-a-bye, baby.—The demonized ragamuffin.

Those who know the word *edu-ma-cation* hardly ever think of the source of the inserted syllable ("infix") *-ma-* or remember its kin. *Razzmatazz,* a synonym of *razzle-dazzle* (showiness), is part of the *edumacation* family. It once referred to old-fashioned (and, by implication, "corny") jazz and extravagant display (fuss, commotion, garishness). The word was coined in the United States at the end of the nineteenth century. The *Oxford English Dictionary* informs us that the origin of *razzmatazz* is unknown: perhaps, we are told, it is an alteration of *razzle-dazzle.* Since the origin of *razzle-dazzle,* another American coinage, is also unknown (the earliest citation is dated 1889), we learn nothing about the derivation of *razzmatazz.* The syllables *razz-, dazz-,* and *tazz-* rhyme with *jazz,* an early-twentieth-century word and the object of endless debate among etymologists. Dazzling razors lighten up the path of *razzle-dazzle* from obscurity (*The Century Dictionary* says "a varied reduplication of *dazzle*"), but we will resist the lures of folk etymology and concentrate on *-ma-.*

Nils Thun, who collected close to two thousand reduplicative words of English, cites *figmajig* (a toy, trifle; anything which moves or works about).[1] Its obscene meaning stands out a mile, as the idiom goes. Thun does not say so, but mentions dialectal *frigabob* (to dance or jerk up and down; anything which dances or jerks up and down or from side to side). A modern counterpart of *frigmajig* would be *fashizzle my nizzle*. *Shagrag* (rabble, riffraff, tagrag) (people who are shaggy and ragged?) has the variant *shag-me-rag* (a mean person), recorded in a British dialect in 1854. It is hardly a blend of *shagrag* and *shagmarelle* (an idle good-for-nothing), as Thun thinks; rather we have *shagrag* with an infix. The Cumberland word *fligmagary* means "a tawdrily dressed woman." From the structural point of view, it is *flig-ma-gary*, for *fligary* has also been attested, and also in the North, with nearly the same meaning. Another synonym of *frigary* ~ *fligmagary* is *flig-me-jig* (a girl of doubtful character), in the parlance of late Victorian England. The verb *jig* (to jerk up and down) arose as slang and has continued into the present: Farmer and Henley give *jig-a-jig* (to copulate); Lighter's examples testify to the international reputation of the phrase.[2] *Fligmejig* and *frigmajig* are, for all intents and purposes, variations of the same word. *Frig* was at one time as unprintable as the other (now printable and pronounceable) *F*-word, and unless *flig-* is a deliberate alteration of *frig*, to make it sound more genteel and fit for use in mixed company (like *Gosh!* for *God!*), it may be its regular phonetic variant.[3]

    In the previous chapter, *hoddy-mandoddy* and other names of the snail were mentioned (see p. 55). Now we can add *odd-me-dod* to that list. The existence of the infix *-ma-* ~ *-me-* is a fact. That is why *arithmetic* so easily turned into *rick-ma-tick* in a dialect of Scots and why *clish-clash* (idle gossip, scandal; to gossip) has a by-form *clish-ma-clash*.[4]

    Probably *-ma-* has come from compounds like *frigmajig* in which *-ma-* is a dialectal pronunciation of *my*. We may find some confirmation of this hypothesis in the history of the word *rigmarole*, an alteration of *Ragman* (or *Ragman's*) *roll* (a parchment roll, an official catalog or register). John Jamieson says the following about the oldest Ragman roll: "The name was applied specifically, and perhaps originally (in the supposed invidious sense 'the Cravens' Roll'), to the collection of those instruments by which the nobility and gentry of Scotland were tyrannically constrained to subscribe allegiance to Edward I of England in 1296, and which were more particularly recorded in four large rolls of parchment, consisting of thirty-five pieces bound together, and kept in the Tower of London."[5] Jamieson explained *Ragman* as "craven" because the roll included the names of the Scottish barons who knuckled under to the English king (Icelandic *ragmenni* means "coward," and, given that interpretation, *Ragman* turns out to be a word of Scandinavian descent). According to *The Oxford Dictionary of English Etymology,* the reference is rather to "a ragged man." However, a likelier etymon of *Ragman* in *Ragman roll* is *Ragman,* one of the many medieval names of the Devil: to the Scottish feudals Edward's long document was indeed the Devil's list. With time, *Ragman's roll* began to designate any endless and tedious register and was used as the name of a parlor game. The entertainment was provided by a roll of parchment containing verses descriptive of character (often shockingly indecent). To each verse a string with a pendant was attached. The parchment was rolled up and each player selected one of the projecting strings; the verse to which it led was taken as his or her description. When people forgot the meaning of *Ragman,* folk etymology changed the word into *rig-my-role, rig-me-role* (something unintelligible but with vaguely scurrilous overtones), and into *rigmarole* (balderdash), in which *-ma-* looked like an infix.

We will return to both *Ragman* and *rigmarole* at the end of this chapter. At the moment, suffice it to note that infixation brought to life such dissimilar forms as *daffydowndilly* (daffodil) (first recorded in 1573 and immortalized in *Mother Goose:* "Daffy-down-dilly is new come to town, / With a yellow petticoat, and a green gown"), *fan-damn-tastic* and *abso—lutely,* with various expletives in the place of my demure dash.[6] (Dorothy Parker's story "Too Bad" is about a husband and wife who have nothing to say to each other. The woman is trying to find some subject for conversation. "'See my pretty daffy-down-dillies?' she said. . . . To anyone else, she would have referred to them as daffodils." Those silences irritated her: "It makes you nervous and self-conscious, and you talk desperately about tomato soup, and say things like 'daffy-down-dilly'.") Not all forms with infixes reveal their structure as easily as does *edumacation. Daffydowndilly,* for example, is transparent *(daff-y-down-dill-y),* but who coined this word and why? The *Oxford English Dictionary* says:

"A playful expansion of *daffodil*." Strangely, **maggy-down-nolia* or **hary-down-belly* do not exist.[7]

In 1903, Heinrich Schröder, a German linguist, who was as prolific as he was talented, published an article entitled *Streckformen*.[8] Since *strecken* means "to stretch," Schröder's term can be translated as "extended forms." The article contained 53 examples, most of them culled from German dialects. A few years later, he brought out a book on the same subject, in which he discussed about 350 words. All of them are trisyllabic, with stress falling in the middle, and practically all are expressive.[9] Schröder compared words like *'klastern* and *kla'dastern* (to run about aimlessly) and concluded that the latter is *kl-ad-astern*, though *kla-da-stern* would have been a more natural division. As long as *klastern* and *kladastern* occur in the same dialect, no one can contest Schröder's etymology: apparently, to reinforce a word or to achieve a humorous effect, people "pull aside" a word and insert an extra syllable. Engl. *shagrag* and *fantastic*, alongside *shagmerag* and *fandamntastic*, are comparable to *klastern ~ kla-da-stern*, but *shagmerag* and *kladastern* differ in two respects: the German word changes the place of stress and its insert is meaningless even from a historical point of view (*-ad-* or *-da-* has no etymon). Schröder discovered a long list of such inserts. Unfortunately, he went too far and cited as extended many words that probably have a different origin. If *shagrag* had not been attested, the derivation *shagmerag* from *shag-me-rag* would have carried little conviction. The partners in Schröder's pairs often differ widely in meaning and form, and critics lost no time in attacking his conclusions.[10] Despite the initial rebuttal, Schröder's idea has gained recognition. His term *Streckform* became familiar,[11] and his discovery helped to explain the origin of some hard words. As always, false leads abound: *clishmaclash* and *razzmatazz* are extended forms, while *rigmarole* only looks like one.

English is poor in colloquial words resembling German *kladastern*, but a few seem to exist. Dialectal *fineney* (to mince, simper) is a synonym of *finey*, so that perhaps it is *fi(ne)ney*. *Fandangle* (ornaments, trinkets; capers) has stress on the first syllable; yet it looks

like an extended form of *fangle,* as in *newfangled,* with stress transferred to *fan-; fangle* means "a conceit, whim; to trim showily, en-
tangle; hang about, trifle, waste time." The association with *dangle*
may be due to folk etymology. *Fundawdle* (to caress) and *gamawedled*
(tipsy) are probably extensions of *fondle* (to caress) and *gaddle* (to
drink greedily and hastily). *Fundawdle* may, of course, be simply
fun + dawdle, but in such a compound stress would have been on the
first syllable: compare *browbeat, proofread, spoonfeed, wirepull,* and
the like.

   Perhaps *finagle* is another extended form: *fi-na-gle.* This verb was
first recorded in 1926 in the United States. In dialectal pronunciation, *-dle* often alternates with *-gle. Figgle* is a doublet of *fiddle* (to
fidget about). Except in dictionaries, *finagle* has almost never been
discussed.[12] In contrast, *skedaddle,* still another American word, has
been in the limelight almost since the day it surfaced in an American
newspaper in 1861 and kept appearing in letters to the editors of
popular magazines on both sides of the Atlantic for years. *Skedaddle*
has been traced to Classical Greek (a favored hypothesis for more
than a century), Irish (the suggested source was a form in the Irish
Bible that, as it turned out, does not exist), Welsh, Swedish, and Danish
(in fact, no Scandinavian verb sounds like *skedaddle.*)[13] Only northern Engl. *skedaddle* (to spill milk) sheds light on that so-called Ameri-
canism (so-called, because American words alien to the British
Standard often turn out to be regionalisms brought to the New World
from England). As native speakers of northern dialects explained,
one can skedaddle coals, potatoes, apples, and other substances falling from a cart. English dialectal *scaddle* means "to scare, frighten;
run off in a fright." American *skedaddle* is, most likely, an extended
form of *scaddle* (or **skeddle,* if such a pronunciation of *scaddle* existed), that is, *ska(da)ddle* or *ske(da)ddle.*

   The harvest is slim: Schröder's model has yielded a half-dozen
words like *finagle,* all of them of questionable origin. When reading
a dictionary, one occasionally runs into verbs resembling extended
forms, but, as pointed out above, some leads are false. *Bamboozle*
rhymes with *foozle* but is clearly not *bam(boo)zzle. Boondoggle* has
stress on the first syllable and did not develop from a shorter verb.

Shillaber (American slang), for which the *Oxford English Dictionary* has only one 1913 citation and whose putative stub has survived as *shill* (to decoy an accomplice, especially one posing as a customer to encourage other buyers), may be an extended form of German *Schieber* (black marketeer) (then *shi-la-ber*), but this reconstruction is not particularly strong, and so it goes. The indubitable inserts in English are *de* (or *te*) and *a*.

Here we find words that have been dead for centuries like *simper-de-cocket,* a term of mild abuse for women (originally *"a simpering coquette"?*), and the fairly recent *gobbledegook ~ gobbledygook* (one more piece of American slang, not attested before 1944). Assembled together, they look like exhibits from a linguistic museum of freaks: *flipper-de-flapper* (noise and confusion), *tatterdemalian* (a ragged person), *grizzle-de-mundy* (a stupid person who is always grinning), *hubble-te-chives* (confusion), *Flibber-ti-gibbet* (one of many names of evil spirits in *King Lear; Flibberdigibbet* occurs, too), *dandiprat* (an insignificant person), and *slabberdegullion* or *slubberdegullion* (lout) (compare the shorter form *gullion* [fool; nonentity]). Engl. *helter-skelter* is "a rhyming jingle." Its northern German counterpart is *hulterpulter,* but extended forms are close by: northern German *helter-de-fulter* (beside *helterfulter)* and *hullerdebuller.* The Dutch say *holder-de-bolder* (helter-skelter), and Germans have *holter-di-polter* (also spelled *holter-die-polter*) (upside down).

The infix *-de-* may have come to English with French words like *dandelion* (*dent-de-lion* [lion's tooth]), from northern German, or from Dutch. (For future reference we may remember that the popular name of this plant—also influenced by French usage—is *piss-a-bed:* the dandelion is a diuretic.) In English, *-de-* is especially common in words denoting ruckus and in the names of demons and people considered worthless. Some of them are next of kin to the compounds that occupied us in Chapter 6, for instance, *flipperdeflapper.* When Christopher Robin knighted Winnie, he said: "Rise, Sir Pooh de Bear." In similar fashion, the slobbering gullion (a worthless sloven) arose one day as *slubberdegullion* (I do not understand why the *Oxford English Dictionary* calls *-gullion* a fanciful addition), and the grizzling mundy (that is, "a grinning good-for-nothing"; *mundy* seems to contain an opprobrious allusion) was elevated to the status of *grizzledemundy*. The humor inherent in such formations is their most noticeable feature.

The French and Dutch origin of *-de-* ~ *-te-* does not mean that every word having an infix was borrowed from those languages: it is enough to have a model for new forms to appear. *Gobbledegook* is simply *gobble* and *gook* with *-de-* between them. The structure of such supposedly extended forms as *finagle* and *skedaddle* is obscure (perhaps *fi-na-gle* and *ske-da-ddle*), whereas *Flibberdigibbet* is obviously *Flibber-de-gibbit*. But what are *Flibber, gibbet, Flipper,* and *gibbit?* Is the first element of *dandiprat* identical with *dandy,* and is *-prat* "trick" or "buttock," or somebody's name, or none of the above? Some such questions cannot be answered—a minor inconvenience in this context, for here our only concern is the infix.

A curious word is *hobbledehoy* (an awkward youth). The earliest citation of it in the *Oxford English Dictionary* is dated 1540. One of the fiends in *King Lear* is called Hobbididance. *Hobidy-booby* (only one 1720 example of its use has been found) possibly means "scarecrow." In older books and in dialects, *hobbledehoy* appears in at least eight variants, with *hoble-, hoba-, hobbe-, hobo-, hobly-, hobbi-, hobbard-,* and *haber-* as its first element. Two of them (*hobble-* and *hobbard-*) reflect different pronunciations and not only vagaries of spelling. At present, *hobbledehoy* is associated with hobbling (hence the idea of clumsiness), but it probably owes the association to folk etymology.[14]

Hobble- must be related to *hob-,* the first element of *hobgoblin,* the popular variant of *Rob* (see p. 101, below), still another name of the Devil in the late Middle Ages. In 1557 Thomas Tusser published the book *Fiue Hundred Pointes of Good Husbandrie.* One of its chapters is about twelve periods of human life, each lasting seven years. It begins so:

The first seuen years, bring vp a childe;
The next, to learning, for waxing too wilde;
The next, keepe under sir hobbard-de-hoy.[15]

The meaning is: until the age of seven, bring up (that is, take care of) your child; between seven and fourteen, teach him, lest he get out of hand; between fourteen and twenty-one, "keep under," that is, suppress Sir Hobbard de Hoy. Sir Hobbard de Hoy is the Devil, the temptation of lust, for Tusser had a clear notion of when the sexual urge should be kept in check, when it should be satisfied, when it is too late to begin, and when sex is no longer attractive. Evidently, before a young man turns twenty-one, this particular devil should be "kept under." Thus *Hobbard* is a side-form of *Robert.*

The origin of *-dehoy-* is less clear. Perhaps *Robert le Diable* was also known under the name **Robert le Roy* (Robert the King, King Robert). After *Robert* became *Hobard, Roy* followed suit and changed to *Hoy,* to preserve the alliteration, and since the devils' names usually had *-de-* or *-te-* in the middle (*Hobberdidance, Haberdicut,* and the rest), **Hobard le Hoy* became *Hobbard-de-Hoy.* Although this is guesswork, the way from the unattested **Robert le Roy* to *Hobbard-de-Hoy* can be reconstructed with some confidence at a distance of more than half a millennium.[16] *Hobbledehoy* is an extended form, but only an etymologist can discern its devilry.

Another infix of extended forms in English is *-a-.* We again enter a museum of freaks: *jackanapes* (coxcomb), *blackamoor* (now offensive and gone out of use), *jackadandy, grinagog,* a synonym of *grizzledemundy, muck-a-muck* (a person of importance), *ragabash* (an idle ragged person), *pit-a-pat, pick-a-pack ~ pick-a-back* (on the shoulders), and a profusion of words with *cock-,* some of them obsolete or dialectal: *cockagrice* (a cock and a pig cooked together) (a dish favored in the fifteenth century), *cok-a-leekie* (soup made from a fowl boiled with leeks) (the *Oxford English Dictionary* cites a phrase from the *Daily Telegraph,* December 7, 1865: "The savory haggis and the unassuming cock-a-leekie"), *cock-a-bondy* (a fly for angling), *cock-a-bendy* (an instrument for twisting ropes), *cock-a-hoop* (in a state of elation), and so forth. Only *cock-a-doodle-do* does not need a gloss. *Hullabaloo,* a close relative of *hurly-burly,* discussed in the previous chapter, is another word with *-a-,* and there are *peek-a-boo* and words familiar from nursery rhymes: *rub-a-dub-dub, rock-a-by ~ hush-a-bye,* and the like. Even Anglicized borrowings are prone to acquiring *-a-* in the middle. The Dutch phrase *ter kaap varen* (to go privateering) became *copabare* (to misappropriate government stores), a piece of well-formed gibberish.[17] Spanish *jáquima* (halter) turned into *hackamore* (halter with a loop), as though it were part of a verse from *Mother Goose:* "Hick-a-more, hack-a-more, / Hung on the kitchen door."[18] Words like *ragabash* and *pit-a-pat* resemble *claptrap* and *tip-top,* the only difference being that they have an infix.[19]

The infix *-de-,* as pointed out, probably had two sources, French *de* and Dutch *de.* The infix *-a-* is not a purebred either: sometimes it goes back to the English prepositions *on* or *of* and sometimes to French *a. Jackanapes* emerged as *Jack on* or *of Napes* (the origin of *Napes* is unascertained, but William de la Pole, first Duke of Suffolk, whose nickname was Jack Napes, had a badge with an ape's clog and chain), whereas *cap-a-pie* (from head to foot) is from French. As with *-de-,* once *-a-* was felt to be a legitimate English infix, new extended forms arose that owe nothing to *on ~ of* or French *a.* Surely, **cock-on-doodle-do* never existed, and French roosters crow *cocorico.* Most people I polled prefer *rigamarole* to *rigmarole* (some of them profess English). The rhythmically perfect word *rigamarole* has thus undergone two extensions since the beginning of the eighteenth century (the earliest citation of *rigmarole* in the *Oxford English Dictionary* is dated 1726). With the recent appearance of a board game called *Rigamarole,* the older form will probably disappear altogether, at least in the United States.

I will conclude the chapter on extended forms with a short history of the word *ragamuffin.* We must return to the fiends of the Middle Ages. There was a devil called Ragamoffin, and William Langland (ca. 1332–ca. 1400), the supposed author of *The Vision of William concerning Piers Plowman,* an allegorical and satirical poem, mentioned Ragamoffin in the part of the work dated 1393. According to the multivolume *Middle English Dictionary,*[20] the most complete repository of English words recorded between the Norman Conquest (1066) and the printing of the first English book (1475), in 1344 a certain Isabella Ragamoffyn lived in England. We can only make conjectures about that woman's character, occupation, or looks. The

Oxford English Dictionary, despite its excellence, sometimes says strange things; for example, as noted, it resorts to the concept of a fanciful addition. In *slabberdegullion* it is *gullion;* in *ragamuffin*, it is *-amuffin;* in *ragabush*, it is *-abush*. What is a fanciful addition? An arbitrary group of meaningless sounds? Some sort of *hickamore, hackamore?*

The Devil was often portrayed as having a ragged appearance, but, more probably, *Ragamoffin ~ Ragamoffyn* has the same root as *Ragman* (Langland spells *rageman*), the devil's name we encountered in the history of *rigmarole* (from *Ragman* or *Ragman's Roll*). Like *Robert ~ Hobard*, *Rageman* seems to be a French word, though many centuries earlier the French may have borrowed it from German. The second part of *ragamuffin* remained unexplained for a long time. Here is the solution. E. W. Prevost, the author of a dialectal dictionary, noted the phrase *Auld Muffy*, used by the older dalesmen in Cumberland for the Devil. This *Muffy* is identical with French *maufé* (ugly, ill-featured), used in medieval England for the Evil One, a creature notoriously hideous and deformed.[21] Apparently, both parts of *ragamuffin* mean "devil"; *-n* must have been added under the influence of words like *guardian, warden,* or *slabbedegullion*. Shakespeare has *rag of Muffin* or *rag of Muffian* in 1 Henry IV, IV, iii:272. *Ragamuffin* is thus a tautological extended form with the original sense "devil-a-devil," a coinage not unlike *muck-a-muck* and *hobble-de-hoy*. Later *ragamuffin* was associated with rags and acquired the meaning of "a ragged street urchin."

We do not know why some words have the infix *-a-*, whereas others have *-de-*. Hardly any rule ever regulated their use. In 1612 the form *raggedemuffin* turned up. In dialects, *cater-a-fran* and *cater-de-flamp* have been recorded; both mean "askew" (compare p. 45, above).[22] English extended forms have always been colloquial or slangy. Yet they are not fanciful. The origin of *-gullion, -bash, -mundy, -muffin, -hoy,* and so forth is often obscure. With a bit of good luck, we can succeed in retracing their development and observe how they attach themselves to other "worthless" words like *slubber-* and *grizzle-* and insert a buffer (*-a-, -de-*) between themselves and their neighbors.

Chapter Eight

which makes it clear that
although swelling is good,
shrinking is also good, or

Disguised Compounds

Imperturbability is much too long for an English speaker.—*Hubbard* rhymes with *cupboard,* but *fore-head* does not rhyme with *horrid.*—On husbandry and soldiery.—Heifers come to the foreground again.—More of the same: *cow-slip* or *cow's lip?*—What is *cheeselip?*—Strawberries and straw.—Is a woman a man?

Few lines from Shakespeare have been quoted more often than Enobarbus's characterization of Cleopatra: "Age does not wither her, nor custom cloy her infinite variety." Unlike Cleopatra, words wither with age, but by shrinking they conceal their past and begin to look younger. An easily observable law governs the progress of words through history: with time, they get shorter and shorter. Sanskrit, spoken in Ancient India, and the language of King Alfred are related, though not directly. One needs no previous exposure to philology to open books in those languages and compare the length of words in them. The difference is astounding: a page of Old English accommodates about three times as many words as does a page of Sanskrit. But in comparison to Modern English, Old English looks almost like Sanskrit. It is hard to imagine that sixteen centuries ago (a short period, considering the entire history of human speech) a Goth, a speaker of another language related to English, this time closely, could pronounce without effort a verbal form consisting of six syllables. Today, native English words are, as a rule, monosyllabic: *stand, go, eye, hand, small, strong,* and so on (compare pp. 9–10, above, on Plato's

Greek and Modern English). Monsters like *imperturbability* and *trans-mogrification* exist, but no one uses them in conversation, and when a word of Romance origin contains more than three syllables, it often has an additional stress: *ˌfundaˈmentally, ˌreconˈnoiter, ˌinterdigiˈtations.* Clipping is universal: *gym, prof, doc, lab, math, Fred, Rick, Al, Sam.* ("What's your name?" "Becky Thatcher. What's yours? Oh, I know. It's Thomas Sawyer." "That's the name they lick me by. I'm Tom when I'm good. You call me Tom, will you?" "Yes.") Gone is the glory of Latin *laudavissēmus* and Gothic *ˈmikilidedeima* (both mean "[we] would have praised" or "had we praised"). Various theories have been offered to explain what force makes words lose weight. They need not delay us here, for it is the phenomenon rather than its causes that we have to examine.

Nowhere can the traces of wear and tear be seen more clearly than in compounds. Those who pronounce *Sunday* as *sun* + *day* use a regular compound. But, as we remember, Solomon Grundy was born on a Monday. The rhyme presupposes the pronunciation *Mondy* (and, of course, *Sundy:* ". . . buried on a Sunday / This was the end of Solomon Grundy"). To some people *Sunday* and *sundae* are not homonyms. The Old English name of *Sunday (sunnandæg)* began with *sunnan-;* the modern form is one syllable shorter than it once was, but the whole still means "the day of the sun." In a literate society, and especially in a language like English, with its conservative spelling, a word's written image may furnish a clue to its etymology: *write, wright, right,* and *rite* have the same pronunciation but reveal their past on paper. Likewise, the spelling of *yesterday, birthday, holiday,* and the names of the days of the week does not allow us to forget the origin of the second element. *Holiday* is clearly "a holy day."

We can observe the "weathering" of compounds step by step. *Breakfast* is the meal with which we "break (our) fast." Today, neither *break-* nor *-fast* has the vowel of *break* and *fast* (compare the command *break fast!*), but the spelling of the word is traditional. Once we are told what *breakfast* is supposed to mean, we accept the explanation (because it makes sense), though we do not associate the interval between late dinner or supper and the first meal of the next day with fasting. The etymology of *breakfast* is slightly less trivial than that of *Sunday* and *holiday*. (*Holiday* and *breakfast*, from *brekefast*, were trisyllabic words, and in such words the first vowel was shortened; this explains their modern pronunciation.)

Breakfast will lead us to *cupboard*. If old Mother Hubbard had gone to the *kubbard*, the connection between the piece of furniture in which she kept a bone for her dog and cups on boards would have been impossible to detect. *Cupboard* was first recorded in 1375. Some of its alternate spellings were *couborde, cobord,* and *cubberd*. The comment in the *Oxford English Dictionary* is worth quoting in full (as always): "By the 16th c[entury] the second element was phonetically obscured, and the *p* of *cup-* sunk in the following *b,* as in the existing pronunciation, which is indicated by a multitude of more or less phonetic spellings of the *cubberd, cubbert* type, often crossed by etymological reminiscences. Since the 18th c[entury] the analytical spelling has prevailed." The earliest meaning of *cupboard* was "a board [= table] to place cups and other vessels on." In this case, the Middle English word no longer sounds like a compound, and its meaning has changed somewhat. (It has also lost some ground in American English: Americans' skeletons reside in the closet, not in the cupboard.)

Spelling can do more than preserve a relic of a word's bygone structure; occasionally it strikes back, as seen in the history of *forehead,* for example. According to the popular verse, allegedly composed by Longfellow, "There was a little girl, and she had a little curl / Right in the middle of her forehead; / When she was good, she was very, very good, / But when she was bad, she was horrid." The rhyme leaves no doubt about the pronunciation of *forehead,* and it is the only pronunciation given in the *Oxford English Dictionary* (the fascicle with this word appeared in October 1897). Old Engl. *forhēafod* lost its *h* (to say nothing of *f,* pronounced as *v*) four hundred years before Longfellow's birth: the spellings *forred* and *fored* turn up already in the fifteenth century.[1] The pronunciation with -*h*- must have been reintroduced by pedants who had perverse ideas of clear delivery or by those who believed that the more letters they could turn into sounds the better. The first group was too learned, the second barely literate, but the result happened to be the same. There is no virtue in sounding *h* in *shepherd* or *annihilate* for fear of appearing indistinct or uneducated. However, the variant *forehead* spread and seems to have always had greater currency in American than in British English. *The Century Dictionary* (New York, 1911) lists both variants. *The Universal Dictionary of the English Language* (London, 1932), edited by Henry Cecil Wyld, calls the pronunciation with *h* vulgar or modern. The editors of other dictionaries register what they hear and do not dare appear judgmental. Yet they still list *forid* as the first variant. Under the influence of spelling, a disguised compound has doffed its disguise, and now anyone can see *and* hear that the forehead is indeed the "fore" part of the head. Some people find this return to the past horrid, but no one cares about their opinion. In all probability, five centuries ago, their ancestors impotently mocked the lower orders for slurring *h* in *forehēafod.* It is interesting to study the history of language but depressing to be part of it.

The following two examples will show that a change of spelling, such as *cupboard* to *cubberd* and *cubbert,* really makes the inner form of a word inscrutable to native speakers, who rely not only on an aural but also on a visual image of the words they use. *Shepherd,* mentioned in passing above, has retained a few traces of its origin. The structure of Old Engl. *scēaphierde* (a tender of sheep) (*scēap* [sheep] + *hierde* [herd]) was as obvious as that of Modern Engl. *swineherd* or *cowboy* to us. (The shortening of the first vowel produced *shep-* instead of *sheep;* then *h* became mute.) But the corresponding family name is spelled *Shepard,* and the connection of its bearer with herding sheep is no longer felt. A similar event happened in the history of the word *gossip.* Old Engl. *godsibb* (a sponsor in baptism) (= "a sponsor in God") is a compound of the same type as *godfather, godmother,* and *godchild,* with the only difference that *-sibb* (akin, related) was not a noun but an adjective turned into a noun. Later, *gossip* came to mean "a familiar acquaintance of either sex, now principally female" (in folk tales, *old gossip* is "old woman") and "tattler; idle talk." Two minor phonetic processes (the dropping of -*d-* and the substitution of -*p-* for final -*b-*), accompanied by a radical change of meaning (from "a sponsor in God" to "ill-founded rumors" and "trivial tittle-tattle") severed the tie between the modern word and its former constituents.

Gospel bears a superficial resemblance to *gossip* but goes back to an Old English word for "good," not "god" (+ *spell* [news, tidings]); *gōdspel* initially meant "good news." The vowel in the first syllable was long, and long vowels were shortened not only in trisyllabic words like *holiday* but also before two consonants; compare the loss of length by *ēa* in *scēaphierde* (shepherd) before *ph* and by *ō* in *bonfire* before *nf.* That is why *gōdspel* yielded *godspell* (rather than **goodspell*) and *gospel,* with *d* shed, as in *gossip.* The same shortening drove a wedge between *goose* and *gosling.* Not improbably, *gossamer,* first recorded in the fourteenth century, also developed from *goose* + *summer,* but the allusion is obscure. Among the disguised compounds in which the first vowel has lost length, we find *Christmas,* originally "the mass (= festival) of Christ," and *husband.*

Whether native or Scandinavian, late Old Engl. *hūsbonda* meant "the master of a house."[2] A look at the senses of *husband* and its derivatives will show that "the male spouse" does not exhaust its meaning. *To father* is "to be the father (of)," whereas *to husband* is "to marry" (now archaic) and "to manage, especially with prudent economy." Jane Eyre spoke of husbanding her mother's allowance. The noun *husbandry* refers to domestic management, not a group of married men or the state of being married, as one could expect from the comparison with *soldiery* and *slavery.* Nor is *ship's husband* married to a ship, though a ship is traditionally referred to as *she:* he is an agent appointed by the owners to attend to the business of a ship while in port, especially to attend to her stores, equipment, and repairs and see that the ship is in all respects well found. (Having given this definition, the *Oxford English Dictionary* adds: "Now little used, the duties being generally performed by a 'Marine Superintendent'.") Finally, there is *husbandman* (farmer), an odd compound from the modern point of view. With time, "the master of the house" developed into "householder" and "a man joined to a woman in marriage." Before two consonants (-*sb*-), *ū* shortened, and this led to the modern pronunciation of *hus*- in *husband.* The spelling -*band* does not antedate the fourteenth century (*a* and *o* often alternated before *n*), and some naïve people think that *band* is the genuine element of *husband*. They are mistaken. The root of *bondage* is the same as in *(hus)band:* it goes back to Old Engl. *bonda* (an occupier and tiller of the soil; husbandman). *Bondage* meant the condition of being a *bonda,* a bondman, or bondsman—after the Norman Conquest, not a small landowner but a so-called villeine, holding his land from the lord of the manor and with his liberties curtailed; the meanings "lack of freedom, servitude, subjugation" reflect his changed social status. The proximity of *bond* (shackle) also contributed to the deterioration of meaning, and *bondsman* began to denote "serf, a person in bonds" instead of "freeman."

Hussif, sometimes spelled *huzzif,* is rarely seen or heard today. It arose in the form *hūswīf* (housewife) and narrowed its meaning to "sewing kit." That same *huzzif,* when it lost the final consonant, became *hussy,* or *huzzy* (a pert girl, compare *goody,* defined as "a lowly form of address to a [married] woman," from *goodwife*). *Husband* and *hussy ~ huzzy* have the same first syllable going back to *hūs* (house).

The word *heifer,* glorified in Chapter 1 of this book, is another disguised compound: its original form (to the extent that we can judge) was *heahfore.* One should think that an animal name coined by speakers of Old English, especially a compound, a sum of *heah* and *fore,* would not be too hard to decipher. But this is not so. Is *heah-* "high" and *-fore* "fore," or is *-fore* related to the verb *fare?* *Heahfore* has been explained as "highstepper," "a calf with long front legs," and even "stepping superbly." But a heifer is a one-year-old cow that has not calved. Those who called the animal *heahfore* would not have looked on its long legs (front or hind) or high steps (leaping?) as its most noteworthy features. Scots *farrow* (not in calf) (distinct from *farrow* [a litter of pigs]), if it is akin to *-fore,* looks like a cognate we need, but *heah-* remains unexplained; it cannot be understood as "full-grown," for such an epithet does not fit a young cow.

In dialects, the form *heckfore* occurs. Perhaps *heah-* is related to *haw* (as in *hawthorn*), from Old Engl. *haga.* Both *heah-* and *heck-* may at one time have meant "enclosure." The second element of *heahfore* is reminiscent of *-fare* in the bird name *fieldfare* and of *-ver* (from *-fer*) in *elver* (a young eel) (*el-* is a shortened variant of *eel*), possibly a suffix meaning "occupant." If in the days of King Alfred heifers were kept in special enclosures, this may be the reason *heahfore* got its name. The word seems to be transparent; yet all the suggested etymologies of it leave us dissatisfied.[3]

Cushat (it rhymes with *rush at*) is a similarly deceptive compound. Robert Burns and Walter Scott popularized this name of the wild pigeon. Its Old English form was *cusceote*. We think that we understand the meaning of both elements (*cū* [cow] + *sceote* [shot]), but the whole does not amount to a bird name. Opinions differ, and the conjectures are almost as varied as those about *heifer*. A desperate attempt has been made to present the Old English word as *cusc-eote* rather than *cu-sceote,* with *cusc-* meaning "chaste" (like German *keusch;* a chaste bird?!) or "quick" (= "a quick darter"), but what is *eote?* The most reasonable hypothesis seems to be that *cusceote* is an Anglicized variant of Welsh **cusguthan* (unattested; its modern Welsh reflex *coed* means "forest").[4] If so, we are again victims of folk etymology.

Some compounds disguise their past more ingeniously than others. If we know the plant name *cowslip* only from reading, we cannot decide whether it is *cow's lip* or *cow slip.* The second variant is right. *Slyppe,* in Old Engl. *cūslyppe,* meant "a slimy substance," and the whole must have been understood as "cow slobber" or "cow dung." Another plant name with *-slip, oxslip,* is traceable to *oxanslyppe;* compare *Oxenford* or *Oxenaford,* the medieval name of Oxford, and its Latinized name *Oxonia.* (A curious parallel. The Old English plant name *lustmoce* [cuckooflower] means literally "pleasure muck." Now it is called *lady-smock, lady's smock,* or *ladies' smock.* The modern word was first recorded in 1588, whereas *lustmoce* did not continue even into Middle English. Yet is it not possible that *-smock* is here *-s-mock?* Once the word was misdivided, *lady-* came in easily. Or am I falling into the same trap as those who saw *folk's glove* in *foxglove?*) In contrast, *cheeselip,* now obsolete except in dialects, contains neither *lip* nor *slip.* The word means "rennet," that is, "a mass of curdled milk in making cheese" or "the fourth stomach of a calf prepared for curdling milk." Its first element is indeed *cheese,* but the second was *lyb* or *lybb* (poison) and, apparently, "antidote." Final *p* in *cheeselip* seems to be of the same origin as in *gossip* (from *b* at the end of the second part of a compound). A variant with a shortened vowel before two consonants *(cheslip)* is known, but *cowslip* did not turn into **cuslip* or **cuzlip*. For some reason, speakers never forgot the association of that plant name with the cow, though other associations (for instance, with *good* in *gospel* and *god* in *gossip*) have been lost.

Words like *husband, gospel,* and *cheeselip* (the latter with its misleading -*lip*) yield to etymological analysis and present themselves as sums of two old words that fused and have partly or wholly changed their form in the process. But sometimes the second element is added to an unexpected or incomprehensible first one. This is what happens in the names of some berries. Obviously, *strawberry* is *straw* + *berry*. The question is: Why *straw?* If we disregard attempts to pass off *straw*- in *strawberry* as a cognate of *frag*- in Latin *fragola* (the same berry),[5] the main attempts have been as follows: perhaps from its propagation by runners, in which case Old Engl. *strēaw*- in *strēawberige* is related to *strew*[6] (but it is unlikely that the first element of *strawberry* is a verb); or from the old practice of using straw to protect the fruit (but this would be valid only in gardening, not in naming wild strawberries); or from tiny straw-like particles that cover it;[7] or because of the custom of stringing strawberries;[8] or, because the wild strawberry grows chiefly in grassy places and in hay fields (the most sensible idea of all).[9] The word is often explained as a corruption of a supposed **strayberry,*[10] and it has been suggested that *strēaw*- in the old name of *strawberry* is neither *straw* nor *stray* but the product of folk etymology.[11] (The case would not be unique: *gooseberry,* for example, possibly called this because its rough bristly surface resembles gooseskin, is not the original name of the berry, though the details are hard to trace.) The circumspect editor of *The Oxford Dictionary of English Etymology* concludes the entry with the melancholy verdict: ". . . the reason for the name is unknown." I think the reason that Harold H. Bender offered *(strawberry = grassberry)* should be accepted.

What are *rasp-, bil-, huckle-,* and *whortle-* in the names of the berries? An inquisitive student will find only conflicting hypotheses in dictionaries and special publications. Even when we see light, it is usually dim. Thus *cranberry* is a borrowing of German dialectal *Kranbeere* (or some similar form) (craneberry). But are cranes particularly greedy consumers of cranberries? In the Scandinavian languages, *cranberry* is also "craneberry" (Swedish *tranbär,* Danish and Norwegian *tranebœr,* from *trana, trane* [crane]), a fact that does not make the reason for naming cranberry any clearer. Another trick of folk etymology?[12] Life would be easier if our vocabulary consisted only of words like *blueberry,* or at least *loganberrry* (it was first grown by James H. Logan, an American judge and horticulturist) and *wineberry,* but it would be much duller.

Phonetic change and all kinds of unpredictable events may destroy similarities and create new associations. *Daisy,* as we remember, is "day's eye." *Window* is "wind's eye," but it is a Scandinavian word: its Old English equivalents were *ēagþyrel* (eye hole) (*þ = th,* as in Engl. *through,* to which *þyrel* is related) and *ēagduru* (eye door) (*þyrel* was also the second element of *nosþyrel* [nosehole], Modern Engl. *nostril*). Scandinavian *windauga* superseded both its native rivals. The phonetic difference between Old Engl. *ēage* and Old Scandinavian *auga,* although not too great, was sufficient for *daisy* and *window,* those two "eyes," to sound differently in the modern language. Conversely, *fellow* has the same "ending" as does *window. Fellow* is another loan from Scandinavian, where it had the form *félagi* (*é = ē*), a derivative of *félag,* that is, *fé* (property) (one of its reflexes is Engl. *fee*) + *lag* (something lying). A *félagi* was the person who laid down money in a joint undertaking. Both *window* and *fellow* are disguised compounds, but *-ow* in them has different sources—contrary to *window* and *daisy,* in which *-ow* and *-y* have the same etymon.

The element *man,* like *-berry,* is sometimes added to obscure words. *Chapman* is a twin brother of German *Kaufmann.* The Old English form was *cēapman* (merchant), from *cēap* (price; bargain), whose relic is the modern adjective *cheap* (and compare place names like *Cheapside,* the name of an old market place). The ineradicable habit of English speakers to clip long words turned *chapman* into *chap* (buyer, purchaser), after which *chap* shared the fate of *customer* (as in *a rum customer*) and acquired the meaning "fellow, lad." So *chapman* is not *chap* plus *man:* rather *chapman* minus *man* gave us *chap* (we have already seen another example of back formation in *sleaze* from *sleazy*). *Henchman* is the continuation of *hengestman* (horse attendant) (from Old Engl. *hengest* [stallion]). The names of feudal titles often go back to what seems today humble pursuits. An officer of the stable (Late Latin *comes stabuli*) is Modern Engl. *constable* (via French), and *mariscalcus* (a Latinized Frankish word), literally "mare servant," is now *marshal*. *Maid* may also be the second element in a compound whose first one has dropped out of the language. *Mer-* in *mermaid* meant "sea," and it was in the *mere* that Grendel and his mother, Beowulf's opponents, lived (though Grendel's habitat may have been a swamp).

Men and maids bring us to the most "famous" disguised compound in English, namely, *woman*. No talk show on words is broadcast without someone's asking why *woman* ends in *-man*. The question has been answered as often as it has been asked (because the history of *woman* is known), but the level of excitement remains steady. *Wīfman*, the Old English for "woman," was opposed to *wǣpnedman* (man). Both words ended in *-man*. The adjective *wǣpned* (pertaining to weapons or "armed"), but recorded only with the adjectival meaning "male," entered into several compounds, for instance, *wǣpnedcild* (a male child) and *wǣpnedhand* (male line). There were also *wǣpnedhād* (male sex; sexual power) (*-hād* = *-hood,* as in *manhood*) and *wǣpned-wīfstre* (hermaphrodite) (a nonce word). Some scholars contend that *wǣpen* could mean "penis." However, it is not inconceivable that *wǣpnedman* and its doublet *wǣpnman* originally meant "warrior" and, by inference, "male." One thing is clear: *man,* whose etymology will be discussed in the next chapter, originally referred to adult human beings of both sexes.

That the Germanic word for *man* was not coined with the meaning "male" is clear, for otherwise *wīfman* would have been impossible and *wǣpnedman* redundant. In Old Icelandic, the words for "man" and "woman" were *karl* and *kona* (or *kvenna*), respectively; yet Icelandic, too, made use of the compounds *karlmaður* and *kvennmaðr* (*maðr* [man]; ð = *th* as in Engl. *this*). It did not seem odd to speakers of English and Icelandic that *wīfman* and *kvennmaðr* were masculine nouns; the generalized meaning of *-man* and *-maðr* must have overshadowed the incongruity of the grammatical gender. (People take such situations in stride. German *Mensch* [a human being] was at one time either masculine or neuter,[13] *Weib* [woman], a cognate of *wife,* is also neuter, and so is *Mädchen* [a young girl] because of its diminutive suffix *-chen.* In Modern English, we do not notice the incongruity of: "This is my *daughter* Mary John*son.*")

In Old English, the incongruity is especially remarkable, because *wīf,* like its modern German cognate *Weib,* was neuter (so that a combination of a neuter and a masculine noun yielded the meaning "female"!), but it did not bother anyone until modern linguists expressed their surprise. Like *man, wīf* is a word of debatable origin. In the old languages that had three genders, the ending of the feminine singular (as in Latin *vita* [life]) coincided with that of the neuter plural (as in Latin *verba* [words], the plural of *verbum*). It appears as though *wīf* was at one time a collective neuter plural, designating "womankind" or "a family belonging to a woman," rather than a single woman. Similar changes are not so rare. The German cognate of Engl. *stud* is *Stute* (mare). The original meaning of *stud* was "a place where horses for breeding are kept," not "a herd of horses," and German has a corresponding noun *(Gestüt); Stute* began to designate a female horse only in the late Middle Ages. Romanian *feméie,* from Latin *familia,* meant "family" in the old language, but now it means "woman."[14] German *Imme* developed like *Stute:* first "a swarm of bees" and much later "bee." For tracing the recorded history of *woman,* the origin of *wīf* and *man* is of marginal importance. Suffice it to say that the existence of the compound *wīfman* does not imply an inferior position of women at the remote epoch when this word was coined.

Later developments are less dramatic. The vowel *ī* in *wīfman* was shortened before two consonants, and *-fm-* became long *m,* as it did in *leman,* an archaic word for "lover, sweetheart" (from *lēofman,* that is, *liefman* [a dear, beloved one]; pronounced like *lemon*), and *Lammas* (the 1st of August, the feast of St. Peter in Chains, observed in Anglo-Saxon England by the consecration of bread made from the first ripe grain) (Old Engl. *hlāfmæsse,* that is, "loaf mass"; loaf =

bread, see also the end of Chapter 5 on *Lammas*). The usual pronunciation became *wimmin*. When English lost long consonants, *wimmin* changed to *wimin*. In Old English and later, the combination *wi-* sometimes turned into *wu-*. This happened in the history of *wudu* (wood), from *widu*, and of *wuman*, from *wimin*. When *i* in the first syllable went over to *u*, the pronunciation of the second syllable did not remain quite the same: *i* between *m* and *n* began to resemble a weak *a* (as in the modern indefinite article).

With or without *wi-* becoming *wu-*, the singular and the plural should have merged: either *wimin* or *wuman* for both. (Compare words like *ragman* and *ragmen:* their pronunciation is identical.) The spelling *uuuman* must have been avoided, because in medieval texts *uuu* (the first two letters for *double u*) would have been inconvenient to read, though, in principle, a succession of three *u*'s was allowed. Since *o* before *m* designated *u* in other words (for example, in *some* from *sum,* and *come* from *cuman*), *u* in *wuman* was replaced by *o*. The distinction between *woman* and *women* in present-day English was due to the effort to differentiate the singular from the plural. Today the singular has the later pronunciation of the word (with *wu-* from *wi-*), whereas the plural retained the ancient form (with *wi-*). In the written form of the word *woman,* the original second element *-man* has survived, and the spelling *women* was introduced for the plural: *wo-man ~ wo-men* like *man ~ men*. Unlike German *Weib,* Engl. *wife* has not retained its meaning "female" (it survives only in compounds like *midwife* and *fisherwife*, as well as in the idiom *old wives' tale*) and entered into the partnership with *husband* (which ousted Old Engl. *ceorl, wer,* and occasionally *bonda* in that role). The story ends here unless we want to pursue it into the *womyn* stage and watch the obliteration of the human element in the once "gender-neutral" word *wīfman*. Incidentally, *man* and the second syllable of *human* (from Latin *hūm-ān-us*) are not related, but Old French *femelle* changed into *female* under the influence of *male*.[15]

The number of disguised compounds in Modern English is neither overwhelming nor too small. Some are hard to detect. Consider *leman* and *Lammas,* which turned up above. Having learned the history of *Christmas* and *woman,* we may half-guess the origin of

Lammas and *leman,* though only dictionaries will tell us what to do with *La-* and *le-*. Many words shrink beyond recognition. For example, both *lord* and *lady* once began with *hlāf* (bread), like *Lammas.* In Old English, they had the forms *hlāfweard* (bread keeper) (from *hlāf,* as in *loaf,* and *weard,* as in *ward*) and *hlǣfdige* (bread kneader) (the root *-dig* [knead] has survived in *dairy,* originally "a female servant," not "milkmaid," and its archaic synonym *daymaid,* or *deymaid,* in which *day- ~ dey-* are distinct from *day* in *daytime* and the like).

Barn was a disguised compound already a thousand years ago. It developed from *berern,* that is, from *bere* (barley) + *ern* (house). *Ern* has left only one more trace in Modern English (the historical word *saltern* [salt works]), but its cognate is *ran-* in the verb *ransack,* a borrowing from Scandinavian. Surprisingly, *-sack* has no relation to *sack* (plundering). The etymon of *ransack* is Scandinavian *rannsaka* (to attack a house) (hence "to rob"), whereas *sack* (plundering) is a borrowing of French *sac* in phrases like *mettre à sac* (to put to sack). The French took over those phrases from Italian: what was put into the sack became the plunderer's booty. Icelandic *saka* is akin to Engl. *seek,* not to *sack* (bag). *Bridal* was once a noun: *brȳdealu* (bride ale; ale drinking). With time, *-al* was mistaken for a suffix of an adjective (as in *tidal,* for instance). *Barley* moved in the opposite direction. *Bærlīc* was first an adjective ("like barley, pertaining to barley") but became a noun, though it still has an adjectival suffix, as in *comely* and *friendly.* Nightmares have no relation to horses. *Mare* (from Old Engl. *mære*) is a female incubus. French *cauchemar* (nightmare) contains the same second element. Peacocks neither consume peas nor have pea-like dots in their plumage; *pea-* goes back to Latin *pāvō,* which itself meant "peacock." *Garlic* (Old Engl. *gārlēac*) is literally "spear leek" (called this for its tall, sharp stalk; *gar-,* as in *garfish* [spearfish]), and for a long time the best etymologists believed that Old Engl. *bærlīc* (barley) also ended in *-lēac.* Only James A. H. Murray, the great first editor of the *Oxford English Dictionary,* explained it correctly; *bærlic* is not a disguised compound.

No revelations in this chapter have been particularly startling. The art of etymology consists in seeing through a word's disguise. Whether the mask is simple or compound is a matter of detail.[16]

Chapter Nine

*which proves beyond reasonable doubt
that disguise and treason are everywhere, or*

Suffixes, Prefixes,
Misdivision, and Blends

On maidenhood and boyhood.—On sloth, warmth, and coolth.—*Sizzle
– fizzle – drizzle* and other frequentative verbs.—Intrusive *r.*—*Riddle
– needle – beetle.—Fickle – mickle – brittle.*—The fugitive *s-mobile.*—
On hneezing, neezing, fneezing, and sneezing.—How aphetic forms
fend for themselves.—A balanced view of daffodils (without *-down-*
in their middle).—My Nuncle Ned Thelme.—Tawdry but admirable.—
Brunch survives the derision of highbrows.—More blends.

The previous chapter ended with an allusion to disguise in several
forms. Not only compounds but also words with prefixes and suffixes tend to shrink. A compound in English is usually made up of
two elements, each of which functions as a separate word. A few
have a connecting vowel or consonant *hand-i-work, fist-i-cuffs,
politic-o-economic, bond-s-man, land-s-man, state-s-man,* but most
are like *bondman, handbook, footnote,* and *landlubber.*
A compound may behave like a phrase, and then the question is:
Are we dealing with one word or two? Or the fusion of the elements
may be such that all the traces of "compounding" are gone. The dilemma "one word or two" is brought home to every literate person
by inconsistent hyphenation. *Half brother* needs no hyphen in American English, whereas *half-life* does. *Home base* is two words, *housewife* is one, and *home-brew* presumably a word and a half (note two
hyphens in *half-and-half*). In some cases, initial stress is a marker of
a compound: '*redcoat* is not the same as '*red* '*coat.* But '*Green Peace*

has one stress, and so do innumerable groups like '*White House,* '*welcome week* and '*birthday present,* without necessarily becoming compounds.

Etymologists are not interested in *half brother* and *housewife,* both of which proved to be immune to wear and tear. They volunteer their services when *halfpenny* becomes *ha 'p 'ny* and *housewife* becomes *huzzif* or *huzzy.* However, between full preservation *(housewife)* and a wreck *(huzzy),* several intermediate stages may occur. Words ending in -*man* are a case in point. The origin of *snowman* is not controversial, though -*man* is almost a suffix in it (like -*ful* in *beautiful,* -*most* in *uppermost,* and -*worthy* in *praiseworthy*). In *doorman, chairman, ragman,* and *gentleman* (the latter modeled on Old French *gentils hom;* Modern French *gentilhomme*), the suffix-like role of -*man* is probably felt more strongly than in *snowman.* In *leman* (lover) (from *lēofman*), -*man* is fully submerged (p. 84), and in *woman,* phonetic change has produced adverse results (speakers do not understand why *woman* should end in -*man*). In disguised compounds, we can sometimes isolate one element even when the other is opaque: *bilberry, linchpin,* and *lukewarm* are understood to end in -*berry, -pin,* and -*warm* despite the fact that *bil-, linch-,* and *luke-* carry no meaning in Modern English. Likewise, we identify -*ment,* the tail end in *segment, fragment,* and *ornament,* and are left with meaningless *seg-, frag-,* and *orna-.*

One can assume that, in the past, all suffixes were words, like -*man* in *chairman* and -*ful* in *beautiful.* A look at older forms sometimes confirms that assumption. For example, Old English had the noun *hād;* one of its meanings was "state, condition." The noun has been lost, but the suffix derived from it survived. *Hād* was already a suffix in Old English, as follows from *cildhād* (childhood), *prēosthād* (priesthood), and *mægdenhād* (maidenhood), to name a few. Later it appeared in *boyhood, neighborhood, falsehood,* and so forth. Another noun, used as the second element of *līflād* (the course of life), also edged into this suffix. In the sixteenth century, the would-be legitimate reflex of *līflād,* that is, **livelode,* gave way to *livelihood,* as though from *lively + hood,* and began to rhyme with *likelihood.* A form related to -*hood* was -*head,* now only in *maidenhead* (the hymen) and *godhead* (divinity). Words with Old Engl. *ā* today have a reflex of *ō* (as in *stone* from *stān*), so that *hād* could be expected to become *-hōde*. The present-day form is irregular. The suffixes *-hood* and *-head* are not cognate with the nouns *hood* and *head*.

The most "treacherous" words end in a suffix that has become almost inseparable from the root. The advantage of *-ment, -hood, -ling* (in *changeling* and *starveling*), and *-less* (in *fearless*) is that they are long and cannot be missed. In similar fashion, *-ster* is "detachable" not only in *gamester, trickster, teamster, rhymester, punster,* and *jokester* but also in *spinster* and *Webster* (in which the association with spinning and weaving webs is all but lost) and in *huckster,* though *huck-* is not a meaningful unit of English vocabulary. But who will guess that *bath* contains a relic of an old verb meaning "to warm up" and the suffix *-th?* That suffix is often hard to isolate in words more transparent than *bath.* In British English, *sloth* has the vowel of *slow,* so that the structure of the noun is clear, but in American English, *sloth* rhymes with *cloth,* and its original tie with the adjective is weak. Nobody will be surprised to learn that *width, breadth, length,* and *depth* are related to *wide, broad, long,* and *deep;* yet the difference in their vowels obscures the connection. In dealing with *health* and *wealth,* an effort is needed to realize that they are akin to *heal* and *weal,* partly because *weal,* as in *public weal,* occurs rarely. The vowel in *health* and *wealth* was shortened before two consonants; the same happened in *width, breadth, length,* and *depth.*

A noticeable suffix need not be productive. It is productive only if new words can be easily formed with its help. Consider *-er.* No matter whether the words *shouter* and *squeaker* have been attested: in certain circumstances they may arise, as did *speaker* and *crier* long ago. The same holds for *-less: computerless* and *e-mail-less* are potential words; their only drawback (or merit, depending on the situation) is that they have been coined on the spur of the moment. But *-th* disallows such experiments: although *warmth* and *truth* are well-established words of Modern English, **coldth, *hotth, *wrongth,* and **falsth* are moderately funny oddities. *Coolth,* as the *Oxford English Dictionary* shows, has been tried many times, for some reason, without success.

Birth and *mirth* are cognate with the verb *to bear* and the adjective *merry,* respectively. Here, too, the feeling of unity is lost: phonetic change and an unproductive suffix have disunited the families. *Berth* may be derived from the same verb as *birth,* but it is even less analyzable than *birth. Dearth* traces back to *dear* (scarce) (from "precious, costly" to "obtainable with difficulty"); we do not associate them, because *dear* is no longer synonymous with "wanting." The root of a simple word sometimes conveys no more than do *linch-, bil-,* and *luke-.* For example, *bir- ~ ber-* in *birth* and *berth* convey nothing. Such roots are stubs left after taking away the ending (if there is one) and the suffix. We vaguely detect a common feature present in *chuckle, cackle, jiggle, joggle, fizzle, sizzle, drizzle,* and *tootle.* All of them denote repeated actions or actions that last long, and they owe their meaning to *-le* (such verbs are therefore called frequentative or iterative). Subtracting *-le* usually leaves us with an identifiable base. For instance, *tootle* means "to keep on tooting." *Jiggle* and *joggle,* without their suffixes, yield *jig* and *jog. Chuckle* is from *chuck* (such a noun and a sound imitative verb existed in the fourteenth century; *chuckle* surfaced 200 years later), *dabble* is from *dab, dazzle* is from *daze* (with the usual shortening of the vowel before two consonants), *topple* is from *top,* and *sparkle* is from *spark. Fizzle* has been derived from its synonym *fizz,* an onomatopoeia, whereas *drizzle* may be akin to Old Engl. *drēosan* (to fall) (*drizzle* [to fall in small raindrops]). However, *sizzle* and *giggle* were modeled on the likes of *drizzle,* bypassing **sizz* and **gigg.* Inasmuch as **sizz* and **gigg* do not seem to have existed, a suffix is identifiable in them only thanks to what may be called "peer pressure."

Many frequentative verbs came to English from northern German and Dutch, where they are extremely common.[1] *Wriggle* is such a word, though a cognate of *wrig-* can be seen in Old Engl. *wrīgian* (to bend, turn, twist). One of its synonyms is *wiggle,* also of German or Dutch origin; another is *waggle,* from *wag.* In the Germanic languages, the root *weg-* (with variants) has always occurred in words designating rocking movement. Unlike *pad, pat,* and *tap, weg-* does not imitate any sound, but its origin need not concern us at the moment; we only observe that *wiggle* ~ *waggle*, like *wriggle*, which may have the same root, "extended" by *r* for emphasis, are frequentative verbs. ("Intrusive *r*" is not so rare. Shakespeare used *scamble* [to scramble]; dialects have preserved this form. The verb *fitter* preceded *fritter* in recorded texts. The infamous verb *frig* may be a variant of *fig*, as in dialectal *figgle*, that is, *fiddle* [to move back and forth]. Across language borders, the number of such examples increases. The best-known of them is Engl. *speak* versus German *sprechen*. The situation is the same in Romance.) *Hobble* (to move unsteadily) resembles *hop* but may also be of German origin. Words with short, inconspicuous suffixes *(bath, berth, dearth; drizzle, fizzle)* resemble disguised compounds.

Despite the derivational transparence of frequentative verbs, *-le* is unproductive in Modern English, though *tootle* must have been coined toward the middle of the nineteenth century (apparently, as a joke that refused to go away). Attempts to produce new verbs (**beggle* [to beg importunately], **rockle* [to swing, rock incessantly], **naggle* [to keep nagging at someone]) result in lifeless creations, though they are not worse than *prickle* or *figgle*. False leads abound everywhere in etymology, and suffixed words are not an exception. *Fondling* was derived from *fond* with the help of the suffix *-ling*, and then *fondling*, by back formation, yielded *fondle*, which now looks as though it is *fond* + *le*. *Suckle* may have had a similar fate (from *suckling*).

Unlike *-hood*, *-le* has always been a suffix in English: no noun, adjective, or verb stands behind it. At one time, it was longer. The verbs with *-le*, to the extent that they are traceable to Old English, ended in *-li-* followed by *-an*, a marker of the infinitive. Still earlier, *-li-* may have had the form **-lōi-*, not a meaningful word either. In *payment, sisterhood*, and *warmth*, the word's structure is obvious, but *-le* can be identified and isolated mainly because it occurs in several dozen frequentative verbs and adds the same shade of meaning to them. Without that it would have been fully "disguised" and *tootle* would not have been coined. *Get, cut, put, set, fit, bet, wet, whet*, and *let* also look similar, yet we do not ascribe any function to their final -*t.* (Here the factor of "peer pressure" is felt only in grammar: under the influence of *set—let—put—cut, fit* and *wet* have lost their preterit -*ed* ending in American English.)[2]

The presence of -*le* unites *garble, warble, juggle, smuggle,* and *struggle* with *wriggle, giggle,* and the rest. *Warble* is akin to some verbs with -*le* that have been attested only in languages other than English. *Smuggle* may have the root *mug-* with *s-* appended to it (see what is said about *hugger-mugger* on p. 58), but its history is obscure; in any case, the adjective *smug* is not its etymon. Engl. **strug-,* the sought-for base of *struggle,* has not turned up (a similar Scandinavian word exists, however). *Garble* and *juggle* are verbs of Romance origin. The first is not related to *garb,* and the second has not been, in some fantastic way, derived from *jug*; flanked by *jaggle* and *joggle,* it has become their near synonym.

Not only verbs end in the suffix -*l(e).* In nouns, it most often characterizes the names of appliances and instruments. Sometimes it is disguised so well that it has become an inseparable element of the root. This is what happened in the words *tool* and *towel,* in which -*l* was added to the roots of the now extinct verbs meaning "to make" and "to wash" (though *towel* went from Germanic to French and came back to English slightly Frenchified). In present-day English, *tool* and *towel* have no suffix. Their case is similar to that of *bath.* The degrees of obscurity are the same in nouns as in verbs. *Sparkle* is transparent, *dazzle* (from *daze*) is less so owing to the short vowel, *drizzle* is opaque because the verb *drēosan* has dropped out of the language, and *wriggle* is, most likely, a borrowing. We can easily construct such a ladder for nouns, except that words like *handle, girdle* (from *hand* and *gird*), and *ladle* (perhaps less obviously from *lade*) will be in the minority here.

Beetle has the root of the verb *bite; weevil* and *weave* are similarly related. Few people will associate them today. *Needle* was derived from a verb meaning "to sew," and if *d* were lost in it, it would become as monolithic as *tool.* Icelandic *nál* (needle) is such a monolith. *Need-* in *needle* has no connection with seams or stitches, and we "hear" the suffix only against the background of the equally unanalyzable nouns *beadle, bridle, saddle,* and *label.* From the historical perspective, all of them are like *needle*. The lost verb from which *needle* was once derived is akin to Latin *nēre* (to spin), whence Latin *nervus* (sinew, bowstring); the adjective *neural* is from a Greek cognate of *nervus*. Only an etymological dictionary can restore the unity between Engl. *nerve* and *needle*.

Riddle is another old word with a suffix. Old English had the noun *rǣdels* (usually masculine, with the plural *rǣdelsas*) and the feminine noun *rǣdelse* (with the plural *rǣdelsan*). The verb *rǣdan* meant "to advise, counsel, persuade; consult; decide," and so forth; we know its continuation *read* (in *read a dream* and *read a riddle*, it has retained the ancient meaning "to discern, interpret"). German *raten* (to advise), a cognate of *read*, and especially *erraten* (to guess) have changed little since the Middle Ages. *Rǣdels(e)* had a spectrum of meanings corresponding to those of *rǣdan*, namely "consideration, discussion, imagination, conjecture, interpretation"; "riddle" was among them. Later, *-e* in *rǣdelse* was dropped and *s* understood as a marker of the plural of a noun with a suffix *-el*, rather than *-els*. Two phonetic processes turned *ǣ* into *i*, and the modern form *riddle* appeared (with plural *riddles*). Of all its meanings only "enigma" is extant. The verb *read*, the reflex of *rǣdan*, is still pronounced with a long vowel, but it has narrowed its meaning so drastically that nothing connects it with *riddle* any longer. The homonym of *riddle* (enigma) is *riddle* (a coarse-meshed sieve), from *hriddel*. Its suffix is the same as in *ladle* (the verb *hrīdrian* meant "to sift").

Here, as everywhere, phonetic processes separate words that would otherwise have sounded alike. *Thimble* is related to *thumb*. Speakers of Old English sensed their affinity; we usually don't. The reason is not only different vowels but also the changed relation of words to things: our thimbles are not meant for the thumb. *Bramble* is cognate with *broom*, and perhaps twelve centuries ago people realized this. (The consonant *b* is "parasitic" in *thumb, thimble,* and *bramble. Thumb* with *b* emerged toward the end of the thirteenth century. Presumably, *b* was pronounced at the time. *Numb* had a similar history, but in *dumb, b* has not always been mute.) Already in the remotest past, *riddle* was impenetrable. Modern linguists understand its derivation quite well, but *darnel* and *thistle* baffle them.

The ability of English to form verbs from nouns and nouns from verbs often makes it hard to decide which came first. The verb *handle* is a derivative of the corresponding noun, but did the noun *shuttle* precede the verb *shuttle* or are they parallel formations, both from *shoot:* one the name of an appliance, the other a frequentative verb? (Those who would trace *shuttle* to *shut* would be wrong but not dismally so, because *shut* and *shoot* are related.) *Shuffle, scuffle,* and *shovel* go back to *shove* or its cognates in German or Scandinavian. However, the verb *shovel* has been derived from the noun, whereas the nouns *shuffle* and *scuffle* were formed as partners of the verb. Since here we are trying only to "undisguise" suffixes, we need not go into the distant origin of each word.

Adjectives ending in *-le* are few: the best known of them are *fickle, mickle, little, idle, nimble,* and *brittle.* Unlike Romance *-al* in *beneficial, pivotal,* and *dialectal, -le* is native. Its descent did not contribute to its productivity, whereas *-al* enjoys some freedom and occasionally differentiates meanings: compare *analytic* and *analytical, classic* and *classical, historic* and *historical, poetic* and *poetical.* The origin of some adjectives in the *fickle—mickle* group is not devoid of interest. Old Engl. *ficol,* the etymon of *fickle,* meant "cunning, tricky," its underlying sense being "changeable, inconstant." The root *fic-* recurs in German *ficken,* a cognate and synonym of the English *F*-word. In dialects, *ficken* has other meanings, for example, "to flog lightly; scratch," in addition to the main one, all of which developed from "move back and forth" (compare *frig* and *fiddle,* above). A fickle person was ready to shift his or her loyalties, as follows from Old Engl. *gefic* (deceit) (German dialectal *Gefick* means "people running in different directions").

Brittle, first recorded in the fourteenth century, is akin to Old Engl. *(ge)bryttan* (to break to pieces). It shares an onomatopoeic beginning (*br-*) with *break* (from *brecan*), and it has always meant "fragile." Since *bryttan,* like *(ge)fic,* exists no longer, the derivatives of both are now mere "conventional signs"; no other words in the language support them. *Nimble* is less isolated, but its siblings have lost touch with it. The Old English for "take" was *niman,* a cognate of German *nehmen.* Scandinavian *taka* superseded it, and all that is left of the

root of *niman* are *nimble* (with "parasitic" *b*, as in *thimble* and
bramble), whose ancient meaning must have been "receptive, quick
at sizing," and *numb*, literally "taken." In the consciousness of modern speakers, *nimble* and *numb* are not even close. Dictionaries cite
nim (to take; steal) (slang); it brings joy only to lexicographers and
those who remember Shakespeare's Corporal Nym.

The roots of *little* and *idle* are unknown. *Mickle*, of which the
standard form *much* is a phonetic variant, is related to Greek *mégas*,[3]
as in *megaphone* and *megalomania*, and Latin *magnus* (great). A few
adjectives that came to English from French, for instance, *supple*
and *subtle*, align themselves with *fickle—mickle—brittle—nimble*,
but a look at their etymons (Latin *supplex* [submissive] and *subtilis*
[slender, delicate]) reveals the nature of the disguise. The same is
true of *simple* and *double*.

A story resembling that of the verbs ending in *-le* can be told about
the verbs with the suffix *-er*. A list containing them is long and includes *chatter, clatter, patter, stutter, bicker, flicker, flutter, blunder,
bluster, shudder, jabber, swagger, scatter, shatter, shiver, quiver, qua-
ver,* and *waver* among others. From the historical point of view, their
most remarkable features are their late appearance and obscure origin; their sources are often German, Dutch, and Scandinavian. *Jabber* (not from *jab*) and *chatter* are probably onomatopoeic. *Flitter*
and *flicker* are two of many sound symbolic words in which initial *fl-*
denotes inconstant motion. Few have credible cognates, and only the
frequentative suffix lends the group an illusion of unity, though it is
appended to stems that seldom occur in English without *-er* (*clat-,
scat-, blust-,* and so forth). *Chat* and *flit* are not the etymons of *chatter* and *flitter* but rather back formations from the longer verbs. However, *patter* (to tap) is *pat* + *er,* and *swagger* is perhaps *swag* (which
in dialects means "to move unsteadily") + er. An ancient root or two
can sometimes be excavated, for instance, **skud-* (to shake) for *shudder, *stut-* (to strike against) for *stutter,* and **wav-* (to move about)
for *waver.* I suspect that *bicker* is akin to *bitch* (from Old Engl. *bicce*).
Dictionaries do not confirm my guess, but they have little to say
about this verb, so I may be right.

Another dead suffix is -*k* in *talk, smirk, stalk, walk*, and *lurk. Talk* and *smirk* are cognate with *tale* and *smile, stalk* is presumably related to *steal*. A comparison of *wal-k*, Old Icelandic *vel-ta* (to roll), and German *wal-zen* (the same meaning) shows that *k* and *t* ~ *z* are suffixes added to the root *wal* ~ *wel-*, though roots that have not been attested without suffixes look suspicious (see Chapter 16). From *walzen* we have the name of the dance *waltz* (German *Walzer*). *Lurk* is possibly akin to *lour* (to look threateningly). In Modern English, *talk, smirk*, and the other *k*-verbs are pure roots like *chalk, work*, and *murk*. The existence of a frequentative suffix in them is a fact of history.

Prefixes are less prominent in the history of English, but a few things should be said about them, too. Those who have had a chance to browse through the supplement to *The American Heritage Dictionary of the English Language*, which is a list of reconstructed roots and their modern English reflexes, will have noticed roots like "***spen-***, also **pen**"; "***slagw-***, also **lagw-*," and "*smer*, also **mer-*." Hundreds of seemingly related words differ in that they appear with or without initial *s-*. One such word turned up above: *mug* (to waylay and rob), it was suggested, is cognate with *smug-* in *smuggle*. That enigmatic, elusive *s-* has been called *s-mobile* (movable *s*). Its productivity remained the same after the emergence of the earliest written documents. Observers of modern dialects register *sclash* for *clash, sclimb* for *climb*, and other similar formations.

The verb *sneeze* first turned up in the fifteenth century in the form *snese* and replaced *fnese*, from Old Engl. *fnesan;* its by-form was *nese* (modern dialectal *neeze*). *Nese* is believed to be a borrowing from Scandinavian (Old Icelandic had *hnjósa*), with *h-* lost. Likewise, German *niesen* and Dutch *niezen* must have had *h-*. *Fnese* and **(h)njósa* are onomatopoeias, whose most audible sounds echo those of the word *nose*. The *Oxford English Dictionary* says the following on the change from *neeze* to *sneeze:* "The adoption of *sneeze* was probably assisted by its phonetic appropriateness; it may have been felt as a strengthened form of *neeze*." *The Oxford Dictionary of English Etymology* suggests that *snese* ~ *sneeze* were substituted for *neeze* "as more expressive." The expressive nature of *s* (a voiceless, fricative consonant) is far from clear, and many researchers have grappled with this prefix. Some trace it to hoary antiquity. Others refuse to believe that it was a regular prefix, because adding and subtracting initial consonants for etymological purposes is a dangerous procedure, but the number of words with alleged *s-mobile* is so great that one shies at ascribing it in all cases to chance.[4] Perhaps sclimbing and sneezing really presupposes a greater effort than climbing and neezing. If so, the power of *s-* has not diminished for millennia. (To return to *smile* and *smirk:* their probable Greek cognate is *meidiáō*[5] [to smile], without *s-*).

Unstressed prefixes tend to disappear. Words with lost prefixes (so-called aphetic forms—a term coined by James A. H. Murray) may coexist with full forms, and their affinity is then felt. For example, *lone* and *squire* are aphetic doublets of *alone* and *esquire.* (*Alone* comes from *al one* [all by oneself], so that *a-* is not a prefix here, but it was interpreted as such: *a-lone* from *al-one.*) Sometimes the related words, one of which is aphetic, are no longer synonyms: compare *mend* and *amend, fend* (in *to fend for oneself*) and *defend,* and especially *maze* and *amaze. Plot* "conspiracy" is believed to be a shortening of French *complot,* but French etymologists doubt the connection. Despite the simplicity of the situation, jumping to conclusions should be avoided: *fend* is indeed a prefixless variant of *defend,* whereas *cry* is not the stub of *decry* and *rear* resembles but probably is not an aphetic form of *arrear. Atone* rhymes with *alone* for a reason: it goes back to *at one* (in harmony). In contrast to *lone,* it has kept both syllables intact and did not become **tone.* This, however, could have happened, as the history of *twit* shows. Old English had *æt-'wītan* (to reproach). Later the unstressed vowel was shed, and *twit,* with a shortened vowel, came into being. Nothing betrays its origin; it is now a homonym of *twit* (to understand). In the form known to us, *twit* was first recorded in 1530. In the same year *atwite* turned up for the last time in the database of the *Oxford English Dictionary*—an elegant coincidence. (This is perhaps the best place to mention *enough:* *e-* is a relic of an old prefix, as follows from Old Engl. *genōg,* and from its German synonym *genug,* that is, *ge-nug.* Although *-nug* is meaningless, *ge-* is a living prefix in German, whereas in English, only the archaism *yclept* [called] has *y-* allied to *ge-*.)

A note on a disguised prefix in a French word may be of some interest here. Latin had the phrase *lībra bilanx* (a balance having two scales) (*bilanx,* from *bis* [two] and *lanx* [scale]). Its Italian continuation *bilancia* goes back to a similar Vulgar (that is Late, Popular) Latin form. But in Spanish and French we find *balanza* and *balance,* respectively, perhaps under the influence of *ballāre* (to dance) (with reference to the "dancing" movement of weighing scales before they come to a standstill). English borrowed the French word in the thirteenth century with the meaning "uncertainty, doubt, risk"; "weighing scales" was recorded later. Since that time, stress, as usual in English, shifted to the first syllable, and the ancient prefix *bi-* is no longer possible to discern in *balance.* French borrowed Italian *bilancio* among many other banking terms at the end of the sixteenth century and turned it into *bilan* (balance), so that French speakers may realize what the etymon of their *balance* is, but English lacks the support of a corresponding Latin, Latinized, or Italian form.

Daffodil is not a French word: its "base" is *affodil* from Medieval Latin *affodilus* (Classical Late Latin *asphodelus*). The mysterious initial *d-* has been compared with the equally mysterious *t-* in *Ted* for *Edward* and with Dutch *de* (as though from *de affodil*), but it remains unexplained. Walter W. Skeat, in a supplement to the first edition of his *English Etymological Dictionary,* p. 787, quotes James A. H. Murray's article on the history of *daffodil.* Whatever the origin of *d-,* it is probably not a submerged prefix despite Skeat's later suggestion that Middle French *fleur d'affrodille* may have influenced the form of the English word.

Other than that, prefixes are never disguised in Modern English the way they sometimes are in German. German *bleiben* and *glauben* are akin to and synonymous with Engl. *leave* and *believe* (though *bleiben* means "to stay, remain" rather than "to cause to remain"). Initial *b-* and *g-* are relics of the prefixes *be-* and *ge-.* English words like *belittle* do not turn into **blittle,* and, in looking for the origin of *blithe* or *bristle,* the question whether **belithe* or **beristle* are their etymons does not arise. The most common English prefixes are of Romance origin (*dis-, mis-, in-, re-, pre-,* and all the negative ones except *un-*). In *disqualify, misspell, influx, reread,* and *preshrunk,* the first element is perfectly clear. Shakespeare used spellings like *i'th'paste* (= *in the paste*) and *'t* for *at;* they resemble *'sblood,* a familiar variant of *His blood,* and *'tis* (= *it is),* and are colloquial variants typical of everyday speech. They are like *bo's'n* and *fo'c's'le.* However, as pointed out, disguised prefixes do not occur in English, and we can leave them at this.

Disguise is rampant when a phrase like *mine uncle* yields *my nuncle* and the word *nuncle* begins to lead an independent existence. The change of *mine uncle* to *my nuncle* is of the same type as the change of *al-one* and *at-one* to *a-lone* and *a-tone,* the main difference being that in the second case the redistribution of boundaries occurs within the word, whereas in the first, two words are involved. As long as both *uncle* and *nuncle* are in use, the origin of the word that arose by misdivision (the technical term for it is metanalysis) poses no problems. But the parent form and the product of metanalysis may diverge. Old French *naperon* (table cloth) (Modern French *napperon*) has the same root as do *napery* and *napkin* (French *nappe* [linen cloth]). *A naperon* became *an aperon* (apron). To an English speaker *napkin* and *apron* are unrelated. In this instance, the noun lost *n-;* in *nuncle,* it gained an initial consonant. Likewise, *adder* (viper) was *nǣd(d)re* in Old English. Its German cognate is *Natter,* and compare Latin *natrix* (not a viper but a harmless water snake, from *natāre* [to swim]). Dutch *adder* (adder) shed its *n-* in the phrase *den nadder* (*den* is an article). The two languages arrived at identical forms by different processes. *An ewt* (to stay with aquatic animals for a while) was mistaken for *a newt.*

Auger is a disguised, misdivided compound. The second element of Old Engl. *nafogār* ended in *gār* (spear, piercer, borer) (Modern Engl. *gore* [a triangular piece of cloth]; see the history of *garlic* on p. 86, where *garfish* [spearfish] is mentioned). *Nafu* has come down to us as *nave* (in a wheel). The *nafogār* was originally a pointed tool for boring the naves of wheels. Here, too, Modern German *Näber* (a dialectal word) resembles its etymon *(nabagēr),* whereas Dutch *avegaar* is *n*-less. Engl. *an auger* is from *a nauger.* Old French *nomper* means "non-peer" (a third party called in to decide between two; *-mp-* from *-np-,* as in *impossible*). In English, it gradually changed to *umpire. Nickname* is still a name, but *nick-* needs an explanation. Here the original form was *an ekename,* with *eke* as in *eke out one's salary (eke* [to augment], *eke out* [to supplement]); thus, "an additional name." *A nekename* from *an ekename* yielded the meaningless compound *nickname.* The expression *for the nonce* is a reshaping of something like **for then anes (anes* [once]). The most striking example of misdivision is *aitchbone,* earlier *nachebone* (Old French *nache,* ultimately from Latin *nates* [buttocks]). The loss of *n-* resulted in the spelling *Hbone.*

A few proper names owe their origin to misdivision. *Ned,* like *nuncle,* must have arisen from *mine Ed.* However, in *nanny* two words have merged. In *nanny goat, nanny* can be understood as *Anny* (with *n-* from *mine*), a pair to *Billy* in *billy goat,* but *nanny* (nursemaid) is a typical baby word: compare Russian *niania* (nursemaid), Welsh *nain* (grandmother), and Latin *nonna* (aunt) (the last continues as *nun* in English, from *nonna,* a title given to an elderly person; Italian *nonna* means "grandmother"). Charles P. G. Scott, the etymologist for *The Century Dictionary,* wrote what amounts to a book (three papers, about 250 pages, featuring approximately 350 words) on misdivision.[6] Most of his examples are "nonce words" that turned up in old texts (*nabbey* for *abbey,* and the like) and provincial (dialectal) words that occur in colloquial speech, like *nidget* (idiot), from *an idiot* (compare *did you* pronounced as *didju).* Scott's most interesting entries are *jackanapes* and *Cockney,*[7] and he had an original idea about people dressed up "to the nines" (*to the nines* [perfectly] is not restricted to dressing). The few dictionaries that venture an explanation of that idiom say that the allusion is to the Nine Muses. Scott suggested that the starting point is *to then īne* "to the eyes."[8]

Another consonant that shifts between words is *t. John atte Elme* became *John Telme,* as *John atten Elme* became *John Nelme.* (It is now easy to guess where the ancestors of Messers Nokes, Nash, Nalder, and Norchard once lived.) Many houses stood *atte welle* or *atte welles* (at the well or "near the spring"), whence the family name *Twells.*[9] *Saint* often let its final *t* go to the name that followed. *Stabbs* in Oxfordshire and *St. Tabbe,* the Prioress of Coldingham, are from *St. Abb* or *St. Ebb.*[10] Tooley Street in London is St. "Oley" Street

(Oley is St. Olave). It is "famous for its three 'tailors', who, we are told, once met, and signed a petition beginning 'We the people of England'. But it seems that one of the three tailors was a grocer, and that only one of the two remaining had a shop in Tooley Street."[11]

In the saint category, the most often cited case is *tawdry*. The word goes back to *Saint Audrey* (Ethelrēada):

> It implies, therefore, that the things so called had been bought at the fair of saint Audrey, where gay toys of all sorts were sold. This fair was held in the Isle of Ely (and probably at other places), on the day of the fair saint, which was the 17th of October. . . . An old English historian makes saint Audrey die of a swelling in her throat, which she considered as a particular judgment, for having been in her youth much addicted to wearing fine necklaces.[12]

This historian, Nicholas Harpsfield, Archdeacon of Canterbury (died 1588), adds in his *Historia Anglicana Ecclesiastica:* "Our women of England are wont to wear about the neck a certain necklace, perchance in memory of what we have told."[13] First, only the phrase *tawdry lace* was current, then *tawdry* came to mean "vulgarily showy, ostentatious but of inferior quality; flashy, gaudy."

The loss and addition of other consonants in the process of misdivision are of little importance. I will only reproduce an explanation Scott gives in the section on *r.* In tracing the origin of *hobby* and *hobbledehoy* (pp. 70 and 115), we observed that *Hob* is a by-form of *Rob.* The consonants *r* and *h* often form a union in the history of the Germanic languages. Scott conjectured that in phases like *our Rob, our Rick,* and *our Rodge,* pronounced *our 'Ob, 'Ick, 'Odge,* aspiration was added on the analogy of names like *Henry* and *Harry,* after which *Hob, Hick,* and *Hodge* appeared as the familiar names of *Robert, Richard,* and *Roger.*[14] This hypothesis, although not fully persuasive, is not worse than any other. Scott assumed that with two *r*'s in succession, one was lost and metanalysis followed. A parallel case would be *Riding,* historically the name of the three districts of Yorkshire. The phrase *North Thriding* (that is, the northern third part) became *North 'Riding.* Then *East Riding* and *West Riding* sprang up. Folk etymology granted legitimacy to the idea of riding all over Yorkshire.[15]

To a varying degree, metanalysis occurs in most, if not all, European languages. In French, the definite article often merges with its noun, as in *lierre* (ivy) from *l'ierre* (from Latin *hedera*). Of "misdivided" French words in English one example will suffice. Latin *lamella* is a diminutive of *lamina* (a thin plate of metal). It yielded French *lemelle,* and *la lemelle* was mistaken for *l'alemelle.* Emancipated *alemelle* acquired various forms, including another diminutive, *amelette,* with *-le-* and *-me* transposed. Later *amelette* became *omelette* (spelled in various ways), and in the seventeenth century, it reached English. At that time, one could say *aumelette d'œufs* (an omelette, or pancake made of eggs). The omelette was supposedly named from its thin flat shape. Old French *alemele* meant "the blade of a knife," and Modern French *alumelle* is glossed in English dictionaries as "sheathing of a ship." Folk etymology traces *omelette* to *œufs mélés* "mixed eggs." The story of this remarkable word shows that in etymology, as in other endeavors, to reach one's goal, one has to break a good number of eggs. *On ne fait pas d'omelette sans casser des œufs.*

Words disguise their past by shrinking, making productive affixes (that is, prefixes and suffixes) unproductive and dead, exchanging sounds with their neighbors, and in many other ways. Two words may also fuse, and the seamless grace of the resulting products (so-called blends) often deceives the shrewdest observer, who fails to notice the head of one "animal" joined to the tail of another. The most successful blends probably known to all English speakers are *smog* (= *s[moke]* + *[f]og*), *brunch* (= *br[eakfast]* + *[l]unch*), and *motel* (= *mo[tor]* + *[ho]tel*). (*Brunch,* initially university slang, was coined in 1895 in England and, like most such novelties, incurred the wrath of the purists. It is a pleasure to quote a passage written in 1901 and proving the futility of predictions about language: "A few years ago the word *five-o'clocker* seemed likely to be permanently adopted in Paris, as *ennui* has been here. But I cannot suppose that the mongrel word *brunch* for a meal combining breakfast and lunch, which has recently shown signs of temporary popularity, is likely to be accepted as true coin in either capital."[16] The capitals are London and Paris. Events on the other side of the ocean did not interest the author.) Lewis Carroll, a great lover of blends, called them portmanteau words, because a portmanteau opens into two halves and two words can be packed into it. His comment, in the preface to his *Hunting of the Snark* (a snark is half-snake, half-shark), is as follows:

> For instance take the two words "fuming" and "furious". Make up your mind that you will say both words, but leave it unsettled which you say first. Now open your mouth and speak. If your thoughts incline ever so little towards "fuming", you will say "fuming-furious"; if they turn even by a hair's breadth toward "furious", you will say "furious-fuming"; but if you have that rarest of gifts, a perfectly balanced mind, you will say frumious.[17]

Two of his coinages—*galumph* (*gallop* + *triumph*) and *chortle* (*chuckle* + *snort*)—have found their way into familiar usage.

Smog, brunch, motel, galumph, and *chortle* are an etymologist's dream: their origin is beyond dispute. But we cannot be present at the birth of every blend, as happened in the history of *gerrymander* (to manipulate election districts unfairly so as to secure disproportionate representation). The story of this verb has been told many times:

> The term, says Norton, is derived from the name of Governor Gerry, of Massachusetts, who in 1811 signed a bill readjusting the representative districts so to as favor the democrats and weaken the Federalists, although the last named party polled nearly two thirds of the votes cast. A fancied resemblance of a map of the districts thus treated led Stuart, the painter, to add a few lines with his pencil, and say to Mr. Russell, editor of the *Boston Sentinel,* 'That will do for a Salamander'. Russell glanced at it: "Salamander", said he, "call it Gerrymander!" The epithet took at once, and became a Federalist war cry, the caricature being published as a campaign document.[18]

According to another version, quoted in the *Oxford English Dictionary,* Russell was the editor of the *Continent,* and Stuart added not "a few lines" but a head, wings, and claws. However, the punch line is the same. *The Century Dictionary* supplies an anticlimactic detail that the redistribution of the districts was only believed to be Gerry's idea; in fact, he was opposed to the measure. Be that as it may, we have here a "pretty etymological tale" from Massachusetts (the other one from the same state concerns *schooner:* p. 128).

"It is to be expected that whimsical or conscious or unconscious fusions of this sort that caught the popular fancy, and in the course of time established themselves, will prove difficult to trace."[19] Many blends originated in slang, and unless we have contemporary testimony about the elements of the coinage, we cannot be sure that we are dealing with amalgam words. The adjective *slender* appeared in a fourteenth-century poem in which it rhymes with *tender* and means "lean." A French and a Dutch etymon of *slender* have been proposed, but perhaps it is the sum of *slight* and *tender.* The verb *snooze* emerged in texts at the end of the eighteenth century. It must always have been a colloquialism reminiscent of *sneeze, snore,* and *doze.* Another blend? *Blotch* looks like a composite of *blot* and *botch.*

Here are a few putative blends. *Dumbfound = dumb + confound?* (Most likely.) *Scurry,* originally the second element of the rhyming jingle *hurry-scurry,* may be *scour + hurry,* probably part of a formation like *harum-scarum* that succeeded in prying itself loose from its "master." *Blurt = blow* (or *blare*) + *spurt? Flounder = founder* (to stumble, go lame) + *blunder? Squirm = squir* (to throw with a jerk) (dialectal) + *worm? Binge = bung* (the orifice in the *bilge* of a cask, through which it is fitted)? *Doldrum = dull* or *dolt + tantrums? Flurry = flaw + hurry?* (Unlikely.) *Cantankerous = cankerous + contentious? Flaunt = fly + vaunt? Flush = flare + blush?* One can fill pages with similar questions.[20]

Jespersen insisted that blending plays a greater role in word formation than most people believe. The etymology of *slender* from *slight* or *slim + tender* is his. He suggested *scroll = scrow + roll; slash = slay* (or *sling,* or *slat*) *+ gash* or *dash; gruff = grim + rough; troll* (verb) *= trill* or *trundle + roll; twirl = twist + whirl; blot = blemish* or *black + spot, plot,* or *dot.*[21] We have no way of verifying such derivations; but most of them are plausible. Blends are especially popular in humorous place names (like *Oxbridge = Oxford + Cambridge*) and in brand names like *Texaco (Texas + Company*). Viable terms like *Amerind* (said about American Indian languages) have come from blends. Anyone can coin a blend: *Eurasia (Europe + Asia), Benelux (Belgium + Netherlands + Luxembourg); frenemies* (friends who act more like enemies); *fictionary* (a dictionary of fiction; this is my coinage, but, no doubt, I have predecessors); *gliberal* (a beautiful blend I found in a local newspaper); *Tolstoevsky* (*Tolstoy* + *Dostoevsky*), a joke of Russian scholars that has worn rather thin; *argle* = *argue* + *haggle; dispread* = *disperse* + *spread;* and so forth. At the risk of irritating all serious philologists I would like to propose an etymology of *doe* (the female of the fallow deer) from a blend. Engl. *roe* means not only "the milt or spawn of a fish" (from Old Engl. *rā*, with several ancient cognates) but also "a small species of deer," a different word. Cannot *doe,* a word of unknown origin, from Old Engl. *dā,* be a blend of *deer* (from *dēor*) and *roe?* The female of the deer is smaller than the male. Perhaps *dā* was the sum of *dēor* and *rā,* with the accent laid on the animal's size.

The elephant's child (if I can be allowed to return to Kipling's *Just So Stories* for the last time) was full of 'satiable curtiosity, and all his relatives spanked him for it. We are no less courteous and curious, and our reward is words, unhurriedly but with a good grace, revealing their secrets to us. *Bath, tool, walk, twit, nidget, balance, tawdry, omelette,* and *doldrums* emerged to us in their pristine simplicity, and this, as already suggested at the end of Chapter 2, is what etymology is for and about.

Chapter Ten

which suggests that in the world of words anonymity is the greatest reward, or

Words and Names

Going nap.—A dish of jemmies.—Jack-of-all-trades needs a john.—
Tom, Dick, and Harry.—Big guns.—A tribute to Earnest Weekley.—
The sorry plight of nincompoops.—If a woman is not exactly a man,
what is (a) man?—Robin Hood and his hobby horse.—Donkeys all
the way through.—Codlins and cream.—Hooligans, hoodlums, and
larrikins.—The Poles dance, the Flemings produce fine fabrics.—On
being carried in a sedan and riding a hackney.—A shepherd called
Syphilis.

Before computers became part of our life, everybody knew that a
macintosh (also spelled, or rather misspelled, *mackintosh*) is a rain-
coat. In 1836 Charles Macintosh (1766–1843) invented a waterproof
material that bears his name. Even those who are far from linguistic
pursuits will guess that *Macintosh* or *Mac* (whether Big Mac or the
computer) goes back to a name. Such words, usually spelled with a
small ("lowercase") letter, are all around us. *Sandwich, diesel,* and
volt, among hundreds of others, are familiar examples. Their origin
is clear when we know the circumstances in which they came into
being. But sometimes those circumstances have to be reconstructed
from a few fossils. In still other cases, even such fossils are absent.

Dictionaries inform us that *napoleon* is "a rectangular piece of
pastry, iced on top, with crisp, flaky layers, filled with custard
cream"—an admirable definition. But why should a piece of pastry
with flaky layers be called *napoleon?* The man was not iced on top;
nor was he made of sugar and spice, and all that's nice. Equally enigmatic is the reference to the French emperor in the name of the card

game napoleon, which is always called *nap*. Once *nap* supplanted *napoleon,* its origin became as obscure as that of *nap* (sleep) and *nap* (the surface of cloth)—except to those who know it. Scholarly and popular books tend to hide behind a smoke screen; for example, "card-game in which the player who calls five is said to *go nap,* formerly *go the Napoleon*" (for the uninitiated: "Short for *Napoleon,* Christian name of certain emperors of the French, esp. Napoleon I [1769–1821], after whom the coin so named was called").[1]

When the smoke clears, we discover the following: "Nap . . . evidently commemorates Napoleon III, who retired to Britain after losing the Franco-Prussian War in 1870, and has since been described as 'the nearest thing Europe ever produced to a Mississippi riverboat gambler'." In some way, Napoleon III was confused with his illustrious predecessor, for otherwise the appearance of two other dignitaries would be hard to explain: "As optional extras not suitable for less than five players, Nap may be overcalled by 'Wellington', a five-trick bid that pays 10 each if lost, and Wellington by 'Blücher', also a five-trick bid but paying out 20 each if lost." (Each player may raise the bidding in the following series: one, two, three, miz, four, five. *To go five* is called *to go nap; miz* is a no-trump misère.) As long as we are in such distinguished company, it can be mentioned that Swedes play "an unusual cross between Nap and Rams" called Rödskägg, that is, "Redbeard," or "Barbarossa."[2]

To return to pastry, not necessarily rectangular. Depending on where you live or travel in the United States, you may be treated to a bismarck, either a jelly doughnut or a fried cruller. A drink called Bismarck (a mixture of champagne and stout, that is, strong beer) emerged "in the colonies" at the beginning of the twentieth century. The allusion may have been to the Chancellor's power (I am guessing; perhaps the mixture was invented by a man nicknamed Bismarck), but *bismarck* for a jelly doughnut?! Our ignorance in such cases is all the more annoying because the words in question are late, coined almost within recent memory. The *Oxford English Dictionary* has no examples of *napoleon* (cake) before 1892, and the earliest citation of *bismarck* in the splendid *Dictionary of American Regional English* is dated 1930. Both words must have found their way into print soon after they were invented. The one good thing about Napoleon and Bismarck is that such people undoubtedly existed, a fact that provides an etymologist with a starting point. The contours of the picture become blurred when instead of the French emperor and the German statesman we encounter the faceless Jack, him of all trades, the proverbial every man jack. A long list of compounds (*Jack-a-dandy, Jack-o-lantern, Jack-in-the-box,* and so forth) merges with phrases like *Jack Tar* (a common sailor). Some male animals are jacks, *jackass* being foremost in this herd, and the knave of hearts (in cards), the character given to stealing . . . pastry, is *jack.* Having fallen so low (an ass and a pilferer with a sweet tooth), Jack rose to distinction in the phrase *Union Jack.*

Implements and machines cannot do without Jack either. He is not alone. *Jenny* is not only a female donkey and a wren but also part of various mechanical devices. The spinning-jenny, as *The Century Dictionary* explains, is said to have been so named by Arkwright after his wife, Jenny. But according to a grandson of James, or Jacob Hargreaves, the inventor, it is a "corruption" of *gin,* a contraction of *engine. Gin* would easily suggest *Jin, Jinny,* and *Jenny.* The dictionary continues: ". . . but in the present case there is probably an allusion to E[ngl.] dial[ectal] *jenny-spinner, jinny-spinner,* the crane-fly, also called in Sc[ots] *spinning-Maggie* and *Jenny Nettles." Betty* was at one time synonymous with *bess* and *jenny* (a short bar used by thieves to wrench doors open). As though that is not enough, *jemmy* turns up with the meaning "a sheep's head baked," a source of innocent joy to the thieves' company in *Oliver Twist:* "Nancy . . . returned with a pot of porter and a dish of sheep's heads: which gave occasion to several pleasant witticisms on the part of Mr. Sikes founded upon the singular coincidence of 'jemmies' being a cant name common to them and also an ingenious instrument much used in his profession."[3]

Jack and its French counterpart have been in vogue among commoners for centuries. In France, peasants were nicknamed *Jacques;* hence *Jacquerie,* a revolt of French peasants (1358) against nobles and pillaging soldiers. If *Jack* is almost synonymous with *man, jack-of-all-trades* and *all work and no play make Jack a dull boy* find an explanation: may *Jack* enjoy his near anonymity with *Jill. Jack,* as the name of a tool, seems to be an arbitrary creation, and so do *betty* and *jemmy*. The question is the same as about Napoleon and Bismarck (that is, why Jack, Jemmy, and so on?), except that here we will hardly find an answer, "Jacques" being so undistinguished. Burglars are sentimental, and naming a favorite tool after a sweetheart must have been common practice. It would be interesting to meet the first Jenny/ Betty/ Maggie, the mothers of all crane flies and skeleton keys, but such a meeting would not enrich the science of etymology.

Of the trio *Tom, Dick, and Harry,* only the last escaped the process of decapitalization, but *Harry* suggested harrying and harrowing; hence probably *Old Harry* (the Devil). It was Tom's fate to watch his name appended to big and clumsy creatures and objects. We have *tomboy, tomcat* (the ancestor of Tom the Cat was Gib, that is, Gilbert), *Great Toms* (in the belfries of Oxford, Lincoln, and Exeter), *Long Tom* (a gun), and even *tom toe* (the great toe) and *tom plow*.[4] *Tomfoolery* contains the same inexplicable reference. Dick and John fared worse than anyone else. Privies bear human names (often female) in many languages, but in England, *john* succeeded *jakes*. On the other hand, William of *sweet william* did extremely well.

However little we may know about the reasons why *tom, john, jack,* and *jenny* ended up where they are now, we are confident that they go back to *Tom, John,* and so on. The situation is worse than with Napoleon and Bismarck, but the principle is the same. Fortunately, the fact that the Colt (a revolver) was patented by Samuel Colt of Hartford, Connecticut, cannot be called into question. Likewise, Big Bertha and Katyusha, two cannons, were certainly named after women (Bertha is obscure, but Katyusha, that is, Katya, was the heroine of a popular Russian war song). The more murderous the device or the weapon, the gentler its name (compare what is said about *jenny,* above). One of the recorded meanings of *maiden* is "guillotine."

Scavenger's daughter, an instrument of torture, is the invention of Sir Leonard Skevington (or Skeffington), Lieutenant of the Tower, in the reign of Henry VIII. *Skevington* changed to *Scavenger* under the influence of the word *scavenger* (an officer who took "scavage" and [later] kept the streets clean) (*scavage* meant the toll formerly levied in London on merchant strangers and had originally nothing to do with filth). The "daughter" compressed the body, so as to cause haemorrhaging. The history of the word has been documented. A harder case is the origin of *gun,* a fourteenth-century noun. It was Skeat who connected *gun* with *Gunilda,* a Latinized form of Scandinavian *Gunnhildr;*[5] a singularly appropriate name for a cannon (the first guns were catapults), because both *gunn-* and *-hildr* mean "battle," and in myth, Gunnr was a valkyrie, "a corpse chooser," a war maiden who invited fallen warriors to Valhalla.

Skeat's hypothesis is excellent, and the *Oxford English Dictionary* accepted it. However, as late as 1899, Friedrich Kluge, the great German etymologist, still preferred the derivation of *gun* from *mangonel* (a machine for throwing stones). *The Oxford Dictionary of English Etymology* reproduces Skeat's explanation but adds "probably," and Ernest Weekley, who was the first to cite "the famous fifteenth-century *Mons Meg* of Edinburgh," as well as *Brown Bess, Long Tom,* and *Hungry Liz* (nor did he forget *Big Bertha* and *die faule* [the lazy] *Grete* of 1414), said "perhaps." This is his conclusion (in the quotation below, his abbreviations have been expanded):

> Connection with Old Norse *gunnr,* war, was even suggested by Lye (1743). Another, and less fanciful, suggestion is that *gun* is for Old French *engon,* variant of *engan,* device (cf. *gin* for *engine*), a form recorded in the region (Mons), whence the first gun constructors came to England; cf. *Mons Meg* . . . probably made at Mons. Perhaps both sources have contributed, the latter having helped to fix the already existing nickname. Egan is from Old French *enganner,* to trick, of unknown origin. It has a variant *engaigne,* missile, engine, whence early Scots *ganyie,* missile, regularly used in association with *gun.*[6]

Although two sources often converge in producing a word, it does not follow that a word can have two or more etymologies. In every case, only one will be correct, but a new coinage may need support to become accepted. *Spinning jenny* (from *Jenny?*) could have died without its homonym *jenny ~ jinny,* and *gun* (from *Gunilda?*) may not have stayed in the language if it had not met *mangonel* and especially *engon,* a similar-sounding synonym. In retrospect, we cannot always decide how the process started.

Multiple references to Ernest Weekley in this chapter have a good reason. He went further than most in tracing common words to names both in his 1921 dictionary and in a special book.[7] In the preface to the dictionary, he said: ". . . I have proposed personal-name origins for many of the hitherto unsolved problems of etymology, and . . . brought the two classes of words into closer connection than earlier etymologists." His statement 12 years later has an even keener edge: ". . . the part played by personal names in the creation of our vocabulary is not yet realized by etymologists." All his suggestions are ingenious, though some are better argued than others. The almost forgotten word *trot* (old woman; hag) may be related to German *Drude* (sorceress, incubus). Weekley thought that the English noun goes back to Dame Trot of Salerno, eleventh-century doctor and witch. If his guess is justified, the case, it seems, can be closed. But such is only the first impression. *Trot* in *Dame Trot* may have been a nickname: perhaps the lady of Salerno was called Trot because she was a trot!

One of Weekley's most successful etymologies is that of *nincompoop,* a word that invariably makes people laugh. Its recorded history begins in 1676, and at that time it was spelled *nincompoop* and *nickumpoop.* Clearly, *poop* was added to *nincom- ~ nickum-.* Except for *poop* (the stern of a ship), all the other meanings of Engl. *poop* ("inside information"; "to quit because of exhaustion," as in *poop out;* "an abrupt sound; a gulping sound," and "excrement") are slangy. Latin *puppis,* the ultimate source of *poop* (stern) (via French), was probably nautical slang 2,000 years ago. The origin of all *poop*s but one is unknown; *poop* "(to make) an abrupt sound" is an indelicate onomatopoeia. *Poop* (fool) was noticed at the beginning of the twentieth century and may have been abstracted from *nincompoop,* but Dutch also has *poep* (pronounced almost like Engl. *poop*), a term of abuse (approximately "asshole").

Judging by its phonetic shape, *poop* is a baby word. Hence both Engl. *poop* (to break wind) (and "to produce a vulgar sound" in general) and French *pupée* (doll) (from Latin *pūpa* [a little girl]; Engl. *puppet* and *puppy,* originally "plaything," are from the same French etymon); the meanings of such words are diverse but to a certain extent predictable. At one time, *nickumpoop* was more offensive than it is now and may have referred to a certain Nickum, a notorious poop. Weekley suggested that *Nickum* is *Nicodemus,* mentioned in John III: 1–4. Nicodemus, "a man of the Pharisees," came to Jesus by night and confessed his faith in Him. Jesus responded that "[e]xcept a man be born again, he cannot see the kingdom of God. Nicodemus saith unto him, How can a man be born when he is old? can he enter the second time into his mother's womb, and be born?" Jesus did not answer the question directly but repeated: "Ye must be born again" (the quotations are from the Authorized Version).

The nocturnal interview did not do Nicodemus any good in the eyes of posterity. He gained the reputation of a blockhead unable to understand the simplest things and became a popular figure in medieval mystery plays. Modern French *nicodème* means "simpleton." Some time later, *nickumpoop* changed to *nincompoop,* perhaps under the influence of *ninny,* a sixteenth-century word for "duffer," supposedly from *Innocent,* by misdivision, like *Ned* and *nuncle* from *Ed* and *uncle.* In Weekley's opinion, *ninny* and its synonym *noddy* are traceable to Nicodemus's name; to boost his hypothesis, he cited *noddypoop,* another word for "fool." (Nor did Nicodemus fare better in later times. The French family name *Nicot* goes back directly to *Nicodemus.* Jacque Nicot, French ambassador at Lisbon, introduced tobacco into France in 1560; hence *nicotine.*)

In deciding whether to accept an etymology, we usually have to weigh probabilities. Someone called Nelme comes from a family that once lived "at an elm." By contrast, *nincompoop* cannot be shown, beyond reasonable doubt, to derive from *Nicodemus,* rather than from, for instance, Nicholas or Old Nick. Weekley's conjecture is good, and that is all we are allowed to say. *The Oxford Dictionary of English Etymology* agreed with it, but Skeat did not, and most modern dictionaries, which tend to follow the principle "better safe than sorry," state that the etymology is unknown or uncertain. The other etymologies of *nincompoop* are mere guesswork. Samuel Johnson derived the first part of the word from Latin *non compos (mentis)* (not sound [in mind])." To be sure, *nincompoop* could have emerged at universities as students' slang. *Chum* and *crony* are believed to have such an origin: allegedly, short for *chamber fellow,* at Oxford, and from

Greek *khrónios*[8] (long-lasting, long-continued), at Cambridge. *Loo* (lavatory) (a place for "ab-loo-tion," like *lava-tory?*) is another "university word," and see p. 102 on *brunch*. Perhaps *nincompoop* is *ninny cum poop*, a joke like M'Choakumchild (a teacher in *Hard Times*), or a fanciful formation, as the *Oxford English Dictionary* says. However, Weekley explained the earliest forms and found a missing link (French *nicodème*). Until someone comes up with a better suggestion, his etymology should stand.

One of the most intricate stories along the same lines can be told about the word *man*. According to the Roman historian Tacitus, some ancient Germanic tribes venerated a god called Mannus. Tacitus wrote his book *Germania* in the first century c.e. The oldest myths, chronicles, and homilies in English and other Germanic languages, all of which were recorded much later, do not mention Mannus. However, *Germania* is a reliable source, and when we can draw on outside information, Tacitus's facts always turn out to be accurate. Personal and place names testify to the cult of Mannus, though it is strange that no tale of him has come down to us.

Apparently, the common name *man* and the proper name *Mannus* are the same word. *Mannus* looks like a form from a Latin grammar book, the more so because the Latin noun *mannus* (pony) existed, but Germanic masculine nouns sometimes ended in *-us*. The usual assumption is that if we discover the origin of *man,* the origin of *Mannus* will take care of itself: the god will emerge as "protoman." Since it is more likely that human beings invented a deity called Mannus than that Mannus created man in his image and after his likeness, we should rather try to learn how the god's name came into being and attempt to derive *man* from it. This approach is more realistic, because several words for "man" were current among the earliest Germanic speakers, so that they did not seem to need another one. Yet it arose.

The origin of *man* has been most often searched for among nouns and verbs designating human activities instead of in the realm of religion and cult, and this is why it has never been found. According to one suggestion, the word **gmono,* akin to Old Engl. *gomo* and Latin *homo,* lost initial g- and yielded *mon,* which alternated with *man.* Another hypothesis related *man* to Latin *manus* (hand), with "hand" developing the meaning "laborer, man" (as in *all hands aboard* and *farmhand*). A third etymology derives *man* from the root present, among others, in Latin *mens* (mind).[9] Since *man* would hardly have been coined with the original meaning "thinker" or "someone endowed with memory" (in those times, human beings were not opposed to animals as thinkers versus dumb creatures), "think" was interpreted as "to breathe" or "to be sexually alert." The same objection remains: neither breath nor the sexual urge is a specifically human feature.

Even if one of those etymologies (or a similar one) gained universal acceptance, the biggest difficulty would have remained, for we would have ended up with the result that speakers of Early Germanic called their supreme deity "(the) man." This is like having a god Homo or a god Anthropos. Beginning at the other end holds out greater promise. In several languages, words with the root *man* mean "ghost, apparition." The earliest gods of humanity do not resemble Zeus, Athena, Bacchus, Eros, and the rest known to us from Greek and Latin literature. They were envisioned as a multitude of spirits inflicting diseases and driving people mad. Someone called *Man-* (ghost, bogey) would be part and parcel of such a host. In Ancient India, the progenitor of the human race was called *Mánu,* Mannus's namesake. As time went on, the frightening ghost must have acquired anthropomorphic features, relented (as it were), and become the object of cult worship.

Gothic, a Germanic language, recorded in the fourth century c.e., had the word *gaman;* it meant "partnership, fellowship" and "partner" (*ga-* is a prefix; having the same word designating a group and one of its members is not unusual: compare Engl. *youth* [the state of being young, young people and a young man]). Perhaps its original meaning was "a circle of Mannus's votaries." In the earliest texts of Old English, German, and Icelandic, the word *man ~ mann ~ mon* referred to servants and persons of inferior status; it translated Latin *servus* (slave). In relation to a god, everybody is inferior. It is from the *gaman,* a group of Mannus's worshippers, that *man,* first "a partner" in such a group, then "slave; servant," and finally, "a human being, a person of either sex" seems to have emerged. Modern German *Mensch* (a human being) goes back to an adjective that probably meant "belonging to Mannus."[10] Martin Eden, the protagonist of Jack London's semi-autobiographical novel, wrote an essay entitled "God and Clod." His title would fit a story about the origin of the word *man*.

In some areas, common and proper names are often indistinguishable. One of them is animal names, with tomcats, jackasses, and billy goats at every corner. Etymologies seem to lie on the surface—a circumstance that invites caution, as a few examples will show. Among the cases of folk etymological reshaping of foreign words (Chapter 5), *Morris dance* turned up. Its central figure is Robin Hood. Opinions differ on whether historical Robin Hood existed, but "[t]he identity of the man matters less than the persistence of the legend."[11] Robin Hood was adopted into the May Games, and the legend mingled with the old myths of forest sprites and the Wild Hunt. The beloved outlaw invariably appeared on a hobby horse. *Hob* is a popular pronunciation of *Rob* (see more about the alternation *Rob* ~ *Hob* on p. 101), and *hobby horse* is the same as *robby horse, only with alliteration. The May Games were rough, and the procession of those who participated in them turned really wild; hence the expression *horse play*.[12] Yet it does not follow that because the hobby is an indispensable part of the Morris dance, the word *hobby* emerged with the games or owes its existence to *Hob*.

Animal names often have the root *rob-*. In several Germanic languages, including German, *robbe* means "seal." In some Flemish dialects, *robbe* is "rabbit," whereas Icelandic *robbi* means "sheep, ram." Also, the English bird name *robin* is close by. If we change the vowel, Engl. *rabbit* will join its Flemish counterpart. Although *hobby* is a variant of *robby, *robby need not be a derivative of *Robert* or *Robin:* their connection may be due to folk etymology.

It is the same with donkeys as it is with horses. We will look at *donkey, cuddy, dicky, moke,* and *neddy. Donkey* appeared first in Francis Grose's *A Classical Dictionary of the Vulgar Tongue* (1785), in which the definition is: "Donkey *or* Donkey Dick, he or Jackass."

For several decades, *donkey* remained slang and rhymed with *monkey*. Dictionaries offer two etymologies of *donkey*. One derives the word from the color *dun,* with *-kie* being a diminutive suffix common in northern dialects (compare *lassikie* [lass, lassie]; Skeat cites *horsikie* and *beastikie*). Dun is a common color of horses and donkeys. The Russian for *dun* is *savrasyi* (stress on the second syllable), and *Savraska* is a popular name for a horse (*-k-* is a diminutive suffix, *-a* is an ending).[13] According to another etymology, *donkey* is a nickname of *Duncan.* That derivation seems to be less probable. In the phrase *donkey Dick,* both elements were hardly proper names.

Old, established animal names tend to yield to upstarts that usually mean "a small round soft thing." *Rob, lob, lop,* and *bop* are among such newcomers. In the past, they were disyllabic: *lobbe, loppe,* and the like, with a long consonant between the vowels. They resemble nicknames and at times exchange roles, as happened to *Dobbin* (a male name and a patient draught horse). Compare "Dobbin of Ours," Amelia's lifelong admirer in Thackeray's *Vanity Fair.* At school (which he detested), "[t]he latter youth (who used to be called Heigh-ho Dobbin, Gee-ho Dobbin, and by many other names indicative of puerile contempt) was the quietest, the clumsiest, and, as it seemed, the dullest of all Dr. Swishtail's young gentlemen" (the beginning of Chapter 5). We have *hobby horse;* *dobby horse is not unthinkable. Engl. *cub* is one of such *kob—rob—lob* words. *Cob* (head swan; a stout short-legged horse; seagull; spider) (the last now dialectal, except in *cobweb*) may partly belong here, too. Which baby word would designate which "beastikie" depends on chance. In German, the seal is called *Robbe.* In Icelandic, it is *kobbi.* The hypocoristic name (that is, a nickname) of *Kolbeinn* and *Kolbrandur* is *kobbi;* many Icelanders think that *kobbi* (seal) was called after some Kolbeinn.

In the pairs *swine – pig, hound – dog,* and *deer – stag,* the words that emerged later (*pig, dog,* and *stag*) sound somewhat alike; the Old English forms were *pigga (with an asterisk because only Middle Engl. *pigge* has been recorded), *docga* (*cg* = *gg*), and *stagga (first recorded in the twelfth century). Like *robbi – kobbi,* they may be applied to various animals. Icelandic *steggur* means "tomcat," while English northern dialectal *steg* means "gander." The syllable *dog-*

occurs in the names of at least two varieties of fish: the dogfish is a small shark, and the Dutch *dogger* is a cod fisher, whence *Dogger Bank* (a great shoal in the North Sea). Words of the same structure (*cob-cub-rob-dog*), to which *hog* and *frog* can be added, are characteristic not only of Germanic: in like manner, Latin *catus* (of African origin), apparently a baby word, appeared alongside *fēlēs* and partly superseded it. *Kitten* is cuddlier than *cat,* and *kitty* even more so.

We are now fully equipped to deal with *moke* (donkey) and are not surprised to learn that *mok(e)* is a typical name for lambs and pigs in German dialects and that Irish and Welsh have the same word for "pig." Our *cob – dog* list expands by one more word. Weekley thought that *moke* could be some proper name like *Moggy* applied to the ass and cited thirteenth-century *Mock, Mok, Mog, Mug,* and the modern family names *Mokes* and *Moxon.*[14] Eric Partridge says that Weekley hit the etymological nail on the head.[15] He forgot that etymology is a hydra with many heads, none of which is easily hittable. In light of the evidence from German, Weekley's derivation is improbable. **Muck- ~ mok-* have meant "soft" for thousands of years; their reflexes in Modern English are *meek, muck,* and *moke.* The Moxons were named after pigs, not the other way around.

Cuddy (or *cuddy ass*) is a nineteenth-century addition to the Standard. Here Cuthbert obliges us. The logic is familiar: since *Cuthbert* is *Cuddy, cuddy* must be from *Cuthbert* (compare *Kolbeinn ~ kobbi,* above). However, *cuddy,* like *kitty,* may be one more cuddly baby word. *Cuddy* means not only "donkey" but also "the young of the coalfish or seath" and "the local name for the hedge sparrow or 'dunnock' and for the moor hen" (incidentally, the dunnock is dun, which explains its name). Our next ass is *dicky,* a distant relative of *dicky bird. Dicky,* the animal, and *dick* (penis) hardly go back to *Dick.* The penis is more probably "a little fellow." In Yorkshire, *dick* or *dickie* means "louse." In Hampshire, little lice are called *bobs;* in these parts a pincer bob is a stag beetle, and their males, like other male animals, are referred to as toms.[16] *Dick* appears to be related to *dink,* a northern word, which means "trim, nifty"; its origin, as could be expected, is unknown. *Dinky,* derived from *dink,* means "small, insignificant" (compare *dinkey* [a small locomotive]). My campus is situated in a neighborhood called *Dinky Town*. Some stores ("shoppes") bear the signboard "Dinky Town, U.S.A." Perhaps *dink* is a so-called expressive variant of *dick,* as *clink, clank,* and *tinkle* are expressive, reinforced variants of *click, clack,* and *tick.* Only *neddy* is probably *Neddy,* though donkeys, on account of their obstinacy, are believed to be noddies. (It would be fair to note that donkeys were venerated in ancient societies, despite the fact that their character must have been the same at all times.)

Eric Partridge, in the book mentioned above, says the following about *cuddy:* "Not from *cuddy,* a swain, for that word and 'our' cuddy both represent Cuddy, the pet-form of the male given-name *Cuthbert,* which owes much of its (former) popularity to St. Cuthbert." *Ass* is an embarrassing word to pronounce. This is the reason it gave way to a whole bunch of synonyms, but Partridge's statement contains a serious flaw: why should the name of a popular saint be given to a proverbially stupid animal? We may not be able to discover why *tom* and *jenny* came to be associated with cats and wrens, but unless we manage to reconstruct the link between St. Cuthbert and the donkey, an etymology connecting them is not worth much. Weekley's brief reference: "Cf. *Cuddy Headrigg* in *Old Mortality*," is nothing like the overwhelming mass of analogs in the entry "gun" (*Old Mortality* is a novel by Walter Scott).

Sometimes desired links exist. One of the most unfair words in English is *dunce.* The celebrated scholastic theologian John Duns Scotus died in 1308, but the earliest citation of *dunce* in the *Oxford English Dictionary* is dated 1530. The word acquired the meaning "a caviling sophist, hair splitter; a dull pedant" and "blockhead" under the attack of the humanists and reformers, who called Duns's followers Duns men, Dunses disciples, and simply dunces. Sophists, literally pursuers of wisdom (compare *philosophy* [love of wisdom]), had bad press in the postmedieval period. *Sophism* (a clever statement meant to expose the opponent's weakness in reasoning) turned into "a specious but fallacious argument." *Sophomore,* a combination of "wise" and "foolish" (*-more,* as in *oxymoron,* originally "pointedly foolish" + *moron*) first meant "debater" ("sophister"), that is, "a student learning to argue and distinguish sense from nonsense." A blend of wisdom and stupidity in one and the same word proved fatal to the compound, and it began to designate a student still "fresh" but full of self-importance, one characterized by "sophomore mentality."

The origin of *donkey, moke,* and their kin is hard to discover, because the probability of their going back to human names is not great. Some compounds give the etymologist less trouble. *Magpie* ends in *-pie,* from Old French *pie,* from Latin *pīca* (the same bird); the beginning element, *mag-,* is from *Mag,* the pet name of *Margaret.* Shakespeare spelled *Grimalkin* as *Gray Malkin* (the name of one of his many devils). *Gray* was sometimes confused with *grue-,* as in *gruesome.* Cats in folklore are associated with witches and are seldom tame, so that *Gray Malkin* may have meant "terrible Malkin." *Malkin* is a diminutive of *Malde* (Maud, Matilda). (*Matilda,* like *Gunilda,* is a war-like name: its oldest German form was *Mahthild* = "might" + "battle.")

Almost unbelievable adventures happened in the history of the word *codlin* or *codling* (a variety of apple, especially a variety too harsh to eat raw). The word has been recorded in numerous forms, including *quadling* and *quodling,* and in the fifteenth century, it was spelled *querlyng* and *querdelyng,* as though consisting of *querd* (whatever *querd* may mean) followed by the diminutive suffix *-ling,* as in *codling* (a small cod) and *gosling.* Since codlins are eaten baked, folk etymology derived their name from the verb *coddle:* allegedly, codlins had to be "coddled or stewed."

> Codlins and Cream have been a favourite dish since the days of Elizabeth. An old farmer tells me how his mother used to heat up her wood-oven, bake the loaves of bread, then a batch of cakes and pastries, and finally put in a large bowl full of Codlins and leave them there for the night—that is what is meant by 'coddling,' a slow stewing in a mild oven over a long period.[17]

None of the old etymologies of *querdling ~ codling ~ codlin* is convincing: from Irish *cuerit* (an apple tree), from Medieval Latin *cidonia* (quince), or from Middle Engl. *quert* (safe and sound). Weekley, on the other hand, explained the early forms as alterations of French *cœur-de-lion* (Lion Heart), the soubriquet of Richard I, and cited several close parallels. *Codling* came out as "a fancy name for an esteemed apple." The family names *Querdelioun* and *Querdling* survive in Norfolk as *Quadling* and *Quodling*.[18] This is a fully acceptable etymology, though I am not sure that the name reflects the esteem in which codlings were supposedly held. Codlins, it will be remembered, have to be stewed or baked before they can be eaten: one needs a tremendous effort to make a lion's heart mellow. What a contrast with the depreciatory name *crab apple!* That fruit is as astringent as the *cœur-de-lion,* but no one coddles it. *Crab-* is perhaps from a verb meaning "to scratch," but the allusion to the apple's crabbedness is incontestable. What could the medieval Yorkshire man called *Crabtree* have done or what was he like to deserve such a name?

Every now and then, words actually or allegedly derived from names form groups. Such is, for example, the criminal trio *hooligan – hoodlum – larrikin.* Hooligans made their way into police reports in the summer of 1898, and the word caught the popular fancy at once. Perhaps, as has been suggested, the "progenitor" of these ruffians was a certain Patrick Hooligan, or the real name of the first hooligan was Houlihan, or they were members of Hooley's gang. Hooligan was a favorite name in music hall productions and cartoons. The truth remains hidden. The predominantly Irish slang word *hooley* (a noisy party, spree), first recorded in 1877 (which means that it had existed for some time before that date), makes the combination *hooley gang* (rather than *Hooley's gang*) perfectly clear. In retrospect, the phrase might have been understood as identical with a proper name.

Some time in the early eighteen-seventies, when *hooley* became known to literate people, hoodlums began to terrify San Francisco. Popular magazines and newspapers printed a series of letters on the origin of the new word, most of them offering unsubstantiated guesses. Although here, too, an Irish name was suggested as etymon, it has never been found. The existence of a gangster called *Hoodlum* is in doubt. The third time the Irish were suspected to have struck was in Melbourne (again in the last quarter of the nineteenth century). Australian street rowdies are called larrikins, allegedly because Larry (Lawrence) was a common name among the Irish there. Since the mythical Little Larry did not emerge from historical records, the tale does not inspire confidence, especially because *larrup,* which surfaced in the eighties, means "to beat, thrash, flog"; *-up* resembles the suffix of *wallop, lollop,* and *trollop.* Not only do hooligans and larrikins behave in the same way: the words (*hooli-gan* ~ *larri-kin*) have a somewhat similar structure. If *-kin* is a diminutive suffix, a clever conjecture by A. L. Mayhew should be considered. In some dialects, *d* between vowels turns into a kind of *r* (this is how *porridge* developed from *poddidge,* ultimately from *pottage* [what is put in a pot]), and Mayhew believed that *larrikin* was a vulgar pronunciation of **laddikin* (a little lad).[19] Possibly, none of the three words goes back to a proper name. To find the protohooligan / -hoodlum / -larrikin is more difficult than to trace *man* to *Mannus.*

A great many place names live as the names of things. Three dances—*polka, polonaise,* and *krakowiak*—remind us of Poland, just as *ecossaise* conjures up a picture of Scotland. We consume Brie and Gouda (still capitalized), eat turkey and talk turkey, drink champagne, burgundy, and chianti, wear guernseys and jerseys, and drive in limousines. Especially fine handkerchiefs and cuffs used to be made of lawn. Folk etymology worked hard to connect this lawn with the lawn we mow, either because it was allegedly bleached on a lawn or smooth grassy sward (an allusion to the fabric's fineness) or because as a transparent covering it might be derived from the sense of a vista through trees. (I am referring to such attempts to explain the origin of *lawn* as folk etymology, though professional lexicographers offered both derivations. Folk etymology is rampant every time people, however learned, invent explanations based on a chance similarity between two words.) Skeat showed that *lawn* got its name from Laon, a town in northern France, an important place of linen manufacture, situated not far from Kamerijk, called Cambrai in French (Kamerijk is the Flemish name of the town). From Cambrai (not from Cambridge) we have cambric, which is the same fabric as lawn. The French, however, call cambric *batiste,* in memory of Baptiste, its maker, who lived in Cambrai. *Lawn,* a piece of ground, once had the form *laund* (ultimately related to *land*), and so strong was the attraction between *lawn$_1$* and *lawn$_2$* that *lawn* (cambric) also acquired *-d.*

Later, both words dropped this consonant. As a result, *lawn* (cambric) approached its etymon *(Laon),* but *lawn* (an open space) lost its tie with *land.*

Research into the history of the word *sedan* has been less successful. In England, sedan chairs came into fashion at the beginning of the seventeenth century, and stress on the word's second syllable suggests a French etymon. Since the name of the French town Sedan immediately springs to mind, Samuel Johnson, a great lexicographer but a poor etymologist, derived *sedan* from *Sedan.* However, sedans were manufactured in Italy, not in France. Skeat supported Johnson's idea: in his opinion, the cloth made at Sedan (and called *sedan*) is the link between the chair and the town; his entry is uncharacteristically short. No evidence points to a special role of sedan (the cloth) in making portable chairs. *Sedan* suggests a seat (Latin *sedes* [seat]). Latin *-ll-* sometimes changed to *-dd-* in Italian; for example, Latin *sella* (saddle) became Italian *sedda.* Yet *sedan* does not mean "saddle" and is apparently not an Italian word, because sedans were used in Italy long before they made their appearance in England, and there the portable chair was called *seggietta.* Perhaps Sir Sanders Duncomb, who popularized sedans in London, coined the word himself, that is, took the first two syllables of the rather recent adjective *sedentary* and pronounced them in a French way, with a pun on the name of the town. All this is unprofitable speculation and will remain such unless new facts or new associations shed light on the origin of *sedan.*

We know more about *hackney,* the name of another conveyance. As early as the fourteenth century, it meant "a riding horse for hire"; *hackeneyman* turned up in 1308. Related words exist in French, Spanish, Portuguese, and Italian. Dutch, too, has *hakkenei,* and it is an old word in that language. Although some variant of *hackney* occurs in every major Romance language, the word has no Romance etymology despite its vague similarity with Latin *equīna* (mare). Such facts play an important role in our reasoning. Compare what is said about *zigzag* in Chapter 7. I will deviate from names for a moment and refer to the history of *strumpet,* a fourteenth-century word. *Strumpet* (in which *-et* is a suffix that turned a lowly street woman of Germanic descent into a classy French prostitute) is an isolated word in

English, whereas in German and Icelandic, *strump-* ~ *strumpf-* has a rich and varied environment. Consequently, it is native there and a borrowing in English. Likewise, *hackney* (from *hackeney*) does not resemble any native Romance word that can explain its origin, while in Germanic it is part of a family. There were attempts to derive Middle Dutch *hackeneye* from the verb *hacken* (to chop), with reference to the alternate lifting and dropping of the horse's feet in ambling and the accompanying sound that reminded one of the alternating movement of a pair of chopping knives in chopping cabbage or the like. Skeat preferred to gloss *hakken* as "to jolt."[20]

Later researchers concluded that the Dutch word was an import from French, and the entire structure collapsed. It deserved its fate: the explanation was too fanciful, too "precious." A good etymology is like a work of art, and, as a rule, its worth is immediately obvious. Such a work of art is Skeat's second explanation. The French Francophones, he said, who lived in England after the Conquest of 1066, used the English word *hackeney,* this *Hackeney* (capital *h*) being a place in Middlesex. Horses were raised on the pasture land there and taken to Smithfield market through Mare Street. From Anglo-French the word spread to Continental French, and from there to other languages, including Dutch. At present, Skeat's etymology has no rivals, though some dictionaries still say "origin uncertain." The place name Hackney meant either "Hac(c)a's island" or "an island in the form of a hook."

With time, *hackney* was "clipped" and yielded *hack* (a common drudge and even "prostitute"). Hacks (more or less harmless drudges) are alive and well, and so are hackneyed, that is, trite, shopworn phrases. ("There are thousands for whom the only sound sleep is the *sleep of the just, . . .* all ignorance *blissful,* all isolation *splendid. . . .* It would not matter if these associated reflexes stopped at the mind, but they issue by way of the tongue, which is bad, or of the pen, which is worse.")[21]

Names appear undisguised in derivatives like *Shakespearean, Byronic, Kafkaesque, Bonapartist, Marxism,* and *yperite* (another name of the mustard gas used in 1915 in the battle of Ypres, in Belgium), because we know who Shakespeare, Byron, and others were.

However, Nicolas Chauvain is a forgotten figure, which makes *chauvinist* opaque. But for the dimly remembered imprecation *by Jove, Jove,* that is, Jupiter, would have become a dead word. Astrologists regarded the planet Jupiter as the source of happiness. Hence *jovial,* which is divorced in our mind from the Greek god; perhaps (through phonetic attraction) we think of *joyful* when we pronounce that word. The cocktail *manhattan* must be connected with *Manhattan* (a youngster who was not allowed to drink it asked his father to give him a *boyhattan;* I do not know whether it was his own coinage), but it comes as a surprise that *groggy* (unsteady on one's legs), from *grog,* owes its origin to Admiral Edward Vernon, who, according to legend, had the nickname Old Grog on account of wearing a grogram cloak (*grogram:* French *gros grain* [coarse grain]) and who ordered the Navy's rum to be diluted with water. The story seems to be true. Most people will probably be taken aback when they learn that Syphilis is the name of a shepherd, the central figure in a Latin poem by Girolamo Fracastoro (1530). He called the disease and the young man Syphilis because the shepherd is represented as the first sufferer. This is not exactly the type of setting one expects to find in a bucolic tale. Fracastoro's hero betrayed the sun god and was visited with a new and terrible disease for his apostasy. Perhaps the inspiration for the name was Sipylon of the Niobe myth, with a pun on a Greek word for "pig lover."

Let me repeat what I said at the beginning of this chapter. We are reminded of names at every step: *guy, maudlin, bloomers, colossal, spoonerism, silhouette, vandalize, worsted, currants* (raisins of Corinth)—trying to list them all would be Sisyphean labor (Sisyphus, too, was from Corinth). The less we know about Guy Fawkes and Amelia Bloomer, the less we are aware of the etymology of the words associated with them. They become as anonymous as Gunilda and Bertha. A little knowledge is sometimes worse than ignorance and may result in grave mistakes. Tantalus stole the food of the gods (of which he partook and became immortal) and gave it to humans. Since he could not be killed, the gods, to punish the thief, made him stand in water up to his chin, with fruit-laden trees over his head, but when he tried to drink, the water disappeared, and when he reached for the fruit, the wind blew it away. Therefore, *tantalizing* means "exposed to view but inaccessible." A restaurant in my area invites its prospective customers to try their tantalizing menu. I never risked going there.

All proper names were at one time meaningful: *Gottlieb* (god + dear [to]), *Wulfstān* (wolf + stone), and so forth. This tradition continues in fiction with its Mrs. Malaprop (Sheridan), Mr. Allworthy (Fielding), and Becky Sharp (Thackeray). Discovering the origin of fictional names is no less interesting than tracing the history of "real" words. A specialist in names asks: "I wonder if Dickens realized that Tiny Tim Cratchit's name originally came from *crichet* or *criquet,* a French word that at first was used to mean a crooked man and came to be used to describe a small one. Surely so appropriate a name was no accident . . ."[22] A similar question occurred to me. Is it possible that Oliver Twist's being the thieves' fag ("servant; someone running errands for his senior") contributed to the choice of Fagin's name, even though the vowels are pronounced differently?

It is not good to end a long chapter with a question to which the author does not know the answer, so I will offer an upbeat statement: the science of etymology is vast, and its branch devoted to the origin of names is one of the most intriguing. But then all scholarship is vast and intriguing, and there is enough room for everybody in it.

Chapter Eleven

in which history pretends to raise its veil, or

Coinages by Known Individuals

Mainly boondoggling.—"O, how she scoons!"—Jonathan Swift coins
Lillipute.—Catullus's risky pun.—The jeep wins the war.

Francis Hodgson Burnett's book *Little Lord Fauntleroy* is about a New
York boy destined to inherit his English grandfather's immense for-
tune; the old gentleman is an earl. Cedric (the little lord) and his mother
are on board, ready to sail to England: "And the big steamer moved
away, and the people cheered again, and Cedric's mother drew the veil
over her eyes, and on the shore there was left great confusion . . ." (end
of Chapter 3). Drawing the veil is the main business of history, and it takes
a while to discern something behind it and overcome the confusion.

Chapter 2 of this book began with a fantasy on the theme of the
daisy "day's eye." Who coined the charming word: a child, a poet?
When, in what circumstances, and why, if some other name of that
flower had, most likely, existed? The moment of creation is beyond
recovery. Nor can we learn the name of the person who enriched
English with such a wonderful word—once an image of rare beauty,
a joy forever, though now, to use a technical term, a mere disguised
compound. Yet, as pointed out several times in the preceding pages,
every word owes its existence to an individual act of creativity. It is
the same with *dæges ēage* from Anglo-Saxon England as with *hot
dog* from New York City. Surely, a sausage in a soft roll was not
called this by ancient people who venerated the dog and held a festival in its honor in the middle of summer, on hot days. Some cook,
vendor, cartoonist, or comedian must have likened a sausage to a
dog. Other people first laughed at the phrase and then adopted it.

Today we use it unthinkingly without any canine associations. The history of the hot dog has been investigated in detail, but the identity of the "wordsmith" and the impulse behind the name remain unknown.[1]

Other times we are more fortunate. The Flemish chemist Jan Baptista van Helmont (1577-1644) distinguished gases from solids and liquids and is credited with introducing the term *gas*. He said in plain Latin that he had "called that spirit *gas*, as being not far removed from the *chaos* of the ancients" (in Dutch, *g-* has the phonetic value close to that of Greek χ). *The Oxford Dictionary of English Etymology* adds that van Helmont, in whose teachings gas was an occult principle present in all bodies, may have taken his cue from Paracelsus's use of *chaos* for the proper element of spirits such as gnomes. *Gnome* is a rare word in English: it denotes "a spirit" inhabiting the interior of the earth and occurs in several European languages as a synonym of *dwarf.* Paracelsus (1493?–1541), whose real name was Theophrastus Bombastus von Hohenheim, a Swiss physician, alchemist, and chemist, used the word **Gnom* (without *-e*) only in the plural: *Gnomi*. His gnomes were predominantly the spirits of the earth. It seems that Paracelsus did not invent the word, but only popularized it. However, his sources have not been found. If the coinage is not his, the moment of creation is lost (the usual case). He will not write a letter to the editor of the *Oxford English Dictionary* like the one M. Gell-Mann wrote about the history of the word quark.

Dictionaries state that *blurb* may have been coined in 1907 by Gelett Burgess (1866–1951), an American humorist and illustrator, who drew on a comic book jacket a picture of a young lady dubbed Miss Blinda Blurb. *Boondoggle* was allegedly coined in 1925 by R. H. Link, an American Scoutmaster. Originally, a boondoggle was the plaited leather cord worn around the neck by Scouts; hence any insignificant handicraft and further, pointless, unnecessary work.[2] *Blurb,* almost an onomatopoeia like *blurt* and *burp,* alliterating with *Blinda* (from *Belinda?*), was easier to invent than the trisyllabic verb *boondoggle,* but easy or complicated, all types of authorship should be documented. The time-honored gossip about how a certain person coined this or that word is usually nothing more than folk etymology, though here, too, exceptions are possible.

The following story is told about *schooner.* Allegedly, Captain Andrew Robinson built the first vessel so called at Gloucester, Massachusetts. When the vessel slid off the stocks into the water, a bystander cried out: "O, how she scoons!" Robinson instantly replied: "A scooner let her be!", and from that time vessels like Robinson's have gone under the name thus accidentally imposed. The New England verb **scoon* (to skim along) has not been recorded, but it is a possible variant of dialectal *scun* (the same meaning). Skeat, who warns his readers that pretty tales about word origins should not be trusted, says that the anecdote about Robinson rings true.[3] Even the *Oxford English Dictionary,* despite its aversion to popular fantasies, raises no objections to it. Since a respectable nautical term, unless it came to English from medieval Scandinavia, must look as though it originated in Dutch, an *h* was added to *scooner.* Later *schooner* made its way into Dutch (among many other languages), where it felt perfectly at home. But the word is of American extraction.

Reference to the inventor is only the first step toward discovering the word's origin. Even if it can be shown that Link coined the verb *boondoggle,* we still have no idea how he did it. Why *boon-* plus *doggle?* The most astute conjectures will miss the mark unless some means of verifying them exist. The same holds for *gnome.* A near homonym of *gnome* (spirit) is Engl. *gnomon* (indicator [of a sundial]), from Greek. Its root means "to know" (compare *agnostic, ignore, cognizant,* and so forth), which fits the function of an indicator. Perhaps Paracelsus thought that his *Gnomi* were privy to the wisdom only subterranean dwellers can gain. The *Oxford English Dictionary* prefers to separate the two gnomes, but Paracelsus hardly remained blind to their similarity.

Below, I will recount the attempts to explain the origin of two words, *Lilliputian* and *jeep.* It will become clear that etymologists face the same problems regardless of whether they are dealing with so-called individual coinages like *blurb* and *boondoggle* or with those brought to life by anonymous creators.

Lilliputian is Jonathan Swift's invention, and its official date of birth is 1726. Swift did not leave an account of his creative process, but even if he had done so, it should have been taken with a huge grain of salt, for he treated contemporary etymologists as Molière did contemporary doctors: in his opinion, people pretending to know something about word origins were charlatans. He made his hero ponder two etymologies of *Laputa:* one by local sages and one that occurred to Gulliver. Both seem to ridicule eighteenth-century philologists, though Gulliver's interpretation may contain a clue to Swift's parody. If we could only ask Swift! This is a perennial lament: historians are always born too late. He and Paracelsus, and so many others, are sadly out of reach.

Lille- sounds like an informal pronunciation of *little;* only *-e* is "extraneous matter." However, the Swedish, Norwegian, and Danish for *little* is *lille,* a disyllable. Swift was mildly interested in Swedish affairs and seems to have acquired a smattering of the language. If he went to Swedish for inspiration in coining the word *Lilliputian,* he must have had a good reason for doing so. No one has so far succeeded in unearthing it.[4] In his works, Swift sometimes represented himself as an unlearned man. In reality, he was well educated and loved linguistic games. He could easily have appropriated a word from a foreign language. However, his Latin and French were so much better than his Swedish that the Scandinavian hypothesis does not look too attractive. Be that as it may, the lilliputians, or the lilliputs, were probably little puts. So what is *put?*

Here we are left with several plausible solutions. Latin had *putus* (boy), a word allied to *puer.* In French we find *pute* and *putain* (whore). Their Spanish cognate is *puta,* so that Laputa, the flying island of *Gulliver's Travels,* means "the whore," assuming that the name was to be understood as a Romance noun with the definite article. The similarity between *Lilliput* and *Laputa* cannot be fortuitous: some offensive allusion must have been hidden in both words. *Putte* is a pet name for a little boy not only in Latin but also in Swedish, and since Latin *puto* means "to reckon, suppose, judge, think, imagine," *Lilliput(ian)* can be understood as "petty-minded." Indeed, everything is small among the Lilliputians, not least their conceptions.

In *Gulliver's Travels,* we are exposed to entire sentences in the language of the Lilliputians. One of Swift's favorite books was *Gargantua and Pantagruel,* and the sentences Swift quotes become intelligible when translated from Lilliputian into Rabelais's French.[5] This circumstance reinforces the idea that *Laputa,* for example, wears a Romance garb. But after we have found several foreign words that could have suggested *-put* to Swift, we note that at the end of the seventeenth century, Engl. *put(t)* (blockhead) appeared in printed texts. The earliest recorded example of *put(t)* in the *Oxford English Dictionary* is dated 1688. Swift was born in 1667. He knew and disliked the phrase *country put,* defined in the year 1700 as "a silly, shallow-pated fellow"; he in general disapproved of recent monosyllables.[6] He would probably have relished the idea of endowing the citizens of the great empire of Lilliput and, by implication, of its rival Blefuscu (caricatures of England and possibly France) with the name he detested.

As long as we stay with English, *Lilliput* yields "little (stupid, contemptible?) fellow," though the problem of *-e-* remains. It is not a particularly bothersome problem, for words with so-called infixes are many (see Chapter 9). But even if Swift made up *Lilliput* of two native elements, he probably noticed how lucky his coinage was, for *put-* is the root of the words for "boy, lad" also in the Romance languages, and if his knowledge of Swedish was sufficient, he must have congratulated himself on reaching out to Scandinavia. Then *Laputa* came as a reward for inventing *Lilliput.*

Other attempts to guess the origin of *lilliput(ian)* have been less convincing. Perhaps *-put* is the second syllable of Latin *caput* (head); then the desired gloss would be "people with little heads." Or is *Lilliput* an anagram of *put little* and *Laputa* a near anagram of *utopia?* Also, *putty* is not unthinkable as a baby's pronunciation of *pretty.* Weren't the Lilliputians pretty little?[7] A resourceful man with a bent for decipherment claimed to have discovered an alphabetical-numerical code that allowed him to interpret Swift's place names. He came up with *Lilliput = Nowhere* and *Laputa = Saxony,* that is, England.[8] We are not informed why Swift buried his secret so deep, why only the kingdom of the Lilliputians emerged as some kind of Thomas More's Utopia or Samuel Butler's Erehwon, and (the main point) why *Lilliput* and *Laputa,* despite their near identity, have nothing in common in the world of Swift's fiction.

Swift took the secret of his neologism to his grave. Our lot is to choose the most probable reconstruction. This is the only approach to any reconstruction (in linguistics and elsewhere), which, in a way, is a version of Occam's razor: don't multiply assumptions introduced to explain a thing beyond necessity. Among the choices *putty = pretty, put = (ca)put, lilliput(ian) = put little,* and *Lilliputian = a little put,* the fourth taxes our credulity the least. It is a common occurrence that a single etymology fits several words. In *Gulliver's Travels* we have *Lilliput* and *Laputa.* An etymology that explains both of them is to be preferred. The conjectures centering on *pretty, caput,* and *put little* ignore *Laputa*—a circumstance that diminishes their appeal. In the spirit of Occam an etymologist usually tries to kill two birds with one stone.

We could stop here but for an unexpected lead from Swift to the Roman lyric poet Catullus. In an episode related by Catullus (No. 53 in modern editions), someone who heard Calvus's speech in court exclaimed: "Di magni, salaputium disertum!" ("Great gods! What an articulate [fellow]!"). Something in this exclamation, probably *salaputium,* made Catullus laugh. If the speaker was a visitor from a remote province, he may have used a droll dialectal word. *Salaputium* never turns up anywhere else in the literature of Ancient Rome, and its reflexes (that is, forms going back to it) do not exist in any modern Romance language, though the name or nickname *Salaputis,* in the ablative, occurs in an African inscription. Perhaps *salaputium* was an obscenity; suggestions to this effect abound. Seneca states (it is not known on what authority) that Calvus was short, and the truth of his statement is usually taken for granted. The admiring (or mocking?) visitor may have been impressed by a torrent of eloquence from such a puny figure and said something like: "This (little) fellow can ejaculate, he can!" Two students of Catullus suggested that *-putium* in *salaputium* was the source of Swift's *Lilliput.*[9]

Swift knew and translated Catullus, though not No. 53, and he owned two editions of his poems.[10] However, neither contains a commentary, and if Swift did not read sixteenth-century Italian editions in which the word *salaputium* is discussed at length and the relevant passage from Seneca is quoted, he hardly knew that Calvus was short (I say *hardly* because he may have remembered Seneca's phrase *paruolum statura* (of short stature) about Calvus irrespective of Catullus), and the idea of using *salaputium* in connection with his own little people would not have occurred to him. If Swift wanted his readers to guess the meaning of *Lilliput,* the use of an obscure word from Catullus would have defied its purpose, but considering how impenetrable some of his coinages are and how well he disguised the meaning of the sentences in "Lilliputian," one cannot be sure. All things considered, the likelihood that *-put* derives from *salaputium* is remote.

Swift's word is so pronounceable and has such a common European look that its success was guaranteed, though no one could have predicted how natural it would soon sound to millions of people. We traveled from England to Scandinavia, France, Spain, Italy, and Ancient Rome, only to return home and trace *Lilliput* to a seventeenth-century slangy English word. The journeys were undertaken for the sake of a name invented by a great writer, and the result is satisfactory but not final.

Close to three centuries separate us from 1726, the year in which *Lilliput* made its debut, and our ignorance of its origin causes little surprise. Many eighteenth-century words are etymological cruces, but in this instance we are not dealing with an artless invention of a forgotten wag. One of the most brilliant English speakers in history invented a catchword, possibly based on a multilingual pun. He may have intentionally thrown us off the scent and supplied false clues, so that we would pride ourselves on having reached the shore while being all at sea. Contrary to *Lilliput, jeep* appeared for the first time on a newspaper page *(St. Paul Pioneer Press)* in the memory of many people still living, on August 14, 1940, but we are not much better off with its derivation than with the derivation of Swift's coinage.

On February 22, 1941, "the jeep gave an exhibition of what it could do by climbing the steps of the nation's Capitol. Some reporter asked the driver what he called his vehicle, and the driver said, 'Why, I call it a jeep. Everybody does.'"[11] *Jeep,* the name of a vehicle, could not be older than 1940. Yet as early as 1943, Henry L. Mencken wrote that a great many folk etymologies of the word were in circulation but that they were extremely unconvincing.[12]

"A great many folk etymologies" is an exaggeration, for only two main etymologies of *jeep* compete. One traces the word to the abbreviation *G. P.,* allegedly "General Production,"[13] later reinterpreted as "For General Purpose" or "For General Purposes." According to the other, ". . . the original jeep was designed and manufactured by the Minneapolis-Moline Power Implement Company and was given its name from the 'Popeye' comic strip—during the Fourth Army Maneuvers at Camp Ripley, Minnesota, during the later part of August and first part of September, 1940."[14] Eugene the Jeep is a small fanciful wonder-working animal in the comic strip, known as "Popeye" in the United States and "Thimble Theatre" in England, by Elzie C. Segar. The creature looked like a rodent, and every time it performed a miracle, it squeaked: "Jeep!"

Most dictionaries give credence to the popular derivation of *jeep* from the cartoon character. However, one can read that *jeep* goes back to *G(overnment)* +*P,* designator for 80-inch wheel-base reconnaissance car[15] or that it is a "reduction of Jeepers Creepers! (the exclamation of Major General George Lynch, Chief of Infantry, U.S. Army, upon the occasion of his ride in the prototype model of the vehicle in 1939 at Fort Myer, Virginia, coined at the time by Mr. Charly H. Payne, his companion in, and designer of the vehicle); perhaps later influenced by the initials *G. P.,* for General Purpose, official designation of the vehicle."[16] What sources did the editor of the dictionary that offered such a story have? It is too bad that dictionaries do not give references. One can find mention of *jeep* (recruit) in works devoted to the name of the vehicle, but the existence of the other *jeep* is probably a coincidence. Mencken came to the conclusion that the origin of the word is obscure[17]—a significant fact if we bear in mind that *jeep* was coined in the full light of history and that we have eyewitness reports of the car's production. (Whatever the origin of *jeep,* the English language owes *goon* to Segar, from the comic strip character Alice the Goon. Its alleged etymon is dialectal *gooney* [fool].)

Sometimes words are minted from the requisite stock in trade. A cynophile is "a dog lover," a compound made up of two Greek roots. Swift's *Lilliput* was coined in a similar way, except that the elements are not Greek. Onomatopoeia and sound symbolic words arise in speech spontaneously, as though of their own free will. "Pass a circular saw revolving five hundred times a second through a keg of tenpenny nails. This is *jasm."* On a quieter note, *broodle* means "to cuddle and soothe a little child."[18] As all of us were at one time young, so every word was once brand-new. When it comes to language, even the least eloquent speaker is a potential lawmaker in Plato's sense. Children and poets are the best language gamesters and neologists. In the enormous bucket of relatively recent coinages, *Lilliputian* and *jeep* are mere drops, but theirs is the advantage of having become common property and the charm of being etymologically obscure.

I began this chapter with Cedric Errol and will finish it with Sam Beaver, the hero of E. B. White's book *The Trumpet of the Swan,* who "kept a diary—a daybook about his life. It was just a cheap notebook that was always by his bed. Every night before he turned in, he would write in the book. He wrote about things he had done, things he had seen, and thoughts he had had. Sometimes he drew a picture. He always ended by asking himself a question so he would have something to think about while falling asleep" (end of Chapter 1). If Sam decided to read the previous pages and did not fall asleep at once, instead of asking: "Why does a fox bark?" and "How does a bird know how to build a nest?" he would probably have written: "How does it happen that we are uncertain about the origin of words created by known people at a known time, and not even too long ago?" That would indeed be something to think about.

Chapter Twelve

*whose main theme is the mixed
blessing of globalization, or*

Borrowed Words

People are lazy, or the history of cucumbers.—*Crab, scarab, scorpion,* and other migratory words.—Baskets, cans, and weasels as
ships.—The much-feared typhoon, wandering axes, and soap that did
not wash.—Traces of submerged languages (substrates).—*Flivver* and
clover. When did Germanic speakers see the sea for the first time?—
The reception of Sigmund Feist.—Celtic words in Germanic.—The
Viking raids.—The Norman Conquest.—Wamba and Gurth.—Anglo-
French.—Rabbits in the wild and on a plate.—From Germanic to Old
French and back home.—French or Latin?—On muskets and mosqui-
toes.—Doublets, triplets, and so on.—A Dutch-German invasion that
never took place.—Is English too rich because people are lazy?

Words and germs travel with people, who have always known how
to cover great distances, even though in the Middle Ages and later,
thousands never left their villages and would call a local's wife born
ten miles away "an overflow." Borrowings are monuments to human
beings' physical mobility and mental laziness. In Chapter 4, we examined the sound symbolism of the word *pumpkin.* The ultimate
source of *pumpkin* is Greek; *pépōn*[1] meant "ripe" and, by implication (or so it seems), "large melon." Its opposite, Late Greek *ágouras*
or *aggoúri(on)*[2] (*gg* was pronounced as *ng*) (unripe), became known
to other Europeans as *augurke* (Modern German *Gurke*), *ogorek* ~
ogurek (Polish), and so forth. English borrowed the Dutch word with
a diminutive suffix and ended up with *gherkin* (a cucumber for pick-
ling). Melons, it appears, had to be eaten mellow, whereas cucumbers
were consumed "raw." (The pun *melon* ~ *mellow* is unetymological:

Late Latin *mēlō-* was a shortening of *mēlopēpo* [apple + ripe].) Thus the Greeks had a fruit called "ripe" (the melon or the pumpkin) and a vegetable called "unripe, raw" (the cucumber), but since they were not the first to cultivate either, the word for the cucumber may not have been native with them.

It is not known who taught Ancient Romans to grow cucumbers; in any case, Latin *cucumis* (genitive: *cucumeris*) is not from Greek. *Cucumis* resembles *cucurbita,* from which, by way of French, English has *gourd,* but their similarity may be due to chance, or perhaps both are sound symbolic formations; *cucur-* resembles a baby word for a round object. Europeans (and this is the main point here) could have thought of a native name for an imported object, but it was easier to call a cucumber a cucumber and later clip it to *cumber* (a common form in British dialects) or *cuke* than to invent something new. Plant and animal names and the names of objects of material culture (including those of foodstuffs like *butter, sugar,* and *coffee*) tend to migrate from country to country. They send the etymologist in search of their home and original meaning all over the world. Finding them is no easy task, because, along the way, melons turn into pumpkins, while Greek nouns grow Dutch suffixes, and because the records of early civilizations are scarce and the languages that were the likeliest sources of such words may have died centuries before writing was invented. Often we have to be satisfied with vague references: "probably Mediterranean," "an Alpine word," or "of Oriental origin."

Migratory words (*Wanderwörter,* as they are called in German) show an astounding ability for mimicry and, once admitted into a new language, begin to look like some words of native vocabulary and like other borrowings: *pumpkin* resembles *pump* and *pomp,* and *melon* forms a natural union with *mellow.* Such secondary ties obscure their origin still further. Crustaceans and insects having shards provide a good example of such mimicry. If we look at a string of words—Engl. *crab,* German *Krebs* (crayfish), and Greek *kárabos* (stag beetle; a kind of prickly crab)[3]—we will notice how similar they are. Latin *cancer* (pronounced *kanker*), Greek *karkínos*[4] (both mean "crab"), and Russian *rak* (crayfish) are also close: the same *k-r-k, k-k-r,* and *k-r-b* that suggest scraping and scratching. Two more words of the same type are *scorpion* and *scarab*. *Skorpíos* (later *skorpíon*)[5] made the usual way from Greek to Latin, from there to French, and finally to English. Greek *skarábeios*[6] reached English from Latin *(scarabœus)*, bypassing French. All those creatures have long feelers and bear an almost uncanny resemblance to one another. It is unclear whether we have a migratory word (or perhaps two of them) or many cases of so-called primitive creation, if not of onomatopoeia *(skr-skr)*. Engl. *crab* and its Germanic cognates (Old Engl. *crabba,* Old Icelandic *krabbi,* and Old High German *krebiz*) have been around for a long time and may be native (such is the opinion of some researchers), but a profusion of analogous Greek and Latin words makes this hypothesis suspect; perhaps we are dealing with a borrowing or several borrowings from an unknown language. It remains to be said that French took over some form like *krebiz* as *crevis* (Modern French *écrevisse*). When *crevisse* or *crevis* returned to English, it became *crayfish* and *crawfish* and people did not recognize *crabbe* (later, *crab*), its ancient sibling, in the guest from abroad.

We will pursue crabs and crayfish for a while. Greek *kárabos* meant not only "stag beetle" (that is, "a horned beetle") and "crayfish" but also "a light ship" (a sea crayfish?). Its nautical progeny is famous in pirate literature: Italian *caravella,* Spanish *carabella,* French *caravelle,* and Engl. *carvel ~ caravel* (the last borrowed from French in the fifteenth century). At first sight, the Greek word seems to have developed a metaphorical meaning (from a sea animal to a sea ship), but possibly the development was not so straightforward, and the association with the crab may be a folk etymological trick. Among the words beginning with *kr- ~ gr-* and ending in *b, p, f,* and *v,* many names of receptacles (sacks, baskets, and vessels) occur, originally wickerwork, and less often, carriages. Such are Engl. *crib* (with wide connections in the languages of Europe), Latin *corbis* (basket) (German *Korb* is from Latin), and *carpentum* (a two-wheeled carriage) (a Roman carpenter was a carriage maker, a cartwright), Tigrinya (a Semitic language of northern Ethiopia) *kāribbo* (a small leather sack in the form of a bottle), and numerous Arabic words for "a leather sack," "drum," and "a small vessel" (compare Engl. *carafe,* from Arabic).[7] This is what the vague formula "borrowed from an unknown

Mediterranean language" implies: some words, used by speakers of southern Europe, the Near East, and northern Africa, that originated in the remotest past on or close to the coast of the Mediterranean Sea, traveled with the name of the artifacts, entered Greek and Arabic, and migrated from there to other languages. English usually has them from French.

Primitive boats were hollowed out trees, empty receptacles of sorts. Latin *corbita* meant "a merchant ship" (literally "a little basket"), and at the end of the eighteenth century, French *corvette* appeared, which is probably Dutch *corbe* (a ship, but, from the etymological point of view, "a basket") with a French diminutive suffix and pronounced in a French way. Later the Dutch re-borrowed their own word from French (Modern Dutch *korvet*). Russian has *korob* (basket) (stress on the first syllable) and *korabl'* (ship) (stress on the second syllable); *korob* is more likely related to Latin *corbis* than a borrowing of it.[8] Greek *kárabos* may go back to some migratory word for "receptacle"; if so, then not a metaphor "crayfish" to "ship," but, as suggested above, a trivial case of folk etymology. Russian *korob* and *korabl'* illustrate the situation familiar from the history of Engl. *crab* and its Germanic congeners: perhaps a native word, perhaps a borrowing of a migratory term.

We encounter more wandering vessels in the history of the nouns *can* and *cane*. The phrases "a chair with a cane seat" and "cane sugar" are a reminder of the fact that *cane* is not only "a walking stick." *Cane* entered English in the fourteenth century; at that time, it meant "a hollow stem." Its etymon is Old French *canne,* from Latin *canna* (reed, cane, tube, pipe). However, *canna* also meant "vessel"; it brings us to the English noun *can* (which was known in Old English: *canne*), German *Kanne* (can, pot), and so on. *Canna* (vessel) surfaced in Latin only in the sixth century and could have been borrowed from Germanic. Old Engl. *canne* was recorded once and reemerged in the fourteenth century, possibly imported from the continent after a long period of oblivion, but in Early German, Icelandic, and Dutch, the cognates of Engl. *can* were common words.

If the Germanic word for "can" is not a borrowing from Latin, it needs an etymology, and in case it is, the Latin word requires an explanation of its origin. Outside Germanic and Romance, Greek *káneon* (basket; a votive basket)[9] exists, an ancient word occurring in Homer, presumably a borrowing from some Semitic language and related to Babylo-Assyrian *qarū. Canna* (reed) need not be separated from *canna* (vessel), originally a wicker basket. The name of the vessel was probably coined in Greece, spread with all its meanings from Greek to Latin, and thence in many directions.[10] The modern reflexes of that word designate all kinds of elongated objects ("pipes") and occasionally a vessel. Engl. *canal* and *channel* (both from French) are "pipes," and so is *kennel* (a street gutter), distinct from *kennel* (a dog house). Another "pipe" is *canyon* (in English from Spanish). A canister is a small case or box for tea; the canistrum (Latin), originally made of cane, was used for bread, fruit, and so forth. Canaster (a kind of tobacco) got its name from the rush basket in which it was imported. Italian added a suffix to *canna* (tube) and produced *cannone* (a big reed, a big tube; an object supplied with a big tube; cannon). English and other European languages borrowed this word from Italian. Greek *kanṓn*[11] (rod) is related to *kánna,* whence *canon* (spare the rod . . .). A cannula (or canula) (a tube for inserting medication or draining fluid) is "a small tube," and *cannelon* (a stuffed roll) is Italian *cannellone* (tubular soup noodle), from *cannello,* one more word for "a small tube." The family is large and in plain sight; the progenitor is hard to identify with desired clarity—a classic definition of a migratory word.

A similar tale can be told of the word *galley.* "The story, in brief, is that the Greek name of an animal develops in Byzantine Greek, into the name of a ship; that the Byzantine term is taken over by the West as *galea;* then develops certain variants, among them, through a change of the suffix, *galera;* that *galera* spreads and reconquers part of the *galea* territory."[12] The animal in question is Greek *galéa*[13] (weasel; marten; ferret) (it also meant "rockling," a coastal fish). The Greek word passed into Arabic and penetrated from there into India. The Indian term became Portuguese *jalia,* a colonial word in that language. Readers of European adventure novels in the original are well acquainted with *galera,* a later development of *galea. Gallery* is not related to it.

So far, our rambles have not taken us beyond India. The story of *typhoon* provides a Chinese connection. The ancient Graeco-Latin word *typhoon* (a violent whirlwind) is also the name of the demon Typhon or Typhoeus[14] (a monster with a hundred heads of dragon shape), finally defeated by Zeus. Typhon occurs in Aristotle's *Meteorologia,* which was translated into Latin about 1260. As *typho,* it gained some popularity in Italy. The *Vulgate* mentions *ventus typhonicus* (in the Authorized Version, Acts XXVII: 14, we read: "But not long after there arose against it [= Crete] a tempestuous wind, called Euroclydon."). In the sixteenth century, the word became more frequent. The scanty evidence at our disposal makes it impossible to decide whether *typho* survived outside the learned tradition. We only know that some time later, it appeared in French dictionaries.

Not later than in the seventh century, the Greek word made its way into Arabic; it turns up in two passages of the *Koran* (Sura 7:132 and Sura 29:14). The reference is to a major calamity. Arabic *ṭūfān* came to designate a typical storm raging in the seas between Arabia and China. From Arabic the word spread to Persian, Turkish, and other Oriental languages. Finally, Greek re-borrowed it from Turkish. Somewhere in the East, the Portuguese picked up *tufão* in the sixteenth century. The Western languages must have taken it over from Portuguese as a nautical term. It blended with the Graeco-Latin cognate of *typhon* and acquired the form *tifone* and the like; with time, *typhon* became the standard spelling.

As early as 1560, the Chinese origin of *typhoon* was proposed, with the etymon *tai-fung* (a great wind). But the older forms were *tuffon, tifone,* and so forth. *Typhoon,* with the vowel of long *i* in the first syllable, reflects the traditional school pronunciation of Greek; *-oon* appeared under the influence of *monsoon.* The English, who learned the word at the end of the seventeenth century, could have heard *taifung* from Chinese mariners, and if they did, the Portuguese and the Chinese word blended, but the story of *typhoon* in the other languages did not begin in China. The Arabic term seems to have become so common as a designation for the Chinese storms that its Greek origin was forgotten.[15]

The names of tools migrate especially often. Thus we find Finnish *tapara,* Russian *topor* (stress on the second syllable), Armenian *t'ap'ar,* Persian *teber,* and among them, Old Engl. *taparœx* and Old Icelandic *tapar-øx* (*ø* = German *ö* and French *œ*). All of them mean "ax." The Armenian word is a borrowing from Iranian, the Finns and the Scandinavians learned *tapar-* and *tapara* from East Slavic, and the English adopted the Scandinavian word. No explanation exists why the Scandinavians added *tapar* to their native word *øx*. The migration must have begun in Asia Minor, where *tapa* (stone) has been recorded. Apparently, the first *tabar, tapar,* or *teber* was made of stone. (This is a common case: for example, Russian *kam-en'* [stone] is cognate with Engl. *ham-(m)er;* the hyphen separates the root from the suffix.) Some etymologists believe that the Iranian and the Slavic words are native in their languages, but such a coincidence, although not impossible, would be rare.

At least one migratory culture word may have originated among Germanic speakers. Old English had *sāp,* which meant "amber, unguent" and *sāpbox,* of unclear meaning ("resin box" or "soapbox"?). Another Old English noun *sāpe* (salve) seems to be related to *sāp.* Old High German *seifa* meant "resin," but *seiffa* is usually understood to have designated soap. According to Pliny, Romans learned the use of *sāpo* from Gaul, and modern Latin dictionaries, when they include *sāpo,* sometimes gloss it as "soap," though the pomade that Pliny mentions was used for coloring hair, not for washing. Since *soap* has an acceptable Germanic etymology, it may be a Germanic word even if Romans heard it from Gaul. *Sāpo* and *sāpe* denoted some liquid or viscous substance, assuming that they are akin to the verbs *seep,* its English dialectal synonym *sipe,* and Middle High German *sīfen* (to trickle). *Sip, sup,* and *sap* have been proposed as cognates of *soap,* but the history of each of them is obscure. Perhaps *soap* has the same root as Latin *sēbum* (tallow, grease, suet). Italian *sapone,* French *savon,* and their cognates in the Romance languages are from Latin *sāpo* (the genitive: *sāpōnis*).

Some products are universal. For example, all people need salt. The name for salt is nearly the same in many languages and is probably part of their most ancient vocabulary rather than a migratory word. Its root must be *sal-,* but finding a gloss for it is hard: "something sifted or evaporated?", "a sediment"? Or "gray stuff," as suggested by the meaning of Engl. *sallow* and its cognates? It has even been compared with Latin *sōl* (sun). *Salt* has changed its sphere of application since the earliest times when it designated "condiment, seasoning, relish." The Slavic cognates of *salt* mean "sweet"(!) and "malt," and this makes the search for origins particularly complicated.

Four major questions arise in the study of migratory words. First, when we have a group like *tifone, typhoon,* and so on, where was the oldest of them coined? Second, do all the words we net in each case belong together? Third, what accounts for the original word's popularity? And fourth, what are the paths of migration? As long as we deal with a specific type of ship or a wind associated with one part of the world, some answers are self-evident. But for *tapar* to be borrowed, it must designate an unusual and attractive type of ax, because the word follows the imported object. Twelve centuries ago, the war-like Vikings decided that a *taparøx* was a grander name than *øx* and produced the tautological compound "ax-ax." The Icelandic sagas inform us that the *taparøx* was useful for cleaving enemies' skulls, though the traditional *øx,* a halberd rather than an ax, must have served that purpose equally well. The Russian *topor* is not a battle ax. At the end of the journey between Ancient Persia and Finland, we are not sure whether we are dealing with one migratory word or two and what made people borrow it (or them) from their neighbors. A few other names for choppers—*adz* and *hatchet,* for example—pose similar problems.

As we have seen, the source of a migratory word can sometimes be discovered: Arabic, Portuguese, Greek, and so on. Other references, such as "some Mediterranean language," are vague, but at least they point to the area in which the word originated. The hardest case is a borrowing from unidentifiable quarters. For instance, the earliest historical inhabitants of Britain were the Picts. Since they had no writing, their language is lost. The insular Celts probably borrowed from the Picts, among others, some plant and animal names and some terms related to the local terrain. Such words would have been foreign bodies in their language, as are *typhoon* and *galley* in

English. Germanic invaders could, in their turn, have adopted those words from the Celts. Understandably, etymologists are unable to trace their history. On the other hand, the Angles, Saxons, and Jutes, who settled in Britain in the fifth century, did not speak "pure North Sea Germanic." They could have absorbed any number of words from the languages now extinct, so that Old English may contain accretions from unrecoverable sources. In this sense it is customary to speak about a pre-Celtic and a pre-Germanic substrate (or substratum). The concept of the substrate plays an outstanding role in Romance linguistics. Although Gaul and Iberia were Romanized in antiquity, hundreds of French, Spanish, and Portuguese words are not of Latin origin: they are relics of the native languages of both "provinces." Even Italian is far from being a mere continuation of Latin, for it has numerous words from so-called Alpine languages.

The situation in pre-Germanic is less clear, because the existence of a substrate in its history is at best a hypothesis. Before examining its worth, a short digression is in order. Surprisingly, the science of etymology sometimes acquires political overtones. *Topor* and *korob* are either native Russian words or borrowings from the East. It would be a disaster if the knowledge of origins were allowed to boost the national pride of the Russians (who allegedly did not need foreign models for naming axes and boxes) or to put them down (for allegedly being unable to name a simple tool without the help of their neighbors). Medieval Scandinavians borrowed a few Slavic words (for example, Swedish *tolka* [to interpret] and *torg* [market place] are from Russian), and medieval Slavs borrowed a few Scandinavian words, including the place name *Rus* (ultimately from Finnish) and the name for "an epic hero" (*vitiaz'*, from *víkingr* [viking]). Such borrowings are of inestimable value for reconstructing past contacts but should be used with extreme caution for assessing the superiority of the culture of one tribe (or nation) over that of another. Even good scholars occasionally succumb to the lures of nationalism. In 1916, Friedrich Kluge, the most famous German etymologist of his time, published a newspaper article about the Germanic descent of the French word *garçon* (boy), which he traced to the Germanic word for "hero."[16] Perhaps he was right (though this is doubtful); it is the

ignominy of politicizing an etymology that won't go away. The following passage is from a 1926 article by Eduard Prokosch, an American philologist of German descent, who speaks about Antoine Meillet,
a great French linguist:

> The pre-Germanic substratum is asserted most definitely by A. Meillet. . . .
> To Meillet we are also indebted for a number of lucid and rather complete
> statements of the stock arguments for this view. The whole problem is (un-
> fortunately and absurdly) so much tainted with national bias of one sort or
> another that the opinion of a scholar like Meillet is of double value. For in
> his *Langues dans l'Europe nouvelle,* published at a time when war feeling
> was still running high (1919), he showed such admirable freedom from chau-
> vinism and such judicious control of a wide array of facts that in his case
> there is no room whatever for any insinuation of prejudice. He may justly
> be acknowledged the leader and spokesman of those who argue for a pre-
> Germanic (non-Indo-European) substratum theory in general. Primarily
> through Meillet's sponsorship, this theory is raised from a medley of random
> guesses to the dignity of a scientific theory that must be taken seriously.[17]

No one doubts that the nations of modern Europe are the product
of countless crossings and recrossings of ancient tribes. Here we are
concerned only with the effect of those processes on language. The
origin of some words is more or less clear. Such are onomatopoeias
(cock-a-doodle-doo, moo), possible onomotopoeias *(thump, dump),*
symbolic formations *(flitter, sleazy),* undisguised derivatives (*worker*
= *work + er*), extended forms *(edumacation),* blends *(chortle,
Eurasia),* and words from names *(Colt, diesel).* Some other words
yield their secrets if we happen to find their earlier forms (for example, *tool* consists of a verb that meant "to make" and a suffix used
in the names of implements; *woman = wīf + man*) or succeed in
getting beyond the crust of folk etymological alterations (thus *favor*
in *curry favor* goes back to the French name of a chestnut horse, and
Morris in *Morris dance* means "Moorish"). But some words lack
established cognates outside the language or group of languages in
which they occur. They have no discernible prefixes or suffixes, are
not disguised compounds or blends, and contain no sound symbolic
groups. They are mere "conventional signs." If they were known 12
or 15 centuries ago and (to the best of our knowledge) were as opaque

then as they are today, doesn't this suggest their possible origin in a substrate? Not necessarily.

Several factors have to be taken into account.[18] The other languages may have lost the cognates of our isolated words because words die as fast as they are born. If we compare the vocabulary of Modern English, German, Dutch, and French with the vocabulary they had five and seven centuries ago, we will notice massive losses of words. Any reader of Elizabethan literature, to say nothing of Chaucer, needs a special dictionary. Speakers of Modern Dutch have trouble understanding their seventeenth- and eighteenth-century poets. Even more noticeable than the disappearance of words is the rapid expansion of vocabulary. Nothing justifies the idea that all recent coinages must be etymologically transparent (the opposite seems to be true). The slang in common use today is not ancient. Yet we are seldom able to explain how it came about. Many verbs denoting mockery, that is, synonyms of *scoff* (*taunt, banter, chaff, fleer, jeer, sneer,* and so forth) are of questionable origin. None of them occurred in writing before the fifteenth century. The same holds for the names of various coins (*tanner* [sixpence], *jitney* [nickel]), bad cars *(flivver, jalopy),* dilapidated buildings *(slum),* derogatory or comic appellations like *dweeb, dud, dude, nerd,* and *bloke,* expressive verbs *(drudge, fudge, budge),* and for the impressive number of words meaning "drunk" and "prostitute." Even the history of *booze* is known imperfectly. A complete list of such words is long. Surely, *banter, slum,* and *flivver* have not come to English from some mysterious substrate. It should also be borne in mind that we do not know the origin of some words, because no one has made a good guess, and sometimes good guesses have been ignored or rejected as unconvincing.

To illustrate the last point, I will give three examples, beginning with a contested etymology that I find satisfactory. The word *clover* has cognates in German, Dutch, and Frisian, but in the Scandinavian languages, *klöver ~ kløver* is a borrowing from German. According to one conjecture, *clover* is related to the verb *cleave* (to stick to, adhere), because its thick juice was one of the main ingredients of the honey valued greatly in the past. In some modern dialects, *honeysuckle* means "clover." Those who find the reference to stickiness insufficient (they say that the juice of other plants is equally thick and sticky) suggest borrowing from the substrate and are left without any etymology. The second and the third examples are from my own work. Dictionaries agree that the origin of the verb *chide* is unknown. Old Engl. *cīdan* meant the same as *chide* ("to scold"), *gecīd* meant "strife," and no similar word has been recorded outside English. Once, when leafing through a German dictionary of past centuries, I ran into *kīdel* "wedge." It occurred to me that the root *kīd-* meant "stick, cudgel" and that the original meaning of *gecīd* may have been "an exchange of blows," from *cīdan* (to brandish sticks). Later the idea of a physical fight, as I suspected, yielded to that of a verbal altercation. Likewise, *-buke,* the root of the verb *rebuke,* is akin to *bush* (Old French *bushier* ~ *buchier* ~ *buskier* [to beat, strike], from "to cut down wood"). Less certainly, *trounce* (to censure severely) may be related to *truncheon.* If my hypothesis is right, we have one fewer word of unknown origin. Another time, as related at the beginning of Chapter 1, I came across an article on the ancient divinity of death *Henne* and realized why *henbane* begins with *hen.* A similar idea occurred to two of my predecessors long before my birth, but no one remembered that. The moral of the story is that many acceptable etymologies are simply undiscovered or forgotten and that luck (or serendipity) plays an important role in an etymologist's work.

The most often cited Germanic words, presumably borrowed from some indigenous language, are *sea, ship, sail, boat,* and more like them pertaining to maritime vocabulary. Their etymology is speculative, a circumstance that resulted in the idea that the ancestors of the earliest Germanic tribes were not the first inhabitants of northern Europe and learned about the sea and seafaring late. The idea aroused passionate resistance and was "unfortunately and absurdly tainted with national bias," to quote Prokosch. Few people in Germany wanted Germans to be newcomers in their modern home (as though millennia later it mattered a tiny bit). To exacerbate matters, Sigmund Feist, the originator of the baleful theory, was a Jew. His view of Germanic and Celtic migrations led to his ostracism. That venom is now spent, but the origin of *ship, sail, sea,* and so on remains one of the most debatable questions of Germanic historical linguistics.[19]

And now an example of a wise use of the idea of the substrate. The origin of the word *ivy* remained undiscovered for a long time. In 1903, Johannes Hoops, an eminent scholar and a specialist in the history of plant names, proposed the equation Old Engl. *īfig* / Old High German *ebah* ~ Latin *ibex* (a wild goat), because both are "climbers."[20] His etymology was received with enthusiasm, but it turned out that Latin borrowed *ibex* from some indigenous Alpine language, and since it is not a native Latin word, it cannot be compared with *ivy.* Dictionaries still mention Hoops's equation (though invariably with a sour disclaimer); yet the case is hopeless. In all probability, *ivy* is related to Old Engl. *āfor* (bitter, pungent) (because of the taste of the plant's leaves).[21] It is, of course, possible to say that the closeness between *ivy* and *āfor* is due to a coincidence and that *ivy,* like *ibex,* is a substrate word whose origin will never be known, but an approach that takes the existence of a substrate for its starting point is unprofitable. If a good "native" etymology has been proposed, the substrate need not come into the picture. Among the languages closely connected with English, Dutch has especially many isolated words, and some Dutch scholars pursue the idea of the substrate with great zeal (see the end of note 19).

Migratory words and relics of the substrate are the hardest cases students of lexical borrowings encounter in their work. The rest is less complicated. English offers an exceptional opportunity for investigating the routes and fortunes of borrowings. Germanic invaders appeared in Britain around the year 450 and came into contact with the Celtic population of the island. However, ancient Celtic words in English are few and entered Germanic on the continent from Gaul. *Iron* and *lead* (the metal) are believed to be among them. Old Engl. *rīce* (power; powerful), from Celtic, has survived only in the last syllable of the disguised compound *bishopric* and in the proper names *Fredrick* and *Roderick,* but its German cognate *Reich* is widely known (Engl. *rich* is akin to *-rick). Breeches* and *bin,* from Gaul, must also have been borrowed on the continent before the invasion. The other early Celtic words, such as *down* (hill) (possibly preserved in the name of *London*), *brock,* the northern name of the badger, and *bannock* (a flat round cake), stay on the outskirts of the Standard.

The paucity of ancient Celtic words in Old English has not received a convincing explanation. It is usually said that the conquerors did not need to learn the language of the natives, who were either ejected from their home or reduced to dependent status, but the history of all invasions (except those that resulted in the total extermination of the autocthonous inhabitants) shows that people, whatever their position in society, cannot live long without borrowing words from their neighbors. The entire theory of the substrate is based on the tenacity of the language of conquered tribes. Historians know not only substrates but also superstrates (the language of the conquerors disappears but leaves traces in the language of the aborigines) and adstrates (the two languages continue to develop side by side). However, the fact remains: English words from Celtic are, as a rule, the product of later contacts. In the eighteenth and the first half of the nineteenth century, it was customary to declare every etymologically obscure English word to be of Celtic origin and in general to derive English vocabulary from Celtic. Two typical examples are John Cleland's *The Way to Things by Words . . .*[22] and a dictionary by Charles Mackay bearing the preposterous title *The Gaelic Etymology of the Languages of Western Europe and More Especially of the English and Lowland Scotch, and of their Slang, Cant, and Colloquial Dialects.*[23]

Serious philologists dubbed this practice Celtomania and eradicated it so efficiently that some reasonable Celtic etymologies of English words fell by the wayside. Modern researchers show greater restraint. Once again, we witness politics interfering with etymology. It seemed to some that by showing the Celtic origin of English words (or as Mackay wanted it, of words of all European languages) they would do good service to their countrymen. Heaven protect us from patriotism in historical linguistics![24]

The insular Celts and the continental "Germans" lived side by side with Romans from the days of Julius Caesar. Both learned a certain number of Latin words. About two hundred borrowings from everyday Latin preserved in Old English partly go back to the pre-invasion period, but quite a few entered English later through Celtic mediation. *Anchor, cheese, oil, pepper, pear, wall, street, kettle, table, pillow,* and *wine* belong to those strata (Germanic peoples drank ale and beer, but not wine). Latin returned to the island with the conversion of the Anglo-Saxons to Christianity. The introduction of the words *pope, priest, shrine, altar, mass,* and *creed* is an obvious result of Christianization. However, the later borrowings from Latin into Old English include some nonreligious words, for example, *crystal, verse, theater; rose, lily, cucumber; circle, grammar,* and *paper.*[25]

In the eighth century, the Viking raids began. The Danes settled on the northern coast of France and attacked Britain from there. The arrival of a huge Danish fleet ("the heathen men" and "that army" of the *Anglo-Saxon Chronicle*) goes back to 850. Despite the success of King Alfred in repelling the invaders, by 878 the Danes had control of two-thirds of the island, and in the eleventh century, England became a province of Canute's empire (though with London as its capital). Old Danish was close to Old English, and at an elementary level, the conquered and the conquerors must have understood each other. The farther away from Winchester, Alfred's southern capital, the closer the dialects of Old English were to the dialects of the invaders. Yet Old English and Old Danish were different languages. A modern reader of the Icelandic sagas who knows both of them, though, of course, passively, reacts with surprise to the episodes in which Scandinavians experience no difficulty in speaking with the English king and his retainers. In an anthologized passage from the *Anglo-Saxon Chronicle,* Ohthere, that is, Óttar, tells King Alfred about his travels. Opinions differ, but today we are inclined to believe that the interview could not have been carried on without an interpreter.

Modern English is full of borrowings from Scandinavian. They are especially prominent in northern dialects, but the Standard, too, absorbed many of them. They pertain to warfare at sea (especially the names of ships), law and administration (including the word *law,* literally "something laid down"), and to everyday life (for example, *cast* and *take*), and, the greatest surprise of all, the pronouns *they, them,* and *their* (*she,* despite many uncertainties attending its history, is probably English.)[26] In principle, borrowings from Scandinavian have merged with the rest of English vocabulary. *Fellow, window,* and *husband,* the disguised compounds mentioned in Chapter 8, look native (and, as we know, *window* is half-native, while *husband* may have only modified its meaning under the influence of *húsbóndi*), and so do *law* and *cast.* Unexpectedly, *take* superseded *neman,* and *give* and *get* (unless *g-* in them owes its origin to the pronunciation of northern dialects) may be from Scandinavian, because if they had continued the forms of "classical" Old English, their initial sound would have been the same as in *yield* and *yoke.*

Initial *sk-* (as in the word *Scandinavia*) and final *-g* are telltale signs of Scandinavian words: English has *sh-* and *-(d)ge ~ -ow /-aw* in their place. Thus *skirt, sky, ski; rig, egg* (both the noun *egg* and the verb *egg on*), *drag,* and *tug* are Scandinavian words, whereas *shirt, ship, shelf; ridge, edge, draw* and *tow* are English. However, this rule does not apply to all cases. *Skate* is from Dutch, *skillet* is probably from French (unlike *skill,* which is from Danish), *skeleton* is a bookish borrowing from Greek via Latin. *Fig* (the fruit and the opprobrious gesture) came from Old French; *plug* was borrowed from German or Dutch; *beg* is a back formation from *beggar;* the history of *dig* is obscure; *pig, frog, dog,* and *stag* are native; and *wig,* a shortening of *periwig,* is an Anglicized variant of *peruke* (French *perruque,* from Italian *perrucca*). The first impulse on seeing *rug, snag,* and *slug* is to suggest Scandinavian descent. I have chosen those three words, because they surfaced in texts late, mostly in the sixteenth century, too late for typical borrowings from Scandinavian, and dictionaries are careful in adding "probably" to the phrase "of Scandinavian origin." Some cases are bound to remain controversial. Thus, although the verb *die* has been known from texts only since the twelfth century and has an Old Icelandic synonym *deyja,* it is perhaps a native English word.[27]

Many things fall rather naturally into three parts: north – center – south, hot – warm – cold, black – gray – white, and the like. It has also been customary to divide the history of languages into three periods: old, middle, and modern. In English, a catastrophic event marks the end of its oldest period, namely the Norman Conquest. Although for scholarly purposes it is said that Old English lasted from 450 to 1066, the first records of the Germanic invaders' language do not antedate the year 750, and they are extremely sparse. There is little to read in Old English before the ninth century. The Battle of Hastings took place on October 14, 1066. On the next day, people did not begin to speak a different language and did not realize that they had gone over to the next period, but the events that followed the Conquest justify the role ascribed to it in retrospect.

From 1066 until the dukedom of Normandy was lost to the British crown and the French under King John, now Lackland, discovered that they were foreigners at home (who did not know the language of their country and spoke a dialect of French ridiculed in Paris) and began to learn English (Middle English as it is called), England was bilingual. Old French, unlike Old Danish, had nothing in common with Old English, except their distant origin from the same protolanguage—a fact of which both the English and the French were unaware (and if they had been privy to our knowledge of comparative linguistics, their communication would not have been facilitated). One of history's little ironies is that William and his soldiers were the descendants of the Norwegian Vikings, who had, in the past, conquered Normandy (whence its name), as the Danish Vikings had conquered two-thirds of England and later all of it. By 1066, the Danes who settled in Britain had been assimilated into English culture (which they first partly destroyed and then enriched by their presence), and the Norwegians had become French in language and customs. This means that the conquerors and the conquered at Hastings were ethnically very close, but blood turned out to be thinner than the water in the channel that separated England from France.

For a long time, French remained the language of the upper echelon of British society. Otto Jespersen must have been the first to quote the dialogue from Chapter 1 of Walter Scott's *Ivanhoe*. The action is set in the days of Richard I, that is, shortly after 1189. Wamba, the fool (jester) and Gurth, the swineherd, are slaves of Cedric the

Saxon. Many books on the history of English retell or reproduce part of this dialogue. Here it is in full:

"I advise thee . . . to leave the herd to their destiny, which, whether they meet with bands of travelling soldiers, or of outlaws, or of wandering pilgrims, can be little else than to be converted into Normans before morning, to thy no small ease and comfort," quoth Wamba. "The swine turned Normans to my comfort! Expound that to me, Wamba, for my brain is too dull, and my mind too vexed, to read riddles." "Why, how call you those grunting brutes running about on their four legs?" demanded Wamba. "Swine, fool, swine," said the lad; "every fool knows that." "And swine is good Saxon," said the Jester; "but how call you the sow when she is flayed, and drawn, and quartered, and hung up by the heels, like a traitor?" "Pork," answered the swineherd. "I am very glad every fool knows that too. . . ." said Wamba, "and pork, I think, is good Norman-French; and so when the brute lives, and is in the charge of a Saxon slave, she goes by her Saxon name; but becomes a Norman and is called pork, when she is carried to the Castle-hall to feast among the nobles; what dost thou think of this, friend Gurth, ha?" "It is but too true doctrine, friend Wamba, however it got into thy fool's pate." "Nay, I can tell you more," said Wamba, in the same tone; "there is old Alderman Ox continues to hold his Saxon epithet, while he is under the charge of serfs and bondsmen such as thou, but becomes Beef, a fiery French gallant, when he arrives before the worshipful jaws that are destined to consume him. Mynheer Calf, too, becomes Monsieur de Veau in the like manner; he is Saxon when he requires tendance, and takes a Norman name when he becomes matter of enjoyment."

This witty conversation has no foundation in reality, because a hundred years after Hastings, Gurth would not have called swine's flesh *pork* but rather *swīnflǣsc, *picflǣsc, flicce ("flitch"), or *baco ("bacon"). A Saxon serf would not have heard the word *pork* until the mid-thirteenth century at the earliest, and *mynheer* is Dutch, not Old English (incidentally, note the phrase *read riddles,* in which *read* has the old meaning "to guess"), but from the modern point of view the idea is absolutely correct: *pig (swine, hog, boar), cow (bull, ox), calf, sheep, ewe (lamb),* and *deer (stag, doe, roe)* are English words, whereas *pork, beef, veal, mutton,* and *venison* are French. Today, *pig* and *pork* belong to the same style, and no one would think that *veal cutlet* (both words are French) sounds more genteel than *lamb chop* (both words are English), but when we have pairs of synonyms (*be-*

gin ~ commence, depth ~ profundity, happiness ~ felicity, meal ~ repast, believe ~ trust, friendly ~ amicable, and so on), the French one is reserved for an elevated style or abstract concepts. This, however, is not always the case. In the triad *chief – main – principal,* all three words are from French. The distinction between *help ~ aid, freedom ~ liberty,* and *hearty ~ cordial* is one of usage rather than of style. *Enemy* (from French) is neutral, *foe* (English), contrary to expectation, elevated. In the pair *enmity ~ hostility,* both nouns are French, and in the pair *begin ~ start,* both verbs are English.

It is enough to open any page of an English dictionary, to see that, numerically, words of Romance origin predominate in the vocabulary of the modern language, even though the most frequent words *(come, go, do, make, foot, hand, eye, bread, water)* are usually Germanic. Several problems confront a student of the Romance element in English. To make sure that a word has come to English from French, one has to discover the French etymon. This is sometimes impossible, because in our search, we move back and forth between Old French and Anglo-French, or Anglo-Norman, as it is sometimes called, the French dialect spoken by the Normans in England. In the first two centuries after the Conquest, the language of the rulers was almost closed to English words, but later the situation changed, so that a word known to us only from Anglo-French may, despite that fact, have been a borrowing from Middle English and have had a Germanic rather than a Romance past. *Rabbit* is a common Middle English word; it first occurs in contexts dealing with French cuisine. The suffix *-it* is French, and several French etymons of the word have been proposed, but the root of *rabbit* is probably the syllable *rab ~ rob* occurring in various animal names (see p. 116). The same seems to be true of *strumpet,* mentioned on pp. 122–23: the suffix is French, but the root is, most likely, Germanic. *Trot* (an old woman, hag) first turned up in a French poem by John Gower (died in 1308); yet it does not resemble any French noun having a comparable meaning; evidently, it is not French at all.

Many words penetrated Early French from their Germanic neighbors (the Franks) and returned to English. Detecting an ancient semi-obliterated Frankish word parading in French guise requires a good deal of detective work. We have observed the Germanic crab "crawl-ing" to France and coming back to England under the name of *crevis,* where the English demoted it to *crayfish.* *Baco* (pork), which I ex-pected Gurth to use, meant "pig" and "ham." This is an old word in the Germanic languages, and it resembles Modern Dutch *big* (pig). After a long stay in French, it reemerged in English as *bacon.* An-other traveler is Middle Dutch *trecken* (to pull, draw), familiar from Afrikaans *trek* (a journey by ox wagon); its doublet is *track,* a bor-rowing from French. (The noun *trekker,* this time bypassing French, became Engl. *trigger,* literally "a puller.") And now two best-known examples. Engl. *yard* (from *geard*) meant "fence, enclosure." It is related to the Slavic word for "town" (as in *Novgorod* [new town]), but its closest cognate *garden* is a borrowing of Old Northern French *gardin,* a variant of Old French *jardin,* ultimately from Germanic. The native reflex of Germanic *warðo* (ð = *th,* as in *this*) is *ward;* it was re-borrowed from French as *guard. Warden* and *guardian* are related in the same way.

Finally, one has to learn to distinguish between the French words that flooded English in the Middle Ages and their doublets borrowed much later from French and Latin books. The Latin words are usu-ally longer and more "literary." Compare two short lists. From French: *balm, benison* (now obsolete), *blame, chance, chieftain, fancy, palsy, ransom, ray, reason,* and *sure.* Their twins from Latin: *balsam, bene-diction, blasphemy, cadence, captain, fantasy (phantasy), paralysis, redemption, radius, ration,* and *secure. Fever* was borrowed from Latin in the Old English period. In the fourteenth century, *-ish* was tacked on to it. *Febrile,* a synonym of *feverish,* is also from Latin. It appeared in the seventeenth century. Some Romance doublets are unexpected. Skeat explains in his dictionary that Middle French *mousquet,* which English borrowed as *musket* in the sixteenth cen-tury, designated originally a kind of hawk (a regular case: another sort of gun was called a *falconet* [a small falcon], and another a *saker,* again "a kind of hawk"). The French took it over from Italian *mosquetto* (musket), originally also "a kind of hawk," so called from its small size (Latin *musca,* a cognate of *midge,* means "a fly"). It follows that *mosquito* (from Spanish), once more "a little fly," is, historically, the same word as *musket*. Their meanings are so dis-similar and the metaphor on which the name of the musket is based is so far from obvious that despite the nearly complete coincidence of their sound shape *(musket, mosquito)*, their affinity is concealed.

Since speakers of Northern and Central French differed in their pronunciation of certain words, Modern English may have two bor-rowings, both from Old French, reflecting those differences, for ex-ample, *wage* and *gage*, *catch* and *chase*, *launch* and *lance*. To the pairs *cattle* ~ *chattels* and *catch* ~ *chase*, *capital* and *capture* were added. The root of *cattle*, *chattels*, and *capital* goes back to Latin *caput* (head). The combined meaning "wealth, property" and "live-stock" has several parallels. Thus, *pecuniary* (pertaining to money) is a sixteenth-century borrowing of Latin *pecūniārius*, from *pecūnia* (money, originally "riches in cattle") (Latin *pecu* [cattle, money]; compare *peculiar*, from Latin *pecūliāris* [one's own]). *Fee* is related to the Germanic word for "cattle," as seen in German *Vieh* (cattle). Russian *skot* (cattle) is related to or is a borrowing of a Germanic word for "treasure" (German *Schatz*). An extreme case of five English words reflecting the same etymon is *discus* (an eighteenth-century borrowing from Latin), *disk* or *disc* (from French *disque* or straight from Latin), *desk* (from Medieval Latin but with the vowel changed under the influence of an Italian or a Provençal form), *dish* (bor-rowed from Latin by Old English), and *dais* (from Old French).[28]

The innocuous-looking phrase "from French or straight from Latin" returns us to the advice given above to learn to distinguish early French from later French and Latin borrowings. *Balm* and *balsam* are easy to distinguish, and so are *disc* ~ *disk* and *dish*, because their history can be traced in sufficient detail. But more than once a French etymon would have yielded the same result in English as the Latin etymon from which the French word is derived. Both French *disque* and Latin *discus* (without an ending) would have become Engl. *disc* *(disk)*. Time and again, historians of English repeat the same state-ment: "From French or its Latin source." *Facile* can be from French *facile* or Latin *facilis*. Old French *prophane* and Latin *profānus* are equally probable etymons of *profane*. In most such cases, the question—French or Latin?—has no definitive solution.

A browser of an English etymological dictionary may conclude that some time around the sixteenth century a combined Dutch-German invasion followed the Viking raids and the Norman Conquest. The number of Middle Dutch words, homonymous with their cognates in Northern German (or Low German, as it is called in linguistic works), that entered English and became fully domesticated in it is astounding, and they are not limited to seafaring, warfare, or trade. Most of the frequentative verbs discussed in Chapter 9 are of Dutch or Low German origin. *Brackish, drawl, drill, groove, loiter, snip, snap,* and hundreds of others have the same source. The dictionary in which they are featured is 660 pages thick.[29]

No modern European language has received so many words from so many languages as has English.[30] Whether this openness has always been a blessing is a matter of opinion. Foreigners groan under the burden of English vocabulary. Native speakers, who, as time goes on, read less and less of their classical literature, understand it worse and worse. Both language and literature develop by canonizing their lower (popular) forms and rejecting some of the achievements of past epochs. Fewer and fewer people remember the difference between *timorous* and *temerarious,* but at the moment, everyone knows the difference between *nerd* and *geek* and between *awful* and *awesome,* and that is the way it has always been. Most words branded in Samuel Johnson's 1755 dictionary as low are now respectable, whereas Shakespeare must be read with a sizable glossary. Some borrowings had their day and disappeared, others stayed and gladden both a discriminating user and an etymologist who know the difference between *doughty, bold, stalwart* (from English), *stout* (from Anglo-Norman, originally Germanic, like German *stolz* [proud]), and *brave, valiant, valorous, courageous,* and *intrepid* (from French), and are not afraid to add the English suffix *-less* to both Engl. *fear-* and French *daunt-.* Mastering a language, even one's own, especially such a rich language as English, is a gallant deed.

Chapter Thirteen

in which the plot does not thicken, or

A Retrospect:
The Methods of Etymology

Language changes, but we take no notice.—Internal reconstruction.—
Cognates, congeners, and other family business.—On galleys and
galleries.—Chuck Taylor endorses Converse brand tennis shoes.—
Cognates versus borrowings.—The first summing up.—Say no to look-
alikes.—The more, the better.—If possible, stay at home.—A waif
arouses pity.—From things to words.—Good wine needs no bush.

My story is approaching the culmination, and the time has come to
throw a retrospective glance at the strivings and achievements of
etymology, the better to appreciate the revolution in historical linguistics that will be discussed in the next chapter. Etymology finds
its justification in the belief that words are, or, at a certain stage in
the development of language, were, not arbitrary but meaningful
combinations of sounds. Every decipherment presupposes that the
code can be broken; in this respect, an etymologist is like a decoder.

Words change both their phonetic shape and meaning (see especially Chapter 2). This is not a trivial statement. We understand the
oldest people around us and our great-grandchildren, and the ease of
communication emphasizes the stability of language. Some words
appear and disappear in our lifetime, stress can shift from the second
syllable to the first, and usage does not remain the same from decade
to decade, but those are details not comparable with social upheav-
als, revolutions in the style of clothes, and the collapse of age-old
taboos. The paradox of language is that it changes fast and radically,
without our noticing it. *Barn* (from *bere* + *ærn*) and *daisy* (from

dæges ēage) have lost half of their sounds. Several centuries ago, *stone* was pronounced with the vowel of *store* and before that with the vowel of *spa*. *Book* and *fight* had the vowels of modern *Bork* and *feet*, respectively. Most of the oldest words of English are now mono-syllabic (*see, speak, cat, dog, head, mouth,* and so on; see p. 74) and often remain such in declension and conjugation *(saw, speaks, dogs, mouthed),* in contrast to what they were in Chaucer's days, let alone in the days of Hengist and Horsa, the semi-legendary leaders of the fifth-century Germanic invasion of Britain. Evidently, to be success-ful, etymologists should try to uncover the oldest recorded form of the words they are researching.

Human memory is short, and our historical intuition, when it comes to words, is unreliable. We learn with surprise that the *Oxford English Dictionary* has no citation for *fake* (called slang) before 1812 (can the word be so recent?) and that *floozy* was known in 1911 (could it be around so long?). The naive idea that one can discover the origin of a word by looking at it attentively and thinking hard yielded to the demand for studying Old and Middle English, Old French, and so on. The first professional etymologists in Western Europe (and they appeared about four hundred years ago) were partly aware of the situation, but their knowledge of the earlier stages of the modern languages was limited; proficiency in Latin, Greek, and Hebrew could not make up for that gap in their education. With few exceptions, the grammars, dictionaries, and editions in our libraries do not antedate the middle of the nineteenth century. The amateurs who, as late as 1900, filled the pages of popular journals with their conjectures on word origins, had no idea that they should have used their time read-ing rather than writing.

The earliest attested English words return us to the beginning of literacy in Britain. Some of them were coined after 450, but most were brought by the invaders to their new home from the continent. They are millennia away from any primordial utterances and mono-syllabic grunts that allegedly mark the rise of human speech. How-ever, we must be grateful for what we have. Without the evidence of Old Engl. *hūswīf* (literally "housewife") and *heahfore,* etymologists would have been hard put to reconstruct the history of *hussy* and *heifer.* Not everybody is so fortunate. For untold centuries, all culture was oral, and in many cases, historical linguists have no texts to work with and depend entirely on so-called internal reconstruction. For example, they note words like *to husband* and *husbandry* and conclude that "the male spouse" could not have been the first meaning of the noun *husband.* Every language has such significant accretions from the past, but they seldom go far back. Or we compare several modern languages and try to guess which forms are more archaic. (Thus we can compare Engl. *do* and German *tun,* and decide that at one time English infinitives ended in *-n* but later lost it.)

Terms like *Germanic* and *Romance* presuppose the existence of language groups. The members of a group are related, that is, they go back to the same ancestor and share certain features inherited from that ancestor and absent elsewhere. The parent of the Romance languages is Latin (the substrates are taken for granted), and both French and Spanish etymologists must be fine Latinists. The parent of Germanic (the Scandinavian subgroup, English, Dutch, Afrikaans, German, Yiddish, and a few dead languages like Gothic) has not been recorded. No texts exist in it, and here our position is less advantageous, but the situation with Romance is an exception: all the other protolanguages are the product of reconstruction. A historian of Germanic words compares forms from the languages belonging to the group and, considering how long Germanic speakers were the neighbors of the Celts and Romans, needs more than a smattering of Celtic and Romance linguistics. In practice, all-encompassing erudition is rare, but the ideal remains.

A term that has frequently occurred in the pages of this book is *cognate,* a noun or an adjective (for example, *flatter* is cognate with, or a cognate of, German *flattern*). In the same sense, *allied, akin,* and *related to* have been used. The noun *cognate* has a synonym *congener.* We spot some cognates without any difficulty, for example, Engl. *house,* German *Haus,* Dutch *huis,* Swedish *hus.* Others are less obvious: Engl. *tooth, four, love* and *go* versus German *Zahn, vier, lieben,* and *gehen.* Cognates are offspring of a protoword (reconstructed but not attested, whence the warning asterisk), which may stay ossified in one language and change its sounds and meaning in another. Icelandic *hús* (*ú* designates long *ú*, as in Engl. *who*) has the same pronunciation today that it had 2,000 years ago. Of the two words—*tooth* and *Zahn*—the German one has preserved its shape better than its English cognate, but it, too, has lost a consonant (the original form of *Zahn* was *zand*).

Selecting cognates is an indispensable first step of every etymology, but a string of related forms may not solve the question about the word's "nonconventional" meaning. Our aim is to learn how the combination of sounds *h-ū-s* came to mean "dwelling." By discovering *Haus* and *huis*, we do not come any closer to the solution, though we realize that the diphthongs in English, German, and Dutch developed by later phonetic processes: in medieval texts, the word appeared as *h ūs*. We are in better shape with Engl. *flatter* and German *flattern* (to flutter), because thanks to the German cognate (assuming that it is indeed a cognate of the English verb and of *flutter*), the shift of meaning becomes clear: from "fluttering" around the person whose good graces are our objective to insincere praise. Note the parentheses in the previous sentence: it is helpful that *flatter* and *flattern,* unlike *house* and *Haus,* mean different things, but this benefit has a shady side: we are now no longer certain that the words we paired are cognates. Thus, we either face an uninspiring set of words nearly or wholly identical in form and meaning *(house ~ Haus ~ huis ~ hús)* or clusters like Engl. *flatter* / *flutter* ~ German *flattern,* whose members are not necessarily related to one another. Every attempt to find an etymology depends on the selection of cognates. Is *clover* really akin to *cleave* (to stick to), and *chide* to *kīd* (wedge)? I think they are, but not everybody will agree, because the connection between *clover ~ cleave* and *chide ~ kīd* is not self-evident.

The passage on *galley* (p. 139) ended with the statement that *galley* is not related to *gallery.* To make such a statement, one has to investigate the history of both words. *Galley* was originally a Greek animal name. When the letter *G* in the *Oxford English Dictionary* was going to print, nothing worth repeating was known about the origin of *gallery.* Since that time, Romance scholars have made a few suggestions, and *The Oxford Dictionary of English Etymology* was able to state the following: "Perh[aps] alteration of *galilea* GALILEE . . ."

Galilee (a porch or chapel at the entrance of a church) derives from the name of a province of Palestine, "perh[aps] used in allusion to it as being an outlying portion of the Holy Land; first recorded of Durham cathedral and taken up thence by antiquarian writers of [the nineteenth century]." The origin of *gallery* is still unknown. A porch is not a gallery, and in the wanderings from Medieval Latin *(galeria)* to Italian *(galleria),* northward to French, and to English, a good deal of information has been lost. Earlier researchers did connect *galley* and *gallery,* but they based their conjecture on a wrong etymology of *galley* (which they traced to Greek *kālon* [wood; lumber; fleet]).[1] With that etymology discredited, we can say that *gallery,* despite its obscurity, is not a cognate of *galley.*

It is clear why isolated words are the hardest to etymologize, though isolation is a relative concept. *Chide* (if *kīdel* does not belong with it) is only English, *clover* (if unrelated to *cleave* [to stick to]) is limited to a few Germanic languages, *house* (if all the non-Germanic cognates proposed for it are wrong) occurs only in Germanic, unlike *father* or *eight,* with connections from Norway to India. It is such isolated words that may be fragments of a substrate. As pointed out, the one precious cognate we need may not have been recorded or the obscure word we are studying was coined in a way incomprehensible to us.

> For instance, the development of *ragged* to mean 'exhausted, edgy' and used to refer to males shows that the original allusion to menstruation, *on the rag,* has been lost. The slang *chucks* for 'high topped tennis shoes' seems entirely arbitrary without the information that Converse brand tennis shoes carry the endorsement of Chuck Taylor. The verb root of *wanker* 'loser' is puzzling without the information that *wank* is an imitation of the sound of the buzzer on Truth or Consequences.[2]

Hundreds, if not thousands, of words similar to *chucks* and *wank* must have been in circulation for centuries. Our chance of guessing their origin is slim. *Ship,* in the politely subdued jargon of modern researchers, is a word of doubtful etymology, which means that the hypotheses on its origin advanced so far are not fully convincing, though the comparison with Latin *scīpio* (staff, pole) is not bad (a vessel we call "ship" may have been a hollowed log or a dugout). But perhaps its etymon (the form from which it is derived) meant "basket" or "can." Words for such containers are numerous. Even we, with our miniscule command of Old English vocabulary, know about two dozen; at least as many may have been lost. Yet the problem remains: to discover the origin of a word, we need cognates with comparable but nonidentical meanings.

Compounds and words with prefixes and suffixes form a special group. *Bridal* goes back to a sum of two nouns: *bride* and *ale*. *Nimble* is *nim-b-le,* and *balance* is traceable to **bilancia.* Nothing else can be said about them. The next step would be a search for the origin of *bride, ale, nim, -b-, -le, bi-,* and *lancia,* but the results of that search are of no consequence for understanding *bridal, nimble,* and *balance.* In dealing with such words, etymology merges with word formation. Transparent words like *undo, shipment,* and *statesman* do not interest etymologists, who step in only when questions arise, for example, about what is *orna-* in *ornament, -couth* in *uncouth, cran-* in *cranberry,* and *straw-* in *strawberry,* and why we say *spokesman* rather than **speaksman.*[3]

In theory, cognates (descendants of the same parent) are easy to distinguish from borrowings (guests from another language). But let us look at two examples. A thousand years ago, English and German had the word *hūs* (house). Today, English and German have the word *nylon.* English and German *nylon* are not cognates. Engl. *nylon* was invented in 1938 by the DuPont Chemical Co., a coinage that makes one think of the textile (compare *rayon*) and perhaps vaguely suggests the fabric's novel character (compare *new*). Both the product and its name became popular in many countries. Is it possible that a special type of dwelling called *hūs* originated in some one Germanic language and spread to its neighbors, as *nylon* did in the twentieth century?

The earliest Germanic word for "house" seems to have been *razn* (recorded in Gothic). Its cognates have been mentioned above in connection with Engl. *barn, saltern,* and *ransack.* The Germanic *hūs* was, in all likelihood, different from the *razn* (compare the differences between Modern Engl. *house, building,* and *edifice*). In Gothic, a language recorded 16 centuries ago, *hūs* occurs only in the compound *gud-hūs* (godhouse), that is, "temple." *Hūs* is not a maritime word, but its origin is no less obscure than that of *ship*. Since a prehistoric counterpart of the DuPont Chemical Co. is hard to imagine, we assume that *hūs* is not a borrowing in any of the older Germanic languages but a reflex of a Proto-Germanic word. Although this assumption is justified, it cannot be proved. In the thirty-seventh century, someone who will write a book like the present one may suggest that *nylon* is a Proto-European noun consisting of the negation *n-*, the root of the Greek word *hýle* (forest)[4] (with *h* dropped), and a suffix of probably substrate origin, the whole meaning either "containing no fibers" or "not to be worn in a wooded area." We have seen that Engl. *crab* and Russian *korob* (basket) may be either native words in their languages or borrowings. Engl. *garden* is a cognate of Slavic *gorod* (town), but borrowing (from Germanic into Slavic or from Slavic into Germanic) is not inconceivable. "The great problem of comparative philology is to distinguish between those resemblances which are the result of common parentage and those which are the result of influence, or what is called 'borrowing'."[5] Every student of historical linguistics comes to the same conclusion.

An etymologist deals with probabilities. As long as we have the support of documents, we are historians. *Heifer* undoubtedly developed from *heahfore* because the Old English form *heahfore* and its later reflexes (continuations) have been recorded, but this form is opaque. Why did it mean "a one-year-old cow that has not calved"? Both *ea* and *o* could be short or long. To produce an etymology, we will try to choose the most promising variant of four *(hēahfore, heahfore, hēahfōre, heahfōre)*, though opinions about what is promising differ.

Heifer is a notoriously hard case, but probability is the foundation of most etymologies. *Snark* is certainly, not probably, a blend of *snake* and *shark*, because Lewis Carroll explained his coinage. By contrast, Swift did not bother to tell us why he called his little people *Lilliputs,* and we are not better off with that name than with *heifer.* The name of the person who introduced *slender* into English is irrelevant. The probability of a blend *(slight + tender)* is rather high, but it is still only a probability. Although unanimity is rare among etymologists, the degree of their success is impressive. The origin of thousands of words has been discovered and codified in excellent dictionaries. The mechanisms of phonetic and semantic change (to be discussed in the next chapters) and the role of the ludic element (language at play) are today understood so much better than they were even two centuries ago that the science of etymology can be proud of its achievements.

From the foregoing exposition a few principles of etymological analysis have emerged. It may be useful to summarize them and list them in one place.

- Etymology does not depend on look-alikes. Engl. *house* and German *Haus* are similar (nearly identical) and related, whereas *galley* (from Greek) and *gallery* (a reshaped Hebrew place name?) are similar and unrelated. On the other hand, Engl. *tooth* and German *Zahn* belong together, though today all their sounds are different. Their relatedness or the lack thereof can be established only by comparing the oldest extant or reconstructed forms of each word. Folk etymology suggests ties based on chance resemblances. It will explain *gossip* as *go sip* and invent a plausible yarn about how *sirloin* originated in the phrase *Sir Loin.* Indulging in amateurish fantasies should be discouraged (which does not exclude the possibility that someone without any training in linguistics may know a story or a local custom of real value to an etymologist: see the explanation of *chucks* and *wanker,* above).

- An etymology that can "decode" several words is, in principle (note the hedging), preferable to the one that offers a separate explanation for each word of what seems to be a set. For example, if the choice is between an etymology of *Lilliputian* that fits only this word and an etymology that sheds light on both *Lilliputian* and *Laputa,* it is advisable to accept the second one. However, a hypothesis that purports to explain dozens or even hundreds of words is usually suspect. The immutable law—the broader the volume, the more narrow the content—is valid for all formulations. Hence the danger of hearing onomatopoeias and ideophones everywhere, overstating the role of sound symbolism, detecting blends in all obscure words, and in reducing the entire vocabulary of a language to a few roots (the last point, like the mechanisms of change, will be discussed later).

• It is often unclear whether a word is native or borrowed. In such cases, the probability factor plays an especially important role. *Crab* may be of Germanic descent, but the existence of numerous similar words elsewhere makes the idea of borrowing more appealing (not proven but only more appealing; our evidence is inconclusive by definition: words are not characters in a Conan Doyle or an Agatha Christie story and are not in a hurry to confess even on the last page). A bad etymology is not better (in fact, it is much worse) than no etymology at all ("origin unknown," a resigned acquiescence in inevitable ignorance, as Jespersen put it in a Micawberian way), but given a high probability that a word has an ascertainable origin in its language, caution is needed in suggesting a foreign source, be it a neighboring language, the language of ancient colonizers, or an unidentifiable substrate.

• When a word occurs in several languages and the question arises where it originated, its home should be sought in the language in which it has ties with other words. This is why *zigzag* seems to have been coined in German and *hackney* in English.

• Every word was coined by a resourceful individual or borrowed as a result of language contact in a certain place at a certain time. It has an etymon, a sound complex endowed with meaning. Some words are short-lived, others become a permanent part of the vocabulary. Newcomers may oust their synonyms that have existed for centuries. The staying power of words increases if they form ties with other words. *Bob* (an insect) merged with the name *Bob*, *gun* from *Gunilda* (assuming that this derivation is right) pretended to be a clipped form of Old French *mangonne,* so that upstarts began to look like old-timers. This should not be interpreted in the sense that *bob* and *gun* have two etymologies each, but it means that the survival of a word may depend on the soil from which it springs up. Our inability to choose among several equally reasonable solutions should not be used as a plea for the ability of a word to have multiple etymologies.

- The knowledge of things around us cannot be derived from words (or names, as Plato called them), but the sidelight from etymology occasionally illuminates the past. If *ship* is really cognate with Latin *scīpio* (staff, pole), this fact confirms our notion of the most primitive sailing vessels. However, in research, the process starts at the opposite end: to arrive at a plausible etymology of *ship,* we must have an idea about primitive ship building. Etymology is not about the word's "true meaning," because any meaning acceptable to a given community is "true." Its goal is to break through the conventional nature of the linguistic sign. When success crowns this endeavor, *cuckoo* emerges as an onomatopoeia, *balance* as "two weighing scales," and *lord* as "the guardian of bread."

- As a general rule, a good etymology is simple (only finding it is hard). Name givers use the material close at hand: a husband is a homeowner, a lady is a bread kneader, a galley is a weasel, and a cloak is a bell-shaped (clock-shaped) garment. Etymologies presupposing many complicated moves need not be wrong but usually are.

It appears that we already know a good deal about an etymologist's work. Yet the most rewarding part of the story lies ahead.

Chapter Fourteen

in which etymology becomes a science,
rejoices, and then has second thoughts, or

Sound Laws

Basi as the ancestor of *berry.*—Latin *pater* and English *father.*—
Rasmus Rask, Jacob Grimm, and Grimm's Law.—*Indo-European* and
Germanic.—Two consonant shifts.—Language trees, waves, and
unions.—From Zeus to Týr.—The nonoverlapping tracks of vocalic
alternations.—What cannot be done should not be done: the dilemma
of *ai* and *a.*—Voltaire's unattested joke.—What cannot be done is done
all the time: Grimm's Law violated, and vocalic alternations not observed.—Big pigs, bacon, packing up bags, nipples, nibbling, tredging,
trudging, and other matters of great pitch (or pith) and moment.—
Taboo.—Margaret becomes Peg.—Coming to terms with chaos.

The etymology of *bridal* consists of "undisguising" it. In *tool,* an
ancient suffix has to be isolated. In *strawberry,* the meaning of *straw*
craves an explanation. Those are worthy tasks. But, as pointed out in
the previous chapter, we hit etymological bedrock when we try to
discover the origin of *bride, ale, straw, berry,* and other short words
that do not look like compounds, have no suffixes, and are not based
on poorly understood meanings (*straw = grass?*) or metaphors. Why
berry, for example? Here our only hope is to find a set of illuminating
cognates. The Dutch and German for "berry" is *bes ~ bezie* and *Beere,*
respectively. In Low (that is, Northern) German, *besing* (blueberry)
has been recorded. The old forms do not differ much from those current today: Old English had *berie ~ berige* (the latter pronounced as
beriye). Old Icelandic *ber* sounds nearly the same as the word for
"berry" in the Modern Scandinavian languages. Gothic preserved the
compound *weina-basi* (wineberry, grape). Since Norwegian dialectal

bas and *base* mean "shrub," it has been suggested that at one time *berry* meant "belonging to, growing on a shrub" or "growing on a blueberry shrub" (compare Low German *besing,* above). Later, "blueberry" might have become the generic name for "berry." Even if this conclusion is right, we still need to understand how the sound complex *bas-* or *bes-,* or *ber-* acquired the meaning "shrub." Here the Old English adjective *basu* "purple, scarlet, crimson," though at variance with the color of blueberries, comes in. Perhaps, in spite of the discrepancy in meaning ("red" versus "blue"), *berry* was originally a color word.

Someone with a bent for puns may find such speculation fruitless, but let us repeat: a word's earliest meaning is usually impossible to reconstruct if all the available cognates are absolute synonyms. Unlike the string Engl. *berry* – German *Beere* – Icelandic *ber,* all of them meaning "berry," the string "berry" – "shrub" – "red" (or "reddish") provides some leeway for a hypothesis, however tentative, about sense development.[1] Yet the aim of the excursus on the origin of *berry* was to highlight the difference in sounds rather than meaning. Gothic *basi,* Old Engl. *basu,* and Norwegian dialectal *bas* ~ *base* have *a* and *s.* The other words have *e* and *r* in the root, and in Dutch, *bezie* competes with *bes.* How broad is the permissible spectrum of such deviations among the cognates? Today we are well informed about these things. For example, the kinship of Gothic *basi,* Dutch *bezie,* and Engl. *berry* is indubitable. A special rule governs the relations between *s, z* ~ *r,* and *a* ~ *e* in Germanic: compare Engl. *was* ~ *were* and *man* ~ *men.* Training in historical linguistics is devoted largely to recognizing such alternations.

The one evergreen example of cognates is Engl. *father* and Latin *pater.* Of a similar type are Engl. *three* and Latin *trēs,* along with Engl. *what* (when pronounced as *h-wat;* the Old English form was *hwæt*) and Latin *quod* (that is, *k-wod*). It is impossible to prove (in the mathematical sense of the word) that *pater* and *father* are cognates. One can only suggest that the difference in the consonants does not prevent them being akin and then group other words with *f, th (þ), h* in English versus *p, t, k* in Latin, to check whether the same correspondence recurs again and again. This is exactly what has been done. Despite some difficulties, most of which were accounted for later, it turned out that at their oldest stages, English, German, Dutch, Icelandic, and Gothic had *f, þ, h* where Latin, Greek, Slavic, Celtic, and some other languages had *p, t, k.* Similar relations obtained between *p, t, k* and *b, d, g* and in one more series of consonants.

The phonetic differences between *pater, trēs, quod* and *father, three, what* was noticed long ago, but their regular character and all-important role became clear only at the beginning of the nineteenth century after the publications by Rasmus Rask (a Dane) and Jacob Grimm (a German).[2] The correspondence of which *p, t, k* versus *f, þ, h* constitutes one part is sometimes referred to as Grimm's Law. Rather than citing a few pairs like *pater – father* and *trēs – three,* historical linguists had to sift the vocabulary of one language after another and decide for which of them such correspondences are valid. Do they exist only between Latin and English (Dutch, Scandinavian, Gothic)? Are there other "laws" of the same type? Before the nineteenth century was over, most such questions received convincing answers. It appeared that the languages of the world form clusters ("families") characterized by similar features, each family being presumably a descendant of a parent language. The largest family encompasses the enormous territory from Norway to India. Since the greatest philologists of the 1900s were Germans, they called that family Indo-Germanic *(Indogermanisch)*—an inappropriate term, because the Romance, Celtic, and Slavic languages, as well as Armenian, Albanian, and a few others, belong with Sanskrit (a language of Ancient India) and Germanic. The English term *Indo-European* is much better.

Germanic is a group within Indo-European. The term *Germanic* turned up early in the pages of this book and was defined in passing and briefly. It can now be re-defined. Within Germanic, the closeness of Swedish to Norwegian, of German to Yiddish and Dutch, and so forth, is apparent to all who can speak or read those languages. Even the affinity between German and English arouses no doubts, though English has lost most endings and borrowed thousands of French and Latin words at the expense of native vocabulary. The borders between the various groups (Romance versus Germanic, Germanic versus Celtic, Slavic versus Indo-Iranian, and so on) are relatively easy to draw. It is less obvious whether all of them belong to the same family. For example, Rask at first concluded that Celtic should not be classified with Indo-European. A student of Irish and Armenian or Frisian and Albanian has to look hard for any similarities between them. Only when we begin to learn Turkish, Vietnamese, or Algonquin, do we realize that we are in an entirely different linguistic world.

In the Eurasian belt between Ceylon and Scandinavia, only Basque, Sami, Hungarian, Finnish, and Estonian are not Indo-European (while Latvian and Lithuanian, the Baltic neighbors of Estonian, "stay in the family"). *Indo-European* is a term of linguistics; it does not refer to race, ethnicity, or culture. We do not know how that unity came about. The origin of separate groups, that is, the ethnogenesis of Greek, Slavic, Germanic, and other tribes and the conditions under which they began to speak what we now call proto-Germanic, proto-Celtic, and so forth, is also unknown; compare what is said about substrates in Chapter 12. Archeologists, historians, and language historians work together to retrace the ways of ancient migrations, but their resources are limited. The oldest attested documents of Indo-European do not antedate the second millennium B.C.E.

The Germanic group of languages, which is at the center of our interest, because English belongs to it, has several features that characterize it uniquely. If English had lost them, it would have stopped being Germanic, but both its basic vocabulary and some peculiarities of grammar survived the Norman Conquest. In phonetics, it is the shift from *p, t, k* to *f, þ, h* and from *b, d, g,* to *p, t, k* (the third move has not been discussed here) that gives away a Germanic language. The causes of the shift and its partly unexpected circular results (why change **p, *t, *k* and then restore them from **b, *d, *g?*) have generated a mountain of articles and books. We will only note that the shift is old. The recorded texts in Germanic have all the "new" consonants in place. The earliest extant book in a Germanic language is the Gothic Bible. But beginning in the first century, in the north, Scandinavians carved runes (runes are letters of a special, so-called runic alphabet). They knew neither parchment nor paper. Their writing materials were stone, wood, and metal. To the extent that we can reconstruct their pronunciation from those inscriptions, their consonants were Germanic. By the time when Romans came into contact with Germanic tribes, the shift had been completed. Later, Germans kept on changing their consonants: with them *tip* became *Zipf,* *water* became *Wasser,* and so on. Therefore, it is customary to speak about the Germanic, or the First, Consonant Shift (this is Grimm's Law), and the German, or the Second, Consonant Shift. The first separates all the Germanic languages from their non-Germanic "relatives" within Indo-European, the second isolates German within the Germanic group. Low German is distinct from High German in that, among other things, it did not undergo the Second Consonant Shift or has only a few traces of it.

The discovery of the First Consonant Shift led to the idea that sound correspondences have the force of laws, as in physics. The most famous statement of nineteenth-century linguistics was: "Sound laws have no exceptions." This statement revolutionized etymology. A search for words somehow connected with the word whose origin was being investigated lost its character of a ramble among look-alikes, and a surprising realization came that look-alikes are deceptive. For example, some early etymologists viewed Welsh *kau* (to close) as a possible cognate of Engl. *key.* But Welsh, although Indo-European, is not a Germanic language. It follows that a Welsh cognate of *key,* if it exists, must begin with *g,* and conversely, if *kau* has a related form in English, its initial consonant should be *h. Key* and *kau* are not related.

The idea of cognates and language families does not antedate Rask and Grimm. Grimm's contemporaries thought that the Proto-Indo-European language, as real as Modern German, existed in the remote past. It allegedly disintegrated with time: groups emerged, then subgroups, then individual languages, and then dialects. The process was likened to the growth of a tree with its trunk, branches, and twigs. However, no agreement was then reached on the original home of the Indo-Europeans. Their language we purport to reconstruct resembles the firmament in a planetarium in which the "stars" of various brightness have been projected onto a spherical ceiling, and we think that they are equidistant from us (this is an image by I. M. Tronskii, a Russian classical scholar). The model of a tree with its offshoots gave way to a more realistic one, according to which language groups are like overlapping waves. It is now recognized that the people whom we call Indo-Europeans, wherever they first lived, spread over Eurasia and superimposed their language on the indigenous populations, wiping out local speech and absorbing substrates. The Indo-Europeanization of two continents had a later analog in the Romanization of Europe at the time when the Romans added ever new lands to their empire.

According to a third conjecture, speakers of different languages lived so long in close proximity that they formed a so-called language union, that is, borrowed the most conspicuous features of phonetics, grammar, and vocabulary from one another (actual, not reconstructed, language unions are known).[3] The theories mentioned here were advanced in the nineteenth and twentieth centuries. Earlier linguists, on the other hand, took their inspiration from the Bible. They traced as many words as possible to Hebrew (the language allegedly spoken in Paradise), derived Latin from Greek, German from Gothic, and English from German. Adam begat Seth, Seth begat Enos, and so on. They could only list words that resemble one another and posit borrowing (for instance, Engl. *key* from Welsh *kau*). More than once, they compared words that are indeed related, but they were unable to stratify the facts at their disposal. The following examples will show how modern linguists look for cognates.

Old English had the word *fǣmne* (maid, virgin, bride; woman; virago). Similar words have been attested elsewhere in Old Germanic, one of them being Old Icelandic *feima* (a shy woman). It is easy "to compare" *fǣmne ~ feima* and Latin *fēmina* (woman), but as we now know, Germanic *f* corresponds to non-Germanic *p,* which rules out the kinship between *fēmina* and *fǣmne.* That is why some etymologists paired *fǣmne* with Lithuanian *pienas* (milk) (perhaps the original meaning of the Germanic word was "a feeding mother"?), Lithuanian *piemuõ* "shepherd" (what if the starting point was "a woman tending sheep"?), and Dutch *veem* (trade company, storehouse company) (its *v-* is from *f-;* couldn't *fǣmne* be "a woman introduced into a group; bride"?).

All those etymologies look unimpressive. The last is especially shaky, also because the history of Dutch *veem* has not been clarified, and, as a rule, a word of questionable origin can do little to illuminate another obscure word: the posited connection nearly always turns out to be false. None of the proposed derivations accounts for the fact that Old Engl. *fǣmne* has such divergent meanings as "woman, bride" and "virago," whereas Old Icelandic *feima* (a poorly attested word) meant "a shy girl." Brides, shy girls, and viragoes do not suckle babies and are hardly the best shepherdesses. Germanic had two main words for "woman." Their Modern English continuations are *wife* (from *wīf*) and *quean* (hussy) (from *cwene* [woman; female serf; prostitute], related to but distinct from *queen,* from *cwēn* [woman; wife; queen]). *Bride* is also an old word. Initially, *cwene* must have referred to the woman's child-bearing function, and *wīf* probably emphasized her belonging to the sex opposite to the male. The numerous, partly incompatible meanings of *fǣmne ~ feima* are a riddle.

Phonetic correspondences indicate that *fǣmne* is not a cognate of *fēmina,* but they do not disqualify *fēmina* as a possible borrowing into Old Germanic. A word for "woman," when borrowed, is either elevated ("a female person of superior rank") or derogatory ("prostitute"). Perhaps *fēmina* reached the Germanic-speaking world with Roman soldiers, and first meant "beldam," occasionally "whore," and (with a touch of irony) "prude." Amazing changes attend the history of words for "a female person." *Girl* surfaced in English with the meaning "a child of either sex" (in Chaucer's days, the word was used predominantly in the plural). Final *-l* in it is a diminutive suffix, and the root, attested from Switzerland to Norway in several forms (*gir-, ger-, gur-,* and *gor-*) occurred in the names of all kinds of creatures and objects considered immature and worthless. The root of *lass* seems to have meant "rag" (not a unique case). If the current etymology of *wench* is right, this word meant "an unsteady one" ("a flirt"?). *Qino,* the Gothic cognate of *quean,* meant only "woman," but "hussy" and "prostitute" are both among the meanings of Old Engl. *cwene.* Likewise, the postulated *fǣmne ~ feima* from *fēmina* could have "gone up" ("a modest, bashful girl"), "down" ("virago"), or remained neutral ("woman").[4] The confusing story of *fǣmne* has been told here to show that the discovery of sound correspondences opened etymologists' eyes to hidden connections, killed their trust in look-alikes, and made many tempting conclusions unacceptable.

The second example along the same lines will be a verb. Dutch *trekken* means "to pull, draw, tug" (it has been mentioned on p. 154 in connection with *treck, track,* and *trigger*). *Trekken* may be related to its Latvian synonym *dragât*. But one cannot help remembering Engl. *drag* and Latin *trahere*, both of which also mean "to pull, draw, tug." Pre-nineteenth-century researchers would have lumped them together as a matter of course. But modern etymologists must obey Grimm's Law. Dutch and English are Germanic languages. Consequently, *draga* and *trekken* are supposed to have matching *d ~ t* and *g ~ k*. Long *k* in *trekken* can be explained as expressive (see pp. 39–40), the more so as Dutch *treken* once existed, but the other discrepancies remain. *Trahere* is equally puzzling: its initial *t* corresponds to neither *t* in *trekken* nor *d-* in *drag*. The disconcerting conclusion is that the three verbs are not related. No one is happy about it, and an attempt has been made to posit a rule whereby *drag* and *trahere* could be combined; another attempt refers *trekken* to the substrate. Numerous megalithic structures exist in the Netherlands, Germany, and Denmark. They were supposedly built by pre-Indo-European settlers. Those who erected such monuments must have needed special vocabulary for dragging and piling up slabs. Since nothing is known about those builders, reference to their language does not go far. Nor is it clear why people with much humbler architectural ambitions should have borrowed a technical term they did not need. If we are facing a migratory word of great antiquity, its source is irretrievably lost.

Incompatible forms like *drag – trekken – trahere* do not emerge in overwhelming numbers, but they are not rare. The English preposition *to* is cognate with Slavic *do* (*t ~ d,* by Grimm's Law). They correspond to Gothic *du;* its *d-* is inexplicable. Dutch *plat* and German *platt* mean "flat." Initial *p-* in Greek *platús*[5] and Medieval Latin **plattus* (the root of *plate,* from French, and *platitude*) matches *f-* in *flat,* but **t* should have been shifted to *þ (th)*. In the Dutch and German forms, neither *p* nor *t* is shifted. Predictably, both words have been explained as borrowings of French *plat* or referred to the substrate. Alongside *plat ~ platt,* Dutch *vlaak* (*v-* is from *f-*) ~ German *flach* exist (all of them mean "flat"). In Chapter 16, we will see how etymologists account for the alternation *-t ~ -k.* Regardless of their success in dealing with the end of the words, the mismatch Engl. *t ~* Greek *t* will remain. Old Engl. *pǣcan* (to deceive) resembles *fǣcne* (deceitful) (also Old English). If they are related and some non-Germanic word of comparable meaning beginning with *p* or *f* is their supposed cognate, either *pǣcan* or *fǣcne* violates Grimm's Law (to put it differently, they cannot be related), and if they are not, their similarity is due to chance. The Old English for *knave* was *cnafa* (squire) (see p. 197). Its synonym *cnapa* is not a "corruption" of *cnafa,* for it has cognates in other Germanic languages. Some dictionaries call *cnafa* and *cnapa* "obscurely related." This phrase means nothing. Equally unrevealing is the formulation that *flat* is "of uncertain relationship" to Greek *platús.* Like *plat, cnapa* has been referred to the substrate. No etymology is preferable to a wrong one. As long as we realize that we have a problem, we will keep trying to solve it.

Sound correspondences can be found between any two related languages. I have chosen Grimm's Law because of its systemic nature and importance. When an old word survives in many languages, an etymologist works with such strings as Gothic *qiman,* Latin *venīre,* and Greek *báinein*[6] ("to come"). The protoform, which is assembled like the least common multiple, to account for all variants, must have begun with **gw-.* In Germanic, **gw-* became *kw-* (spelled *q* in Gothic) by Grimm's Law. In Latin, **gw-* lost **g-,* and **w-* turned into *v-* *(venīre),* while in Greek **gw-* yielded *b-* *(báinein).* Such rules are counted by the hundred, and etymologists in search of cognates should be aware of all of them.

The posited changes (**gw* to *kw,* **gw* to *w,* and **gw* to *b*) did not "disfigure" the protoform beyond recognition. But students think I am joking when I tell them that in the pantheon of the Scandinavian gods, in which Odin (Óðinn) steals the mead of poetry and learns the secret of runes, Thor (Þórr) kills giants, Frey (Freyr) woos a giantess, and Balder (Baldr) is killed with the mistletoe, only the one-handed Tyr (Týr) has an Indo-European name cognate with *Zeus* and

Jupiter (that is, *Jū-piter; piter* is a variant of *pater*).Yet this fact is incontestable. In the Indo-European root **diēu-* (pronounced as '*dyēw*), *d-* before *i* (= *y*) became *dz* in Greek and *dj* in Latin, which is not surprising if we take into account how speakers of Modern English pronounce *did you* and *soldier* (see the history of *nidget* [idiot] on p. 100). The ending *s* in Greek developed from **z*, but in Germanic, **z* became *r*. By Grimm's Law, **d* changed to **t*, so that the protoform of *Týr* sounded approximately like **tīwar*. In Old English, the name has been attested as *Tīg* and *Tīw;* the latter lives on in Modern Engl. *Tuesday*. A beginner views such procedures as legerdemain: *d* to *t*, *d* to *dz*, *s* to *r*, and so on, but those are regular changes. We are in trouble when they do not occur where we expect them.

Vowels alternate according to the rules that manifest themselves with especial clarity in the principal parts of so-called strong verbs (weak verbs form their principal parts with the help of the ending -*ed*, pronounced as *t*, *d*, or *ed: kick – kicked – kicked, rig – rigged – rigged, pet – petted – petted;* their vowels are not affected). We will consider six classes:

I	rise – rose – risen
II	choose – chose – chosen
III	bind – bound – bound
IV	steal – stole – stolen
V	give – gave – given
VI	wake – woke –woken

Old Germanic distinguished four rather than three principal parts: the infinitive, the preterit singular, the preterit plural, and the past participle. In Modern English, only the verb *to be* has preserved all four: *be – was – were – been*. This is how those six classes must have looked about two thousand years ago (I will let the 3rd person represent the preterit plural).

I	**rīsan – *rais – *risun – *risans*
II	**kēosan – *kaus – *kusun – *kusans*
III	**bindan – *band – *bundun – *bundans*

IV   *stelan – *stal – *stālun – *stulans
V   *geban – *gab – *gābun – *gibans
VI   *wakan – *wōk –*wōkun – *wakans

Old English had approximately such forms, except that *ai* became *ā* in it (hence *rīsan* – *rās* in the first class), *ā* became *ǣ*, and *au* turned into *ēa*. Of the other changes only one has to be mentioned. The vowel of the infinitive in the third class was originally *e;* it became *i* before *n*. An extant verb that shows the old state of affairs is *helpan* – *halp* – *hulpun* – *hulpans* (compare German *helfen* – *half* – *geholfen*), but in Modern English, *help* is weak *(help – helped – helped)*.

Each class was like a railroad track: for example, *i* alternated with *ī* (Class I), *e* alternated with *a* (Classes III, IV, and V), *a* alternated with *ō* (Class VI) and *u* (in several classes), but, for example, not with *ai* (= Old Engl. *ā*). Jacob Grimm called the entire system of such vocalic alternations *ablaut*. The English term is either ablaut or gradation; the French call ablaut *apophonie*. Ablaut is one of the most conspicuous features of the Indo-European languages. In Germanic, the main alternating pairs are *e ~ a* and *i ~ a*. Outside Germanic, their counterpart is *e ~ o:* compare Latin *tegēre* (to hide, cover) *~ toga* (toga, robe).

Vowels entered into similar relations in all parts of speech, but in strong verbs, the "tracks" have a particularly graphic form. The non-overlapping of the tracks has serious consequences for etymology. Certain vowels, as pointed out, are allowed to alternate; others are not. To see how this rule works, we can return to the word *key.* Its Old English form *cǣg* developed from *kaig:* *ǣ* traces back to *ā,* which is, as usual, a later reflex of *ai.* Since Old Frisian *kāi,* the only cognate of *cǣg,* has nearly the same form and exactly the same meaning as the English noun, it provides no help in searching for the origin of the word. But in northern British dialects, the adjective *key* (twisted) (rhyming with *way*) has wide currency. It is related to Swedish dialectal *kaja* and Danish dialectal *kei* (the left hand) (the Standard Danish for the "left hand" is *kejte*) and appears in compounds, for example, *key-legged* (knock-kneed, crooked). *Key* (the adjective) and its congeners have the same root as *cater* in *cater-corner* (p. 45). "Left" and "crooked" are synonyms in many languages: what is right is right (that is, straight, correct), and what is left is twisted and threatening (compare Latin *sinister* [situated on the left side] and Engl. *sinister,* from Latin or French).

The implement called *cēg ~ kāi* must have been a stick (pin, peg) with a bent end. Borrowing from a remote language is less likely. Alongside **kaig-,* many words with the root **kag-* existed, and they also meant "stick, pin" (but hardly twisted, crooked, or bent) or objects made of pieces of wood. Such are Southern German *Kag* (stalk; cabbage stump), Norwegian *kage* (a low bush), Old Icelandic *kaggi* (cask) (the etymon of Engl. *keg*), and English dialectal *cag* (stump), from Scandinavian. Despite the similarity in form and meaning, **kaig-* and **kag-* are not related, because **ai* does not alternate with **a.*

A pseudo-cognate of the same type haunts the history of *oat*. Old Engl. *āte* meant "wild oats" *(avena fatua),* and its Middle English continuation meant the cultivated variety *(avena sativa).* (The phrase *to sow one's wild oats,* with reference to sowing weeds instead of good grain, surfaced in texts only at the end of the sixteenth century. Its inventor has not been found.) From wherever oat migrated to the Germanic speaking world, it must have been used both as fodder and for human consumption. The cognates of *āte* have been attested only in Frisian and in some Dutch dialects. A plant name of such limited geographical distribution may have been borrowed from a substrate language, though a reasonable Germanic etymology of the word exists too. We will leave the main question open and look at one detail only.

In Luke VI:1 (the Authorized Version), we read: "And it came to pass on the second Sabbath after the first, that he went through the corn fields; and his disciples plucked the ears of corn, and did eat, rubbing them in their hands." This verse is almost identical with Mark II:23. For *corn field* (that is, *grain field*), Gothic has *atisk,* in which *-isk* is a collective suffix. The *atisk* was a place in which *at-* grew, but whether oats or some other culture we do not know. *At-* would be an ideal match for *āte,* but the same barrier as between *key* and *cag* separates them: we assume that *āte* goes back to **aite-,* and **ai* is not a partner of **a* in any of the ablaut series.

The English word *heather* provides perhaps the most striking example of the **ai* ~ **a* dilemma: as far as we can judge, *heather* is not related to *heath*. The cognates of the latter are secure: German *Heide*, Dutch *heide*, Old Icelandic *heiðr* (*ð* = *th* in Engl. *this*), and Gothic *haiþi* (*þ* = *th* in Engl. *thin*). Their oldest root has **ai*. Contrary to *heath, heather* was first recorded only in the eighteenth century. However, in the fourteenth century, *hathir* emerged; its more recent forms are *hadyr, hather,* and the like, including *hether,* the etymon of *heather. Hathir* was originally confined to Scotland with the contiguous part of the English border, that is, to the region in which *heath* was unknown. It may be a borrowing from Scandinavian, though the most common Scandinavian word for "heather" is *lyng* (with some variants), and **haðr* did not turn up among its regional synonyms. The etymology of *Hadaland,* the old name of the Norwegian province now called Hadeland, is debatable. I believe it meant "Heatherland." If Scandinavian **haðr* existed and Middle English borrowed it, it was naturally associated with *heath* and -*r* was reinterpreted as the ending of the plural, typical of the Scandinavian languages, or as a suffix of plant names, as in *clover* and *madder.* Whatever the origin of *heather, heath* and *heather* should be disconnected, because we cannot bridge the gulf between *ai* and *a*. Perhaps there was a time when it became fashionable ("classy"?) to pronounce **ai* as **a,* or the alternation *ai* ~ *a,* impossible in Germanic, was inherited from a substrate language. No hard evidence supports either hypothesis.

Not only amateurs but also professional linguists rebel against the tyranny of sound correspondences. Excellent scholars tried to connect Old Icelandic *meta* "to measure" and *mót* "stamp, mark; manner" (*ó* = *ō*), as though *mót* were something marked off, estimated; Engl. *break,* from *brecan,* and *brook* (rivulet), from *brōc; lie* (to recline), from *licgan* (*cg* = *gg*), and Old Engl. *lōgian* (to place, arrange, settle) (thus: *metan – mōt, brecan – brōc,* and *licgan – lōgian*).[7] A glance at the inexorable scheme of ablaut will tell us that *ō* occurs only in Class VI and does not alternate with *e* or *i* (the series is *a – ō – ō – a*). Consequently, all such pairs have to be dismissed as unrelated. An association between them is secondary, as between *heath* and *heather.* According to one of the principles of word history mentioned in the previous chapter, a word has a better chance of staying in the language if it happens to end up in a "friendly" environment. No doubt, *heather* aligned itself with *heath* in the speakers' linguistic intuition, and, quite possibly, *licgan* and *lōgian* were felt to be cognates, but that feeling has nothing to do with origins. After years of living together, husband and wife begin to look like brother and sister; yet they had different parents.

Few etymologists are witty people. (Reading dead languages does not necessarily refine one's sense of humor.) They have a single great joke for all. Voltaire is reputed to have said that in etymology, vowels count for nothing and consonants for very little *(c'est une science où les voyelles ne font rien et les consonnes fort peu de chose).* The joke has been repeated hundreds of times. No one ever refers to the page in Voltaire's *Œvres* in which this dictum appears; it has long since become folklore. Voltaire may have said so but probably did not.[8] For a long time, doctors and etymologists were among the favorite objects of public ridicule. As we know, Swift laughed heartily at the attempts of his contemporaries to discover the origin of words, but he laughs best who laughs last. Today every vowel and every consonant counts. The discovery of sound correspondences turned etymology from intelligent and unintelligent guessing into a respectable branch of knowledge.

We could have finished on this self-congratulatory note if everything in language obeyed "sound laws" and if all such laws were equally sound. However, in the interplay of choice and chance that determines the life of words, phonetic algebra does not reign alone. Several troublesome cases have already been discussed (*cnafa ~ cnapa, flat ~ platús,* and so on). Sound correspondences are supposed to affect great layers of vocabulary, but some changes occur in a few words. They seem to be random and are therefore the hardest to explain. As stated above, *trigger* is a borrowing of Dutch *trekker* (puller). Even if we disregard the confusion between *e* and *i,* common in English dialects, the question remains why the English form is not *tricker.* The *Oxford English Dictionary* informs us that *tricker* was current until approximately the middle of the eighteenth century and is still in dialect use from Scotland to the English Midlands. Only two more Standard English words have *g* in place of etymological *k* between vowels: *flagon* and *sugar*.[9] Late Middle Engl. *flagon* occurred side by side with *flacon* (it is a Romance word). Likewise, Middle Engl. *suker*, also from French, coexisted with *sucre* and *sugre*. Both are relatively old borrowings into English, whereas the earliest recorded citation of *trecker* goes back to 1621, so that the voicing of *k* happened in the modern period.

The change from *tricker* to *trigger* may worry a student of historical phonetics, but it does not complicate an etymologist's work, for the identity of the word, despite its two forms, has not suffered. Other cases are less transparent. Skeat believed that *quib,* the root of *quibble,* is "a weakened form" of *quip* and that *hobble* (to walk unsteadily) is a frequentative form of *hop.* His derivations presuppose the change of *p* to *b* and of *pl* to *bl.* (*Hobble* [to fasten together the legs of a horse] does go back to *hopple.*) The *Oxford English Dictionary* disagrees on both counts, but *The Oxford Dictionary of English Etymology* admits that *dribble* (not related to but influenced in sense by *drivel*) is "a modified form of *drip + le.*" The phrases "a weakened form" and "a modified form" have no explanatory value: they are simply names given to an observable fact. (Compare what is said above about the phrases "obscurely related" and "of uncertain relationship.")

No "law" turns *-pl-* into *-bl-* in English, as the words *apple, topple, steeple, ripple,* and *tipple,* let alone *couple, supple,* and *triple* of Romance origin, show (however, *abble* [apple] has been recorded). An honest statement appears in *The Oxford Dictionary of English Etymology,* in the entry devoted to *nipple,* a noun whose early forms were also *neble* and *nible:* "The change from *b* to *p* is unexplained." Perhaps *nipple* is the diminutive of *nib ~ neb* (point)—*perhaps,* because reference to the sporadic devoicing of *b* makes this hypothesis unsafe. Surrounded by words like *dribble* and *quibble* on one side and Old Engl. *nypel* (the trunk of an elephant), Low German *nippen* (to sip), and the English verb *nip, nibble* has equal chances of being related to *nib* and to *nip.* Dictionaries and books on the history of English have nothing to say about how late Old Engl. *papel ~ popel* became *pebble. Pebble, dribble,* and so on, sound like English words pronounced by a Dane. We are faced with the useless rule: "Engl. *pl* sometimes alternates with and becomes *bl*." As long as the word's identity cannot be called into question (as was also the case with *tricker* ~ *trigger*), everything is fine, for no doubt arises that *pebble* is the continuation of *papel.* But the etymology of *hobble* and *nibble* is bound to remain debatable. The situation becomes even more difficult when words of different languages are compared and phonetic correspondences prove shaky.

In Chapter 4, mention was made of the sound symbolic value of the final consonant in *nudge, budge,* and so forth. Many English dialectal words referring to pushing, pulling, and a careless manner resemble *nudge,* with *nud* and *nug* being among them. Scots *dod* ~ *dodd* (to jog) seem to be akin to *dodge. Trudge* had the variants *tridge* and *tredge,* and it is tempting to relate them to *tread* and Gothic *trudan* (the same meaning), whose etymology, although uncertain, is known much better than that of *trudge.* But Engl. *d* is not supposed to alternate with *-dge,* except before *y* (pronounced as in *yes, you, yet).* Perhaps (again perhaps) *dodge* and *tredge* are expressive, reinforced forms of *dod* and *tread.* Sound symbolism, so obvious in living speech, is not the sharpest tool in etymology.

An observant reader could not help noticing a cavalier treatment of vowels in stringing together the variants *tridge* ~ *tredge* ~ *trudge.* We were so particular about not letting **a* and **ai* (Old Engl. *a* and *ā*) mix, and here suddenly everything goes. The reason is that sound laws and sound correspondences are not valid for all times. Like suffixes and prefixes, they can be productive or dead. At one time, Germanic *z* became *r,* but today we do not turn *easy* and *zip* into *eery* and *rip.* The principle governing alternations of vowels by ablaut was productive in a remote epoch. It has long since lost its productivity. A new verb like *snooze* or *peal* will not be conjugated **snooze* – **snozen* or **pole* – **polen* on the model or analogy of *choose* – *chosen* and *stole* – *stolen* (though in American English, *dove* ousted *dived* and joined *drove,* British *chode* at one time competed with *chided,* and earlier, *strive,* a French verb, was assigned to the same class: *strive* – *strove;* such forms are mere curiosities). It would not occur to anyone to say **pet* – **pot* – **pot(ten)* like *get* – *got* – *got(ten).*

The alternation *rab-* (in *rabbit*) ~ *rob* (as in the German animal name *Robbe* [seal]) is familiar from the previous chapters. In West Flemish, both *rabbe* and *robbe* mean "rabbit," and when a rabbit is called, people say: "ribbe, ribbe."[10] Examples of this type are plentiful. Thus, English words beginning with *t* and ending in *d* or *t*, especially common in dialects, designate small quantities, small objects, and the like. Almost any short vowel can occur between *t* and *d* ~ *t*. Here is an incomplete list of *t* – *d* ~ *t* words: *tid-* (as in *tidbit; titbit* also exists), *tod* "a small cake," *toddle* (a verb), *tud* (a very small person), *tad* (a very small boy), *tit* (a small horse), *tit-* as in *titmouse* and *tit for tat* (compare *tittle-tattle*), *tot* (anything very small; a tiny child); *tut* has numerous meanings, including "a small seat made of straw," and the interjection *tut-tut!* looks like one of the words listed above. To differentiate an uncontrollable alternation of vowels from the one subject to the strict rules going back to the Indo-European past, it was called secondary, or false, ablaut.[11]

Old words changed and were formed in English according to the six-class scheme, which means that *tod* – *tud* are not related quite in the same way as are *ride* – *rode* – *ridden* (and *road*). They are a set of words united by a common meaning and held together by a consonantal carcass, but in the absence of rigid "tracks," their appearance is less predictable and the ties among them are loose. An etymologist has a hard life when confronted with dozens of words like *tid* – *tad* – *tod* – *tud* in many languages.

The following story will show a combined use of secondary ablaut and of consonants defying Grimm's Law. We will tread (trudge) all the way from the pig to the poke and cross several language borders. The word *pig* seems to have existed in Old English, for *picbrēd* (mast, swinefood), literally "swinebread," possibly a misspelling of **pigbrēd*, turns up in a gloss, and a twelfth-century last name *Pigman* may have some relevance. The common Germanic word for *pig* was *swīn*. The recorded history of *pig* begins only in the thirteenth century (Middle Engl. *pigge*, a possible continuation of Old Engl. **pigga*; see p. 40, above). Its earliest meaning is "young of swine," a fact of no small importance, for some new animal names were apparently baby words, coined by or for the benefit of small children who played with chickens, puppies, kittens, "piglets," and calves. Mary had a little lamb at all times.

Next to *pig,* we see *pug.* Between 1566 and 1664, it turns up with the meanings "a short person, doll" (as a term of endearment), "imp, monkey, ape," and "a dwarf breed of dog." In dialects, it designates all kinds of small animals, including the fox, the rabbit, and the squirrel, but in towns, judging by *pug* "harlot" and, unexpectedly "bargeman," it became part of street slang. *Pugge* also existed in West Flemish as a substitute for any Christian name, a sort of *guy. Pug* (imp) is reminiscent of *Puck,* but "devil" was hardly the kernel from which the other senses developed. *Pig* is as enigmatic as *pug.* Older age lends it respectability, without making it any clearer from the etymological point of view.

Pig is isolated in Germanic unless Dutch *big* (pig) is brought into play. This quasi-cognate of Engl. *pig* is an embarrassment, because Engl. *p-* corresponds to *p-,* not *b-* in Dutch: compare the English verb *pick* and Dutch *pikken.* Sound laws suggest that the similarity between Engl. *pig* and Dutch *big* is due to chance, but such a coincidence is almost unbelievable. According to an opinion that goes back to the *Oxford English Dictionary,* the connection between Engl. *pig* and Dutch *big* "cannot be made out," because "the phonology is difficult." Dutch dictionaries list numerous side forms of *big,* namely *bik, bag, bagge,* and *pogge* (see what is said about *bacon* on pp. 152 and 154). One notes with growing unease that Low German has *pogge,* but it means "toad, frog," while Norwegian dialectal *bagg* is glossed as "a one-year-old calf," and Swedish *bagge* as "ram, wether" and "beetle, bug" (in compounds). Meanings and sounds are equally fluid in this group of words.

The next question is what Dutch *big* has to do with Engl. *big.* No records of Engl. *big* predate the thirteenth century. At that time, it meant "strong, stout"; the earliest examples are from northern texts, and this fact accords well with the preservation of final *-g. Big,* as we remember, is aberrant in that it contains *i* but means "large." Engl. dialectal *bug* (big) (compare Norwegian dialectal *bugge* [a strong man]) and *bog* (boastful) set the record straight. Dutch dialectal *bagge* and Norwegian dialectal *bag* make one think of Engl. *bag,* where-upon we find ourselves in an even deeper morass than before. Engl. *bag,* like *big,* may be of Scandinavian origin, whereas Old Icelandic *baggi* may have come from French, for Old French had *bague* (bundle), from which English got *baggage* (= *bague* + the suffix *-age*). The Romance noun may have been borrowed from Germanic. If so, then it is one of the words that entered French from Franconian and later returned home.

Young animals are often characterized as shapeless, "swollen" things, and when they grow up, some of them become huge, so again "swollen." There seems to have been a sound complex *b - g (big, bag, bug, bog)* meaning approximately "puffed up," a complex of the same order as *t - d* "small." *Big* was a near universal animal name, applied most often to pigs, but occasionally a ram could be called a *big,* and among the 77 names of a hare (all of them uncom-plimentary), listed in a late-thirteenth-century English poem, one is *bigge.*[12] *Bog* (boastful) is an obvious case of "puffed up." *Big* (pig) and *big* (strong, stout; large) are, from the etymological viewpoint, indistinguishable.

The problem of *p- ~ b-* is duplicated in the history of *baggi,* for *bag* and *baggage* alternate with *pack* and *package.* While Engl. *bag* is credited with Scandinavian ancestry, *pack* is believed to be a bor-rowing from Flemish. German *Pack,* Icelandic *pakki,* Italian *pacco,* and their analogs may also be of Flemish origin. We keep stumbling against the fateful *b- ~ p-* threshold. Are *bag* and *pack* related? And what about other similar words, all of which denote "swollen" ob-jects? Not only *pack* but also *pock* (pustule) (compare *pox = pock + s* and *smallpox), poke,* and *pocket* belong here. If we are dealing with baby words, phonetic laws have hardly any power over their produc-tion. A child's creations like *pooh-pooh, pooga-pooga,* or *booga-booga* are immune to those laws, and adults, to the extent that they appropriate *pooh-pooh* and their kin, end up with neologisms that can come into fashion in any place at any time. Very little children speak a universal language: babbling has no dialects.

As noted earlier, Dutch dialectal *pogge* means "pig," whereas Low German *pogge* means "toad, frog." Frogs are famous for being able to make themselves swell up, and in Aesop's fable, a frog bursts trying to emulate a bull. If it had known how close *pogge* is to *bagge* (which, let it be repeated, means "ram" in Swedish), it might have stopped worrying. More disorienting is the circumstance that the English counterpart of Low German *pogge* is *pad* (or *paddock; -ock* is a suffix, as in *bullock* and *hillock*). Are they also related? The question is not about the real world in which Steve and Tom, unbeknownst to themselves, turn out to be cousins and have a family reunion but about the limits of linguistic patience.

It is a tremendous concession to chaos to say that Dutch *big* and Engl. *pig,* let alone Low German *pogge* and Engl. *pad,* are related. The bond between Engl. *father* and Latin *pater* is of a different type: those words are traceable to a protoform, whereas *big* and *pig* are not. But refusing to budge will leave us repeating that the connection between Engl. *pig* and Dutch *big* cannot be made out (and it will never be made out), that *pack* may be akin to *bag,* but the change from *b* to *p* (or from *p* to *b*) has not been explained, and that Low German *pogge* and Engl. *pad(dock)* are obscurely related, are of uncertain relationship, or are of unknown origin. Several dozen words in Germanic and Romance begin with *p* or *b* and end in *k, g,* or *d* (to mention only the consonants that have been discussed here) and refer to bundles, swellings, and animals understood as swollen things. They arose as baby words (or so it seems), influenced one another, traveled from country to country, and merged with the native background. The details are lost, but the outlines of the process are not beyond reconstruction.

Pig, big, pogge, and *pad* are not the only members of this union. First of all, various bugs attract our attention. A bug is an object of dread, something that bugs us, makes us ill, ruins our telephones and computers. It frightens people, because it can acquire prodigious dimensions and become BIG. *Big bug* has been recorded with the meaning "an important person." In dialects, the adjective *bug* (swaggering, pompous) is known. *Bog* (boastful) is almost the same word. Middle Engl. *bigg* (rich) existed, too. A lot of swell fellows have been called *big(g)* over the centuries. In the Scandinavian languages, numerous nouns, verbs, and adjectives with the root *bag- ~ bāg-* refer to various harmful and unpleasant things. They are glossed as "to torment, pester, press; hinder, hamper," "trouble(s)," "cripple; fool, shrew; resistance, struggle." Old High German *bāga* (strife, fight, quarrel) is related to them. Engl. *bug* has a sizable following: *bugaboo, bugbear, bogey, boggard* (archaic), and so forth. These (hob)goblins (one is almost tempted to write *boglins)* boggle the mind not only of benighted rustics but also of unimpressionable etymologists who would not know a ghost when they saw one. Engl. *bogey,* Welsh *bwg(an),* Russian *buka* (pronounced '*bookah*), along with Engl. *Puck* and German *Butz,* exist in gleeful defiance of linguistic borders and sound laws, as specters and apparitions should.

A *bug* is of course also a beetle and, in American English, any insect. Bugs, especially bedbugs, swell famously. Strangely, the Old English form was not **bugga* but *budda.* Buds resemble bugs, and in spring they also swell. Confused by the arbitrariness of sound changes, we turn to *The Oxford Dictionary of English Etymology.* Under *bud[1]* we are told that this word was recorded only in the fourteenth century, when its forms were *bodde* and *budde,* and that it is of unknown origin. "The synon[ymous] M[iddle] Du[tch] *botte,* Du[tch] *bot* cannot be connected." The editor of the dictionary chose not to get over the -*d* and -*t* hurdle *(bud ~ bot).* Engl. *bud* is akin to Old Saxon *būdil* (bag, purse) (= German *Beutel;* Old Saxon is a Germanic language close to Old English and Middle Dutch), and it would be strange if Dutch *bot* were unrelated to it. If Low German *pogge* (frog, toad) belongs with Engl. *pad(dock),* then *bug* and *bud* form a group, too. Those curious about Romance parallels are invited to look up *button* and *bottle* in etymological dictionaries and compare Engl. *pudding* with its French synonym *boudin.*

Still other words with ties to the *pig* family have *n* in the root. Not only *poke,* a variant of *pouch,* but also Old Engl. *pung* means "small bag, sack, purse." "Harlot, prostitute" was one of the meanings of *pug* in seventeenth-century English. Predictably, the earliest recorded meaning of *punk* (the chronological range in the *Oxford English Dictionary* is 1596–1781) was "strumpet." *Punk* must have been the name of a swollen thing and a low-class person, as follows from the occurrence of this noun in Scandinavian languages and dialects, in which it designates multifarious junk and occasionally stands for "thingy." Engl. *punk* lay dormant for a century and a half and then re-emerged in American English to conquer the world in recent memory.

By taking one step at a time, we progressed from *pig* to *big,* from *big* to *bug,* from *bug* to *bud* and by another road from *pig* to *pogge* and from *pogge* to *pad.* English, Dutch, German, Scandinavian, Welsh, Russian, and Romance words form an underground culture, like the subculture of punks, not bothered by its lack of recognition and showing no concern for sound correspondences. It is no wonder that circumspect researchers prefer to say that the origin of each of those words is obscure or unknown. No one is in a hurry to return to eighteenth-century etymology with its dead-end *laissez-faire.* Yet we are bound to admit the rivalry of two types of word families. The first type is aristocratic, and its members can be counted. Consider Latin *pater,* Greek *patēr,*[13] Sanskrit *pitár,* Gothic *fadar,* and so on ("father"). The other is plebeian and amorphous. Its members look as though they are related, but their kinship is loose, and their number is hard to determine. Such words are like creeping plants without a clear starting point and lacking direction. Where we think we have detected one family, there can be several: *pig – pug – pogge, big – bug – bag – bog, bud – pad* or perhaps *pig – big, pug – bug, pogge – bog,* with *bud* and *pad* being outsiders. What matters is not the minutiae but the disturbing fact that such multitudes exist and flourish. The plebeians are, as always, more vital and more aggressive. More about them will be said in Chapter 16.

Language teems with *tid – tad – tod – tud* formations. They do not abolish sound correspondences; they do not even weaken the great pronouncement of nineteenth-century philologists that "sound laws" (or established sound correspondences) admit no exceptions. Latin *pater* is indeed a legitimate congener of Engl. *father,* whereas Latin *fēmina* cannot be related to Old Engl. *fœmne,* and Latin *trahere,* Dutch *trekken,* and Engl. *drag* give us pause, precisely because their consonants do not match. Likewise, to the best of our knowledge, *heath* is not akin to *heather* on account of **ai ~ *a,* which belong to non-overlapping ablaut series and are therefore not allowed to alternate in one and the same ancient root. If we make light of the ruthless sound laws, we will find ourselves in the epoch of Swift. Those laws are valid as long as we deal with protoforms and their continuations. But big pigs and toddling tots, onomatopoeias, and sound symbolic words are not part of Indo-European heritage, and we have an imperfect understanding of the rules that govern their emergence, proliferation, and spread. Yet those rules can be studied and grasped. It would be unrealistic to expect that we know everything about the immense complexity of language.

Sound laws can be broken deliberately. Human beings have always (and rightly) believed in the power of speech. In some languages, the words for "doctor, healer," and "speak" are derived from the same stem. At one time, people believed that knowing someone's name gave them power over that person and that certain creatures and objects should not be mentioned for fear of damaging them or bringing out the evil inherent in them. Therefore, designations of the parts of the body, diseases, and physical deformities are among the toughest etymological cruces: sounds were often scrambled in them, and we cannot reconstruct the words' original form.

The same type of taboo affected animals: call a wolf or a bear by its name, and it will come, but say "honey-eater" (so in Russian: *medved'*; stress on the second syllable) or "the brown one" (so in Germanic: *bear* is, most likely, related to *brown*), and the euphemism will deceive the beast. A curious assortment of forms meets us when we examine the cognates of *flea* (Old Engl. *flēah,* from **flauh-*): Greek *psýlla,*[14] Latin *pūlex,* Old Slavic *blukha,* and Lithuanian *blusà.* They resemble one another but do not match: Greek *ps-*, Latin *p-*, Slavic and Baltic *bl,* as well as *lu* alternating with *ul.* English dictionaries assert that *flea* is related to *flee,* but this is probably folk etymology. The other interpretation is more convincing: whatever the ancient name of the insect may have been, speakers seem to have changed it (transposed syllables and altered sounds) in the hope of keeping fleas away. The efficacy of this measure can no longer be assessed.

Proper names are a regular playground. How did *Margaret* become *Peg*? An amateur who coyly signed his letters to the editor with a Greek pseudonym, suggested in 1850 the progression from

Margaret to *Madge, Meggy, Meg, Peggy,* and *Peg* on account of "the natural affinity" between *m* and *p*. As proof, he cited other similar cases: *Martha – Matty – Patty* and *Mary – Molly – Polly – Poll*.[15] It would be nice to pity the man's mid-nineteenth-century ignorance and naiveté, but he was probably right. Modern specialists in onomastics (the study of names) are unable to offer a better explanation. The other changes, also mentioned in the letter, are no less erratic: *Richard* (~ *Rick*) ~ *Dick; William* (~ *Will*) ~ *Bill; Christopher* (~ *Chris/Kris*) ~ *Kit;* and *Robert* (~ *Rob*) ~ *Bob.* I have added intermediate links in parentheses. The alternation *r* ~ *h* in men's names (*Rob* ~ *Hob, Rick* ~ *Hick*) is almost a "law," and an attempt has been made to explain it on phonetic grounds (see p. 101).

The more linguists learned about living speech, the more skeptical they grew about sound laws. After the inebriation caused by the discoveries of the nineteenth century, came a hangover. Students of dialects listed numerous words that preserved unshifted consonants and "wrong" vowels. New settlers, it was shown, mixed with the native population, and hybrid forms emerged, with a consonant of one dialect and a vowel of another. Apparently, the same things have happened throughout history. A bird's eye view of language change yielded to detailed maps. By now we have seen the terrain from above and around us. The task consists of combining both pictures. All etymologists will agree to work toward this aim, for even the most vociferous critics of exceptionless sound laws, when they come to their students, begin their first lecture by writing *pater – father* on the blackboard and explaining the immortal truth of that equation.

Chapter Fifteen

in which nothing means what it says, or

Change of Meaning
in Language History

Meanings are as unstable as sounds.—From the concrete to the abstract.—Words narrow their meanings.—Words broaden their meanings.—What was bad and wrong is now good and right.—What was good and right is now bad and wrong.—What was neither bad nor good is now either one or the other.—Attitudes change, meanings follow suit.—Metonymy and metaphor.—From a couch to a couch potato and other horror stories.—One word or two?—"Bow to the board."—Words meaning the opposite of what they used to mean and words combining two opposite meanings.—An unfulfilled dream of regular semantic laws.—Reasoning from analogy.—110 ways of beating one up and the importance of this fact for etymology.—The second summing up.—Phonetics and semantics at cross-purposes.—On words and things for the next to last time.

The few attempts to penetrate the history of *fǣmne* recounted in Chapter 14, teach a student of etymology an important lesson: in looking for cognates, language historians follow both synonyms and sense associations: from "woman" to "milk" or to "shepherdess," or to "a new member of a group (family)." Such travels scare away the uninitiated, but they are not capricious, even if often misguided. The path from *Zeus* to *Týr* is a product of reconstruction, for only two points on a line are given in direct observation. The development of meaning can often be retraced step by step. The examples in this chapter will show what adventures await the etymologist in the area of historical semantics.

Almost every meaning can become more specialized or expand its volume. It can also engender other meanings through associations that appear natural only in retrospect. Words designating such general concepts as love, hatred, and fear usually refer, in the beginning, to concrete sensations. For instance, *anger* is a Scandinavian word in English (Old Icelandic *angr*). It first meant "affliction" and is related to Old Engl. *enge* (narrow; vexed, anxious; painful; cruel) and Latin *angor* (strangling; distress) (compare Latin *angina pectoris* [a spasm of the chest]). The starting point must have been "the sensation one experiences when being throttled or finding oneself in a narrow place." Latin *angustia* (straitness) (in the plural, "straits, distress") reached English as *anguish,* via Old French. The answer about the original meaning of *anger* ~ *angr* ~ *angor* came from the adjective *enge,* not from looking at a string of synonyms for "hot displeasure."

A similar procedure works for the etymology of *speed.* Here internal reconstruction shows us the way (see p. 159 on internal reconstruction). Among the meanings of *speed,* "success, prosperity" has been preserved in the Standard in the phrases *to wish good speed (to)* and *God send (give) you good speed.* This is an archaic meaning. Old Engl. *spēd,* from **spōdi,* belongs to a large family of words that refer to long time, large areas, and realizing one's potential (compare German *spät* [late], Latin *spatium* [space], and Old Engl. *spōwan* [to thrive] ~ Old Slavic *spēti* [to thrive, mature]). Their probable congeners are nouns and verbs denoting movement toward reaching one's goal, such as Latin *spēs* (hope) and Old Slavic *spēti* (to hasten). Each of the Modern Germanic languages retains a fragment or two of that wealth. In English, *speed* means only "rapidity," without suggesting why one should be in a hurry or what awaits "the speeder" at the end of the way.

Other abstract concepts are war and peace, and they, too, tend to go back to more concrete ones. German *Krieg* at first designated any commotion, Dutch *oorlog* is associated with words for fate, destiny, and the disruption of order. Latin *bellum* goes back to **duellum,* that is, to the idea of a duel, a combat between two parties, while French *guerre,* Italian *guerra,* and Spanish *guerra* (as in *guerrilla*) are Germanic *werra* in Romance guise (compare *ward* ~ *guard,* above, p. 154). The Germanic word has the same root as Engl. *wor-se,* German *Wirrwarr* (confusion), and German *(ver)wirren* (to confuse).

Confusion is thus the underlying idea of *war*. On the other hand, the notion of peace can develop from such concepts as "communal living" and "union." Latin *pax,* which, via French, yielded Middle Engl. *pais ~ pes* (Modern Engl. *peace*) and ousted the native word *frith* (compare German *Frieden*), is believed to be related to Latin *pangere* (to join), *pāgus* (community), and *pāgina* (strips of papyrus fastened together; page) (whence, of course, Engl. *page,* also from French). The development was from "a united group" to "the freedom from strife." *Rest* is like *peace.* Its original meaning was concrete. In the biblical verse: "Whosoever shall compel thee to go a mile, go with him twain" (Matthew V: 41, the Authorized Version), Gothic has *rasta* for "mile." In Old Saxon, *rasta* meant "resting place; grave," in Old High German, "peace, rest," in Old Engl. *ræset,* "repose, sleep; resting place, bed, couch; grave." Here the development must have been from "a stage of the journey, stretch of the way" to "a distance between two resting places," "resting place," and "peace, repose."

The changes we have observed so far have been from "throttling" to "hot displeasure," from "great dimensions" to "success" and "rapidity," from "confusion, commotion" to "war," and from "a united group" to "peace." A comprehensive dictionary of such changes has not been written, though it would be of inestimable value. The etymologist turning to the history of an unexplored word for "anger, wrath, vexation, displeasure," for example, would have looked at the development of meaning recorded in the languages of the world and would have probably found an illuminating precedent.

In addition to becoming more abstract, words often narrow their meaning, that is, become more specialized. The ancestor of *meal* designated "a thing measured," still felt in *piecemeal* (one piece at a time, gradually), and could refer to both space and time, though reference to time predominated ("occasion, season"). "Time for eating" was only one of the senses of Old Engl. *mæl,* but it must have played a greater role than we can imagine today, for it soon suppressed its rivals. The way from "time for eating" to "the food served," with time not even implied ("a solid meal," "three meals a day"), was short, and the compound *mealtime,* a tautological word from the historical point of view (almost "time time"), came into being.

Unlike *meal, season* is an example of a word that has become less specialized in its application. Latin *satiō(n)* (time for sowing) eventually developed into the name for any period (*-n* in parentheses is part of the ending of the accusative: most Latin words continued their existence in the Romance languages in this form). Difficulties arise when we try to understand how *seasoning* (addition of spices) fits the picture and why the Italian equivalent of French *saison* is *stagione.* Italian *stagione* goes back to Latin *statio(n)* "station" (from which Italian also has *stazione)* "the point occupied by the sun in relation to the signs of the zodiac"; hence "a period of seeming immobility." Although the etymon of *season* is Latin *satio,* French *saison* and Engl. *season* seem to combine the meanings of both Latin *satio* and *statio.* The Old French verb *saisonner* (Modern French *assaisonner*) meant "to add flavor" in the earliest texts. The progression may have been from "become adapted to a climate (season)" to "accustom," "bring to the best state for use" (compare *to season wood, timber*), and to "render more agreeable, render palatable, give a higher relish by adding condiments."

In a word that has existed for millennia, meaning can broaden and then narrow: there is enough time for going back and forth. Presumably, both processes have occurred in the long history of *hold.* All the meanings of this verb can be subsumed under "keep," but its earliest recorded sense was "to tend cattle." In Old English, *heorde haldan* (to graze [keep] herds) has been attested, and similar phrases turn up in other Germanic languages. If, as is usually believed, *hold* is akin to Latin *celer* (swift, rapid), the development was from "run fast, drive" (in general) to "follow flocks" and "tend, graze cattle." But this is no more than a conjecture. In any case, later, the process went in the opposite direction: from the specific meaning "take care of a herd" to "watch, guard" (compare *behold* [to watch, look from "keep, retain"]) and to "possess, maintain," perhaps under the influence of some other verb or verbs.

Caught by a stream of consciousness, I would like to devote a few lines to the history of *condiment.* It may not be immediately obvious that *condiment* is an almost exact equivalent of *preservative* (as in "no preservatives added"). Latin *condīre,* from which *condimentum* was formed, meant "to pickle, embalm; preserve." In the past, the main condiments were salt (for it prevents food from spoiling) and herbs. Later, condiments were associated with spices. But it so happened that Medieval Latin *conditor* (one who makes spicy [= tasty] dishes; a purveyor of spices) crossed the path of Old Italian *zucchero condito* (cane sugar) (from Arabic *sukkar qandī*), whence French *sucre candi* and Engl. *sugar candy*. In English, *condiment* and *candy* did not affect each other, but a German *Konditorei* sells all kinds of sweets and pastry; it should have been called *Kanditorei*.

None of the changes of meaning mentioned here (from concrete to abstract, narrowing, and broadening) has been accompanied by the change of attitude toward the object named. We know that strangulation, being in a tight spot, anger, confusion, and war are bad, whereas success is good, but our knowledge is the result of our experience; it has nothing to do with language. Seasons, meals, running fast, following flocks, and possessing something are neither good nor bad in and of themselves. But many words reflect people's view of the world: to be stupid, miserly, and fickle is bad, contrary to being clever, generous, and loyal. Each of the six epithets carries an emotional charge. Time and again, words denoting neutral concepts begin to refer to praiseworthy qualities and desirable things (this is called the amelioration of meaning), or the sign is reversed (from plus to minus; or occasionally from minus to plus).

Two instances of amelioration are *fond* and *nice*. Obscurity envelops the early history of *fond*. This adjective, which may be allied to *fun* but is not connected with *fawn,* looks like the past participle of a little-known Middle English verb meaning "to lose savor." However, **fonned* may never have existed. *Wretched* and *wicked* also resemble participles, yet they are not related to any verbs. In *fond,* sense development was from "foolish" to "having a strong liking." In Shakespeare, *fond* means "foolishly affectionate" (an epithet King Lear applies to himself), "trifling, trivial," and "eager." Later, all the negative overtones disappeared. One can now be fond of music and be a fond (doting) husband without making a fool of oneself. Latin *nescius* (not knowing, ignorant) yielded Old French *nice* (silly, simple-minded), which passed through the stages "foolish; shy; subtle, dainty;

appetizing; agreeable," until it acquired the familiar present-day meaning "delightful, pleasant." In connection with *nice, tidy* can be mentioned. *Tide* must originally have meant the same as Icelandic *tíð* and German *Zeit,* that is, "time." But as early as the thirteenth century, we find *tidy* (in good condition, not *"timely" or *"seasonable").

Either because it is easier to fall and run to seed than to fly high and thrive, or because people are more inclined to scold and belittle others than to praise and admire them, examples of semantic deterioration seem to occur with greater frequency than those showing amelioration.[1] An instructive case is the decline of the adjective *mean.* In the course of a few decades of the twentieth century, the epithet *elitist* became a term of abuse. Yet throughout history, those things have been considered contemptible and offensive which can be "pawed over by the canaille," to use Jack London's phrase. The Germanic cognates of *mean,* including German *gemein,* may be glossed as "common"; compare German *Gemeinschaft* (community). But German *gemein* is also "base, nasty," whence *Gemeinheit* (meanness, vulgarity). The root of *gemein* (preserved in Gothic *ga-mains* and Latin *com-mūnis*) (to [ex]change), with the implication of "passing through many hands, shared by a multitude," had the sense "treacherous, false" already in the ancient epoch, as follows from Old Engl. *mān* (crime, sin; bad; false oath, perjury), a counterpart of German *Meineid* (*Eid* [oath]). The fortunes of the borrowed adjective *common* have been similar: from "belonging to *or* shared by many" to "ordinary, of inferior quality," and the same is true of *vulgar* from L *vulgus* (the public, crowd) and, by extension, "rabble." Since antiquity the prevailing point of view has been militantly elitist. Hence the way from "belonging to all" to "base."

(By way of compensation, it can be mentioned that keeping to oneself is no good, either. Greek *idiótes*[2] meant "a private person, one not engaged in public affairs; one without professional knowledge, a layman" and "an ignorant, uneducated person." It entered Latin, continued into French, and appeared in thirteenth-century English as "idiot," though "an ignorant person, clown" was recorded some time later—a sad process of deterioration from "a private individual" to "a natural fool." The root *idio-* [peculiar, personal] looks harmless in *idiom* and *idiosyncrasy*, but students are amused when they come across the bookish German word *Idiotikon* [a dialectal dictionary]. Being "native," that is, natural, is another defect, judging by its modern reflex *naive*, from French, from Latin *nativus*.)

Knaves, like idiots, knew better days. Old Engl. *cnafa* meant "boy; male servant" (its German cognate is *Knabe* [boy]³). The dissolution of medieval knighthood brought about the change from "servant" to "villain." Knaves were originally squires, knights' young attendants. The collapse of chivalric institutions resulted in the degradation of squires, who found themselves unemployed and became part of the urban riffraff, whence the catastrophic shift of meaning. Only the lowest court card of a suit reminds us of the respectable status knaves once enjoyed in society.

Less trivial is the history of Germanic **wrakjō-* (the word from which Kluge derived French *garçon*). Its meaning improved in one language and deteriorated in another. The English continuation of **wrakjo-* is *wretch*, related to *wreak*, as in *wreak one's vengeance* (to take revenge). A **wrakjō* was a banished person, and no misfortune seemed worse than exile. Thus German *elend* (miserable) is the disguised compound *eli-lenti* (being outside one's land), from *eli-*, a cognate of Engl. *el-se*. However, in Middle High German, this word was upgraded, and *recke* began to mean "a hero" and even "a giant" (properly, "a solitary warrior, adventurer," the precursor of the knight errant), whereas English produced *wretch* (an unhappy *or* despicable creature). (Compare the development of Latin *captivus* [captive] to French *chétif* [wretched]; Engl. *caitiff* [villain], from thirteenth-century French, also first meant "prisoner, poor wretch.")

As long as we stay with words pertaining to the structure of medieval society, mention can be made of *knight*. It shows how the changing conditions of life and especially changing attitudes toward social institutions influence the meaning of words. *Knight* is a cognate of German *Knecht*, at one time a synonym of *Knabe* (boy, youngster), later, "squire" and "mercenary." The compound *Landsknecht* (mercenary) had some currency beyond the borders of the German-speaking area. Modern German-English dictionaries gloss *Knecht* as "servant;

laborer." The German for *knight* is *Ritter,* that is, "horse rider, horseman." Ernest Weekley summarized the relationship between *knight* and *Knecht* in an elegant way (his abbreviations are expanded below): "In English the word has risen as *knave* has fallen, while German *knecht,* formerly soldier (see *lansquenet*), has now reverted to original servile sense." Weekley's entry *lansquenet* (mercenary soldier, card game) is so little known that I will reproduce part of it, too: . . . *landsknecht,* soldier of the country, 'land's knight', originally contrasted with Swiss mercenaries. . . . Often *lanzknecht, lance-knight,* as though from *lance,* and thus wrongly explained by Scott, *Quentin Durward,* ch. xvii." The spelling *lansquenet* bears a visible trace of the word's sojourn in France, but *lanzknecht,* with *z* in the middle, is proof of an early intrusion of folk etymology also in German: the German for *lance* is *Lanze.*

Perhaps the best-known victims of social degradation attended by linguistic deterioration are *churl* (Old Engl. *ceorl* [a free man without rank]), once synonymous with "man" and "husband," and *villain,* originally "villein," almost the same as "villager" ("a feudal serf, a peasant cultivator in subjection to a lord"), despised by aristocrats, who were partly urban and urbane, for being rustics (Latin *rūs* [village]). *Rustic* still means "boorish, uncouth, unsophisticated," as opposed to *rural,* with its associations of far-from-the-madding-crowd tranquility. Berserks (the semi-legendary troops of early Norwegian kings) and vikings (Scandinavian raiders who once enjoyed the greatest respect of their countrymen) mean only "robbers, violent criminals, and marauders" in later narratives. They went the way of all outdated military flesh: knaves, wretches, and other warriors of that ilk.

We can now turn to less combustible subjects. German *Knabe* no longer means "servant," but other than that, it has not changed since the twelfth century when it was first recorded. Sometimes a word attested in the Middle Ages in two languages does not stay intact in either and, surprisingly, acquires the same or approximately the same negative meaning in both. This is what happened to the adjective *slight* in English and German. Its original meaning was "smooth; of light texture," not "small in amount, of little importance." The negative overtones probably developed from the association between "smooth" and "level to the ground," that is, through either "low" or "accessible to all, common" (again "common"). German has *schlicht* (simple) and *schlecht* (bad), related to each other and to *slight*. The verb *slight* also meant "to make smooth *or* level" before it acquired its figurative sense "to treat contemptuously," first recorded in Shakespeare.

It is dangerous to be smooth, but being slanting is no better, for what is slanting and sloping (that is, oblique, not straight) may be unsteady. Middle Low German *slim(m)* and Middle Dutch *slim(p)* meant "slanting." When applied to humans, this adjective acquired partly positive connotations: "cunning, wily" rather than "crooked." In Modern Dutch, *slim* is ambiguous: "artful, crafty" and "cunning, sly." In any case, it is not an unqualified term of abuse. In the seventeenth century, the Dutch word was borrowed into English, and one of its recorded senses is "small, slight; of little substance; poor." To this day, we say *slim evidence, slim hopes,* and *slim chances of success* (compare *with slender success,* now outdated). The *Oxford English Dictionary* records two examples of *slim* (malicious), said about jokes (1668 and 1681), but from the start (the earliest citation goes back to 1657), Engl. *slim* meant "gracefully thin"—an incredible amelioration of meaning, for we could have expected the progression toward *"lean, meager, emaciated." This change is all the more astounding because in German, in which *slimp ~ slimb* once meant "slanting, oblique," *schlimm* means only "bad, wicked." Thus, from "slanting" to "cunning" (Dutch), "insignificant, slight," hence "thin, graceful" (English), and "bad" (German). In an age obsessed with dieting, one is complimented on a slim waist, but not too long ago being corpulent and buxom signified social weight and attractiveness. Who would admire Mr. Pickwick if he were "gracefully thin"?

The names of enviable qualities not infrequently have less than semantically pleasing roots; they are like flowers bursting into bloom on rubbish. If, for the sake of the argument, we agree that being cunning and crafty ("slim") is not an unconditionally bad thing *(schlimm), smart* will be an analog, and a more convincing one, for this is a case of dramatic amelioration. Words designating "clever" and "clear" are often metaphors with the original sense "cutting." Compare *incisive, penetrating, sharp*. But *smart* developed from "painful," as follows from both German *Schmerz* (pain) and the English verb *smart* (to suffer severely). One can observe the consecutive steps of the development: "biting; vigorous; brisk; prompt, quick." The leap from "causing pain" to "intelligent" (= "sharp") would cause distrust, if it were part of a reconstruction, but this leap is a fact. *Slim (slimp, slimb)* (slanting) has not only risen in one language ("astute; sagacious and sly") and fallen in another ("bad"). It has forfeited its direct meaning and yielded it to several metaphorical ones, which are neither broader, more narrow, more concrete, nor more abstract than "slanting," unless we decide that every metaphorical meaning is broader than its literal source by definition. Metaphor (the transference of a name by perceived analogy), metonymy (the substitution of the name of an attribute for the name of a thing), and synecdoche (*pars pro toto* [part for the whole] or vice versa) are among the most powerful motors of semantic change. An etymologist is constantly on the lookout for them, trying to peel off later layers of meaning from a recorded form.

Latin *penna* meant "feather." Quills were made from feathers, then metal nibs were invented, but the old name remained and survived the introduction of fountain and ballpoint pens. Old Engl. *spōn* meant "sliver, chip, shaving," and so did its Germanic cognates. Old Icelandic *spánn ~ spónn* also meant an object made from slivers, namely "spoon." The Modern English word retains the phonetic shape of its etymon, but it owes its meaning to Scandinavian. Authors of books on the growth of vocabulary and vicissitudes of words enjoy discussing phrases like *plastic silverware*.

Metonymy, sometimes in combination with metaphor, can take a word in almost any direction. A case in point is a group of borrowings with the root *temp-*. *Tempest, tempo,* and so on go back to *temp-*, as in Latin *tempus* (time). But the meaning of the root does not provide sufficient information on the meaning of the derivatives. *Tempo, temporal,* and *temporary* need no explanation, whereas ties between "time" and the group *temper, temperament,* and *temperature* are hard to discern. We are reminded of the fact that one and the same word may have a neutral, a positive, and a negative meaning. Thus weather can be good or bad: Engl. *weather* is neutral, Old Engl. *weder* usually meant "storm," and its Slavic counterpart *vedro* meant only "good weather." Likewise, Latin *tempus,* in addition to "time," could designate "good *or* bad time." Apparently, Latin *temperāre* had positive connotations and referred to mingling things in due proportion, whereas *tempestas* combined the senses "season, period" and "bad time, storm." That is why *temperate* (moderate) and *tempest* ended up at the opposite ends of the semantic spectrum. As in phonetics: step by step (from *pig* to *big,* from *big* to *bug,* and so on) we progress here from "time" to "good time," from "good time" to "moderate" or from "time" to "bad time," and from "bad time, rough times" to "a violent storm." Or we can stay in the middle *(temperature).* To be sure, in these shifts, suffixes played a noticeable role.

The ways of metonymy are unpredictable, because every object has an infinite number of attributes. Consider the history of *poltroon* (a spiritless coward, a mean-spirited wretch), in which we may be able to observe the development from "a piece of furniture" to "a person attached to it." This rare and bookish word in the modern language reached English from French, where Rabelais was the first to use it *(poltron).* In French it is from Italian *(poltrone* means "idler," while *poltrona* means "a lazy woman" and "an easy chair," not unlike *poltro* [bed]). Perhaps at one time, Italians borrowed *poltrone ~ poltrona* from German: German *Polster* "cushion" (a cognate of Engl. *bolster*) sounds somewhat like *poltrone.* If so, a poltroon was originally a couch and a couch potato, and the riddle is solved. But contemporary etymologists prefer to trace French *poltron* to **pulliter,* from Latin *pullus* [a young animal]" via Vulgar Latin. This is also a reasonable approach, except that foals, although timorous creatures, are neither cowardly nor lazy. A "fearful animal" becoming "a craven" is hard to imagine. Some difficulties will go away if we note that animal names are easily transferred to all kinds of objects (compare *horse* [a gymnastic device] and *ram* [a battering device]). From **pulliter* French has *poutre* (rafter, beam), the embodiment of immobility. The association must have been between a rafter and a lying, resting, rather than shy, horse. From the historical perspective, *poltrone* (foal and "idler") were the same word. Either way, the earliest poltroons seem to have been lie-in-beds, and sloth, as we know, is the mother of vice.

Both a series of short steps and one magnificent leap can take meaning so far that a word falls apart. Are *poltrona* (a lazy woman) and *poltrona* (an easy chair) two meanings of the same Italian word, or homonyms? In dealing with several languages, we avoid this problem, because, for example, Dutch *slim,* Engl. *slim,* and German *schlimm* ended up in different dictionaries, but etymologists view the entire nest and wonder whether they need to offer three etymologies for three words or whether perhaps two or even one will suffice.

The situation with *poltrona* is typical. For example, the two modern meanings of *nail* (a covering of the finger or toe and "a metal spike") were already known in Old English and Old High German *(nægl, nagal).* Old Icelandic had *nagl* (finger nail) and *nagli* (spike), but the distinction, whenever it arose, must have been due to the speakers' wish to separate the homonyms by grammatical means (*nagl* and *nagli* belong to different declensions). Since people needed words for body parts before they invented metal spikes, the meaning "a covering of the finger or toe" should be viewed as primary and "spike" as a product of metaphor. The most illuminating cognate of *nail* is Old Church Slavonic *noga* (leg) (*nog-a;* Germanic **naglaz* is **nag-l-az,* so that the root is the same, with a regular alternation between non-Germanic *o* and Germanic *a*). Apparently, Indo-European **nog-* designated something elongated and hard, and indeed, we find words meaning "hoof" and "claw" among the cognates of *nail*. A human nail hardly resembles a metal spike, but it is enough to substitute *claw* or *talon* for it, to see the connection. Thus we succeeded in finding the same etymon for *nail[1]* and *nail[2],* the words that, from the semantic point of view, are far apart in the modern language and have been homonyms for thousands of years. Our dictionaries list them as two meanings of the same word. Only etymological considerations make them do so.

However controversial the treatment by dictionary makers of the word *nail* may be, this noun has only two meanings, a circumstance that facilitates the etymologist's task. As a rule, in researching the history of words, we encounter a welter of meanings, most of them probably metaphorical. This is what appears in the entry *litter:* "scattered rubbish," "a number of young brought forth by a pig, cat, etc. at one birth," "stretcher," "straw, hay, or the like, used as bedding for animals or as protection for plants" (this is a condensed version of the entry in *Random House Unabridged Dictionary,* 2nd ed.). "Rubbish" and "straw" are more or less related senses. However, a litter of six kittens can hardly be equated with trash, while *litter* (stretcher) does not refer to material (like straw) or a group of similar objects (like kittens). The question is the same as about *nail:* Do all those meanings belong together?

At first sight, they are loosely or even not at all connected, and themselves look like pieces of semantic litter, but if instead of presenting them in the order of their frequency in Modern English, we arrange them in the order of appearance, everything will fall into place. A borrowing from Anglo-French, *litter* ultimately goes back to Medieval Latin *lectāria,* from Latin *lectus* (bed). (Compare French *lit* [bed]), and "bed" is the earliest recorded meaning of the English word. Old beds were mattresses filled with straw; in the daytime, people stowed them away. So next we see *litter* [a portable couch and "straw for bedding".] From "a straw mattress" we get to "bedding for animals," "all the young of a sow, etc. brought forth at a birth" (as *stallion* is from *stall,* so a litter of pigs, kittens, and puppies is called after the litter on which they are born), further to "a disorderly accumulation of straw, hay, bracken, and the like," and finally to "trash, rubbish." If our evidence were not so detailed, no one would have been able to draw a bridge from "a stretcher" to "waste matter scattered about."

The noun *stock* is a quagmire: "a supply of goods, the outstanding capital of a company," "trunk, race, lineage," "a kind of liquor or broth," "any of several plants belonging to the genus *Matthiola,*" "an adjustable wrench," and so on. We will try to find the nuclear meaning from which all the others can be derived by a procedure familiar from the discussion of *nail* and *litter.* The difference between this procedure and reconstructing the phonetic protoform of Greek *báinein,* Latin *venīre,* and Gothic *qiman* (to come) (see the previous chapter, p. 175) is that in semantics, the earliest meaning (compare *nog-* [something elongated and hard]; the attested forms mean "leg," "hoof," claw," and "nail") can be not only reconstructed but also preserved in one of the related languages.

If we turn to German, we will see that *Stock* is much poorer in content than Engl. *stock:* its main meanings are "stick" (*stick* and *stock* are related by ablaut), "vine, bush," and "beehive" (the last easily derivable from "a hollow trunk"). Either the German word has lost three-quarters of its meanings or Engl. *stock* has expanded over the centuries. Historical dictionaries show that the second suggestion is right. The senses accrued in the following order: "trunk, stem" (Old English; no visible development until the fourteenth century); "a supporting structure," "a hollow receptacle"; "the line of descent"; "fund, store"; "an object of contemptuous treatment"; and "a stiff neckcloth." Predictably, "trunk, stem" turned out to be the earliest recorded meaning in English. It must have been the basic one. From it we get "descent, lineage," "a stem into which a graft is inserted," as well as the names of various objects made of wood and several plants. In financial dealings, a stock was originally a wooden tally representing a sum of money lent to the king. *Stock* (equipment, effects) may have developed from the idea of a branch growing on a trunk. Soup stock and paper stock are similar in that their base is some raw material "supply": bones, vegetables, and so on in the first case; rags, pulp, and the like in the second. Yet, however adroitly we may jump over semantic sticks (stocks) and stones, we stop in wonder at *stock* (udder) (a source of sustenance?) and *stock* (rabbit burrow) (long and straight as a trunk?), both in dialectal use. For good or ill, language is clearly more ingenious than the most resourceful linguists.

A short supplement to the *stick – stock* argument will show that an etymologist must sometimes reckon with unexpected interruptions and that outside influences have to be taken into account. From the etymological perspective, *staff* (a body of officers) is the same word as *staff* (stick), but the first meaning, which became popular not earlier than the 1780s, owes its existence to German (perhaps also Dutch) military usage. Apparently, the staff (German *Stab,* Dutch *staf*) was made up of people obeying a person in authority, the symbol of which was the wand or the baton. *Baton* can also mean "a club, staff, or truncheon, especially one serving as a mark of office or authority." A group of soldiers that derives its name from a symbol is not an uncommon occurrence. For instance, Medieval Latin had *banda* (scarf) and *bandum* (banner; company, crowd) (possibly from Germanic). A band was a military unit following the same *bandum* (banner).

In more cases than one, uncertainty remains whether we have a set of homonyms or a word with divergent meanings. This difficulty makes itself felt in the analysis of a modern language and in historical investigations. While looking through the words beginning with *spa* in *The Oxford Dictionary of English Etymology* I find *spade¹* (a tool for digging) and *spade²* (a suit of playing cards); *span¹* (the distance from the tip of the thumb to the extended tip of the little finger) and *span²* (harness, yoke); *spank¹* (to smack or slap with the open hand) and *spank²* (dialectal) (to travel with vigor and speed); *spar¹* (dialectal) (the rafter of a roof), *spar²* (to fight with prelusive strokes) (Samuel Johnson's definition), and *spar³* (a general term for certain crystalline minerals); *spat¹* (the spawn of the shellfish) and *spat²* (a short gaiter worn over the instep)—five sets on a page and a half. And these are only the words about which the editor had no doubts: in his opinion, they are certainly homonyms, not the result of a semantic split. Other words that are homonyms in most people's linguistic intuition appear in the same entries, separated by capital letters, for example, *spring* (rivulet) and *spring* (a season), whereas *spring* (to leap) is given an entry of its own, possibly because it is a verb, though it has the same root as the noun *spring* (*fall* [descent] and *fall* [to descend] are, likewise, treated in separate entries). Still other words are not merged, for the editor preferred to be on the safe side. Such are *sprig¹* (a small slender nail) and *sprig²* (twig). Both are said to be of unknown origin. Yet their meanings are not incompatible.

Jacob Grimm believed that homonymous roots in old languages should be traced to the same etymon.[4] This is a good recommendation (as, of course, could be expected from such a scholar). We will re-examine briefly the homonyms beginning with *spa*. *Spade* (a tool for digging) is a Germanic word related to Greek *spáthe*[5] (broad sword; a broad stalk; blade; shoulder-blade). *Spade* (a suit of playing cards) is a borrowing of Italian *spade* (the plural of *spada*), which, via Latin, goes back to the same Greek noun. *Span* (a measure of space) and *span* (to harness) are both Germanic and related; it is unclear why the dictionary does not say so. *Spank* (to slap) surfaced in the eighteenth century (1727), *spank* (to move quickly) emerged even later (1807–1810). They may be related (Skeat thought so). All three words under *spar* are Germanic. The etymologies of *spar* (to fight) and *spar* (mineral) have not been clarified; it is therefore anybody's guess whether these words are cognate with each other and with *spar* (rafter). *Spat* (the spawn of the shellfish) appeared in Anglo-Norman in the fourteenth century, and nothing else is known about it. *Spat* (gaiter) is a shortening of *spatterdash*. *Spatter* is probably an onomatopoeia like *sputter, splutter, splash, spit, spew,* and others. If Anglo-Norman *spat* is a loan from Middle English, it can also be one of such words.

Consequently, even in Modern English, homonyms may be traced to the same distant etymon. Today, *stock* (gillyflower) and *stock* (stump), *nail* (part of a finger) and *nail* (spike), *staff* (stick) and *staff* (a body of employees) are homonyms, pairwise. They are as different as *hair* and *hare*. Their former unity (not of *hair* and *hare!*) opens up only to an etymologist. Sometimes history allows us to connect the words that have strayed surprisingly far from their source. Such are *nail, stock,* and *litter.* As a final example, we can look at *metal* and *mettle.* The modern meaning of *mettle* goes back to the figurative use of *metal* (hard stuff, whence "courage, temperament"). In Elizabethan English, the spellings *metal* and *mettle* were used indiscriminately. For Shakespeare *metal* (or *mettle)* was a synonym of "any substance" *(the metal of my speech; of your metal, of your very blood; I am made of that self metal as my sister).* With time, "natural vigor and ardor; fortitude" ousted the neutral meanings, and that is why *mettelsome* is synonymous with *courageous,* and *to be on one's mettle* means "roused to do one's best."

In other cases, the evidence is insufficient, and no answer about the origin of homonyms can be given. In the entry *cob,* we find meanings containing the notions "big; stout," "roundish mass; lump," and "head, top." Even if, for etymological purposes, we divide the meanings of *cob* into those referring to animals, round or lumpy objects, and the head, it will be hard to decide whether we are dealing with one etymon or more (the head is "a lump," or perhaps it is round; small animals are also lumpy and round; on the other hand, lumps are not round, and so on). Not a single word spelled *cob* emerged in English texts before the fifteenth century. Their ties with similar-sounding words in other languages are doubtful, and their age is, as Skeat said on another occasion, past all guessing. A statement like the following in *The Oxford Dictionary of English Etymology* is not uncommon: "BAT A. club, stout, stick O[ld] E[nglish]; B. lump (as in *brickbat*) XIV [that is, first recorded in the fourteenth century]. . . . the source of sense B is entirely obscure and it may belong to a different word" (the entry *bat¹*). *Brickbat* is a piece or fragment of a brick, especially a piece of brick used as a missile, and it is only this secondary function that suggests its tie to *bat* (club, stick).

Occasionally, a pair of homonyms merges so closely that the product of the merger begins to look like one word with different meanings. Then it becomes necessary to separate the twins rather than assemble a word whose meanings have strayed in several directions. Dictionaries of Old English list several meanings of *bord:* "board, plank, table" and "the side of a ship, ship, shield." Almost the same glosses can be found in dictionaries of other Old Germanic languages. In fact, we are dealing with two different words that may not even be related, one denoting "plank," the other "edge." The second of them frequently occurs in early literature because of the synecdoche (the part stands for the whole) "the edge of a shield" to "shield." It was borrowed into Romance and later returned to English as *border;* in Modern English, it is extant only in *board* (a side of a ship) and in the verb *board. Board* "plank" has done much better and developed numerous new meanings, some of them confusing to the uninitiated. "'Bow to the board,' said Bumble. Oliver brushed away two or three tears that were lingering in his eyes; and seeing no board but the table, fortunately bowed to that." This passage occurs in Chapter 2 of Dickens's novel, titled ironically "Treats of Oliver Twist's Growth, Education, and Board."

A word can even change into its own antonym. This happened in the history of the adjective *restive,* which, when it was borrowed from French in the sixteenth century, meant "stationary." Horses were called restive when they did not want to move. Thus *restive* acquired the meaning "stubborn." A stubborn creature refuses compliance, shows signs of impatience, and objects to being restrained. In the course of two centuries, "restive," almost a synonym of "restful," began to mean "restless."

The zigzag in the development of *restive,* along with many more similar twists, is covered by the term enantiosemy (a combination of two opposite meanings in one word) (compare *enantiosis* [a figure of speech in which what is meant is the opposite of what is said; irony]). Extreme cases of enantiosemy are rare, because people cannot expect the same word to mean "good" and "bad," for example (hence the surprise of English speakers when as tourists they discover that Italian *caldo* means "hot"). Yet this phenomenon is not wholly uncommon. We rent an apartment from the landlord (what a word for our time!) who rents it to us. In American English, even the set phrase *to let* has given way to its synonym *for rent. Let* also combines the seemingly irreconcilable meanings "to allow" (as in *let me do it*) and "to prevent" (as in *without let or hindrance*). They were different words in Old English, but phonetic change has turned them into homonyms. The loss of prefixes resulted in that Icelandic *fá* means "to give" and "to get." *Fá¹* and *fá²*, as well as *let¹* and *let²*, owe their existence to chance, but enantiosemy may have more serious causes.

Clashes of antonyms often arise because a neutral concept has developed in the opposite directions. The most anthologized example is Latin *hostis* (enemy), originally "a stranger who in early Rome had the rights of a Roman," and its Germanic cognate **gastiz* (guest) (German *Gast,* Gothic *gasts*). The word's underlying meaning must have been "foreigner, outsider." Latin *hospes* (host, guest, stranger), related to *hostis,* is the etymon of *hospitable,* whereas the root of *hostis* can be seen in *host* and *hostile.* Luck is a neutral concept *(good luck, bad luck),* though *in luck, out of luck,* and *to have no luck* refer to its beneficial aspect. German *Glück (g-* is part of a prefix) presupposes unreserved happiness. Being close to or possessed by a god is a questionable blessing, and for this reason Latin *sacer* meant both "sacred, venerable" and "accursed." *Gistradagis,* the Gothic cognate of Engl. *yesterday* and Latin *hester-nus* (yesterday's), meant "tomorrow." Was the initial meaning of the Indo-European word "(on) another day"? Greek *némein* (to give)[6] is akin to Germanic *neman* (Modern German *nehmen*) (to take). This situation differs from what we see in Icelandic *fá,* for no prefixes have been lost here. Latin *altus* meant "high" and "deep." Everything depends on the point of view. The end of the road, if we turn around, will be its beginning. One takes in stride the fact that *kon-* in Russian *konets* (end) (stress on the second syllable) is believed to be related to *-gin* in Engl. *begin.*

As follows from the above examples, enantiosemy need not be connected with the amelioration and deterioration of meaning, but it often is. Etymologists come across cognates meaning "stench" in one language and "fragrance" in another. The inoffensive source of both may have been "smell." Among the cognates of Engl. *stink,* "strike against, bounce, leap," and the like occur. They refer to collision, sudden movement, running, and sprinkling. Apparently, *stink* could designate "attacking with water" (besprinkling) and "an attack of the air on the nostrils." Germanic *stincan* and *stinkan* have been recorded as meaning "to emit a smell; sniff" (a neutral odor) and "smell sweetly" (a pleasant odor). Old Engl. *stenc,* the ancestor of *stench,* could mean "scent, fragrance," while a *stencfæt (fæt* = Modern Engl. *vat*) was "a smelling bottle." Enantiosemy should be neither dismissed as an aberration nor made too much of.[7]

Ever since regular sound correspondences were discovered and tabulated, linguists have tried to formulate laws, however approximate, that govern semantic change. At first sight, the picture looks chaotic. Metaphor and metonymy have limitless possibilities: from "easy chair" to "a base coward" *(poltroon)* and from "bed" to "rubbish" *(litter).* Meanings can be broadened and narrowed to such an extent that new words arise. Although such moves make sense in retrospect, they are impossible to predict. The German cognate of *starve* is *sterben* (to die). English has narrowed the meaning of this verb: from "die" to "die of hunger." Old Engl. *steorfan* meant the same as German *sterben*. Latin *ponere* (to place, put, set) yielded French *pondre* (to lay eggs).

The change can also go from a specialized meaning to a more general one. If Engl. *bow* (to bend the head or body) (Old Engl. *bugan*) is akin to Latin *fugere* (to flee) and Lithuanian *búgti* (to frighten), the development was from "cower in fear" to "bend the head" (regardless of the circumstances in which the gesture is made). A similar, well-documented case is the progression of meaning in *truckle (under)* (to cringe, act in a servile manner). Its original meaning could not be more concrete: "to sleep in a truckle bed." A truckle bed, that is, a small, low bed, especially on wheels, was formerly occupied by a servant and could be pushed under that of the master in the daytime. The verb meant "to sleep on a truckle bed"; hence the predictable development to "behave in an obsequious manner." *Truckle to* (to submit to a person as a servant to his master) retains an echo of the old meaning. Also *cringe,* used above in glossing *truckle,* has had a comparable history: from Old Engl. *cringan* (fall [in battle], die) (it occurred only in poetry) to "shrink, cower," then "bend the body timorously or servilely," and, to borrow the definition from Wyld's *The Universal Dictionary of the English Language,* "to behave to another in a servile, abject manner, betokening exaggerated and timid respect for him, and a lack of self-respect, to fawn, play the sycophant." Engl. *crank* and German *krank* (ill, sick) (in Middle High German, "weak"), as well as similar adjectives in Icelandic and Dutch, are its cognates.

Students of semantics have classified and explained the recorded instances of the change of meaning; nothing like Grimm's Law has emerged in their material. Here we depend on precedent and analogy. Above, a connection has been offered between *staff* (stick) and *staff* (a body of soldiers, a body of employees). Since the connection may have appeared strained, I added a saving reference to *band* (a group of soldiers following the same banner) and *baton* (a symbol of authority). The parallels made the argument more persuasive, though they did not clinch it: what is true in two cases may be false in a third. Despite its weakness, analogy lends a touch of realism to conjectures on word origins.

Let us suppose we decide to investigate the origin of the verb *beat*. The Old English and Old Icelandic for "beat" was *bēatan* and *bauta*, respectively. Some form like **bautan* was the ancestor of both, and knowing this, we can ask ourselves why **baut-*, that is, why the combination of sound *b-au-t* meant "to strike; to give blows." In phonetics (as long as it deals with etymology), the first question is whether any known sound correspondences will allow us to find the word's cognates. In semantics, we have to inquire how other words meaning "beat" came into existence.

My database, in which words, in addition to being supplied with bibliographical references (who wrote about their derivation and where) are also marked for meaning. One hundred and ten synonyms of "beat, strike" have turned up—a sad testimony to people's fixation on fighting. Among such nice words as *tang ~ whang* and *dozz ~ duzz*, about 20 begin with *b*, including, *baff, beff, biff, boff, buffet, bam,* and *bash. Buffet* (and its cognate *rebuff*) are borrowings from French, in which they are believed to be onomatopoeias. *Baff* and *boff* are from Low German or Dutch; *biff* and *beff* may be native. From Romance, English has *batter* and *battle* (see pp. 24–25, above, where more is said about the onomatopoeic nature of *beat*). With *l* after *b*, the *bluff* group belongs here. Against this background, the suggestion that **bautan*, too, is an imitative (echoic) verb will not look too daring. Apparently, many people associate *b* with punching.

An etymological dictionary of synonyms is a most valuable resource for anyone who investigates the origin of words. A thesaurus of semantic changes, a book that would tell us how often, in the languages of the world, the name of a lazybones is derived from the name of a couch or easy chair and what are the recorded figurative meanings of verbs for "beat; exchange blows," does not exist, but an excellent etymological dictionary of synonyms, albeit limited to the Indo-European languages, does. Only the main words have been included (nothing like 110 synonyms for "beat").[8] However, a few works tracing the development of individual semantic spheres have been written.

Chapter 13 ended with a preliminary set of theses about the methods and principles of etymology. Having discussed the role of sounds and meanings in reconstructing words' past, we can expand that set.

- By definition, cognates are words that have the same root. When a search involves several languages, the assembled cognates are supposed (also by definition) to derive from the same protoform. The statement "Engl. *father* is related (or akin, allied) to Latin *pater*" implies that both are traceable to (have been derived from) the same asterisked etymon.

- After developing from the protoform, words go their separate ways, and in each language, their sounds may change. When they do, they change according to certain rules, and phonetic correspondences arise. Such correspondences exist between any two related languages and any two groups of languages within a family. Sound changes are regular. If we notice that Old Engl. *ā* becomes Middle Engl. *ō* (as in *stōn* [stone] from *stān*) or that a long vowel is shortened in the first syllable of a trisyllabic word (as in *holiday*) or before two consonants (as in *shepherd*), we expect the same changes to occur in all words of similar structure. Once the "law" is established that *f* in Germanic corresponds to *p* in a non-Germanic Indo-European language, we also expect it to work systematically: the protoform must have begun with **p,* which remained *p* in Greek, Latin, Slavic, and so forth, but was shifted to *f* in Germanic. Every time the "law" does not work in putative cognates (for example, both English and Latin words have *f*), we must either explain what caused the exception, suggest borrowing, or admit that given the present state of our knowledge, the selection has been wrong.

- However, words are not military units on parade. Numerous factors disrupt the regularity of sound correspondences. Among them are onomatopoeia (and other kinds of imitation), primitive creation, sound symbolism, the adoption of baby talk, blending, taboo, effects of humor ("language at play"), hybrid forms, and borrowing from a substrate language. Etymologists invoke those factors whenever "sound laws" fail them. The recommendation is not to deny any connection between Dutch *trekken* and Latin *trahere* or between them and Engl. *drag* but to try to explain the derailment of the "law" (though the suggested connection may indeed prove to be nonexistent). Engl. *heath* and *heather,* Old Engl. *fœmne* and Latin *fēmina* (woman), and Old Engl. *cnafa* and *cnapa* (boy, attendant) cannot be "obscurely related": they either go back to the same etymon or not.

- Similar words need not be reflexes (continuations) of a protoform. Engl. *pig* and Dutch *big* belong together, and they are part of the *pig – pug – pog – pok – ~ big – bag – bug – bog* nests. They emerged by variation of the loose structure *p/b* + vowel (usually short) + consonant (mainly *k, g, d*). It is better not to call Engl. *pad* and Low German *Poge* (frog) related, in order to avoid confusion with the *father – pater* type. *Pad* and *Poge* should perhaps be identified as the forms of the same word. The task consists in differentiating the old layer, represented by *father – pater,* and the (younger?) one, represented by *pad – Poge* (more about the meaning of the question mark will be said in the next chapter).

- If a sound correspondence exists, related words should be assembled on the phonetic principle: an English word beginning with *f* should be paired with a non-Germanic word having initial *p* and compatible vowels. But a sound correspondence is only a compass. Along the way, we will look for words that have a semantic bond with the word we are investigating. A semantic bond is a vague concept: private citizens turn into idiots, exiles into giants, and pain becomes intelligence. The patterns of semantic change do not defy classification, but, as a rule, their results cannot be foreseen.

- All the congeners may be synonyms (*father, pater . . . , beat, bauta . . . ,* and so on). To discover how they acquired their meaning, we should examine as many words in various languages as possible in the hope of uncovering the underlying concept. What features do people choose when they coin a name for "beat," "berry," "man," and "woman"? If the net is cast broadly, we can expect the search to be successful. Analogy is all we have here. Nearly identical semantic devices are used all over the world in inventing words (for instance, young animals are called little swollen things), and similar sounds of human speech imitate similar noises in different cultures. If the forms believed to be related are not synonyms (for example, "girl" and "milk"), the proposed etymology is bound to remain inconclusive. Here analogy is especially important. The existence of several instances in the same or in some other language in which a word for "girl" is undoubtedly derived from a word for "milk," the discovery of a recurring metaphor, a widespread metonymic connection (for example, from an exile and a captive to misery), or a typical direction of the broadening (narrowing, amelioration, deterioration) of meaning (from "possessed by all" to "unworthy," from "sloping" to "crafty," and the like) will reinforce our hypothesis. The absence of such parallels will weaken it.

- The meanings of a word can drift so far apart that its unity becomes endangered (so *stock*), and, conversely, different words with vaguely similar meanings can merge and begin to look as though they have always belonged together (so *board* and possibly *cob*). The question—one word or two?—haunts etymological research, as it also does the analysis of present-day vocabulary and lexicographic practice (dictionary making). Jacob Grimm's advice is sound. Begin by assuming the presence of one etymon (especially so in approaching the oldest periods). If necessary, modify your results later.[9]

An etymologist expects phonetics and semantics to work in harmony, but they are often at cross-purposes. Here is an example of how relatively small differences between meanings undermine a perfect phonetic fit. Anyone who is aware of the existence of the verbs *biff, beff, boff,* and *baff* (to beat) will conclude that *baffle* is a frequentative form of *baff* (to beat repeatedly or vigorously; to beat up) that later acquired a figurative meaning. However, *baffle* never meant "beat." The verb emerged in texts in the sixteenth century; at that time, it meant "to disgrace" (specifically a perjured knight) and "to hoodwink, confound"; the sense "to foil the plans" was attested almost a century later. Perhaps they originally were homonyms rather than two meanings of the same word, but this is unlikely.

We are dealing with an international slang word. The source of the English verb is Germany or the Netherlands. *Buffet* and *rebuff* are French; French *beffer* (to mock, deceive) in the form *beffler* was current in Rabelais's days. Italian *beffari* and Spanish *befar* continued into the present. The development may have been from "beat, exchange blows" to "leave one beaten and dazed," hence "to stupefy; disgrace; mock; foil the plans." *Rebuke* provides an analogy. *Chide* (to scold), presumably from "exchange blows," would be another parallel, and so would be *trounce* (p. 146), but in the spirit of the Latin aphorism *obscurum per obscurius*, one word of uncertain etymology should not be pressed into elucidating another obscure word: *chide* and *trounce* themselves need support. Reference to international slang is useful. Yet "to beat repeatedly" would have become "to disgrace" (in a chivalric context) only with the help of French *beffer* or *beffler:* knights were not fist fighters. Since the intermediate links are lost, the etymology of *baffle* cannot be considered solved beyond reasonable doubt.

Phonetic "laws" invalidate otherwise plausible etymologies all the time: compare again *trekken – trahere – drag, heath – heather,* and *fæmne – fēmina.* Sometimes the unprofitable question is debated: "Which is more important in etymology: sound correspondences or meaning?" Obviously, both are of equal importance. We should concentrate on method rather than on theory and ask: "What should we do when a flawless semantic derivation (like that of *heather* from *heath*) shatters at a phonetic obstacle?" This is one of the main problems etymologists encounter in their research. A strong controversy along such lines raged in Romance linguistics at the end of the nineteenth and the beginning of the twentieth century between Hugo Schuchardt (a Swiss) and Antoine Thomas (a Frenchman).

Schuchardt's long works, with their mass of digressions, make for slow reading. Yet his brilliance and erudition more than compensate for his stylistic extravagance. Schuchardt was ready to sacrifice a few troubling phonetic details if all the other facts supported his etymology. He easily eclipsed his opponent, a master of solid word histories. But Thomas stood his ground and kept repeating that if vowels and consonants do not match or do not develop according to the rule, the proposed solution is wrong. Today we know better than did our predecessors that various factors interfere with "sound laws" (see an incomplete list of them above), but the etymologist's duty is to explain how they work in every concrete case, not to refer to generalities.

In one of his major works, Schuchardt supported the derivation of French *trouver* (to find) (with cognates in other Romance languages) from Latin *turbāre* (to disturb, confuse). He investigated fishermen's practice of "muddying water," in order to drive fish into a net, reconstructed the development from "muddy water in looking for fish" to "search" and "find," and disregarded the change of *ur* to *ro* and of *b* to *v*. The entire wealth of ethnographic material he brought to bear on defending his solution could not outweigh those two seemingly trifling difficulties (I am leaving out a few other weak points of his reconstruction). According to an earlier derivation, offered by the celebrated French scholar Gaston Paris, the etymon of *trouver* was *tropāre* * (to look for melodies; compose; find). Paris's etymology is impeccable from the phonetic point of view, but it is based on an unattested protoform with a hypothetical meaning.[10] We are not sure why speakers of the Romance languages replaced Latin *invenīre* and *reparīre* (to find) with a third verb (unless their aim was to tease future linguists). The tug of war between phonetic and semantic evidence is typical: some facts always point in one direction and others in another.

Regardless of the outcome of the *trovāre* / *tropāre* controversy, Schuchardt taught etymologists a lesson never to be forgotten. If the origin of a word is to be sought in people's way of life, the more we learn about "things," the better. A linguistic journal called *Wörter und Sachen* ("Words and Things") was started: it dealt with material culture in its relation to linguistics. It existed for 20 years, published articles with excellent illustrations, and is a joy to read. The knowledge of things cannot be derived from names: words lead us to things and thus get an explanation. Socrates and Plato cannot help smiling in content—wherever they may be.

Chapter Sixteen

in which the author meanders a little
(as is his wont) but then comes to the
root of the matter, or

The Origin of the Earliest Words
and Ancient Roots

A question about the origin of language asked but not answered.—
Bow-wow won't be stilled.—The tongue follows the hand.—Richard
Paget and Alexander Jóhannesson.—*Mater* for *milk, pater* for *pānis.*—
Only linguists know next to nothing about the origin of language.—
Wrong does not mean useless.—Deep are the roots.—*Scribo – scribis
– scribit* and *scribble – scribble – scribble.*—Bare roots.—A search
for a few protosyllables.—Etymology and derangement.—Etymology
and Marxism.—Indo-European reconstructed: August Fick, Alois
Walde, and Julius Pokorny. —Homonymous roots.—When amputa-
tion begins, it is hard to stop: Per Persson's enlargements.—Growing
from a root versus gemmation.—Enough work for everyone to do.

As already noted (pp. 40–43), the greatest temptation of etymology is
to go so far as to be able to discover the origin of language. Yet word
historians are not equipped to make such a discovery. The past stages
of the majority of languages spoken today are either unknown or documented for a relatively short period. In some cultures, words keep well,
but in others they are replaced at an almost unbelievable speed. While
modern Icelanders can read their sagas with the help of a small glossary, Norwegian, Swedish, and Danish have modified their ancient
lexicons drastically. The same is true of German. English preserves
only the core of its pre-Conquest riches. If such innovations have happened in the course of a few centuries, one can easily imagine the
scope of the changes that occurred in the previous millennia.

New words constantly supersede old-timers (*pig* for *swine, dog* for *hound,* and so on), but *swine* and *hound,* despite their unquestionable antiquity, need not be the original names of those animals in Indo-European: we may be witnessing the nth generation of such coinages. Primitive creation, as Wilhelm Oehl understood it, is a permanent process. Verbs like *grip, grab,* and *chop* emerge spontaneously, alter beyond recognition, are ousted by native or borrowed synonyms, and come up again in the same form, fresher than ever.

The still-current theories of the distant origin of words, insofar as they lay claim to unveiling the first steps of language, are not many. According to one, words arose from onomatopoeia. In Chapter 4, we let Whitney defend the bow-wow theory against his chief opponent Max Müller. Here is another example of reasoning along the same lines (this time from Germany) by Theodor Curti:

When we stamp with our feet, we hear a sound that can approximately be rendered by *pa.* If we continue to stamp, the ear will register *papapa.* This single primitive word could serve for designating stamping, walking, marching, and tapping the ground; the foot, both feet, and the foot with the leg. The root *dukh* has less obvious associations; we would not be able to ascribe onomatopoeic effects to it. But if we pronounce *dukhdukhdukh* and, in so doing, think of the noise an infant makes at its mother's breast, this sound complex will not seem so unusual to us. *Dukh* could have given its name to the child, breast, mother, as well as to sucking, suckling, milk, sweetness, liquid, and so on. Nor does a root like *ruk* resemble an onomatopoeia. Yet it could have given rise to more than one process. We may, for example, visualize the discovery of fire. When two logs were rubbed one against another or a stick was turned in a tree trunk, a noise was heard that people thought would be best reproduced by *rukrukrukruk.* However, the imitation may have proceeded with the help of consonants *(rrkk)* or of the syllables *arkark,* and those may have yielded *rak, rek,* or *ruk.* The meaning of *ruk* could have been transferred to numerous objects, actions, and states: stick, tree; rub, turn, burn; smoke, kindle, glisten; five, light (noun and adjective), flame, and pain. One thing is undeniable: many roots that do not look like such, may have had an onomatopoeic, sound imitative origin.[1]

According to another theory, as Richard Paget explained it,

Originally man expressed his ideas by gesture, but as he gesticulated with his hands, his tongue, lips and jaw unconsciously followed suit in a ridiculous fashion, 'understudying' . . . the action of the hands. The consequence was that when, owing to pressure of other business, the principal actors (the hands) retired from the stage—as much as principal actors ever do—their understudies—the tongue, lips and jaw—were already proficient in the pantomimic art. . . . If, while pantomiming with tongue, lips and jaw, our ancestors sang, roared or grunted—in order to draw attention to what they were doing—a still louder and remarkable effect was produced, namely, what we call voiced speech. . . . In this way there was developed a new system of conventional gesture of the organs of articulation from which, as I suggest, nearly all human speech took its origin.[2]

We should pay special attention to the statement that as man "gesticulated with his hands, his tongue, lips and jaw unconsciously followed suit." This is what it means in practice (note the special terms used below: velars are the consonants articulatcd in the back of the mouth, for example, *g* and *k;* labials—*m, p, w, b,* and often *f* and *v*— are produced by the lips; the consonants formed between the two extreme positions are called dentals; for the present discussion, palatals can be subsumed under dentals):

The movements of the speaking organs, in a forward direction, as spontaneous imitations of the shape or form of things in nature and of movement show a conformity between form and meaning in a vast number of comparisons in the six 'unrelated' family groups of languages. Thus the type *kap-* with all variations of the velars and the labials (*geb-, gheb-, gem-, (kem-),* etc.) shows that the meaning of most of the roots belonging hereto has either been 'to eat, hold in the mouth, to grasp, to contain, to close, to press together, to complete, to finish' or 'curved, vaulted, round,' etc.

The types *gel-* and *ger-* (with all variations of the velars) show either a similar meaning as for *kap-* 'curved, vaulted, round,' etc. (in such cases the *l* and *r* have been velar sounds) or they imitate nature sounds (in these cases the *l* and *r* have been palatal or dental sounds). The type *gen-* (with all variations of the velar) shows in the same way a double origin of the *n*-sound, that of a velar (mostly in combination with a following velar: *ang-, gengh,* etc. with the meaning 'round, vaulted, curved') and that of a palatal, imitating nature sounds.

The *n*-sound designates also something enduring, continuing, and this is especially seen in the *n*-combinations which express an emotion or imitate a nature sound.

. . . I regard it as proved that the overwhelming majority of all words . . . have come into existence as spontaneous imitations by the speaking organs of the shape or form of things in nature and of movement.[3]

The author of the last statement is Paget's closest ally Alexander Jóhannesson. His book *On the Original Language of the Indo-Europeans and Their Homeland* was written in Icelandic, and despite a four-page summary in French, could not have had many readers. It features an insert (between pp. 152 and 153): illustrations showing the reconstructed conformity between the gesture and the position of the tongue (the arm is stretched out and the tongue moves forward; the arm is bent, with the index finger pointing toward the man's chest, and the tongue retracts, and so on). Later he popularized his ideas in English, but one seldom sees references to them.[4]

"The *n*-sound designates . . . something enduring, continuing," Jóhannesson says. In the formation of *n,* the tongue is pressed against the teeth, and the sound can be prolonged, whence, apparently, endurance and continuity. The complex *geb* begins in the back of the mouth and ends on the compressed lips. The movement from one stop to another along the mouth cavity presumably suggested the idea of eating, holding, and completing.

The onomatopoeic and the gestural theories are mutually exclusive: if nearly all words imitate sounds in nature, they cannot reflect gestures. Jóhannesson examined 2,200 Indo-European roots and estimated that interjections and other "emotional" complexes numbered only 5 percent of them. About 10 percent went to onomatopoeias, whereas gestural complexes (the third stage, as he called it) made up the remaining 85 percent. "It is to be expected," he states, "that the percentage in other languages is similar." And indeed his expectations came true when he turned to Ancient Chinese, Turkic, Polynesian, and Greenlandic. Like Oehl (whose works he does not seem to have known), Jóhannesson noticed the worldwide distribution of the syllables *kap-* ~ *kaf-* ~ *gab-,* which Oehl isolated in verbs of catching and seizing and referred to primitive creation. In Jóhannesson's opinion, already partly known to us,

The gestural sounds seem to be spontaneous imitations by speaking organs of the shape or form of things in nature and of movements. In roots which in this way have come into existence, the most important fact in imitating a shape or form such as straight, flat or round (curved, bent, hollow, swollen, etc.) is not the starting, but the final sound, such as in I[ndo]- E[uropean] *kap*—in Lat[in] *caput* the head, "the round one," Hebrew *gbh-bh* "to be curved," Chinese *kap* "of cyclical character," Polynesian *hapa-* "crooked," Turkish *kafa* "head" (that is, round) and Greenlandic *qup-oq* "keg, jar" (the curved form).

He continues: "Roots of this type (*kap:* velar + vowel + labial) do not only contain the meaning 'round, curved, vaulted', etc. but also 'to eat, to hold in the mouth, to grasp, to contain, to close, to press together and cover' and 'to cut, dig'."[5]

Whitney and other scholars of his persuasion, who traced human speech to onomatopoeia, cited numerous modern words that are or at one time were onomatopoeic. Curti's examples are especially typical. Likewise, Jóhannesson drew heavily on Modern Icelandic, and Paget on Modern English. The latter found "pantomimic words" everywhere. For example, in *awe,* the mouth is open, "suggestive of fear and surprise." Even in words like *ask* and *ass* (which he called less obvious), he detected the process he was looking for:

> ... *ask,* which is due to a tongue grip in front of the mouth—*(as)*—which is, as it were, *transferred* to the back of the mouth *(k)*—the natural meaning of the gesture being 'grip to self,' which is at least consistent with the idea of asking, though more suggestive of taking! In the doubtful case, *ass,* the tongue tip rises from *a* to make the grip *s*—possibly a foot-lifting gesture, since the early forms of this word appear to have been of the type *as-l* or *as-n,* i.e. a double rise of the tongue the first a little in advance *(s)* of the other *(l* or *n).* This, however, is pure hypothesis. It will be seen, therefore, that of these simple words in daily use a very high proportion are still due to a gesture of the tongue, etc., which bears a direct relation to the meaning of the word.[6]

We should not miss the passage in which Paget likens the progression of sounds in *as-l ~ as-n* (ass) to foot lifting or his highly significant *etc.* in the statement that numerous words are "still due to a gesture of the tongue, etc." Jóhannesson compared only the movement of the hand and the tongue. When Paget notes that in *awe,* the mouth is wide open, "suggestive of fear and surprise," we remember Jespersen (who connected the vowel *i* with the designation of small size), ideophones, and everything said about sound symbolism in Chapter 4. But Jespersen was circumspect and did not carry a reasonable idea to absurd extremes. He did not mention sound symbolism a single time while discussing the origin of language.

However, sound symbolism is present in a minimal way in Paget's theory and not at all in Jóhannesson's. Others have made attempts to explain all or most words as sound symbolic creations. For example, it has been noticed that the names of liquid food and soft substances, as well as verbs designating the process of softening, tend to begin with *m* (in English: *milk, milt, melt, mild; manna* from Hebrew; *mollify,* via French, from Latin *mollis* [soft]). By contrast, initial *f* and *b,* though not so regularly, occur in words for hard food (compare Latin *pānis* [bread] and English *bread*). The widespread baby words *mama* and *papa* seem to reflect the distinction between the kinds of food provided by the mother *(mater)* and father *(pater).* Other categories allegedly include *n* + vowel for moisture, *l* + vowel for drinking and eating places (as in Engl. *lake*), and *k* + vowel for animal names (*cat, cow,* and so on).[7] Carl Täuber, from whose article "The Protolanguage and Its Development" the above examples have been borrowed, analyzed place names in similar fashion.[8] He was convinced that "it is possible, on the basis of the available evidence rather than mere speculation, to reconstruct the tree of human languages and to trace it to six roots."[9]

Perhaps the first thing that puts us on our guard when we review the theories touched on here is how ambitious they are.[10] All or a high proportion of words that arose tens (hundreds?) of thousands of years ago, we are told, were onomatopoeic, or gestural, or sound symbolic, and modern languages have retained enough of those characteristics for us to bridge the millennia. Since it is likely that vocabulary has been replaced many times during such a long period, but improbable that the primordial words should not have changed their sounds and meaning (as they have done in the last four and even two thousand years), the only explanation of such a miraculously retentive character of the lexicon can be given in terms of primitive creation and sound symbolism: old words disappeared, but new words were again and again invented according to the ever-present laws with the same results. I think that none of the scholars mentioned above would have agreed with such a proposition. They believed that they had discerned the beginning of language, not its late stage resembling an indefinite number of earlier ones.

Modern researchers trying to understand the emergence of art, literary forms (such as myth, the folk tale, and epic poetry), dance, and rituals have long since given up theories based on a single cause. They speak about the origins rather than the origin of art, folklore, and religion. The same must be true of word history. The rise of language attracts the attention of specialists in the animal forms of communication (titillating news of speaking dolphins and primates regularly reaches the media), paleoanthropologists, neuropsychologists, and semioticians (students of signs), but linguists have few approaches to this problem. Children learn to speak by imitating adults, who have a full command of language, and thus do not resemble mute beasts surrounded by their likes. Pidgins and creolized languages are secondary products based on well-formed systems. The level of material culture has nothing to do with the complexity of the language that corresponds to it (hopes of discovering a kind of protolanguage among the Australian aborigines vanished quickly). And that is all there is.

The human mind can reconstruct only order. As a result, reconstructed languages are always neat and logical. They compare favorably with the chaos of the modern state that serves linguists as their starting point. However, if language arose from cries accompanying gestures, imitation of sounds in nature, instinctive exclamations at work, or babbling, the earliest words must have been so haphazard as to defy reconstruction. The idea that, with time, guttural sounds gradually yielded to those articulated in the front part of the mouth may be true.[11] Yet velar consonants (*g, k,* and glottal stops) are widespread and need not be the relics of prehistory.

The few names that have occurred in the foregoing discussion belong to serious scholars, but the origin of language, because of the insolubility of the problem, is a subject that, for centuries, has been a hunting ground of amateurs. Some of them were not ignorant and yet filled their books with the wildest speculation imaginable. The alternatives, with minor variations, have always been the same (if we disregard the idea of the divine origin of humanity and language):

onomatopoeia, interjections, sound symbolism, and "gesture before sound speech." The hope of detecting an inherent, immutable meaning in every consonant has been especially strong.

In one such deservedly forgotten book, mentioned here only for the sake of the exotic effect, we read that

> Sounds expressive of the simplest actions a *g,* gullet, swallow, *l* to lick, tongue, *p* lip, suck, &c, gradually lost their spontaneous character by constant repetition, and so became the symbols of ideas. At first they were mere noises, produced by a particular organ, naturally calling attention to that organ and its functions. . . . Gradually one complexion of sound, from its more expressive character, would gain the predominance over others, and it would then cease to be spontaneous; it would have become a recognized name, a word, the symbol of an idea.[12]

Later it is said that "*s,* besides its sense of 'being,' is also commonly used to define that which is near, whether the nearness be of likeness or of vicinity." The sound *l* allegedly has "a ligamentous sense."[13] In the book, hundreds of English words are explained in this way.

Imprudent scholars, brave amateurs, and charlatans have one feature in common: they are sensationally original and hope to deliver too much. They also love to deal with roots. *Root* is a term that occurs with some regularity in different theories of the earliest vocabulary. Curti spoke about the roots *ruk* and *dukh.* Täuber's roots, which were six in number, consisted of *m, p, n, t, l/r,* and *k* followed by a vowel. Jóhannesson examined 2,200 roots of Indo-European. None of the authors defined the term, perhaps assuming that such a definition is not needed. As we saw in Chapter 9, the root of a word can be isolated in two ways. *Worker* and *payment* consist of two parts each, because *work* and *pay* are meaningful units; the etymological obscurity of *-er* and *-ment* is viewed as a deplorable but inescapable evil. The root emerged as the part of the word that remains when there are no more elements to subtract. The procedure with short suffixes was the same: *handle* falls into the root *hand-* and the suffix *-le.* It is taken for granted that *work-, pay-,* and *hand-* are linguistic signs (names) of real things.

However, the situation may be more complicated. *Handle* and *payment* are transparent, whereas *bridle* and *raiment* are not, for what are *brid-* and *rai-?* A considerable number of words like *bridle* and *needle* make us think that *-le* has the same function in them as in *handle* (a marker of the names of implements) and that *brid-* and *need-* will find a convincing etymology. The direction of the search has changed: in *handle,* an obscure suffix is an appendage to a clear-cut root, while in *bridle* and *needle,* the sought-for entity is the root and the given (if it can be called this) is a hypothetical suffix. Roots, it appears, are not always easy to obtain.

English has lost most endings (compare: *I / you / we / they speak; I / he / we / you / they spoke*), and the root has become indistinguishable from the word in which it occurs: *write* is what we find in the dictionary. But it is enough to look at the forms of any Latin noun or verb, to discover that their roots have no independent existence. Let us take the verb *scribere* (to write). The forms of the present will suffice: *scribo, scribis, scribit, scribimus, scribitis, scribunt.* Their root is *scrib-,* but there is no Latin word **scrib:* even the shortest forms (*scribo* [I write] and *scribe* [write!]) have endings. We find *scriba* (copyist) and its near synonym *scriptor,* along with several other words beginning with *script-* (from **scrib-t*), in all of which the root is "bound." The question arises whether it ever functioned in its pure form. Those who reconstructed roots like *dukh* as the earliest words of human speech would have said yes and argued that at one time, *scrib* was an onomatopoeia meaning "to scratch" and resembling Russian *skrip* (creak) or a sound symbolic creation, or a gestural formation, or whatever. The hypothesis would have been that, in principle, each word has a history comparable with the history of *scribere.* If so, we will continue the dialogue in Socrates's spirit and ask how many such word-like roots existed in the beginning and whether we can reconstruct them.

Again and again, amateurs and linguists pursue the same utopian project: they look for a few syllables from which the entire lexicon developed. Since "roots" like *la, ma, pa,* and their variants are ubiquitous, the great utopia easily triumphs on paper. Alexander Murray set up nine primitive roots: *ag, bag, thwag, gwag, lag, mag, nag, rag,* and *swag.*[14] A certain Martynov (1856–1900), providentially not known outside Russia and forgotten even there, derived all words of all languages from a protosyllable or protosound. His book *A Discovery of the Secret of Human Language and the Fallacy of Scholarly Linguistics Exposed*[15] is

> a ludicrous treatise combining fantastic etymologies, wild mysticism, and vulgar nutritive materialism, in which he advanced, with a great deal of inventiveness, morbid vituperation, and coarse humor, the idea that all words in all languages derive from the verb "to eat." The last sentence of Martynov's book, a footnote to the word *Amin'* ["amen"] is as good an illustration as any of Martynov's style . . . *"Amin"= jamin' = jamn' = jam's' = ja's' = jas's' = jac'c' = c'! = jas' = jast' = ēēt' = ist' = ist'n' = isten' = istina* ["truth"] . . .[16]

and so on, until *amen* and *istina* (truth) merge with *est'* (to eat).

N. Ia. Marr (1864–1934), a distinguished archeologist, turned to language study, espoused Marxism, and became the dictator of Soviet linguistics. He was a charismatic seducer, and many talented people grew up in his shade and were partly or completely ruined by his teachings. He denounced Indo-European scholars as racists and flunkeys of colonizers (a winning card for decades) and insisted on the importance of semantics in etymology, to the almost total exclusion of phonetic correspondences. Marr allowed four elements (*sal, ber, ion,* and *rosh*) to engender all words. The pun *Martynov ~ Marr* arose early among Moscow linguists. Clandestine machinations behind the Kremlin wall resulted in Stalin's interference and the debunking of Marr. Since one of Stalin's titles, unofficial but repeated on a daily basis, was "the coryphaeus of all sciences," Marr's pupils saw the light and repented. Martynov's book was brought to the students' attention by psychiatrists, and N. S. Trubetzkoy, a great twentieth-century scholar, wondered (in a letter to Roman Jakobson) why Marr was not institutionalized, for even Marr's syntax betrayed a lunatic.[17]

Some etymologists were medical doctors, which did not prevent them from advancing crazy hypotheses. One such medical man was Anton von Velics, who published in Hungarian and German. He taught that the roots *huh, tuh, ruh,* and *suh* were variants of the same unit, namely *huh*. According to his theory, all words were made of nine elements.[18] The tally is: Martynov – one, Marr – four, Täuber – six, Murray and Velics – nine. It is unfair to mention Walter Whiter in one breath with Martynov, because he lived much earlier and was a serious investigator. He, too, traced all words to a single concept; in his case, it was *earth*. Whiter wrote a book of more than 2,000 pages (three thick volumes),[19] but his idea is no more than a guiding principle in his investigation. Wherever possible, he detected the notions "rub," hole," and the like (he understood "earth" broadly). Martynov is funny, Velics almost unreadable. Marr is shallow, often turgid, and unbearably repetitive. But Whiter's manner of writing betrays a dedicated student of language. His word indexes make his conclusions accessible to those who choose to study detours in the advance of scholarship, and one concept is not the same as one root.

The theories that reduce the lexicon to a few elements or one nuclear concept have been useful in only one respect: they have shown that research along these lines is a waste of time, but they have done no harm to the notion of the root, because roots exist, regardless of the abuse they occasionally suffer at the hands of utopians. The botanical metaphor has played a decisive role in the development of historical linguistics. Language was likened to a growing organism, and the multitude of modern dialects was presented as branches on the once monolithic tree trunk (see p. 171). *Root* is such a familiar linguistic term that we no longer notice its indebtedness to botany. (The same is true of *stem*.) Since to Grimm's contemporaries the Proto-Indo-European language was as real as Modern German (they did not realize how little is known about the emergence and spread of the Indo-European family), they saw no reason why they should not have treated them alike. In 1868, August Fick published a dictionary of the roots of Indo-European before its imagined disintegration.[20] He presented his material at the level that philology had reached by his time. The science he practiced was then about 50 years old; he had just turned 35. In a way, his venture determined the course of Indo-European studies for the whole of the next century. The third edition of the dictionary, which took nearly 20 years to complete and which was written in collaboration with a team of outstanding specialists,[21] is still usable.

The procedure for obtaining Indo-European roots is as follows. For example, we assume that the cognates of Old Engl. *siofun ~ seofon* (seven) are Gothic *sibun,* Latin *septem,* Greek *heptá,*[22] Sanskrit *sapta,* and so on. A series of minor phonetic "laws" will explain why Greek and Latin have *e* in the first syllable, as opposed to *a* in Sanskrit, why the Greek word begins with *h,* and why Latin *p* corresponds to Gothic *b* rather then *f.* Then the prototype, the putative Indo-European root, in this case **septm-* (seven), is posited, from which the attested forms are believed to have derived (compare what is said about the least common multiple on p. 175, above). In comparing *scribo, scribis, scribt . . . ,* we stayed with the forms of the same word in the same language, whereas for reconstructing **septm-* it was necessary to compare different words in different languages. By chance, the asterisked root turned out to be almost identical with the Latin word; the work went well, because the cognates were easy to find. But as we have seen, searching for cognates is the hardest part of etymological analysis.

The third edition of Fick's dictionary is a collection of several volumes, with titles like *The Vocabulary of Germanic Language Unity* and *The Vocabulary of Celtic Language Unity.* In the 1920s, a new Indo-European dictionary began to appear in installments, or fascicles, as they are called. All the words in all languages believed to be related were gathered in separate entries united by the root (for example, **bel-, *del-, *kel-,* and **gel-*). For producing this monumental compendium Alois Walde, a classical scholar, sought the assistance of the Celtologist Julius Pokorny, who edited the work after Walde's death.[23] Walde had already brought out a detailed etymological dictionary of Latin in which every word was discussed in terms of its Indo-European heritage. Now the focus shifted to Indo-European.

Understandably, Walde depended on the huge body of research done in every area of Indo-European, and since most etymologies are debatable, he, as appeared later, assigned many words to wrong roots. This, however, is a dismissible blemish, and Walde-Pokorny's dictionary immediately became a standard reference work. If a word is featured in it, one can see the grand picture at a glance, with suggested cognates from Sanskrit and Greek to Lithuanian and Icelandic and references to the most important publications. It is in Walde-Pokorny that Alexander Jóhannesson found his 2,200 roots. He used Indo-European as a springboard and only later extended his theory to other language families.

Pokorny survived Walde by many years and reworked the dictionary.[24] He expunged numerous questionable cognates (some roots disappeared altogether), did away with most references to scholarly sources, simplified the notation, and adopted a more transparent arrangement. Two volumes (not counting the index) were compressed into one. The new product superseded its predecessor, but Walde-Pokorny is still worth consulting, and reprinting it in 1973 was a good idea. In speaking about *s-mobile* (p. 96), I mentioned the etymological supplement to *The American Heritage Dictionary of the English Language.* The roots listed there are from Pokorny. The criticism of Walde-Pokorny and Porkorny is a subject in its own right, but here we are interested only in the reality of the roots in their dictionaries.

Although Proto-Indo-European is a nebulous concept, judging by the facts at our disposal, that language had a rich system of endings, which means that its roots existed not as they do in Modern English (in which *work-,* abstracted from *worker, works, worked,* or *working,* is a homonym of the word *work*), but as in Latin (in which *scribo, scribis, scribit . . .* are forms of the same verb, but *scrib-* is "bound"). One can say that the root is the common part of related words. However, this would be a circular definition, because related words are defined as having the same root. In dealing with *scribere,* we take the unity of the changing word for granted and feign ignorance of the vicious circle. Such liberties are permissible in grammar, at least up to a point, but not in etymology, in which the unity of compared forms is never certain.

Thus, we look at Old Engl. *fæmne* (woman), compare it with Lithuanian *pienas* (milk), then notice Old Engl. *fætan* (to cram, load) (that is, "to make fat"), and reconstruct the Indo-European root *pei-* with the meaning *"to be fat or swell" or *"cram with (liquid?) food," or *"exude moisture." Its reality is hypothetical by definition. Perhaps Latin *pītuīta* (phlegm) (from which we have *pituitary*) and *pīnus* (pine tree) (it yields resin, so that its name may have meant *"moist") belong with *fœmne*. In the formative years of Indo-European linguistics, the idea prevailed that at some time, language consisted of bare roots, and it is bare roots that learned philologists, well-intentioned amateurs, and lunatics reconstructed as the earliest words of human language. We do not know whether, in the remote past, people communicated by means of sound complexes like *bel, del, kel, poi, lei,* and *nei*. The short words of Modern English are the result of the decay of old morphology, not the initial stage of development, and the same may be true of the languages of Southeast Asia.

When Walter W. Skeat published the first edition of his English etymological dictionary (1882), he included "Canons for English Etymology" in the introduction. Canon 5 runs as follows: "It is a rule in all Aryan [= Indo-European] languages that words started from monosyllabic roots or bases, and were built up by supplying new suffixes at the end; and, the greater the number of suffixes, the later the formation."[25] For Skeat, as for Fick, the root of an ancient word was an analog of the root of a plant, but the roots in Indo-European dictionaries have not been recorded as independent entities. They are the common part of words that, according to unprovable but reasonable conjectures, are related, that is, they are pegs on which clusters of words from many languages have been hung. Such pegs have their uses as long as we remember that we ourselves have carved them. The primitive roots, to accommodate all the selected derivatives, are sometimes given such general meaning as "to be, exist, grow," "to constrain," and "to make, prepare," though more often the development is from the concrete to the abstract, for instance, from "make a pot; make a fence" to "make (general)."

Homonyms, which Jacob Grimm tried to avoid in reconstruction, abound in Walde-Pokorny. Pokorny conflated some of them, but he left 11 *wer*'s, as in (1) *wart* (high, raised spot), (3) -*ward* (to turn, bend), (4) *a-ware* (to perceive, watch out for), (5) *weir* (to cover), and (6) *word* (to speak). Numbers 2 (to bind, hang on the scale; heavy), 7 (water), 8 (wide, broad), 9 (to burn), 10 (squirrel), and 11 (to find) are not represented in English. There are four *bhel*'s: *bhel-¹* (to shine, burn), *bhel-²* (to blow, swell), *bhel-³* (to thrive, bloom), and *bhel-⁴* (to cry out, yell). Their reality cannot be verified, and it is not difficult to set up one root in place of four, to gloss it as "increase, grow" (in brightness – **bhel-¹;* in size – **bhel-²;* in health and vigor – **bhel-³;* and in loudness – **bhel-⁴*). Alongside homonyms, synonyms thrive and bloom: for example, time and again, the gloss "to swell" turns up.

In both old and living languages, some synonyms differ only in their last consonants. We are returning to Old Engl. *cnafa* and *cnapa* (attendant, servant) and the adjectives for "flat": Engl. *flat* and German *flach* (*ch* as in Scots *loch*). Their coexistence can be accounted for in two ways: either they arose by varying their final sound (ABC changed to ABD, ABF, and so on) or they developed from the same kernel (AB + C, AB + D, and AB + F). In 1891, the Swedish linguist Per Persson analyzed a great number of words according to the second model, that is, he reconstructed shorter roots than had been done before him.[26] Final consonants and a few vowels emerged as extensions added to the root. Persson wrote his book in German and called extensions *Determinative* (in the plural). The most common English term is *enlargements*.

Persson's analysis runs into several difficulties. Words united by a vague common meaning and having the same initial part are plentiful. I will use the examples familiar from the previous chapters. *Fit-* in *fitful* designates movement in alternate directions, and so do *fick-* in *fickle,* and *fid-* in *fiddle*. It does not follow that the root of those words is or was *fi-* (? *"inconstant, erratic"), capable of taking three enlargements. *Tit* (in *tit for tat*) varies with *tid* (in *tidbit*). Both designate small entities. *Tip* is the name of another small thing, and *tik-* (in *tick-tock* and in the name of the insect) may also be understood as referring to smallness. It seems that no one will want to isolate the root **ti-* in them. But such procedures are applied unhesitatingly to old vocabulary. Second, grammar and word formation recognize prefixes, suffixes, and infixes. Enlargements appear as illegitimate doubles of suffixes. A suffix has a well-defined function. For instance, in adjectives, *-er* forms the comparative degree. In nouns, it denotes the names of agents *(worker, reader, writer),* while verbs ending in

-er are frequentative. But most enlargements are elements devoid of content: just *t, d, k,* and so forth.

The first critics of Persson's book were quick to point out its flaws.[27] However, Persson had great combinatory talent and was not a fanatic of one idea. He offered many excellent etymologies, and his next book, published in 1912,[28] had a lasting influence on Indo-European studies. Walde and Pokorny followed him, and Émile Benveniste, the author of the latest theory of the Indo-European root, left Persson's enlargements intact. Yet the flaws of his reconstruction remained. *Fla-,* the root of *flat* and *flach,* although recognized in this form, is probably as fictitious as would be *fi-* in *fit* and *ti-* in *tip.* Nor do Engl. *pad* and German *Poge* (frog) go back to the root **pa- ~ po-* with the enlargements *g* and *d.* Such words rather seem to derive one from another (ABF from ABD, ABD from ABC, and so on). If this process of "breeding" existed in the past, many words in Persson and Pokorny should be analyzed differently. The following example is as good as any.

Sow (female pig), from Old Engl. *sū,* has cognates in other Germanic languages: Old High German *sū,* Old Saxon *sū,* and Old Icelandic *sýr.* Nearly the same word occurs in Classical Greek, Latin, Armenian, and elsewhere. *Swine* from Old Engl. *swīn* is related to *sow.* Originally a neuter adjective ("pertaining to pigs"), it was later reinterpreted as a noun. Alongside *sū,* words with the enlargement *k* have been posited. Old English had *sū* and *sugu.* Engl. *hog,* possibly of Celtic origin, in which *h-* goes back to *s-,* is akin to *sugu.* The root **sū-,* it was supposed, meant "to give birth," with reference to pigs' extraordinary fertility (*sow* is a female pig). *Sū* and *sugu* have the same meaning, and the role of the enlargement is here even more enigmatic than in other cases. A reconstructed root present in only two words for "pig" has a weak base, and this is where *son* comes in. Like *sū,* Old Engl. *sunu* (son) has numerous cognates in and outside Germanic, including Sanskrit *sunúṣ.* Old Indian grammarians connected *sunúṣ* with a verb meaning "to give birth," so that "son" was understood as "one born," rather than "a male offspring." For a long time the best historical linguists equated the root of *sunu* with *sū* in *sow,* the more so as *sunu* may have had *ū* in the first syllable. *Sow* and *son* were said to have the root "pertaining to birth."

Sanskrit has come down to us in sacral texts and in a series of detailed grammatical descriptions. It was in partial emulation of Old Indian scholars that nineteenth-century linguists reconstructed Proto-Indo-European and made such wide use of the concept of the root. But in Sanskrit, the root unites the forms of a word (as it should), whereas the asterisked roots of Proto-Indo-European were obtained from a multitude of unsafe cognates. The traditional analysis of *son* raises no objections: this word was coined as the past participle of a verb meaning "to give birth"; *n* is a regular suffix in it. But *sū* (sow) and *sugu* are a different matter. *Sū* may have no connection with that verb, and *-g-* need not be an enlargement.

According to another suggestion, *sū* is onomatopoeic, because in some places, *su-su* and *su-ee* are used to call pigs and because pigs produce *sū*-like noises. This etymology of *sū* is also questionable. In most languages, the word imitating pigs' grunt contains the sound *gr-* and *khr-*. *Su-su,* a call to pigs, may have arisen in retrospect, to match the existing word. Thus the Russian call to ducks is *uti-uti,* because the Russian for "duck" is *utka.* The name for "pig" resembling *su* has also been attested in non-Indo-European languages. We may be dealing with an ancient culture word. Sons are not demeaned by a union with sows (let us not say *swine*), nor are sows elevated by finding themselves in the same etymological litter with sons, but enlargements begin to look suspicious in company with real suffixes.

Only suffixes can be separated from the root in good faith. In Gothic *stōjan* (to judge), *-j-* is a common verbal suffix and *-an* is an ending; *stō-* is the root. Old Engl. *stōwian* (to restrain) is a cognate of *stōjan* (it is almost its homonym), and we divide it in a similar fashion: *stō-w-ian.* The Old English for *stool* was *stōl.* Like *tool,* from *tōl,* it ends in a suffix forming the names of devices and implements. The elements *j, w,* and *l* are suffixes appended to the root *stō-* that we also recognize in Old Engl. *stōd* (stood) and *stōd* (stud) ("a place where horses 'stand' and are bred"). The stool "stood" in its place and the judge "stood" for or against the defendant. An enlargement that can be identified with a suffix is simply a suffix. All the other enlargements are questionable, to say the least.[29]

At the end of Chapter 15, mention was made of two types of word families: one exemplified by Sanskrit *pitár,* Latin *pater,* and Gothic *fadar* (father) ("the aristocrats") and the other by *pig – pug – big – bug – punk – pock,* and so forth ("the plebeians"). There the question was asked whether the second family is younger than the first. While Indo-European ablaut existed as a productive model, it served as a barrier to secondary ("false") ablaut (that is why *heath* and *heather* should be kept apart), and while Grimm's Law worked, Old Engl. *fæmne* and Latin *fēmina* could not be cognates. Some "plebeians" are probably late, but, in principle, word formation of the type ABC to ABD to ABF must be as old as AB + C ~ AB + D ~ AB + F. In observing *fit – fid – fik* and *pig – big – bug,* we are reminded not of natural growth (*stō + w + an = stōwan*) but of gemmation. It is as though one word budded off from another: *pug* from *pig, puck* from *pock* (or the other way around), and so forth. There seems to have been a common root or stem, but such a root or stem is an illusion.

The idea of gemmation occurred to me when I was investigating the etymology of the English *F*-word. In the Germanic languages, about two dozen verbs beginning with *fik-, fit-, fid-, fak-, fok-, fop-, fob-, fug-,* and so on have the basic meaning "move back and forth" (*fickle, fitful,* and *fiddle* are a small part of the verbs, nouns, and adjectives united by this meaning and the structure *f* + vowel + consonant). Each of them looks like an etymological mongrel, yet together they form a close-knit pack. Much later, I ran across a passage in a work by Karl Jaberg, a distinguished Romance scholar, in which he refers to Hugo Schuchardt's theory. The most amazing thing for me was that, independent of Schuchardt, I came up with the same botanical image (budding, gemmation) and that Jaberg cited the same layer of words (namely, verbs of moving back and forth) to make his point, though his material was Italian rather than Germanic dialects. This is what he says:

> If I am not mistaken, he [Schuchardt] was the first to suggest the existence of etymological masses. He meant large word families that are in some way

related as true siblings or by other close ties, but whose kinship cannot be established beyond doubt and in all particulars. Etymological masses can develop from the parent word by branching off or budding, approximately as a coral reef develops from the parent body or as does an organism from a single cell. But they can also go back to the merger of words and forms having different origins, the way different genera and species make up a unit. In the first case, we are dealing with etymological masses proper; in the second, with semasiological companionship. A typical example of such companionship is the group 'move back and forth' ('swing, rock, dangle, sway; loiter'). These verbs are connected with nouns whose meaning may be specialized and remote from the basic one. Such concepts are sometimes quite distinct and sometimes have blurred contours. Their names arise and are remodeled in the process of communication between children and adults. In Upper Italy and Tessin, the stems *ball-, baltr, and baltz-* form such a company.[30]

Etymology as a branch of knowledge (another botanical metaphor) lacks an apparatus with which it can solve the riddle of the origin of language, but the older the period with which it deals, the nearer it thinks it can come to the emergence of the first words. Every now and then enthusiasts believed that they had discerned a small number of syllables from which the words of all languages sprang up. They saw a mirage. The relationship between gesture and the spoken word remains a matter of debate; considering how fast words change their form, the large-scale survival of a direct tie between modern words and ancient gestures is unlikely. But onomatopoeia and sound symbolism certainly lie within the purview of etymological inquiry.

At some stage, etymologists reach demotivated sound complexes. For example, they cannot explain why, at one time, the syllable *all* acquired the meaning "whole, entire." Cognates have been listed and a few semantic ties restored, but the question about how, in this complex, the union between sound and meaning arose remains unanswered. Such cases are numerous. Reducing words to their putative roots and dividing them into smaller elements does little to provide the answer, and getting such units is not the ultimate aim of etymology. As this book has shown, a searching mind has enough work even if the beginning of things is hidden.

Chapter Seventeen

*in which the author surveys the scene
and treads the downward slope, or*

The State of English Etymology

Why the downward slope?—From Hebrew as the language in Paradise to the Semitic family in its relation to Indo-European.—The first etymologists of the postmedieval era: Kilianus, Minsheu, Ménage, Helvigius, Skinner, Wachter, Junius, Ihre, and others.—An anonymous pirate.—New philology begins.—Linguists are not expected to know foreign languages.—Hensleigh Wedgwood, the bow-wow man, and Eduard Mueller of historical interest.—Walter W. Skeat's great learning and indefatigable industry.—Polemicists' abrasive style.—Etymologies are discovered, not agreed on.—A good etymological dictionary.—Word histories.—Charles P. G. Scott and Henry Cecil Wyld.—Historical linguistics loses its prestige.—Etymology survives and is here to stay.

It was the hero of Robert Louis Stevenson's epitaph who had "trod the upward and the downward slope." Scholarship, despite all its aberrations and zigzags, moves from peak to peak. Thrillers, on the other hand, must eventually reach the dénouement; hence the borrowed words of the great writer. But before coming down to the valley, we must pay a last symbolic visit to St. Cecilia, whom we left at the mercy of adoring theologians in Chapter 2. It was said there that medieval philosophers did not search for the origin of words the way we do. For them etymology existed "to support—and as they thought prove—preconceived beliefs."[1] The question raised in *Cratylus*—are words arbitrary or natural?—continued to be discussed throughout the Middle Ages (and it is still being discussed). Juggling with words and turning them into charades did not contribute to the progress of philology, but the fanciful view of Hebrew as the source of all languages produced a crude version of comparative linguistics. In the nineteenth century, soon after language families were established, it became clear that the Indo-European and the Semitic languages shared more elements than could be ascribed to chance. Although Hebrew did not regain its position as the mother of tongues, its importance to students of Indo-European increased, and modern scholars look with some interest at the Hebrew-Greek / Latin / Germanic etymologies suggested in the past. A few of them may lead in the right direction. Still later, attempts were made to prove the unity of several language families, and various "global etymologies" gained in popularity. They owe nothing to medieval fantasies; yet the erosion of "provincial" historical linguistics partly vindicates the belief of the Middle Ages in a single kernel of all languages, and the old term *Celto-Scythian* can be understood as a vague counterpart of *Indo-European*.

However, etymology not based on sound correspondences will only arrive at sensible conclusions when the case is trivial (Latin *pater* ~ Engl. *father*), or by chance. Today, the origin of many words remains unknown, but we are able to stay away from unpromising convergences, however tempting they may seem. The closeness of Latin *cura* (care, attention, anxiety) and Engl. *care,* Greek *hólos* (whole, all, entire)[2] and Engl. *whole* (from *hāl; w* has never been sounded in it), or Latin *habēre* and Engl. *have* ~ German *haben* (the same meaning) will deceive no one, because Grimm's Law disqualifies them as possible cognates. (The original meaning of *care* was "grief" and "an expression of grief, lament"; the word is related to Latin *garrīre* [to chatter, to be garrulous.] A cognate of *whole* in Baltic and Slavic begins with *k,* and *have* is akin, in a devious way, to Latin *capio* [to take, capture.])

For a long time, the main method of etymology was dissecting a word and adding, subtracting, and transposing letters. Socrates already used it. (We do the same, but according to rules and guided by the facts of history!) Those procedures are easy to mock, for they are indeed silly. The favorite target of ridicule is Gilles Ménage (1613–1692), the author of the first etymological dictionary of French.[3] Here are some of his derivations: Latin *albus, albicus* (white) to *blaicus, blacus, blancus,* French *blanc,* and by another transposition, *albus, albidus, blaidus, blaydus, blaundus, blondus,* French *blond* (none of the intermediate stages ever existed); Latin *faba* (bean) to *fabaricus, fabaricotus, aricotus,* French *haricot* (bean); Latin *mūs* (mouse) to *muratus, ratus,* French *rat* (rat). But the author of such impossible etymologies was a man of great learning, who knew many old and modern languages and dialects and may be credited with formulating the principles of historical grammar and laying the groundwork for comparative Romance philology.[4]

It is enough to remember that language was at the center of Locke's and Leibnitz's interests to treat seventeenth-century linguistics with respect.[5] Also in the seventeenth century, the first etymological dictionaries of new European languages began to appear. The earliest of them even beat the round date and was published in 1599. In that year, Corneille Kiel, who Latinized his name as Kilianus and is often referred to as Kiliaan, brought out an etymological dictionary of Dutch.[6] His entries seldom exceed three lines, and he gave only the briefest indications to the words' origins, but he knew Dutch dialects and preferred facts to flights of fancy. This made his comments extremely valuable. Kiel has been an object of intense study in Dutch linguistics.

In 1617, John Minsheu (Latinized as Manshæus) published the first etymological dictionary of English.[7] It is half etymological dictionary, half thesaurus. Synonyms in several languages, each with its origin (as Minsheu imagined it), are listed even when, from an etymological point of view, they have nothing to do with the English headword. Although Minsheu showed good sense in selecting cognates and had heard some anecdotes about the history of words, he looked for all etymons in Hebrew, which did not prevent some of his derivations from being repeated two hundred years later. In 1671, Thomas Henshaw edited, supplemented, and published a dictionary by Stephen Skinner.[8] It looks more like a modern etymological dictionary than Minsheu's, for it does not offer an assortment of synonyms in addition to derivations. Whereas Minsheu wanted to trace every word to a Hebrew root, Skinner sought the origins of English in Greek. But he detected cognates with considerable skill, and some of his suggestions turned out to be even more long-lived than Minsheu's.

Between 1617 and 1671, the first German etymological dictionary by Helwig (Latinized as Helvigius) appeared (1620),[9] and Ménage's monumental work came out (1650). Ménage wrote in French. Minsheu used English but gave most glosses in Latin. Skinner and Helvigius, as well as some later authors, wrote only in Latin. An enterprising plagiarist, whose identity remains unknown (his printers, too, hid behind initials) abridged Skinner's *Etymologicum . . .* and translated it into English.[10] All those dictionaries are not simply outdated: they will mislead a modern browser inquiring about word origins. But to a student of the history of ideas they are far from useless. Among other things, we note that words in them are investigated for their own sake, rather than for supporting preconceived ideas—a tremendous step forward in comparison with the Middle Ages.

The linguistic base of seventeenth-century dictionaries is broad. In addition to Hebrew, Greek, and Latin, Minsheu and others knew several modern languages, while Kilianus, as pointed out, felt at home in Dutch dialects. The bulk of the texts in Old and Middle English, Old High German, Old French, and so on lay unpublished. However, Skinner's contemporaries were aware of them and had access to manuscripts. In 1659, an influential dictionary of Old English appeared.[11] Tracing all words to Hebrew and two classical languages was an unprofitable idea, except in dealing with borrowings, but the vocabulary of modern European languages contains such a mass of words, evidently not going back to antiquity, that the search for their origin, of necessity, concentrated on other sources and often resulted in plausible conjectures.

Those who expect to come away from an etymological dictionary with more than a drop of distilled truth will enjoy a survey of old hypotheses and realize that since every etymology is the product of reconstruction, it presupposes a varying margin of error. The tortuous way that leads to a discovery is interesting and instructive to observe. Following it puts our own achievements in perspective and cures us of arrogance. Regardless of the validity of the proposed

solutions, old dictionaries are precious monuments of early lexicography. In the seventeenth and the eighteenth century, etymology was
unabashed guesswork: people compared words and offered their derivations. All of them seemed to be worth discussing, and some entries
contained only an array of older suggestions. Thanks to this method
of presentation, we learn the opinions that would have been next to
impossible for us to dig out (see the subtitle of Lemon's dictionary in
note 12).

In the eighteenth century, the study of word origins continued,
and four new etymological dictionaries of Germanic languages came
out: two of English (Junius, Lemon),[12] one of German (Wachter),[13]
and one of Swedish (Ihre).[14] Lemon's work is insignificant, but the
others reflect every credit on contemporary scholarship. Junius and
Ihre were outstanding philologists and wrote many books beside the
dictionaries (Junius's *Etymologicum* . . . was published posthumously
by Edward Lye, a lexicographer in his own right).[15] Latin remained
the preferred medium, and it was a good thing (even though often
inconvenient to us), for a major contribution to Gothic, English, German, Runic, and the rest easily transcended national borders. One
should have no illusions: an average linguist is not a polyglot.

The "scientific" period in the history of etymology, inaugurated
by Rask and Grimm, did not gain momentum immediately after the
appearance of their works, just as Old English did not turn into Middle
English on October 15, 1066, a day after the Battle of Hastings. Rask
wrote his great investigation in Danish, and if Jacob Grimm had not
known the Scandinavian languages, it might have passed unnoticed.
He at once appreciated the discovery of the consonant shift and developed Rask's ideas in the second edition of his *Deutsche Grammatik
[Germanic Grammar]*. Although he referred to Rask, his colleagues
ignored the reference (whence "Grimm's Law"). The glorious epoch
of Indo-European philology began, but the new methods needed years
to become common property. In the meantime, Skinner, Junius, and
more modern dictionaries at their level continued to satisfy the public, ignorant of sound correspondences, ablaut, and the like. Also,
German was not a popular language in England and France. In the
first half of the nineteenth century, even professional linguists could

not always read convoluted, long-winded German prose and rarely
subscribed to German periodicals.

The most durable etymological dictionaries of English and German are by Walter W. Skeat (1882) and Friedrich Kluge (1883),[16] but
two earlier dictionaries treating the origin of English words deserve
a passing mention. Hensleigh Wedgwood, the author of the first of
them,[17] was expected to prepare the etymologies for what later came
to be known as the *Oxford English Dictionary,* decades before the
letter A went into print. At that time, nearly every volume of the
Proceedings / Transactions of the Philological Society carried an
article by him. He was a dyed in the wool bow-wow man; the introduction to his dictionary is devoted to the role of onomatopoeia in
the origin of language. His articles are more impressive than his dictionary. In them, he listed words of the "plebeian" class (to use the
term from an earlier chapter of this book) and recognized their affinity.[18] But he was not particularly keen on sound correspondences.
Faced with a string of nouns and verbs from languages as remote
from English as Hebrew and Finnish, all of which he gives alongside
Gothic, Icelandic, and German words, one does not know what to do
with them.

However, even his critics admired his gift for ferreting out similar
words from various languages, and George P. March, a distinguished
specialist in the history of English, undertook an American edition
of Wedgwood's dictionary supplied with his corrections. Only one
volume (the letters A–D) was published.[19] Skeat had a low opinion
of Wedgwood, which does not mean that Wedgwood was always
wrong. His book *Contested Etymologies in the Dictionary of the Rev.
W. W. Skeat*[20] is full of insightful remarks. Skeat never responded to
the attack. Later, he drew a rather unsympathetic picture of his "fel-
low-collegian, . . . late Fellow of Christ's College, Cambridge," and
yet the following passage is now worth quoting in full (see part of it
in Chapter 4, p. 35):

. . . the author maintains, with much skill and abundant illustrations, the
theory that language took its rise from imitation of natural sounds and cries
and from expressive interjections, in opposition to the theory of Max Müller

that linguistic roots are 'phonetic types produced by a power inherent in human nature,' whatever that may mean. The theory here advocated by Wedgwood is (as I believe) right in the main, and I may refer the reader to the treatment of it by Whitney and Sweet. Unluckily, it influenced the author far too much in his account of various words; for in many cases the forms in use are too modern or too much altered from their primitive shape for us to be still able to trace how they first arose.[21]

Nowadays, few people consult Wedgwood, which is a pity.

The second dictionary that appeared not long before Skeat's is by Eduard Mueller (sometimes his name is spelled Müller).[22] "This is a thoroughly good and sound work. . . . The results are presented in a brief but usually accurate form, so that most of the articles require little or no correction. But it does not seem to be much known or much used in England, owing, I suppose, to the fact that the text is written in German." Such was Skeat's verdict.[23] "Not much known or much used" is a euphemism. Mueller was well-read and reliable. His references to German dictionaries and compendia are especially valuable today, because some books he knew so well have no word indexes. German scholars of that time managed to keep track of everything their colleagues wrote. Neither a chance remark nor a footnote distant from the subject announced in the title of the article would escape their attention. Only toward the end of the nineteenth century, one begins to find disclaimers of the type: "I am not sure that I am the first to offer this fairly obvious etymology." Mueller's dictionary is now of historical interest only, which means that no one ever opens it.

Walter William Skeat (1835–1912) could have been the name of a factory: the man produced so much. The first short sketch of a linguist's life often appears in an obituary, and I will begin by quoting from one such obituary:

Probably the most familiar face in Cambridge of late years has been that of the veteran who is now gone beyond the sunset. Mentally and physically— he was an expert skater—he seemed to be fashioned out of springs, or like a clock wound up to go for centuries. Nothing daunted him, nothing hindered him for long—his own mistakes as little as anything else . . . Holidays and recreations were an irrelevancy to him, to be tolerated only because without them the springs lost their rebound, not for their own sake. This student's pastime was books, books to be read, perhaps even more, books to be made.[24]

Not waiting for obituaries, Skeat wrote a long introduction to his collection of notes *A Student's Pastime,* largely an account of his studies and scholarly principles, but he also said something about his early years in it, and acted wisely, for without this *curriculum vitae,* his biography would have merged with his bibliography for us.[25] The two are, of course, inseparable, but despite his supernatural assiduity, Skeat was a married man, the father of five children, the author of occasional verses in Old, Middle, and Modern English and Latin, and, as we now know, an expert skater, not a factory. Incidentally, the project to compile Skeat's bibliography has not materialized— I suspect because his editions, glossaries, dictionaries, textbooks, and major articles can be followed, but not his myriad contributions to the most unexpected magazines, *The Hawk*[26] and *The Western Antiquary,* for example.[27]

It is as though an angel guarded Skeat all his life. The young Skeat's ambition was to spend his life as a country curate, and, having completed his degree at Christ's College, Cambridge, he read for holy orders, which he took in 1860. Some curates lived in poverty, but Skeat was comfortably off. He had just moved to another curacy, when, in his words, "an alarming attack of a diphtheric character, totally unfitted" him for clerical work. He does not explain how his organism was affected and why the disease that he ascribed to unsuitable climate never interfered with his future work, but the misfortune turned out to be a blessing in disguise. Skeat went back to Christ's College in the capacity as a mathematical lecturer and, on observing how desolate the field of English philology was, decided to study literature and especially Anglo-Saxon, that is, Old English. He had always liked reading and mathematics. Beginning in 1864, Skeat, the great philologist, appears on the scene. In 1878, he was elected to an endowed chair of Anglo-Saxon at Cambridge. A talented man, with luck always on his side, he lived a happy life, for, as he says, "perhaps no researcher is more fortunate than one whose self-chosen occupation has become his allotted task."[28]

Much has been made of Skeat's arrogance; he has even been called an intellectual bully.[29] But, judging by his participation in the debate, he lost his temper only when he saw complacent ignorance. *Notes and Queries* (a tremendously popular and immensely useful biweekly) printed dozens of uninformed letters whose authors expressed their views on the origin of words. Skeat never tired of repeating that etymology needed professional knowledge, that "opinions" had no value in that area, that it was rash to suggest derivations without consulting the *Oxford English Dictionary* (first called *The New English Dictionary on Historical Principles),* and that Englishmen were unable to understand the simplest truths about scholarship. Everything he said about amateur-etymologists was right, and the last statement, made by an Englishman, could not offend anyone. Sometimes he was wrong and got a taste of his own medicine, but "nothing hindered him for long—his own mistakes as little as anything else." Of course, he was "the establishment" and may not have always been sensitive enough to the woes of the less fortunate.[30] However, snobbery and callousness were hardly typical of him.

As regards the tone of Skeat's attacks on his countrymen's mental sloth, it should be remembered that the journalese of his days was sometimes shockingly rude. One is almost ashamed to read the reviews and rejoinders from the pen of respectable scholars. Here are two samples chosen from James A. H. Murray's legacy. The etymology of the word *Cockney* in *The Century Dictionary* aroused his unrestrained wrath. A huge wheel was set in motion to crush a butterfly. Some of Murray's jibes are as follows:

> Notwithstanding that we have been recently assured, on the high authority of Prof. Whitney [the dictionary's editor-in-chief], that this is 'the only solution of *cockney* phonetically satisfactory,' I think I know Somerville Hall girls, perhaps even Extension Students who would irreverently laugh at it as impossible. . . . Popularization of scholars' work is all very well, provided one has scholarship enough to do it. But surely it should be the broadcasting of truth not of error; it is better not to set up as an authority and 'talk tall' like an expert of what is phonetically satisfactory. One can always say 'I don't know.' Especially important is this in America, where in the absence of liv-

ing English usage, the dictionary occupies a place of authority never conceded to it by educated Englishman. There men swear by the dictionary, its pronunciation, its etymology.[31]

Nine years later, he deigned to recognize an American admirer and unleashed his fury on an "educated Englishman." Now his victim was a certain C. C. B., who complained that the *Oxford English Dictionary* had missed *hennedwole,* one of the names of henbane. Murray offers friendly advice:

> If C. C. B. will rub his eyes, and look again in the "Dictionary," he will, I think, find *hen-dwale* in its alphabetic place on p. 222, col. 3. Some space in "N. & Q" would be saved if people would look twice before writing to say that words are not in the "Dictionary," or if the Editor would himself test such assertions before printing them. It was recently wisely said by an American scholar and critic, "He is a rash man who ventures to say what is not in the 'dictionary'; when you cannot find something there, it is safer to say *you have failed* to find it"

Technically, C. C. B. was right: he looked for *hennedwole,* not *hendwale,* as he stated in his reply, but probably no one took his defense seriously.[32] I doubt that Skeat would ever have derided someone for talking tall or suggested that even the stupidest letter writer should rub his eyes and look again in the dictionary.

Another drawback of which Skeat has often been accused is that he tended to rush his books into print. Murray disapproved of Skeat's idea of bringing out an etymological dictionary before the field had been plowed deep enough. Skeat's first fascicles appeared in 1879, and the last in 1882; the printing of the *Oxford English Dictionary* began in 1884. Skeat, in turn, advised Murray not to wait interminably for a perfect product, publish what he had, and make changes in a later edition. Murray, fortunately, refused to listen. Skeat said in retrospect:

> The preparation for press of this rather ambitious work occupied four years; and it would have occupied a much longer time if I had not made some previous preparation for work of this character, and if, on the other hand, I had exercised fuller research in some cases of unusual difficulty. I

am ready to confess, with all candour, that it seemed to be more necessary that the work should be completed within a somewhat short time than that it should be delayed too long. The publication, soon afterwards, of a second edition enabled me to correct some of the more obvious errors; and several more corrections and additions have been made, from time to time, in the successive editions of the epitome called *A Concise Etymological Dictionary.*

With all its errors, the work has been of much use. The references are numerous and not often incorrect. . . . Many of the etymologies are more correct than in most of the preceding works of a similar character, and point out the immediate sources of words with a greater degree of exactness.

One test of comparative success is imitation; and of this form of compliment the work has had its fair share. Most of the Dictionaries which have appeared since 1882 have borrowed from it more or less.[33]

Sometimes one can read that Skeat was a popularizer rather than an original thinker.[34] I wonder whether anyone who says so has offered a new convincing etymology of a single word or explained even one obscure line in an old author.

The last edition of Skeat's dictionary (1910) marks a peak that English etymological lexicography never transcended. In 1928, the publication of the *Oxford English Dictionary* reached its completion. Etymologies in it are superb and complement Skeat's. Although books with titles like Skeat's continued to appear with some regularity, none of them has become an event in the history of English letters.[35] This is also true of Weekley's contribution. Its author was a first-rate expert in the history of French words in English (and indeed an outstanding popularizer), but his dictionary is original only to the extent that it traces many words to names (see pp. 110–13, above). To this day, someone who wants to know more about the origin of an English word than is given in "thick" dictionaries should consult Skeat and Oxford. This is not said to belittle *The Concise Oxford Dictionary, Webster's Collegiate Dictionary,* and their likes. Etymologies in them are models of brevity and circumspection, but they are an appetizer or dessert (depending on the format), not the main course.

Most of us will probably define a good dictionary as one in which we find answers to all our questions about words. An etymological dictionary cannot live up to such standards. Definitions and usage are often debatable, and the pronunciation and spelling of some words is unstable. Yet all those things are a matter of consensus, whereas the origin of words should be discovered, not agreed on. Unsophisticated browsers are unaware of the difference, and the statement "origin unknown (uncertain)," wherever they may see it, disappoints them. Compilers of modern explanatory dictionaries are not in a position to research anew the origin of all words or even cite the best hypotheses: there are too many to choose from. Those who, in the past, dared to add an etymology to every entry became either authorities, regardless of how trustworthy they were (a classic example is Noah Webster), or objects of bitter criticism (here the best example would be Samuel Johnson, who relied on Skinner).

The followers of Rask and Grimm developed the principles of historical linguistics still in use. By the end of the nineteenth century, new etymological dictionaries of most Indo-European languages had appeared. Ménage, Skinner, and their contemporaries were left behind. The etymology of English, German, French, and so on became part of Indo-European etymology. One could no longer suggest the derivation of Engl. *man,* to give a random example, without learning what is known about its certain and putative cognates elsewhere in Germanic, Slavic, Sanskrit, and Greek. This means that an etymological entry, rather than being compressed into a line or two (when only the bare bones of *man* are visible), should be expanded into an essay (with several pounds of flesh exposed to view). A good etymological dictionary is apparently one that lists all the related forms, explains the nature of the problem, ranges freely over the vast literature on the subject, and judges wisely who is right and who is wrong—with a possible conclusion that the origin of the word remains a matter of debate! As explained in Chapter 1, dictionaries of this type exist, though not for English. A non-philologist does not need such a wealth of detail, and since the production of a comprehensive etymological dictionary takes decades, lexicographers on the staff of "thick" dictionaries copy from the best sources available. For English, as I said, they are Skeat and Oxford.

Occasionally, the editor of an explanatory or encyclopedic dictionary will go far beyond the call of duty and give the etymologies unusual prominence. This is what William Dwight Whitney *(The Century Dictionary)* and Henry Cecil Wyld *(The Universal Dictionary of the English Language)* did.[36] Whitney's etymologist was Charles P. G. Scott. Wyld wrote the etymologies himself. Both achieved spectacular results. But since the origin of an obscure word will often remain problematic, neither was infallible. Their main achievement consisted in providing the history of English words with a Germanic and Indo-European context.

The market is flooded with "word histories." At present, they also recycle the *Oxford English Dictionary* and Skeat. The earliest of such books seems to have been written in 1818.[37] Duane Clayton Barnes begins his *Wordlore* so: "This little volume makes no claim to erudition. There is little in it that anyone with some linguistic background could not dig out of a good dictionary."[38] His "little volume" (135 pages) is excellent. Not many authors will make such a truthful and disarming statement.

Such is the state of English etymology. Before my story draws to a close, I would like to say something about the place of etymology in today's humanities. During roughly the first three quarters of the nineteenth century, thousands of middle-class West Europeans would have eight years of Latin and four years of Greek at school and then go to the university to study more Latin and Greek. Those who remained in philology and specialized in Classics or Germanic (later in Romance) with an emphasis on linguistics usually ended up in historical linguistics, because for a long time the two were synonyms. The core of historical linguistics was etymology; consequently, they wrote dissertations and articles on the origin of words.

That tradition came to an end soon after the First World War. Constructivism in architecture and cubism in painting had their analogs in linguistics. The success of nuclear physics reinforced the linguists' desire to study minimal units and their functions. The age of structuralism and general theory set in. Its first practitioners were gifted people with a strong interest in the growth of language because of the training they received. But their pupils and followers were mostly theoreticians, and language history lost its prestige.

The trend that manifested itself so clearly in the twenties and thirties became prevalent in the fifties and later. New theories, based on mathematical symbols and steeped in jargons incomprehensible to outsiders, sprang up every few years. Despite their forbidding aspect, they were easy to master (much easier than Latin, Icelandic, or Old French) and looked like sciences, and there is nothing a linguist wants more than to be taken for a scientist. However, curricular conservatism saved historical linguistics as an academic discipline from total destruction, and Indo-European studies survived, though mainly in phonetics and grammar, the areas that, for evil or good, lend themselves to formalization (the use of symbols, and so on). Yet a trickle of serious articles and books on etymology never dried up—all that was left of the once powerful stream.

Luckily, the general public knew nothing about the change of attitude among the academicians and kept asking "why we say so." Publishers were happy to satisfy its curiosity, but scholars of Weekley's stature (Weekley's numerous well-written books on the history of English words are still remembered) had died. The vacuum was filled by a rehash of other people's work; research and popularization almost parted company. The acrimonious note 35 to this chapter shows that in English, even etymological dictionaries turned into uninspired compilations. At present, the theoretical boom is on the decline, and although etymology is still a stepdaughter of college departments of linguistics, the number of articles on the history of words in good journals is not inconsiderable, if one compares the situation today with what was going on in the seventies (of the twentieth, not of the nineteenth!) century.[39] Etymology has nothing to fear. It was born with our civilization and will be the last discipline to die.[40]

Chapter Eighteen

in which the author, having reaped the word wind,
comes full circle, and takes farewell of his readers
in the hope of meeting them again, or

Conclusion

For they have sown the wind, and they shall reap the whirlwind.

Hosea VIII: 7

The difference between beginning and end is conventional.—The neglect of vocabulary in books on the history of language.—Books on English etymology.—Scratching the surface is not the same as diving below.—Demand and supply in courses on English words.—Picking up the jewels dropped while treading the upward slope.

This chapter could have been the first in the story of how etymologists reap the wordwind, but it will make more sense here. Those who remember the term enantiosemy will appreciate the merger of beginning and end. Not to make too fine a point of it, this chapter is about the book you have read. Hardly any language has been explored in more detail than English: an annual bibliography devoted to it is a volume that gets thicker every year. Students of English are expected to become familiar with its phonetics, grammar (morphology and syntax), and vocabulary, including the history of all three. The organization of the word system is easy to understand, but hard to represent as a coherent whole, because the lexicon is vast and open-ended; words are born and die incessantly. For this reason, historical grammars traditionally deal with two parts: phonetics and morphology. The number of sound units, declensions, and conjugations is small, and schemes of their development are simple.

Any introduction to the history of English touches on the Germanic origin of English vocabulary, the Scandinavian invasion, the Norman Conquest, and the role of later borrowings. The origin of English words is treated in special books. Some of them have the word *etymology* in their titles. I know of one such book in Russian,[1] two in French,[2] and three in English.[3] Many contain an overview of the development of English vocabulary but do without *etymology* on the cover.[4] Many more deal with various aspects of the history of English words. The notes that begin on p. 253 give only the faintest idea of the literature on the subjects discussed. In the previous chapters (and this includes the references), my aim has been to say as little as possible about the things that can be found in other popular books on English words. Therefore, I devoted minimal space to the Scandinavian and the Romance element in English. Specialists may discover little beyond a few interesting titles in the notes; the others will disregard the small print and follow the plot, which, except in one chapter, thickens from page to page.

Word Origins combines entertainment with instruction. At present, the backbone of our educational system is fun. Where I live, students wish one another a fun class, and to ensure their approval, one has to be a funny guy. I sincerely hope that I have provided word lovers with fun, though I have made no effort to sound "funny"; it is language that is forever at play, and the amusement comes from following the game. But I also had our curricular needs in view. Despite the popularity of courses on the history of words, they are offered rarely, and teaching materials are all but non-existent for them. One has to put together homemade anthologies from journal articles and pieces of manuals no longer protected by copyright. Nothing like Greenough and Kittredge's classic has been written for over a century. If this book stimulates someone to teach the history of English words, it may perhaps serve as the main text. In addition to surveying English vocabulary, I wanted to show how etymologists work, what procedures are standard in their analysis, what mistakes should be avoided, and why the origin of some words remains unknown.

A. T. Hatto, an incomparable translator into English of three great Middle High German poems—*The Nibelungenlied, Tristan,* and *Parzival*—finished *The Nibelungenlied* with an article entitled "An Introduction to a Second Reading." I, too, would like to invite my readers to leaf through this book again. Many things said in the early chapters will appear in a new light now that the end is known. A book not worth rereading is not worth reading even once.

Notes

Chapter One

1. Jacob (sometimes spelled *Jakob*) Grimm, 1785–1863, and Wilhelm Grimm, 1786–1859.
2. See Rudolf Majut, "Himmelsziege und Verwandtes," *Zeitschrift für deutsche Sprache* 19 (1963): 1–38, and my article "The Origin of the Eddic Animal Names *Heiðrún* and *Eikþyrnir,*" *General Linguistics* 28 (1988): 32–48. Reprinted with changes in my collection of essays, *Word Heath. Wortheide. Orðheiði* (Rome: Il Calamo, 1994), pp. 237–252.
3. Walter W. Skeat, *An Etymological Dictionary of the English Language.* 4th ed. (Oxford: Clarendon Press, 1910). James A. H. Murray et al., eds. *Oxford English Dictionary* (Oxford: Clarendon Press, 1884–1928). Since that time the second edition of the *Oxford English Dictionary,* eds. J. A. Simpson and E. S. C. Weiner, has been published, and an updated version is available online.
4. Nathan Bailey, *An Universal Etymological English Dictionary* (London: Printed for E. Bell, *et al.*) Reprinted in the series "Anglistica and Americana," 52 (Hildesheim, New York: G. Olms, 1969).
5. Christian Bartholomae, "Arica XIV," *Indogermanische Forschungen* 12 (1901): 92–150.
6. Theodor Siebs, "Von Henne, Tod und Teufel," *Zeitschrift für Volkskunde* 40 (1930): 49–61.

7. Sigmund Feist, *Vergleichendes Wörterbuch der gotischen Sprache,* 3rd. ed., 1939; 4th ed. (in English), by W. P. Lehmann (Leiden: E. J. Brill, 1986).
8. Manfred Mayrhofer, *Kurzgefaßtes etymologisches Wörterbuch des Altindischen. A Concise Etymological Sanskrit Dictionary* (Heidelberg: Carl Winter, 1956–80); Hjalmar Frisk, *Griechisches etymologisches Wörterbuch* (Heidelberg: Carl Winter, 1960–66); Alois Walde, *Lateinisches etymologisches Wörterbuch.* 3rd ed., by Johann B. Hofmann (Heidelberg: Carl Winter, 1938–54).
9. Walther von Wartburg, *Französisches etymologisches Wörterbuch.* . . . (Leipzig: B. G. Teubner, Basel: Zbinden, 1934–98).
10. Joan Corominas, with the assistance of José A. Pascual, *Diccionario crítico etimológico castellano e hispánico* (Madrid: Gredos, 1980–98).
11. "The English F-Word and Its Kin." In Gerald F. Carr, Wayne Harbert, and Lihua Zhang (eds.), *Interdigitations: Essays for Irmengard Rauch* (New York, *et al.* Peter Lang, 1999), pp. 107–120. One remark is in order here. A good deal of what will be said in this book is based on my research, but I will mention my published work only in a few exceptional cases. The reader will learn more from references to other people's articles and books.
12. James T. Barrs "The Place of Etymology in Linguistics," *College English* 24 (1962): 116–121.
13. The Greek forms of the words mentioned here are ἔντομον (usually in the plural) (insect), ἔτυμος (true), ἔτυμον (etymon; the true, or original, meaning), and ἐτυμολογίᾳ (etymology).

Chapter Two

1. One of the most important goals of the *Oxford English Dictionary* was to find the earliest occurrences of English words. On the whole, the first editors were astoundingly successful, but thanks to the efforts of many people, earlier citations have often been uncovered and incorporated into the second edition. All the dates given in this book are from the online version of the dictionary.
2. Old English vowels could be short or long. In regularized editions, vowel length is designated by a horizontal line over the letter (macron). The letter *g* in *dæges ēage* was pronounced like *y* in Modern Engl. *yes.*
3. "And Adam gave names to all cattle, and to the fowl of the air, and every beast of the field" (Gen. II:20, AV).
4. Greek χαμαί-μηλον: χαμαί (on the earth) (an archaic local case of the unattested form *χαμά [earth]) and μῆλον (apple), named from the apple-like smell of the flower; the form does not occur in Classical Greek. Another time a compound having the same inner form turned up was when potatoes became known in France: French *pomme de terre* (potato).
5. Otta Wenskus, "Platon und die phrygische Sprache. Eine Bemerkung zu Kratylos 410a." In *Studia Celtica et Indogermanica. Festschrift für Wolfgang*

Meid zum 70. Geburtstag, Peter Anreiter and Erzsébet Jerem, eds. (Budapest: Archaeolingua Foundation, 1999), pp. 445–546. An important work on the Greeks' awareness of foreign languages is Jürgen Werner, "Nichtgriechische Sprachen im Bewußtsein der antiken Griechen." In *Festschrift für Robert Muth zum 65. Geburtstag am 1. Januar 1981, dargebracht von Freunden und Kollegen,* Paul Händel and Wolfgang Meid, eds. (Innsbrucker Beiträge zur Kulturwissenschaft 22. Innsbruck: AMŒ, 1983), pp. 583–595.

6. The literature on the *Cratylus* is immense. In two recent books, the reader will find a detailed commentary on Plato's ideas and references to many earlier works: Timothy M. S. Baxter, *The* Cratylus: *Plato's Critique of Naming.* Philosophia Antiqua, vol. 58 (Leiden, New York, Köln: E. J. Brill, 1992), and John E. Joseph, *Limiting the Arbitrary: Linguistic Naturalism and Its Opposites in Plato's* Cratylus *and Modern Theories of Language.* Amsterdam Studies in the Theory and History of Linguistic Science. Series III, vol. 96 (Amsterdam, Philadelphia: John Benjamins, 2000), Part 1. For a lucid and original exposition of Plato's views on the meaning and origin of words, Ernst Heitsch's treatise can be recommended: *Willkür und Problembewußtsein in Platons Kratylus.* Mainz. Akademie der Wissenschaften und der Literatur. Abhandlungen der Geistes- und Sozialwissenschaftlichen Klasse 1984/11 (Wiesbaden, Stuttgart: Franz Steiner). Peter R. Hofstätter's little book *Vom Leben des Wortes. Das Problem an Platons Dialog "Kratylos" dargestellt* (Erkenntnis und Besinnung 11. Wien: Wilhelm Braumüller, 1949) uses the *Cratylus* as a springboard for a broad discussion of language theory, but it makes an important point: those who thought that Plato had offered a parody of etymologists' efforts (and some of the most distinguished scholars thought so) were almost certainly wrong. Heitsch (p. 32) is of the same opinion. My arrangement of the material owes a heavy debt to Hubert Wolanin's article "Plato and the Position of Etymology in Greek Intellectual Culture," published in *Analecta Indoevropaea Cracoviensia, Joannis Safarewicz Memoria Dicata,* Wojciech Smoczyński, ed. (Cracoviae: In officina cvivs nomen vniversitas, 1995), pp. 513–535.

7. See the discussion of the emergence of individual authorship in the literature of the Middle Ages in M. I. Steblin-Kamenskij, *The Saga Mind.* Translated from the Russian by Kenneth H. Ober (Odense: Odense Universitetsforlag, 1973). (The Russian original: *Mir sagi* [Leningrad: Nauka, 1971].)

8. Das Volk dichtet.

9. Isidore of Seville (ca. 560–636) is famous for his theological treatises and for works of encyclopedic nature. His voluminous *Etymologiae* enjoyed tremendous popularity in the Middle Ages.

10. I have borrowed the translation from Mary Carruthers, "Inventional Mnemonics and the Ornaments of Style: The Case of Etymology," *Connotations* 2 (1992): 103–114. The translation (p. 104) precedes her discussion of medieval etymologizing.

11. Most words in Jacopo's tale are Latin, as they were spelled in the late Middle Ages, but *leos* is λεώς, the Ionian-Attic variant of λαός (people, classical Greek). *Lya* is apparently *Leah,* a Hebrew feminine name.
12. θεός.
13. θέω, θερμός, αἶθος.
14. See Roswitha Klinck, *Die lateinische Etymologie des Mittelalters.* Medium Aevum. Philologische Studien 7 (Munich: Wilhelm Fink, 1970).
15. Old Icelandic *fær* can be detected in the name of Faroe Islands.

Chapter Three

1. ὀνοματοποΐα.
2. Beatrix Potter, *The Tale of Little Pig Robinson* (London, New York: Frederick Warne, 1930) (numerous reprints).
3. William B. Lockwood devoted many studies to the origin of bird names, especially in English and Faroese. *The Oxford Book of British Birds* (Oxford, New York: Oxford University Press, 1984), is his most important contribution to the subject. Those interested in Scandinavian data will find detailed discussion in his book *The Faroese Bird Names.* Færoensia, vol. 5 (Copenhagen: Ejnar Munksgaard, 1961).
4. *The Century Dictionary: An Encyclopedic Lexicon of the English Language,* William Dwight Whitney, ed. (New York: The Century Co., 1889–1911). Revised and enlarged by Benjamin E. Smith, 1911. This superb multivolume dictionary had the ill luck of being published at the same time as the *Oxford English Dictionary,* and this is the only reason it does not enjoy greater popularity. It is weak on citations, but its definitions, explanations, illustrations, and etymologies are excellent; it is also a true work of polygraphic art.
5. *The Oxford Dictionary of English Etymology,* C. T. Onions, ed., with the assistance of G. W. S. Friedrichsen and R. W. Burchfield (Oxford: Clarendon Press, 1966) (reprinted many times). Onions and his colleagues summarized the development of senses as they appear in the *Oxford English Dictionary* and provided a clear picture of the semantic history of English words, but their etymologies seldom differ from those in the *Oxford English Dictionary.* One example of their deviation from Murray's view is the entry *boy* (this word will be discussed below, p. 27), where they follow E. J. Dobson and propose a French etymon.
6. See an especially detailed treatment of *gr-* words in Wilhelm Theodor Braune, "Prov. *grinar,* fr. *grigner, rechigner,* fr. *grigne* u. a.," *Zeitschrift für romanische Philologie* [*ZRP*] 38 (1917): 185–192; "Über einige romanische Wörter deutscher Herkunft," *ZRP* 39 (1919): 174–181 (*gr-*words are discussed in section 2: "Frz. *grincer,* it. *grinza, grinzo,* parm. bologn. *grenta,* lomb. ven. *grima,"* pp. 178-181), and "Prov. *grin,* fr. *grime, grimer, grimaud, grimoire,* sp. ptg.

prov. *grina,*" *ZRP* 39 (1919): 366–371. Braune, the famous author of several grammars and a coeditor with Hermann Paul of the equally famous journal *Beiträge zur Geschichte der deutschen Sprache und Literatur*, was also an original etymologist. But since he mainly studied words of Germanic origin in the Romance languages, he published his articles in *Zeitschrift für romanische Philologie,* and references to them in works on English and German etymology are rare (cf. 259n.4). Most of his excurses on word origins are of the type mentioned above. Although known to students of Germanic philology as Wilhelm Braune, he signed his articles with the first name Theodor, a fact that confuses bibliographers but need not cause any doubts about the author's identity.

7. So, for example, in Calvert Watkins's supplement to *The American Heritage Dictionary of the English Language,* William Morris, ed. (Boston, *et al.*: American Heritage and Houghton Mifflin, 1969), p. 1518, **ghrēu-**. See p. 229 on the source of such roots.

8. Brian O'Cuív, "Observations on Irish 'clog' and Some Cognates," *Studia Celtica* 10–11 (1975–76): 312–317. With regard to the view that Engl. *clock* owes something to Flemish, A. G. Rigg says the following: "The word *clock* entered English twice, first (perhaps from Old Irish) in the Old English period, when it clearly meant 'bell'. . . . There is a tradition . . . that the word *clock* was reintroduced into English by the Dutch clockmakers imported by Edward III (Onions [that is, *The Oxford Dictionary of English Etymology*] inadvertently says Edward I) in 1368. In fact, the word occurs in Richard of Wallingford's *Tractatus Horologii* (written between 1327 and 1336) in the section on making a clock strike. . . . The Flemish experts are red herrings: in 1351 three Lombards were engaged on making the clock for Windsor Castle, and North [the editor of Richard of Wallingford's *Tractatus*] discusses the probability of a long tradition of English clock-making even before Rich of Wallingford. The word very probably came from O[ld] N[orthern] F[rench] *cloque. . . .*" ("Clocks, Dials, and Other Terms" in *Middle English Studies Presented to Norman Davis in Honour of his Seventieth Birthday.* Douglas Gray and E. G. Stanley, eds. [Oxford: Clarendon Press, 1983], pp. 156–57.)

9. Wilhelm Oehl, "Elementar-parallele Verwandte zu indogermanischem *ped/pod* "Fuß"—franz. *patte* "Pfote, Fuß"—deutsch *Pfote.*" In: *Festschrift / Publications d'hommage offerte au P. W. Schmidt* (Wien: Mechitharisten-Congregations-Buchdruckerei, 1928), pp. 93–105.

10. Some of the works on "natural voices" are Wilhelm Wackernagel, *Voces variæ animalium.* Programm für die Rectoratsfeier der Universität (Basel: C. Schulze, 1867); Jost Winteler, *Naturlaute und Sprache. Ausführungen zu W. Wackernagels Voces variæ animalium* (Aarau: H. R. Sauerländer, 1892); Oskar Hanschild, "Deutsche Tierstimmen in Schriftsprache und Mundart," *Zeitschrift für deutsche Wortforschung* 11 (1909): 149–180; 12 (1910): 1–47, and Vicente Garcia de Diego, *Diccionario de voces naturales* (Aguilar: no date).

11. *The English Dialect Dictionary,* Joseph Wright, ed. (London, *et al.*: H. Frowde, 1898–1905; reprint London: Oxford University Press, 1970). This is another great dictionary. Its last volume contains *An English Dialect Grammar.*

12. Hermann Hilmer gives an overabundant list of onomatopoeic words in his book *Schallnachahmung, Wortschöpfung und Bedeutungswandel* (Halle: Max Niemeyer, 1914). The lists (German and English) are on pp. 187–355. Glosses of English words appear in English. See pp. 209–211 for the complex BAT. One can learn many interesting things from the forgotten dictionary by Friedrich Koch, *Linguistische Allotria. Laut-, Ablaut- und Reimbildungen der englischen Sprache.* A posthumous edition by Eugen Wilhelm (Eisenach: J. Bacmeister, 1874). Greek αλλοτρία means "a foreign *or* hostile land." Koch's title alludes to the fact that traditional etymological works of his time ignored or "feared" onomatopoeia. Since 1874, the situation has changed, and this area of study is no longer an *allotria* to serious philologists.

13. Jerome Mandel, "'Boy' as Devil in Chaucer," *Papers in Language and Literature* 11 (1975): 407–411.

14. The literature on onomatopoeia is vast. Some of it will be more convenient to list in the notes on the next chapter. The most recent survey of the subject seems to be Michael Groß, *Zur linguistischen Problematisierung des Onomatopoetischen.* Forum Phoneticum 42 (Hamburg: Helmut Buske, 1988).

Chapter Four

1. See a detailed discussion of metaphors in phonetics in the book by Ivan Fónagy, *Die Metaphern in der Phonetik. Ein Beitrag zur Entwicklungsgeschichte des wissenschaftlichen Denkens.* Janua Linguarum, Series minor 25 (The Hague: Mouton, 1963).

2. Reference to this fact can be found in all works dealing with the subject treated here. The earliest classic is Otto Jespersen, "Symbolic value of the vowel *i*," in his book *Linguistica: Selected Papers in English, French and German* (Copenhagen: Levin and Munksgaard, 1933), pp. 283–303. His article was first published in 1922, but Jespersen made a few alterations in it for the 1933 edition. He devoted a special chapter to sound symbolism in his book *Language* (New York: Henry Holt; London: George Allen & Unwin, 1922), in which he investigated traces of sound symbolism in words denoting movement, things, and appearances ("here, too, there is some more or less obvious association of what is only visible with some sound or sounds"), states of mind (with a passage on why *Mrs. Grundy,* a character in Thomas Morton's comedy [1800], was chosen as a representative of boring respectability), size and distance, and some grammatical forms (this is Chapter 20, pp. 396–411). Dwight L. Bolinger ("Word Affinities," *American Speech* 15 [1940]: 62-73) presents a passionate defense of Jespersen's ideas and develops them.

3. As already stated, the literature on sound symbolism is immense. Jozef Boets lists over a thousand titles pertaining to all aspects of sound symbolism. His book, like those by Hermann Hilmer and Vicente García de Diego (see notes 9 and 11 to the previous chapter), opens with a survey of the field: Jozef Boets, *Moderne teorieën in verband met klankexpressie. Een kritische studie met een systematische bibliografie over de jaren 1900 tot 1960* (Gent: Secretariaat van de Koninklijke Vlaamse Academie voor Taal en Letterkunde, 1965). This bibliography covers only the years 1900–1960. Both Ivan Fónagy (note 1, above) and Michael Groß (note 14 to the previous chapter) treat the same subject. No book of this type seems to exist in English, though articles in English on onomatopoeia and sound symbolism are many (see also what is said below on G. V. Smithers). Excellent work on so-called phonosemantics has been done in Russia. Of the books that treat phonosemantics in depth, five can be mentioned: V. V. Levitskii, *Semantika i fonetika [Semantics and Phonetics]* (Chernovtsy: Izdatel'stvo Chernovitskogo gosudarstvennogo universiteta, 1973); A. P. Zhuravlev, *Foneticheskoe znachenie [Phonetic Meaning]* (Leningrad: Izdatel'stvo Leningradskogo universiteta, 1974); S. V. Voronin, *Osnovy fonosemantiki [The Principles of Phonosemantics.* (Leningrad: Izdatel'stvo Leningradskogo universiteta, 1982); V. V. Levitskii [and] I. A. Sternin, *Eksperimental'nye metody v semasiologii [Experimental Methods in Semasiology]* (Voronezh: Izdatel'stvo voronezhskogo universiteta, 1989); and A. B. Mikhalev, *Teoriia fonosemanticheskogo polia [Theory of the Phonosemantic Field]* (Krasnodar: Izdatel'stvo Piatigorskogo gosudarstvennogo lingvisticheskogo universiteta, 1995). Voronin (1982) and Mikhalev (1995) contain numerous references. Voronin's book is especially important. One of the best old books on this subject is in Czech (M. Kořínek, *Studie z oblasti onomatopoje. Příspěvek kotázce indovuropského ablautu. Remarques sur les onomatopées. Une contribution à l'étude des alternances vocaliques en indo-européen.* Arbeiten der wissenschaftlichen Anstalten der Carluniversität zu Prag 36. Prague 1934), but Germanic examples are in the minority in it.

4. G. V. Smithers, "Some English Ideophones," *Archivum Linguisticum* 6 (1954): 73–111. Smithers is one of the few scholars to have recognized the value of Braune's works on etymology (see note 6 to Chapter 3). He speaks of Braune's "great merit" (p. 106, note 1). William J. Samarin's article "Inventory and Choice in Expressive Language" (in *Linguistic and Literary Studies in Honor of Archibald A. Hill,* vol. 2. Trends in Linguistics: Studies and Monographs 8 [The Hague, Paris, New York: Mouton, 1978]: 313–329) deals with African ideophones. It contains many references to his earlier works.

5. πέμπω.

6. πομπή.

7. See *pump* in the *Oxford English Dictionary, The Oxford Dictionary of English Etymology,* and in Walter W. Skeat, *An Etymological Dictionary of the*

English Language, 4th ed. (Oxford: Clarendon Press, 1910; reprint 1963), and *Pumpe* in Friedrich Kluge, *Etymologisches Wörterbuch der deutschen Sprache,* 20th ed. by Walter Mitzka (a more detailed entry than in the later editions by Elmar Seebol, as in note 13). Karl Jaberg has some interesting things to say about "the international root" *bamb-* ~ *bomb-*. See his article "Géographie linguistique et expressevisme phonétique. Les noms de la balançoire en portugais" (in his collection *Sprachwissenschaftliche Forschungen und Erlebnisse. Neue Folge.* S. Heinimann, ed. Romanica Helvetica 75 [Bern: Francke, 1965]): 81–82; first published in 1946.

8. μόλυβδος, μόλυβος, μόλιβος, and three forms beginning with β: βόλυβδος, βόλιμος, and βόλιβος. See μόλυβδος: in Hjalmar Frisk, *Griechisches etymologisches Wörterbuch.* Indogermanische Bibliothek 2 (Heidelberg: Carl Winter, 1960–66).

9. Otto Jespersen, *Language: Its Nature, Development and Origin* (as in note 2), pp. 313–314.

10. Walter W. Skeat, *A Student's Pastime . . .* (Oxford: Clarendon Press, 1896), p. xxxvii.

11. γράμμα, the genitive γράμματος, whence *grammatic(al).*

12. See what is said on the origin of *glaive* in the *Oxford English Dictionary* and in Ernest Weekley, *An Etymological Dictionary of Modern English* (London: John Murray, New York: E. P. Dutton, 1921; reprint New York: Dover Publications, 1967).

13. This is exactly what Seebold says about German *glühen* (to glow) and *glosen* ~ *glosten* (to glimmer). Friedrich Kluge, *Etymologisches Wörterbuch der deutschen Sprache.* 24th ed., by Elmar Seebold (Berlin, New York: Walter de Gruyter, 2003).

14. The best-known work on expressive gemination is André Martinet, *La gémination consonantique d'origine expressive dans les langues germaniques* (Copenhagen: Levin & Munksgaard; Paris: C. Klincksieck, 1937). It contains a long introductory part on the nature and occurrence of expressive, or emphatic, geminates and several lists of words (verbs, adjectives, adverbs of movement, and nouns). However, it is not always clear why Martinet calls certain geminates expressive, that is, sound symbolic. See also many interesting examples and non-trivial suggestions in Georg Gerland, *Intensiva und iterativa und ihr verhältnis zu einander. Eine sprachwiszenschaftliche abhandlung* (Leipzig: Friedrich Fleischer, 1869), and Richard Loewe, *Germanische Sprachwissenschaft,* 4th ed., vol. 1 (Berlin, Leipzig: Walter de Gruyter, 1933), pp. 93–105.

15. See Timothy M. S. Baxter (as in note 6 to Chapter 2) , pp. 62–65.

16. William Dwight Whitney, *Language and the Study of Language: Twelve Lectures on the Principles of Linguistic Science,* 5th ed. (New York: Scribner, Armstrong, 1873), pp. 426–27.

17. Ibid., pp. 429 and 433.
18. Ibid., p. 427.
19. Ibid., p. 427.
20. Ibid., p. 427.
21. Wilhelm Oehl, "Ein Kapitel Sprachschöpfung—*kap* = ‚greifen' *Hand.*" *Innsbrucker Jahrbuch für Völkerkunde und Sprachwissenschaft* 1, 1926, pp. 50–61.

Chapter Five

1. See both quotations in A. Smythe Palmer, *Folk-Etymology: A Dictionary of Verbal Corruptions or Words Perverted in Form or Meaning, by False Derivation or Mistaken Analogy* (London: Henry Holt, 1883; reprint New York: Greenwood Press, 1969), p. 449. Smythe Palmer, the author of several books on English words, is today remembered mainly because of the success of his *Folk-Etymology.* Although on a more moderate scale, he had a predecessor: Julius Charles Hare, *Fragments of Two Essays in English Philology* (London: Macmillan, 1873) (II: "Words Corrupted by False Analogy or False Derivation" pp. 37–80). Note the meaningless (but still current) phrase *false analogy,* as though analogy can be anything but "false," and the accent on corruption and perversion.
2. Johan Storm, *Englische Philologie. Anleitung zum wissenschaftlichen Studium der englischen Sprache 1. Die lebende Sprache* (Heilbronn: Gebr. Henninger, 1881), p. 195 (he doubted the derivation of the phrase from the prayer); Alois Pogatscher, *Zur Volksetymologie.* In *Dreiunddreissigster Jahresbericht der Steiermärkischen Landes-Oberreallschule in Graz über das Studienjahr 1883/ 84* (Graz: Verlag der Steierm. Landes-Oberrealschule, 1884), p. 17 (he did not find that derivation improbable). Storm and Pogatscher were first-rate specialists in historical linguistics and in the history of English. Linda and Roger Flavell *(Dictionary of Idioms and Their Origins* [London: Kyle Cathie, 1992]) give a survey of the conjectures about this phrase.
3. Leonard R. N. Ashley, "Fiction and Folklore, Etymology and Folk Etymology, Linguistics and Literature," *Literary Onomastics Studies* 12 (1985), pp. 5, 6, 9.
4. W. F. H. Nicolaisen, "Some Humorous Folk-Etymological Narratives," *New York Folklore* 3 (1977), pp. 4, 9.
5. ἀφρός.
6. *An Essay on the Archæology of Our Popular Phrases and Nursery Rhymes.* 2 volumes. A new edition (London: Longman, *et al.,* 1837).
7. Walter W. Skeat, *A Student's Pastime.* . . . (Oxford: Clarendon Press, 1896).

8. Pp. lxxiv–lxxv. The derivation of *foxglove* from *folk's glove* was cause for constant irritation in Skeat's life. He wrote about that word three times (see Nos. 203, 474, and 483 in *A Student's Pastime*) and castigated his opponents in the same words: ". . . Englishmen are always making 'suggestions' of this character, being apparently of opinion that unaided guess-work is the only method of value . . ."; "Whenever a writer uses the word 'corruption,' we may commonly suspect him to be guessing. It is the one word that is prized above all others by those who prefer assertion to fact," and so on. But the main point is this: "Our ancestors had a curious habit of connecting the names of plants with those of various well-known animals."

9. Books on German and French folk etymology exist, but they are of little use to a student of English, because the most important thing here is examples (the general principle is clear), and examples are language specific. However, one book should be mentioned. Karl Andresen, although he called his work *Über Deutsche Volksetymologie [On German Folk Etymology]* (Heilbronn a/N: Gebr. Henninger, 1876), drew on the material of several languages, including English. The book enjoyed considerable popularity, ran into several editions, and made the concept of folk etymology widely known. The term *Volksetymologie* was coined by Ernst Förstemann ("Über deutsche volksetymologie." *Zeitschrift für vergleichende Sprachforschung* 1 [1852]: 1–25). See more about English folk etymology in James B. Greenough and George L. Kittredge, *Words and Their Ways in English Speech* (New York: Macmillan, 1901, reprint Boston: Beacon Press, [1962]), Chapter 23) and George H. McKnight, *English Words and Their Background* (New York, London: D. Appleton, 1923), Chapter 13. Almost every book on English words has a few pages on folk etymology, and some examples are familiar from various "Introductions to Linguistics." Several dissertations have been written on English folk etymology in German. The most detailed of them is Erwin Mayer, *Sekundäre Motivation. Untersuchungen zur Volksetymologie und verwandten Erscheinungen im Englischen.* Diss. Köln, 1962. In addition to the "classic" cases of folk etymology, Mayer analyzes all kinds of folk etymological influences, for instance, how *fair, wear,* and *tail* affected the meaning of *fairy, weary,* and *entail,* how the meanings of *ear* (a body part) and *ear* (a spike of grain) interact in the linguistic intuition of English speakers (and in general how homonyms begin to develop similar meanings), and many other subjects of the same type. The dissertation by Alfred Hasse (*Studien über englische Volksetymologie.* Diss. Straßburg. Straßburg i. E.: M. DuMont-Schauberg, 1904) is confusing: a mass of heterogeneous examples. Mayer had a predecessor in Cologne: Karl Rohling, *Englische Volksetymologie.* Diss. Köln. Borna-Leipzig: Robert Noske, 1931, and soon after Rohling another dissertation appeared: Hans-Heinrich Volquartz, *Studien über englische Volksetymologie.* Diss. Hamburg. Quakenbrück: Robert Kleiner, 1935. Neither is of interest (Volquartz's work is particularly unim-

portant). More imaginative is Georg Schröder, *Über den Einfluss der Volks-etymologie auf den Londoner slang-Dialekt.* Diss. Rostock. Rostock: Carl Boldt, 1893. The main drawback of those dissertations is that they conceive folk etymology too broadly: metaphorical expressions, chance mispronuncia-tions recorded in some book, the development of homonyms, and so forth. Invented associations (*Bedlam,* allegedly calling to mind *bed* and *lamb; ram-shackle,* as though shackled by a ram, and the like) turn some of the cited words into charades. An unintended pun is the soul of folk etymology (that is why explanation in this area invites the phrase *has nothing to do with . . .,* as in *"hautboy* has nothing to do with *boy"* and *"reindeer* has nothing to do with *rein,"*), but it is unreasonable to believe that every time the verb *egg on* is used, an image of an egg appears before the speaker's eye. Walter von Wartburg offered a useful classification of processes subsumed under the term *folk ety-mology* in his article "Zur frage der volksetymologie" (*Homenaje ofrecido a Menédez Pidal. Miscelánea de estudios lingüísticos, literarios e historicos,* vol. 1. (Madrid: Hernando [S. A.], pp. 17-27). The most reliable list of English words that come within the purview of folk etymology is Maria E. Houtzager, *Unconscious Sound- and Sense-Assimilations* (Amsterdam: H. J. Paris, 1935), pp. 40–65 (word lists from German, Dutch, and Swedish, as well as a long section on English place names). A much earlier dissertation had a title similar to Houtzager's: R. J. Lloyd, *Phonetic Attraction: An Essay upon the Influence of Similarities in Sound upon the Growth of Language and the Meaning of Words.* Thesis submitted to the University of London, 1888. Liverpool: Turner and Dunnett, 1888. Although published as a separate book, it is part of what must have been a composite volume of dissertations, because it begins on page 97 and ends on p. 152. Not all of it is on folk etymology. Pogatscher's work mentioned in note 2, is an article of 33 pages. It offers word lists from German and English (pp. 16–32), and very short ones from Dutch, French, Italian, Latin, and Classical Greek. Some of Pogatscher's suggestions are use-ful, but later etymologists ignored them. An article by C. Stoffel, "De Volks-etymologie in het Engelsch," *Taalstudie* 1 (1879): 27–44, antedates Smythe Palmer's book by four years, but unlike that book, gives, with a few excep-tions, reliable examples (they begin on p. 33). Most of G. Krüger's words ("Volksetymologien," *Englische Studien* 40 [1909]: 79–86) are exotic, like those in the early twentieth-century German dissertations, mentioned above. A. E. H. Swaen's testy response ("Some Observations on Krüger's *Volks-etymologien," Englische Studien* 41 [1910]: 173–176) deals only with a few words. Folk etymology in place names is a well-developed subject. For initial orientation, see the bibliography in Gail C. Pizzola, *A Sociolinguistic Study of the Folk Etymology of Selected Texas Place Names.* Ph. D. diss. Indiana Uni-versity of Pennsylvania, 2000. Unpublished.

Chapter Six

1. Nils Thun's dissertation *Reduplicative Words in English: A Study of Formations of the Type* Tick-tick, Hurly-burly *and* Shilly-shally (Uppsala: 1963; printed in Lund by Carl Bloms Boktryckeri A.-B.) contains the most complete collection of such words. Thun's predecessors were Henry B. Wheatley, *A Dictionary of Reduplicated Words in the English Language.* Published for the Philological Society by Asher and Co., 1866; Reprint Folcroft Library Editions, 1975; [Karl] Friedrich Koch, *Linguistische Allotria: Laut-, Ablaut- und Reimbildungen der englischen Sprache.* A posthumous edition by Eugen Wilhelm (Eisenach: J. Bacmeister, 1874), pp. 58–94 (see more about Koch's book in note 1 to p. 258); and Max Müller, *Die Reim- und Ablautkomposita des Englischen.* Diss. Strassburg, Straßburg i. Els.: M. DuMont Schauberg. 1909. Yrijö M. Biese gives a sizable list of rhyming words and words with vowel alterations (ablaut) in the article "Neuenglisch *tick-tack* und Verwandtes," *Neuphilologische Mitteilungen* 40 (1939): 146–205. See another list in Hans Marchand, "Motivation by Linguistic Form: English Ablaut and Rime Combinations and their Relevancy to Word-Formation." *Studia Neophilologica* 29 (1957): 54–66. The best bibliography of works on this subject is appended to Thun's book (pp. 305–319). Note especially the articles by Eduard Eckhardt, Gustav Kirchner, and Herbert Koziol. Among more general works, the best-known one is Hermann Güntert, *Über Reimwortbildungen im Arischen und Altgriechischen.* Indogermanische Bibliothek III/1 (Heidelberg: Carl Winter, 1914). A few articles on this subject appeared after the publication of Thun's book, for example, Lillian H. Hornstein, "Reduplicatives *redivivus:* From *Ack-Ack* through *Go-Go* to *Zig-Zag* and a Little Beyond," in *Studies in Honor of J. Alexander Kerns.* Robert C. Lugton and Milton G. Saltzer, eds. (Paris: Mouton, 1970): 59–64.

2. John Stoddart, "Grammar." In *The Encyclopaedia Metropolitana* 1 (London: B. Fellowes, *et al.*, 1845), pp. 120–121. Stoddart gives a survey of some early attempts to explain the origin of *hugger-mugger.* The word appears in all English dictionaries that offer etymological information, and a few shorter works deal with it, for example, L., "Namby-Pamby, and Other Words of the Same Form," *Notes and Queries,* Series 1, vol. VIII (1853): 390–392. The following authors discuss *hugger-mugger* in terms of onomatopoeia or emphasis: Hensleigh Wedgwood, "On Onomatopoeia," *Papers of the Philological Society,* (1844–1846): 113; P. Fijn van Draat, "Reduplicatory Emphasis." *Englische Studien* 74 (1940): 165; G. V. Smithers, "Some English Ideophones," *Archivum Linguisticum* 6 (1954): 86. Willy Krogmann ("Scorlemorle": *Korrespondenzblatt des Vereins für Niederdeutsche Sprachforschung* 59 [1952]: 29) states in connection with *hugger-mugger* that in such words, the basic form is always the first part. This is wrong, as was already clear to L. (the author does not reveal his full name). Walter W. Skeat ("Hoder-moder," *Notes and Queries,*

Series 6, vol. X (1884): 51) took *hugger* as a starting point, traced it to *hoder-*, allegedly from *huddle* and *hide*, and looked on *-moder* (later *-mugger*) as a rhyme for *hoder-*. Wedgwood was the first to note that *mug-* is an international word. See his article "On the Connexion of the Finn and Lapp with Other European Languages," *Transactions of the Philological Society* (1856): 14; and the words *miche* and *hugger-mugger* in his *A Dictionary of English Etymology* (London: Trübner, 1859) (the same in the later editions). Louis H. Gray lists the putative cognates of *mugger* in his article "Indo-European Comparative Linguistics as an Aid to Romance Etymology," in John D. Fitzgerald and Pauline Taylor, eds. *Todd Memorial Volumes: Philological Studies*, vol. 1, p. 195 (#15).

3. Brigittte Christiani, *Zwillingsverbindungen in der altenglischen Dichtung*. Diss. Königsberg. Würzburg: K. Triltsch, 1938.

4. Countless versions of the egg riddle exist. Humpty-Dumpty's kin are French *Boule-Boule* (that is, "glug-glug"), Swedish *Thille Lille* ("little Thille"), Russian *Shaltai-Boltai* (the second half means "toss [the liquid]"), and so forth. The contents of both the drink humpty-dumpty and a fresh egg can be tossed, and this is perhaps the reason they share the name. *Dumpty* may be from the verb *dump*, whereas *humpty* looks like the usual "default" form, as in *hugger-mugger*. The suffix *-ty* resembles *-ty* in *uppity* and *persnickety*.

5. The most important publications on the origin of *hurly-burly* and *hullabaloo* are by Gösta Langenfelt, an advocate of the Turkish origin of *hullabaloo*. Of his three articles on the subject see especially *"Hurly-Burly, Hallaloo, Hullaballoo." Neuphilologische Mitteilungen* 51 (1950): 1–18.

6. In fact, such simple reduplications have been studied extensively, and Thun (as in note 1) lists them. See a survey in A. C. Bouman, "Over reduplicatie en de woordsoorten," *Nieuwe taalgids* 33 (1939): 337–353. Françoise Skoda's book (*Le redoublement expressif: Un universal linguistique. Analyse du procédé en grec ancien et en d'autres langues*. Société d'Études Linguistiques et Anthropologiques de France 15, 1982) is devoted almost entirely to Classical Greek, but the examples are so numerous and so typical that the results of her research are applicable to the expressive words with reduplication in any language. The material of Jacques André's book *Les mots à redoublement en latin. Études et commentaire* 40 (Paris: Klincksieck, 1978) is, as can be expected, mainly Latin. Yet here, too, the examples are of a character that anyone interested in reduplication will be able to apply the author's conclusions to English, French, and so forth.

Chapter Seven

1. Warwickshire; p. 185. See note 1 to the previous chapter.

2. Thun, pp. 112–113, 133. John S. Farmer and W. E. Henley, *Slang and Its Analogues* (London: Printed by Routledge & Kegan Paul for the subscribers,

1890–1904; reprint New York: Kraus Reprint Corporation, 1965). J. E. Lighter, ed., *Random House Historical Dictionary of American Slang* (New York: Random House, 1994–).

3. In Suffolk, they say *flail* for *frail* (basket). See a note on this pronunciation in Edward Gepp, "A Contribution to an Essex Dialect Dictionary: Supplement II," *Essex Review* 30 (1921): 136–137.

4. Thun, pp. 177, 101. Like the other words mentioned here, *rick-ma-tick* appears on p. 223 of Thun's book. It has been recorded in the phrase *the whole rick-ma-tick* (the whole lot, the whole concern, collection) (Thun, p. 146), that is, "the whole kit and caboodle."

5. John Jamieson, *An Etymological Dictionary of the Scottish Language*, John Longmuir, ed. (Paisley: Alexander Gardner, 1879-1882). *Supplement . . .,* by David Donaldson, 1887.

6. See a rich collection of words with infixation in the following articles published in the journal *American Speech:* James B. McMillan, "Infixing and Interposing" (vol. 55, [1980]: 163–183) and Michael Adams, "Infixing and Interposing in English: A New Direction" (vol. 76 [2001]: 326–331). Two more notes by Michael Adams deal with the same subject: "Another Effing Euphemism" (vol. 74 [1999]: 110–112) and "Meaningful Interposing. An Accidental Form" (vol. 77 [2002]: 440–441).

7. As early as 1884, Pogatscher, with reference to the first edition of Skeat's dictionary (p. 787), mentioned a half-dozen explanations of *daffydowndilly* and added his own, learned but implausible. See Alois Pogatscher (as at the end of note 8 to Chapter 5), pp. 21–23.

8. Heinrich Schröder, "Streckformen," *Beiträge zur Geschichte der deutschen Sprache und Literatur* 29 (1903): 346–354.

9. Heinrich Schröder, *Beiträge zur germanischen Sprach- und Kulturgeschichte. I. Streckformen. Ein Beitrag zur Lehre von der Wortentstehung und der germanischen Wortbetonung.* Germanische Bibliothek II/1: Untersuchungen und Texte (Heidelberg: Carl Winter, 1906).

10. Friedrich Kluge, the author of the best etymological dictionary of German (*Etymologisches Wörterbuch der deutschen Sprache*), published an especially virulent review of Schröder's book in *Literaturblatt für germanische und romanische Philologie* 27 (1906): 393–401. However, Otto Behaghel, the editor of *Literaturblatt,* added a short postscript to Kluge's review and suggested that extended forms should not be dismissed out of hand, because sometimes their existence is evident. Years later, he wrote an article on language at play and language humor and mentioned extended forms as a case in point: Otto Behaghel, "Humor und Spieltrieb in der deutschen Sprache," *Neophilologus* 8 (1923): 183.

11. Already in 1910, Francis A. Wood, one of the leading etymologists of his time, wrote an article with the title "Iteratives, Blends, and 'Streckformen'," *Modern Philology* 5: 157–194.

12. See only R. H. Griffith, "Phenagling," *Modern Language Notes* 39 (1954): 291–292.
13. See a near complete survey of opinions in Gerald L. Cohen, "*Skedaddle* Revisited," *Comments on Etymology* VIII/10-11 (1979): 1–42 (it was first "visited" in *Comments on Etymology* V/12-13 (1976): 1–8). Reprinted as "Etymology of *Skedaddle* and Related Forms" in his *Studies in Slang, Part I.* Forum Anglicum 14/1 (Frankfurt am Main: Peter Lang, 1985), pp. 26–63.
14. Some students of English thought differently. One of them was Frank Chance, a talented etymologist, who published dozens of short articles in *Notes and Queries.* The quotation below is from "Hobbledehoy," *Notes and Queries,* Series 7, vol. IV (1887): 524: a lad from 14 upwards, he explains, "is uncertain, physically and morally, whether he will turn out ill or well. And besides this he frequently has an awkward and shambling gait, to which the term may more especially have been applied."
15. See the edition of Tusser's book by W. Payne and Sydney J. Herrtage: English Dialect Society Publications, vol. 8 (London: N. Trübner), 138:60/3. This verse has often been discussed in connection with the origin of *hobbledehoy,* for example, by W. W. E. T. ("Sir Hobbard de Hoy," *Notes and Queries,* Series 1, vol. V [1852]: 468), H. B. F. ("Hobbledehoy," *Notes and Queries,* Series 4, vol. IX [1872]: 147–148), and Walter W. Skeat ("Notes on English Etymology," *Transaction of the Philological Society* 21 (1885–1887): 302–303; reprinted in his *Notes on English Etymology* (Oxford: Clarendon Press, 1901), pp. 131–132.
16. The etymology offered here belongs to John P. Hughes ("On 'h' for 'r' in English Proper Names," *The Journal of English and Germanic Philology* 53 [1954]: 606).
17. Anonymous, "Capabare," *The Mariner's Mirror* 2 (1912): 164.
18. The full text of the rhyme runs as follows: "Hick-a-more, hack-a-more, / Hung on the kitchen door; / Nothing so long, / And nothing so strong, / As hick-a-more, hack-a-more / Hung on the kitchen door." William S. Baring-Gould and Cecil Baring-Gould, the editors of *The Annotated Mother Goose: Nursery Rhymes Old and New, Arranged and Explained* (Cleveland and New York: World Publishing Company, 1962 [1967], p. 271, note 16), explain that a hackamore is a halter usually of plaited horse-hair, used chiefly for breaking horses. "But," they add, "that is not the solution to this riddle. The answer here is 'sunshine'." *Hackamore* surfaced in American books in 1850, and the first citation describes a scene in California. It is improbable that *hackamore* in the nursery rhyme should have anything to do with the word for "halter." Another version of this riddle is less opaque: "Hick-a-more, hack-a-more, / On the King's kitchen door; / All the King's horses, / And all the King's men / Couldn't drive Hick-a-more, Hack-a-more / Off the King's kitchen door!"
19. Nils Thun (as in note 1) has a longer list of such compounds: see p. 223 and the index to his book.

20. *Middle English Dictionary.* Hans Kurath et al., eds. (Ann Arbor: University of Michigan Press, 1956–2001).

21. E. W. Prevost, *A Supplement to the Glossary of the Dialect of Cumberland.* With a Grammar of the Dialect by S. Dicksons Brown (London: Henry Frowde, and Carlisle: C. Thurnam, 1905). Hardly anyone would have found Prevost's note on Old Muffy if A. Smythe Palmer had not discussed it in his article "Folk-Lore in Word-Lore," *The Nineteenth Century and After* 68 (1910): 545–546. Not that historical linguists should expect to find important information in the pages of an old popular magazine like *The Nineteenth Century*, but things happen. Leo Spitzer's article *"Ragamuffin, ragmen, rigmarole* and *rogue" (Modern Language Notes* 62 [1947]: 85–93) is full of interesting ideas, but his etymology of *-muffin* is contrived.

22. When no specific reference is given, my source for dialectal words is Joseph Wright, *The English Dialect Dictionary . . .* (London: H. Frowde, 1898–1905; reprint London: Oxford University Press, 1970).

Chapter Eight

1. Rolf Berndt, *Einführung in das Studium des Mittelenglischen unter Zugrundlegung der "Canterbury Tales"* (Halle [Saale]. VEB Max Niemeyer, 1960), p. 188.

2. It is usually believed that Late Old English *hūsbonda* is a borrowing from Scandinavian. Old Icelandic *húsbóndi,* that is, *hús + bóndi,* means "the head of the house," approximately "homeowner"; Modern Icelandic *bóndi* still means "farmer." (An accent mark in Icelandic words performs the function of the macron in Old English.) According to another opinion, *hūsbonda* is a native word that has changed its meaning under Scandinavian influence. See Klaus Faiss, *Verdunkelte Compounds im Englischen. Ein Beitrag zu Theorie und Praxis der Wortbildung.* Tübinger Beiträge zur Linguistik 104 (Tübingen: Gunter Narr, 1978), p. 138.

3. See a partial survey of opinions in Alan Brown, "Heifer," *Neophilologus* 56 (1972): 79–85. Walter Rye (*A Glossary of Words Used in East Anglia Founded on That of Forby. With Numerous Corrections and Additions.* Publications of the English Dialect Society 26/2 [London: Henry Frowde, 1895]) expunged Forby's etymology of *heifer* (in *The Vocabulary of East Anglia . . .* [London: J. B. Nichols; reprint: New York: A. M. Kelly, Newton Abbot: David and Charles, 1970]), but Forby's long entry is still interesting as an early attempt to guess the origin of the intractable word. The first to suggest that the meaning of *heah-* is "enclosure" was Hensleigh Wedgwood in *A Dictionary of English Etymology. . . .* (London: Trübner, 1859–1865).

4. The suggestion belongs to Heinrich Leo (*Angelsächsisches Glossar . . .* [Halle: Verlag der Buchhandlung des Waisenhauses, 1877], p. 573), but it made no

impression on dictionary makers, though Walter W. Skeat reluctantly admitted that Leo might be right ("Cushat," *The Academy* 29 [1886]: 311).

5. Friedrich Kluge "Germanisches," *Indogermanische Forschungen* 4 (1894): 309. Repeated in F. Kluge and F. Lutz, *English Etymology: A Select Glossary Serving as an Introduction to the History of the English Language* (Boston, New York, Chicago: D. C. Heath, London: Blackie, 1899). See discussion of Kluge's idea in a wide context (similar names of many berries in European languages) in Willy Krogmann's note "Lat. frāgum," *Wörter und Sachen* 20 (1939): 182–184.

6. This is the opinion of Walter W. Skeat, *An Etymological Dictionary of the English Language,* 4th ed. (Oxford: Clarendon Press, 1910). Leonard Bloomfield (*Language* [New York: Henry Holt, 1933], pp. 433–434) also connected *strawberry* with the verb but explained the whole as "strewnberry": in Old English, *strawberry,* he says, "must have described the strawberry-plant as it lies along the ground; as *straw* became specialized to 'dry stalk, dried stalk' and the morphological connection with *strew* disappeared, the prior member of *strawberry* was isolated, with a deviant meaning, as a homonym of *straw.*" And indeed, *strēawberiewīse* (strawberry plant) occurred in Old English, but did not continue into latter periods.

7. Ernest Weekley (*An Etymological Dictionary of Modern English* [New York: E. P. Dutton, 1921]) considered both explanations probable.

8. Carl S. R. Collin, "Eng. *strawberry,*" *Moderna språk* 32 [1938]: 76–79. Collin points out (p. 77) that in some parts of Sweden, strawberry is called *stråbär.* Consequently, the statement repeated in dictionaries that the word *strawberry* has no analogs in other languages should be modified.

9. Harold H. Bender, "English *strawberry,*" *The American Journal of Philology* 55 (1934): 71–74. Except for the idea that *strawberry* should be understood as "hayberry," that is, almost as "grassberry" (an appealing idea in light of the fact that in the other Germanic languages the berry is called "earthberry" and that a corresponding word existed even in Old English but did not survive), all the etymologies mentioned here are old. Andrew S. Fuller (*The Illustrated Strawberry Culturist. . . .* [New York: Orange Judd, 1890], p. 8) knew and rejected them. Bender and Collin give surveys of earlier opinions.

10. As an example of how firm the belief in "strayberries" was, a statement by W. Collett-Sanders in *The Gentleman's Magazine* 1879/II, 116, can be quoted: "The fruit is called *strawberry,* or *straying berry*, from the erratic nature of its runners."

11. Henry Cecil Wyld, *The Universal Dictionary of the English Language* (London: Routledge & Kegan Paul, 1932). Wyld seems to have gravitated toward Kluge's etymology.

12. Such is the opinion of Niels Åge Nielsen in *Dansk etymologisk ordbog. Ordenes historie,* 4th ed. (Copenhagen: Gyldendal, 1997) (*tranebær*).

13. Today *Mensch* (n.) is a term of abuse.
14. I borrowed both examples from Max Niedermann's review of Alois Walde's second edition of *Lateinisches etymologisches Wörterbuch* (Heidelberg: Carl Winter, 1910). *Indogermanische Forschungen (Anzeiger)* 29 (1911): 35 (a comment on *manus*). Niedermann does not touch on the history of *wife*.
15. The literature on the history of *woman* (separate from the history of *wife*) resolves itself into explanations of the phonetic development from *wīfman* to the modern forms of the singular and the plural. Among dictionary entries, the best one is in *The Century Dictionary.*
16. For the material discussed above see, in addition to Faiss's book (as in note 2), Nils Bergsten, *A Study of Compound Substantives in English.* Diss. Uppsala. Uppsala: Almquist & Wiksell, 1911, Erich Klein, *Die verdunkelten Wortzusammensetzungen im Neuenglischen.* Diss. Königsberg i Pr. Königsberg i Pr.: Karg und Mannek, 1911, and Dieter Goetz, *Studien zu den verdunkelten Komposita im Englischen.* Erlanger Beiträge zur Sprach- und Kunstwissenschaft 40 (Nürnberg: H. Carl 1971). Of related interest is Werner Last, *Das Bahuvrîhi-Compositum im Altenglischen, Mittelenglischen und Neuenglischen* (Greifswald: Hans Adler, 1925).

Chapter Nine

1. An excellent dictionary of frequentative verbs in Dutch is A. de Jaeger, *Woordenboek der frequentatieven in het Nederlandsch* (Gouda: G. B. van Goor Zonen, 1875). Among other things, it has an indispensable alphabetical index and a supplement on the verbs that only seem to be frequentative.
2. *It fit last year / it has never fit you better; my brother wet his bed when he was little. The American Heritage Dictionary of the English Language* (1969) gives both *fit* and *fitted* for the past, but only *wetted. Random House Unabridged Dictionary,* Second Edition, 1987, says that *"fitted* is somewhat more common than *fit* in the sense 'to adjust, make conform'," but under *wet*, left without discussion, gives the example: "The dog had wet the carpet." *Fit* and *wet* have joined *cut* and *let*, whereas *whet*, *pet*, and *net* preserve their old forms *whetted* and so forth in the past and in the perfect. *Bet* vacillates between *bet* and *betted.*
3. μέγας.
4. No book on Indo-European ignores *s-mobile.* See an exhaustive treatment of this subject in Mark R. V. Southern, *Subgrammatical Survival: Indo-European s-mobile and Its Regeneration in Germanic.* JIES. Monograph Series 34 (Washington, D.C.: Institute for the Study of Man, 1999). Southern discusses old etymologies and the expressive role of *s-*.
5. μειδιάω.

6. Scott was an active supporter of reformed spelling, which accounts for the odd appearance of his titles. All his three articles are called the same: "English Words which hav Gaind or Lost an Initial Consonant by Attraction." They were published in *Transactions of the American Philological Society* 23 (1892): 179–305; 24 (1893): 89–155; and 25 (1894): 83–139.
7. Vol. 23, 189–195; pp. 206–211.
8. Vol. 23, pp. 284–287.
9. Vol. 24, p. 96.
10. Vol. 24, p. 100
11. Vol. 24, p. 106. See a trustworthy account of the events in Robert Hogg, "Tooley Street," *Notes and Queries,* Series 7, vol. V (1895): 55. Scott refers to it in his article.
12. Robert Nares, *A Glossary; or, Collection of Words, Phrases, Names, and Allusions to Customs, Proverbs, etc., Which have been Thought to Require Illustration, in the Works of English Authors, Particularly Shakespeare and His Contemporaries.* A new edition, by James O. Halliwell and Thomas Wright (London: John Russell Smith, 1872), p. 868 (first published in 1822). Nares quotes St. Ethelreada's words (in Latin) and Harpsfield's comment. See the next note.
13. The English translation is from the *Oxford English Dictionary, tawdry.*
14. Scott, as in note 6, 1893, pp. 110–112.
15. A. Smythe Palmer (see note 1 to Chapter 5) devotes pp. 568–591 to "words corrupted by coalescence of the article with the substantive," but his list from several languages is so chaotic as to be practically useless. Also, many of his etymologies are wrong.
16. Courtenay Boyle, "The Coinage of Words," *MacMillan's Magazine* 83 (1901): 331–332. The earliest citation for *brunch* in the *Oxford English Dictionary* goes back to 1895. The source (the short-lived magazine *Hunter's Weekly*) is almost unavailable. The dictionary refers to Guy Beringer, who allegedly "introduced" the word but quotes only *Punch* for 1896. However, Beringer, in an article entitled "Brunch: A Plea," does not seem to have been the first to use that blend. He says: "The word Brunch is a corruption of breakfast and lunch, and the meal Brunch is one which combines the tea or coffee, marmalade and kindred features of the former institution with the more solid attributes of the latter. It begins between twelve and half-past and consists in the main of fish and one or two meat courses" (vol. 1, no. 2, p. 20).
17. Quoted in Louise Pound, *Blends: Their Relation to English Word Formation.* Anglistische Forschungen 42 (Heidelberg: Carl Winter, 1914), p. 12, footnote.
18. Louise Pound (as in the previous note), p. 55.
19. Louise Pound (as in note 17), p. 4.
20. Three book-length studies are devoted to such examples: Louise Pound (as in note 17), Harold Wentworth, *Blend-Words in English.* Cornell Diss., 1933,

unpublished (only a five-page abstract appeared in print), and Dick Thurner, *Portmanteau Dictionary: Blend Words in the English Language. Incorporating Trademarks and Brand Names* (Jefferson, NC, and London: McFarland, 1993). Two articles by Francis A. Wood deserve special attention: "Iteratives, Blends, and 'Streckformen'," *Modern Philology* (1911–12): 157–194 (it was mentioned in note 11 to chapter 7 in connection with extended forms; pp. 173–177 are on blends: 68 examples) and "Some English Blends," *Modern Language Notes* 27 (1912): 179 (12 examples). G. A. Bergström's book *On Blendings of Synonymous or Cognate Expressions in English: A Contribution to the Study of Contamination.* Diss. Lund. Lund: Hakon Ohlsson, 1906, deals with all kinds of blends (pp. 51–64 are on lexical blends in English). Valerie Adams *(An Introduction to Modern English Word-formation.* [London: Longman, 1973]) discusses blends on pp. 139–160.

21. Most of them are from Otto Jespersen, *Language*... (see note 2 to Chapter 4), pp. 312–313.

Chapter Ten

1. *The Oxford Dictionary of English Etymology, nap*[3].

2. David Parlett, *The Oxford Guide to Card Games* (Oxford, New York: Oxford University Press, 1990), pp. 194–195.

3. *The Century Dictionary* gives part of the quotation. The passage occurs at the end of Chapter 20 of the novel.

4. A. H., "Essex Dialect," *Essex Review* 52 (1943): 157. Dialectal dictionaries give more words of the same type.

5. Walter W. Skeat, *An Etymological Dictionary of the English Language,* 4th ed. (Oxford: Clarendon Press, 1910), *gun.*

6. Ernest Weekley, *An Etymological Dictionary of Modern English* (New York: Dutton, 1921), *gun.*

7. Ernest Weekley, *Words and Names* (New York: E. P. Dutton, 1933), p. vii.

8. χρόνιος.

9. The literature on the origin of *man* is vast. The author of the first hypothesis is Friedrich Kluge *(Etymologisches Wörterbuch der deutschen Sprache,* 4th ed. [Straßburg: Karl J. Trübner, 1889]); it still has some influential supporters. The idea to relate *man* to *manus* goes back to George Hempl ("Etymologies," *American Journal of Philology* 22 [1901]: 426–428). The connection *man – mens* is the oldest of all. Its originator seems to have been Adalbert Kuhn ("Über die durch nasale erweiterten verbalstämme," *Zeitschrift für vergleichende Sprachforschung* 2 [1853]: 466). Those interested in a more detailed bibliography of the question will find numerous references in Norbert Wagner, "Lateinisch-germanisch *Mannus,*" *Historische Sprachforschung* 107 (1994):

143–146, and Alfred Bammesberger, "*Mannus/Manno* bei Tacitus und der Name der *m*-Rune," *Beiträge zur Namenforschung* 34 (NF) (1999): 1–8.

10. This is an inspiring suggestion. See Friedrich Kluge, "Tuisco deus et filius Mannus 2," *Zeitschrift für deutsche Wortforschung* 2 (1901–02): 43–45. The idea that the clue to the origin of *man* is the word's oldest meaning ("slave") occurred to Jacob Grimm, but he did not develop it. See his *Deutsche Rechtsaltertümer* (Darmstadt: Wissenschaftliche Buchgesellschaft, 1983; reprint of the fourth edition by Andreas Heusler and Rudolf Hübner, 1899), pp. 419–420.

11. J. C. Holt, *Robin Hood* (London and New York: Thames and Hudson, 1982), p. 7.

12. See the titles of the early works on Robin Hood in J. Harris Gable, *Bibliography of Robin Hood.* University of Nebraska. Studies in Language, Literature, and Criticism 17 (Lincoln, 1939). I will mention only one pre-1939 article by a representative of the mythological school (its supporters deny the existence of any historical core in the Robin Hood legend) because it gives an excellent description of the games and emphasizes the role of the horse in them: Richard Wolfram, "Robin Hood und Hobby Horse," *Wiener Prähistorische Zeitschrift* 19 *(Festschrift Rudolf Much)* (1932): 357–374.

13. A similar color is *gnedói,* whence a horse name *Gnedkó.* The magic horse of Russian folklore is called *Sívka-búrka, véshchaia kaúrka. Véshchaia* means "knowing all"; the other three words are color names.

14. In his *An Etymological Dictionary of Modern English* (New York: E. P. Dutton, 1921), *moke.*

15. Eric Partridge, *Name into Word: Proper Names That Have Become Common Property* (London: Secker and Warburg, 1949). (This book is a dictionary, and words are arranged alphabetically in it.) Numerous articles have been written on the derivation of English words from place and proper names (including the anonymous *Jack, John,* and *Tom* and biblical and literary characters). However, books with titles like Weekley's and Partridge's are few. See also Julius Charles Hare, *Fragments of Two Essays in English Philology* (London: Macmillan, 1873) (I: "Words Derived from Names of Persons," pp. 1–56).

16. W. M. E. F. "*Bob* = An Insect." *Notes and Queries,* Series 8, vol. XI, 1897.

17. A. H., "Essex Dialect," *Essex Review* 51 (1942): 117.

18. Ernest Weekley, as in note 14, *codlin.*

19. A. L. Mayhew, "Larrikin," *Notes and Queries,* Series 8, vol. V (1894): 447–448.

20. My survey of the early conjectures on the origin of *sedan* and *hackney* is indebted to *The Century Dictionary.*

21. H. W. Fowler, *A Dictionary of Modern English Usage.* Second edition revised by Ernest Gower (Oxford: Clarendon Press, 1965), p. 234.

22. L. R. Ashley, "French Surnames and the English," *Names* 11 (1963): 180.

Chapter Eleven

1. See especially three articles by Gerald L. Cohen (the last of them in collaboration with Bary Popik), all of them entitled "Update on *hot dog*," in the journal *Comments on Etymology* XXII/5 (1993): 1–13; XXIII/2 (1993): 1–15, and XXIII/8 (1994): 22–37.

2. *The American Heritage Dictionary of the English Language.* William Morris, ed. (Boston, *et al.*: American Heritage and Houghton Mifflin, 1969).

3. Walter W. Skeat, *An Etymological Dictionary of the English Language*, 4th ed. (Oxford: Clarendon Press, 1910). *The Century Dictionary . . .* reproduces this story in the form given here, and the *Oxford English Dictionary*, too, quotes it and is ready to accept the anecdote as reflecting the truth.

4. Johannes Söderlind ("The Word *Lilliput*," *Studia Neophilologica* 40 [1968]: 75–79) made the strongest case for the Swedish origin of Swift's word.

5. The most important work along these lines is E. Pons, "Rabelais et Swift. À propos de Lilliputien." In *Mélanges offerts à M. Abel Lefranc, professeur au Collège de France, membre de l'Académie des Inscriptions et Belles-lettres, par ses élèves et ses amis* (Paris: Librairie E. Droz, 1936), pp. 216–228. There is also some truth in the observation that Swift's Lilliputians tend to use short words and their commands sound to a foreigner like a rapid succession of syllables, while the giants' words are long (Julien Vinson, "Le langues du Gulliver," *Revue de Linguistique et de Philologie Comparée* 45 [1912]: 78–79.

6. J. H. Neumann, "Jonathan Swift and the Vocabulary of English," *Modern Language Quarterly* 4 (1943): 200, note 50; Söderlind (as in note 4), p. 75.

7. See all kinds of suggestions on the origin of *Lilliput* in Rudolf Kleinpaul, *Menschen- und Völkernamen. Etymologische Streifzüge auf dem Gebiete der Eigennamen* (Leipzig: Carl Reissner, 1885): 17–18; Frank Chance, "Lilliput." *Notes and Queries*, Series 7, vol. VII (1889): 506; Henry Morley (ed.), *Gulliver's Travels Exactly Reprinted from the First Edition, and Other Works by Jonathan Swift . . .* (London: George Routledge, 1890), pp. 17–18; Paul O. Clark, "A 'Gulliver' Dictionary," *Studies in Philology* 50 (1953): 606; Patricia C. Brückmann, "Lilliputian," *American Notes and Queries* 13 (1974): 4; Keith Crook, *A Preface to Swift* (London and New York: Longman, 1998), p. 171.

8. Pierre Henrion, *Jonathan Swift Confesses: I. Gulliver's Secret / Jonathan Swift Avoue: I. Le secret de Gulliver.* (Versailles: Published by the author, 1962), pp. 53–63.

9. Sheridan Baker, "Swift, 'Lilliputian,' and Catullus," *Notes and Queries* 201 (1956): 477–499. Rachel Torpusman published a few annotated translations of Catullus's lyrics into Russian in the Jerusalem magazine *Solnechnoe spletenie* 2 (1998). On p. 31 she makes the same suggestion (Swift's word perhaps owes

its origin to *salaputium*), without referring to Baker. She may have been unaware of Baker's article.
10. William LeFanu, *A Catalogue of Books Belonging to Dr Jonathan Swift.* . . . (Cambridge: Bibliographical Society, 1988), p. 15.
11. Ralph G. Martin, "The Biography of a Jeep," *The New York Times Magazine* (July 2, 1944): 39.
12. Mencken's question about the origin of *jeep* appeared in *American Notes and Queries* 3 (1943): 119.
13. Richard G. McCloskey, "Jeep," *American Notes and Queries* 3 (1943): 136–137.
14. W. C. McFarlane, "Jeep," *American Notes and Queries* 3 (1943): 155.
15. *The American Heritage Dictionary of the English Language,* 3rd ed. 1992. The second edition traced *jeep* to the comic strip, "an alteration of G. P. (for General Purpose) Vehicle"; the first edition did not mention Segar.
16. *The World Book Dictionary.* Clarence L. Barnhart, editor-in-chief (Chicago, *et al.*: Published for Field Enterprises Educational Corporation, 1963).
17. Henry L. Mencken, *The American Language,* 4th ed. and the Two Supplements . . ., by Raven J. McDavid, Jr., with the assistance of David W. Mauer (New York: Alfred A. Knopf, 1967), p. 759.
18. All three examples are from Leon Mead, *How Words Grow: A Brief Study of Literary Style, Slang, and Provincialisms* (New York: Thomas J. Crowell, 1902) (I was using the 1907 reprint), pp. 83, 87, and 88. The creator of *cynophile* was Professor Richard Burton, the then English Chair at the University of Minnesota, the author of *Dog Literature. Jasm* was defined by E. Benjamin Andrews, Chancellor at the University of Nebraska. *Broodle* is Mrs. Caroline A. Mason's word. Mead devoted 80 pages (30 percent) of his book to neologisms. He wrote letters to people all over the United States, including Theodore Roosevelt and Mark Twain, asking them whether they remember any words they coined. However, the answers reported in his book turned out to be disappointing, for most coinages were stillborn learned freaks like *cynophile*, appealing only to those who prefer *apiarist* to *beekeeper.*

Chapter Twelve

1. πέπων, an adjective. The phrase σίκυος πέπων, occurring in Aristotle, is sometimes glossed as "pumpkin" (with a question mark); σικύα is either "pumpkin" or "melon." Engl. *pepsic* and *peptic* contain the same root.
2. ἄγουρος, ἀγγούριον.
3. κάραβος.
4. καρκίνος.
5. σκορπίος, σκορπίον.

6. σκαράβειος.
7. Marcel Cohen, "Sur le nom d'un contenant à entrelacs dans le monde méditerranéen," *Bulletin de la Société Linguistique de Paris* 27 (1926): 100.
8. The etymology of both Russian words is debatable. See *Etimologicheskii slovar' slavianskikh iazykov. Praslavianskii leksicheskii fond*, vol. 11. O. N. Trubachev, ed. (Moscow: Nauka, 1984), pp. 45–49 and 52–54.
9. κάνεον, from κάννα (reed; plural).
10. Henry and Renée Kahane and Angelina Pietrangeli, "Egyptian Papyri as a Tool in Romance Etymology," *Romance Philology* 17 (1963): 317–318.
11. κανών.
12. Henry and Renée Kahane, "Two Nautical Terms of Greek Origin: *Typhoon* and *Galley.*" In *Etymologica. Walther von Wartburg zum siebzigsten Geburtstag 18. Mai 1958* (Tübingen: Max Niemeyer, 1958), p. 428.
13. γαλέα.
14. Τυφῶν, Τυφωεύς.
15. Henry and Renée Kahane, as in note 12, pp. 417–428.
16. Friedrich Kluge, "Germanisches Reckentum." *Frankfurter Zeitung,* Erstes Morgenblatt, June 21, 1916, p. 2. Later, probably to show that his etymology had no connection with the spirit of 1916, he reprinted his article in an American journal ("Germanisches Reckentum: frz. *garçon,*" *Modern Language Notes* 37 [1922]: 385–390). Kluge derived *garçon* from Germanic **wrakjō-* (hero) (its modern reflex in German is *Recke*).
17. Eduard Prokosh, "The Hypothesis of a Pre-Germanic Substratum," *The Germanic Review* 1 (1926): 50.
18. See Prokosh (as in the previous note): 53–54.
19. Feist's books on this subject are *Kultur, Ausbreitung und Herkunft der Indogermanen* (Berlin: Weidmann, 1913) (a major work), *Indogermanen und Germanen. Ein Beitrag zur europäischen Urgeschichtsforschung* (Halle a. S.: Max Niemeyer, 1914) (70 pages, mainly on etymology), 3rd ed., 1924, and *Germanen und Kelten in der antiken Überlieferung* (Halle [Saale]: Max Niemeyer, 1927) (the same size as the previous one). A bibliography of responses to those books and of works inspired by them would make up a little volume. It is useful to read Viggo Brøndal's early book *Substrater og laan i romansk og germansk. Studier i lyd- og ordhistorie* (Copenhagen: G. E. C. Gad, 1917), because it precedes the fury aroused by Feist's theory. The book is available in French: *Substrat et emprunt en roman et en germanique. Étude sur l'histoire des sons et des mots* (Copenhagen: Ejnar Munksgaard, 1948). Günter Neumann's article "Substrate im Germanischen?" (Nachrichten der Akademie der Wissenschaften in Göttingen). *Philologisch-historische Klasse* 1971/4 (pp. 74–99 of the entire volume) gives an idea of the state of the art. A more recent contribution is: Krysztof T. Witczak, "The Germanic Substrata

and Germanic Maritime Vocabulary." In *The Indo-Europeanization of Northern Europe: Papers Presented at the International Conference Held at the University of Vilnius, Vilnius, Lithuania, September 1–7, 1994.* Karlene Jones-Bley and Martin E. Huld, eds. *Journal of Indo-European Studies.* Monograph Series 17 (Washington, D. C.: Institute for the Study of Man, 1996), pp. 166–180 (with a good bibliography). This is an English version of his 1993 article written in Polish. The words are *sea, sail, steer, breeze, ebb, storm, tide, keel, cliff, strand, net, swim, dune, mast, reef, hoist, boat,* and a few others. An especially ardent defender of a pre-Germanic substrate is Mauritz Gysseling. He usually writes in Dutch, but at least one of his program articles is in German: "Substratwörter in den germanischen Sprachen," *NOWELE* 10 (1987): 47–62. The following is partly a response to Gysseling: Edgar C. Polomé, "Substrate Lexicon in Germanic," *NOWELE* 14 (1989): 53–73.

20. Johannes Hoops, "Alte *k*-Stämme unter den germanischen Baumnamen," *Indogermanische Forschungen* 14 (1903): 483–485.

21. John Loewenthal, "Zur germanischen Wortkunde," *Arkiv för nordisk filologi* 33 (1917): 109, no. 65.

22. John Cleland, *The Way to Things by Words, and to Words by Things; Being a Sketch of an Attempt at the Retrieval of the Antient Celtic, or Primitive Language of Europe . . .* (London: Printed for L. Davis and C. Reymers, 1766; reprinted in the series English Linguistics 1500–1800, No. 122, Menston: The Scolar Press, 1968).

23. London: Published for the author by N. Trübner and Co., 1887. Mackay was a knowledgeable scholar, and his other dictionaries have retained their value to this day. More's the pity he paid such a ludicrous tribute to a preconceived notion.

24. The literature on the Celtic element in English is vast. However, since the material is scanty (*iron, -rick, breeches, bannock,* and so forth), later works add relatively little to those published at an early date. Studies of Celtic words in English range from amateurish (for example, Otto von Knobelsdorff, *Die keltischen Bestandteile in der englischen Sprache* [Berlin: W. Weber 1870], which despite an appropriate epigraph from Goethe is a hotchpotch of old and late borrowings and of words going back to the common past) to serious and highly professional, such as James Hadley, "On Koch's Treatment of the Celtic Element in English," *Transactions of the American Philological Association* (1873): 30–43, and especially Max Förster, "Keltisches Wortgut im Englischen." In *Texte und Forschungen zur englischen Kulturgeschichte. Festgabe für Felix Liebermann zum 20. Juli 1921* (Halle: Max Niemeyer, 1921), pp. 119–242, published in the same year (Halle: Max Niemeyer) as a separate book. John Davies brought out a series of articles in the journal *Archaelogia Cambrensis.* They contain thousands of mainly dialectal words of presumably Celtic origin. There is no index. Davies's etymologies are usually outdated,

but his material is valuable, and his references to Cornish, Welsh, Irish Gaelic, and so on is based on an excellent knowledge of those languages. See "The Celtic Element of the English People," Part 2 (IV/11, [1880], pp. 10–24, 97–109), "Comparison of Celtic Words Found in Old English Literature and English Dialects with Modern Forms" (IV/12, [1881], pp. 81–109, 257–272; VI/13, [1882], pp. 1–18, 81–95, 243–64), "The Celtic Element in the Lancashire Dialect" (IV/14, [1883], pp. 1–13, 84–108), "The Celtic Element in the Dialects of the Counties adjoining Lancashire" (V/1, [1884], pp. 1–31, 105–28), and "The Celtic Element in the Dialectic Words of the Counties of Northampton and Leicester" (V/2, [1885], pp. 1–32, 81–96, 161–182). Of Davies's other works on the subject of English and Celtic, "The Celtic Languages in Relation to Other Aryan Tongues" is the most interesting: *Y Cymmrodor* 3, Part 1, [1880], pp. 1–51; 43 English words are discussed. An important old article is George S. Lane, "The Germano–Celtic Vocabulary," *Language* 9, [1933], pp. 244–264. It is devoted to the common stock. An active contributor to the problem of Germano–Celtic relations is Karl Horst Schmidt. See his articles "Keltisch und Germanisch." In *Das Germanische und die Rekonstruktion der indogermanischen Sprache: Akten des Freiburger Kolloquiums der Indogermanischen Gesellschaft, Freiburg, 26.–27. Februar 1981.* Jürgen Untermann and Bela Brogyanyi, eds. (Amsterdam, Philadelphia: John Benjamins, 1984), pp. 113–153; "Keltisch-germanische Isoglossen und ihre sprachgeschichtlichen Implikationen." In *Germanenprobleme in heutiger Sicht.* Heinrich Beck, ed. Ergänzungsbände zum Reallexikon der Germanischen Altertumskunde, vol. 1 (Berlin, New York: Walter de Gruyter, 1986), pp. 231–247, and "The Celts and the Ethnogenesis of the Germanic People," *Historische Sprachforschung / Historical Linguistics* 104 (1991): 129–147. A. Heiermeier's contribution "Zu den keltisch-germanischen Wortgleichungen. Gedanken zur Indoeuropäisierung Nordwesteuropas (1)." *Istituto Lombardo di Scienze e Lettere. Rendiconti. Classe di Lettere e Scienze Morali e Storiche* 85 (vol. 16 of the 3rd series (1952): 313–340 [the title of this periodical is usually given as *RIL*] is a welcome later discussion of Feist's ideas (see note 19), but it deals almost entirely with place names. A massive evaluation of English vocabulary has been undertaken by Mitsuhiho Ito in the Japanese journals *The Lark Hill: Toyohashi University of Technology. Bulletin of the School of Humanities and Social Engineering* ("Celtic Loanwords in English" 4 [1982], pp. 97–115; 8 [1986], pp. 1–30; 9 [1987], pp. 15–35; 10 [1988], pp. 27–38; 11 [1989], pp. 91–100) and *Journal of Foreign Language Institute* (11 [1987], pp. 97–117 and 12 [1988], pp. 101–112). Each article contains a semantic and etymological analysis of the words cited. Here, too, a cumulative index is absent.

25. For initial orientation see Alois Pogatscher, *Zur Lautlehre der griechischen, lateinischen und romanischen Lehnworte im Altenglischen.* Quellen und Forschungen zur Sprach- und Kulturgeschichte der germanischen Völker 64

(Strassburg: Karl J. Trübner, 1888); Otto Funke, *Die gelehrten lateinischen Lehn- und Fremdwörter in der altenglischen Literatur von der Mitte des X. Jahrhunderts bis um das Jahr 1066. . . .* (Halle a. S.: Max Niemeyer, 1914); Helmut Gneuss, *Lehnbildungen und Lehnbedeutungen im Altenglischen* (Berlin: Erich Schmidt, 1955), and Hugh MacGillivray, *The Influence of Christianity on the Vocabulary of Old English,* Studien zur englischen Philologie 8. (Halle [Saale]: Max Niemeyer, 1902).

26. See a detailed discussion of this thorny problem in Fritz Juengling, "The Origin of the English Pronoun *she.*" *Revista Italiana di Linguistica e di Dialettologia* 3 (2001): 129–151.

27. Scandinavian borrowings in English are a popular topic. The old book by Erik Björkman is excellent: *Scandinavian Loan-Words in Middle English* (Halle a. S.: Max Niemeyer, 1900; reprint Greenwood Press, New York, 1969). (I cannot resist the temptation of pointing out that *loan* is a borrowing from Scandinavian.) See also a popular exposition: John Geipel, *The Viking Legacy: The Scandinavian Influence on the English and Gaelic Languages* (Newton Abbot: David and Charles, 1971). For an idea of the influx of Scandinavian words into more northern dialects of Middle English, see the article by Erik Brate, "Nordische Lehnwörter im Ormulum," *Beiträge zur Geschichte der deutschen Sprache und Literatur* 10 (1885): 1–80. Of related interest is the dissertation by George T. Flom, *Scandinavian Influence on Southern Lowland Scotch: A Contribution to the Study of the Linguistic Relations on English and Scandinavian.* Diss. Columbia University. New York: [no indication of publisher]. Reprint New York: Columbia University Press, 1966. Another dissertation deals with the Scandinavian element in modern English dialects: Georg Xandry, *Das skandinavische Element in den neuenglischen Dialekten.* Diss. Münster i. W. Neu-Isenburg: August Koch, 1914. A useful dictionary is Per Thorson, *Anglo-Norse Studies: An Inquiry into the Scandinavian Elements in the Modern English Dialects,* Part 1 (Amsterdam: N. V. Swets and Zeitlinger, 1936). More references can be found in the books by Sibylle Hug, *Scandinavian Loanwords and their Equivalents in Middle English* (Bern, Frankfurt a.M.: Peter Lang, 1987); Susanne Kries, *Skandinavisch-schottische Sprachbeziehungen im Mittelalter: Der altnordische Lehneinfluss.* North-Western Language Evolution. Supplement, vol. 20, 2003; and Richard Dance, *Words Derived from Old Norse in Early Middle English: Studies in the Vocabulary of the South-Western Midland Texts.* Medieval and Renaissance Texts and Studies, vol. 246 (Tempe, Arizona: Arizona Center for Medieval and Renaissance Studies, 2003).

28. A dictionary of all doublets in English does not seem to exist. Axel Erdmann's work "Båda dubbelformerna härstamma från samma språk. 1. Engelskan" (Upsala Universitets Årsskrift 1882–1885, pp. 135–162) deals, as its title indicates, with doublets, both of which originated in English. It includes pairs like *borough ~ bury, dike ~ ditch, belly ~ bellows, shade ~ shadow,* and some

others that are cognates rather than doublets, for instance, *life ~ alive, drunk ~ drunken, year ~ yore*, and *swoop ~ sweep*. Erdmann also discusses doublets that go back to different dialectal forms of the same word (the *dint ~ dent, nib ~ neb, bond ~ band* type). Special rubrics are devoted to doublets that arose owing to consonantal variation *(fitch ~ vetch)*, differences in sentence stress *(off ~ of, too ~ to, also ~ as)*, the position of a word in a compound *(eye ~ dais-y, each ~ ever-y, moon ~ Mon-day, toad ~ tad-pole)*, apocope, syncope, aphesis, shortening, and analogy. By way of conclusion, he mentions words like *show ~ shew* and *born ~ borne* (homophones but not homographs).

29. J. F. Bense, *A Dictionary of the Low-Dutch Element in the English Vocabulary* (The Hague: Martin Nijhoff, 1939). It was published in installments, beginning in 1926. Four earlier books also deserve mention: W. de Hoog, *Studiën over de Nederlandsche en Engelsche Taal en Letterkunde en haar wederzijdschen invloed* (Dordrecht: J. P. Revers, 1909); T. de Vries, *Holland's Influence on English Language and Literature* (Chicago: C. Grentzebach, 1916); E. E. Llewellyn, *The Influence of Low Dutch on the English Vocabulary* (Oxford: Oxford University Press, 1936), and Johannes-Michael Toll, *Niederländisches Lehngut im Mittelenglischen. Ein Beitrag zur englischen Wortgeschichte mit Benutzung einer von Dr. O. Zippel handschriftlich hinterlassenen Materialsammlung.* Studien zur englischen Philologie 69 (Halle [Saale]: Max Niemeyer, 1926). The last-named book will interest a student of Modern English only insofar as the Middle English words featured in it are still extant. Lists of borrowings in all five books contain numerous rare, obsolete, and local words. G. N. Clark's work *The Dutch Influence on the English Vocabulary* (Oxford: Clarendon Press; London: Milford, 1935 [S.P.E. Tract 44, 161–72]), although published as a separate booklet, is an article that lays no claim to exhausting its material.

30. Works on borrowings in English make up a library. The best compendium of the subject is Mary S. Serjeantson, *A History of Foreign Words in English* (London: Routledge and Kegan Paul, 1935; reprint 1961 and 1962). Numerous monographs are devoted to the words of Greek, Latin, French, Arabic, and Chinese origin in Modern English, as well as to borrowings recorded in Old and Middle English and in almost each of the succeeding centuries. Karl Lokotsch's dictionary (*Etymologisches Wörterbuch der europäischen [germanischen, romanischen und slavischen] Wörter orientalischen Ursprungs.* Indogermanische Bibliothek I/2, 3 [Heidelberg: Carl Winter, 1927]) is arranged by etymon but has word indexes for every language; the English index is on pp. 192–196. Of the other dictionaries only one should be mentioned: Henry Yule and A. N. Burnell, *Hobson-Jobson: A Glossary of Colloquial Anglo-Indian Words and Phrases, and of Kindred Terms, Etymological, Historical, Geographical and Discursive* (London: J. Murray, 1903). 2nd ed. by William Crooke (Dehli: Munshiran Manoharlal, [1968]) (a wonderful and deservedly influential work).

Chapter Thirteen

1. κᾶλον.
2. Connie C. Eble, "Slang: Etymology, Folk Etymology, and Multiple Etymology," *The SECOL Review* 10 (1986): 10.
3. ὕλη.
4. The main books on English word formation are Herbert Koziol, *Handbuch der englischen Wortbildung*. Sammlung germanischer Lehr- und Handbücher I/21 (Heidelberg: Carl Winter, 1937), and Hans Marchand, *The Categories and Types of Present-Day English Word-Formation: A Synchronic-Diachronic Approach*, 2nd ed. (Munich: C. H. Beck). Less detailed are the books by Valerie Adams, *An Introduction to Modern English Word-formation* (London: Longman, 1973), and Laurie Bauer, *English Word-formation* (Cambridge: Cambridge University Press, 1983) (for practical purposes Chapter 7, pp. 201–241, is the most important). See also Osama Fukushima, ed., *An Etymological Dictionary of English Derivatives* (Yamanashi, Japan: Nihon Tosho Lib. Ltd., 1992), and an excellent bibliography: Gabriele Stein, *English Word-formation over Two Centuries. In Honour of Hans Marchand on the Occasion of His Sixty-Fifth Birthday, 1 October 1972* (Tübinger Beiträge zur Linguistik 34. Tübingen: Gunter Narr, 1975).
5. Henry Sweet, *The History of Language* (London: Richard Clay, 1900), pp. 77–78.

Chapter Fourteen

1. Throughout the book, I have refrained from citing my sources in passages of this type. It is taken for granted that the explanations, unless specified otherwise, have come from the best dictionaries. Skeat, the *Oxford English Dictionary, The Century Dictionary*, Weekley, and Wyld have been mentioned more than once. For the other Germanic languages I depended mainly on Sigmund Feist, *Vergleichendes Wörterbuch der gotischen Sprache*, 3rd ed. (Leiden: E. J. Brill, 1939), and 4th ed., by W. P. Lehmann (in English, under the title *A Gothic Etymological Dictionary . . . With bibliography prepared under the direction of Helen-Jo J. Hewitt) (Leiden: E. J. Brill, 1986); Friedrich Kluge, *Etymologisches Wörterbuch der deutschen Sprache*, 20th ed., by Walther Mitzka (Berlin: Walter de Gruyter & Co., 1967), and 24th ed., by Elmar Seebold (Berlin, New York: Walter de Gruyter, 2002); Hjalmar Falk [and] Alf Torp, *Norwegisch-dänisches etymologisches Wörterbuch* (Heidelberg: Carl Winter, 1910–1911). Reprinted as 2nd ed., by the same publisher in cooperation with Universitetsforlaget (Oslo, Bergen), 1960, and two dictionaries by Jan de Vries: *Nederlands etymologisch woordenboek* (Leiden: E. J. Brill, 1971), and *Altnordisches*

etymologisches Wörterbuch, 3rd ed. (Leiden: E. J. Brill, 1977). The following dictionaries of the Germanic languages have also been consulted regularly: Ferdinand Holthausen, *Altenglisches etymologisches Wörterbuch*, 3rd ed. (Heidelberg: Carl Winter, 1971; a reprint of the second edition, 1962); *Franck's Etymologisch Woordenboek der Nederlandsche Taal.* 2nd ed., by Nicolaas van Wijk. ('s-Gravenhage: Martinus Nijhoff, 1912). Supplement by Coenrad B. van Haeringen ('s-Gravenhage: Martinus Nijhoff, 1936). Reissued together by the same publisher in 1949; Alf Torp, *Nynorsk etymologisk ordbok* (Kristiania: Aschehoug, W. Nygaard, 1919; reprinted in Oslo by the same publisher, 1963); Elof Hellquist, *Svensk etymologisk ordbok,* 3rd ed. (Lund: C. W. K. Gleerup, 1948) (several later reprints); Niels Åge Nielsen, *Dansk etymologisk Ordbog. Ordens Historie,* 4th ed. Gyldendal, 1997; Ásgeir Blöndal Magnússon, *Íslensk orðsifjabók.* (Reykjavík: Orðabók Háskólans, 1989), and Jan ten Doornkaat Koolman, *Wörterbuch der ostfriesischen Sprache etymologisch bearbeitet* (Norden: Herm. Braams, 1879–1884; reprint Wiesbaden: Dr. Marin Sändig, 1965). Cf. notes 7–9 to Chapter 1.

2. Rasmus C. Rask, *Undersögelse om det gamle nordiske eller islandske sprogs oprindelse* . . . . (Kjöbenhavn: Gyldendal, 1818). English translation by Niels Ege: *Investigation of the Origin of the Old Norse or Icelandic Language* (Travaux du Cercle Linguistique de Copenhague 26 (Copenhagen, 1993). Jacob Grimm, *Deutsche Grammatik,* 2nd ed. (Göttingen: Dieterich, 1822–1837).

3. This is the opinion of N. S. Trubetzkoy, enthusiastically supported by some and vehemently rejected by others. See the most complete text of Trubetzkoy's article (1939) in his book *Studies in General Linguistics and Language Structure.* Edited, and with an introduction by Anatoly Liberman. Translated by Marvin Taylor and Anatoly Liberman (Durham and London: Duke University Press, 2001), pp. 87–98, 266.

4. See Friedrich Kluge, "Griechisch δέσποινα = angls. *fǣmne?" Indogermanische Forschungen* 39 (1921): 128–129. Regrettably, his opinion has not been accepted, though Jan de Vries (in the Icelandic dictionary, under *feima*) mentions it.

5. πλατύς.

6. βαίνειν.

7. Adolf Noreen, *Abriß der urgermanischen Lautlehre mit besonderer Rücksicht auf die nordischen Sprachen* (Strassburg: Karl J. Trübner, 1894), p. 54.

8. If even one of his characters had said so, Léon Vernier (*Étude sur Voltaire grammarien et la grammaire au XVIIIᵉ siècle* [Paris: Hachette, 1888, reprint Slatkine Reprints, Genève, 1970], pp. 59–64) would probably have quoted it. Voltaire did not shy at offering etymologies, some of them reasonable, others absurd. He traced too many French words to Gaul.

9. Karl Luick, *Historische Grammatik der englischen Sprache,* 2nd ed. (Stuttgart: Bernhard Tauchnitz, 1964), sec. 799, 1/c, and especially Wilhelm Horn, *Laut*

und Leben. Englische Lautgeschichte der neueren Zeit (1400–1950), edited by Martin Lehnert (Berlin: Deutscher Verlag der Wissenschaften, 1954), pp. 1001–1002.

10. L.-L. De Bo, *Westvlaamsch Idioticon,* edited by Joseph Samyn (Gent: Alfons Siffer, 1892).

11. For an especially rich collection of Germanic words related by secondary ablaut, see Leonard Bloomfield, "A Semasiological Differentiation in Germanic Secondary Ablaut," *Modern Philology* 7 (1909–1910): 245–288, 345–382. Also published in book form as Chicago dissertation (Chicago: Chicago University Press, 1909).

12. See the article by Alan S. C. Ross "Names of a Hare," *Proceedings of the Leeds Philosophical and Literary Society* 3 (1932–1935): 347–377.

13. πατήρ.

14. ψύλλα.

15. φιλολόγος, "Origin of the Change of 'Mary' into 'Polly,'" *Notes and Queries* (1850): 299.

Chapter Fifteen

1. A booklet by K. Ahlén (*Om betydelsens försämring och förbättring i äldre och nyare språk. Strödda anteckningar.* [Örebro: Bohlinska boktryckeriet, 1887]) is interesting in that it shows how similar changes (deterioration and amelioration of meaning) in various languages—from Classical Greek to Swedish—affect words of the same categories: the names of groups of people ("rabble"), villagers, outsiders, servants, mercenaries, young women, and so on. Historical semantics, as we have seen, needs such generalizations. Hindrik Schreuder wrote a detailed investigation of the deterioration of meaning in English, *Pejorative Sense Development in English I.* Diss. Amsterdam. Groningen: P. Noordhoff, 1929. In addition to an introductory part on general semantics, it contains chapters on the following subjects: social conditions and contrasts; national, political, ethnological, and racial relations and contrasts; religions and philosophical movements, legal and judicial usages (those are gathered in the part called "The Socio-Cultural Group"); the middle terms (words like *predicament, plight, bias, plot, design, apprehension, incense,* and so forth); and euphemism, irony, and frequent innuendo (*"The Ethic-Aesthetic Group"*). A word index and a detailed bibliography conclude the dissertation. An earlier German dissertation (Johannes Kollberg, *Beiträge zur Lehre vom Bedeutungswandel der Wörter im Englischen I.* Die Qualitätsverschlechterung einiger Wörter. Königsberg i. Pr. Diss. Königsberg: Hartung, 1904) is a collection of 12 word histories (*bedlam, churl, clown, cunning, demure, lewd, libertine, minion, pert, sad, silly,* and *wench*). There is a short introduction. The booklet

is 25 pages long. Kollberg (p. 7) also notes that in the life of words, cases of deterioration by far exceed the recorded cases of amelioration and quotes two statements to this effect by Horace and Samuel Johnson. The latter said: "Tongues like governments have a natural tendency to degeneration." An old work on the aforementioned tendency is interesting to read not only for the sake of its amusing title: Reinhold Bechstein, "Ein pessimistischer Zug in der Entwickelung der Wortbedeutungen," *Germania* (Wien) 8 (1863): 330–354. It contains 42 word histories. Bechstein's epithet *pessimistic* was noticed. Max Müller and Friedrich Schroeder wrote works with it in their titles. Highly recommended is the book by Grzeorz Kleparski, *Semantic Change and Componential Analysis; an Inquiry into Pejorative Developments in English.* Eichstätter Materialien. Schriftreihe der Katholischen Universität Eichstätt 9. Abteilung Sprache und Literatur 4 (Regensburg: Friedrich Pastet, 1986).

2. ἰδιώτης.

3. Now rarely used in this sense. The Modern German words for "boy" are *Junge* in the north and *Bub* in the south.

4. *Deutsches Wörterbuch von Jacob Grimm und Wilhelm Grimm,* vol. 1 (Leipzig: S. Hirzel, 1854), p. XLIX.

5. σπάθη.

6. νέμειν.

7. Karl Abel did not coin the German word *Gegensinn* (the opposite meaning) (literally "'gainst-sense"), but he was the first to study enantiosemy in detail. His essay "Über den Gegensinn der Urworte" (in his book *Sprachwissenschaftliche Abhandlungen* [Leipzig: Wilhelm Friedrich, 1885], pp. 313–367, also published as a separate pamphlet in 1884, but not included in his *Linguistic Essays* [London: Trübner, Boston: Houghton Mifflin,1883]) contained many examples from Egyptian and other old languages. I cannot judge their accuracy, but his examples from Indo-European (the list is given on pp. 348–352), except for the well-known Latin *altus* and *sacer,* are unconvincing or wrong. Abel did not distinguish between words like Engl. *let,* which combine opposite meanings because of phonetic change, words with a wide semantic range (for instance, when a modal verb means both "to have to" and "to be able to"), and real cases of enantiosemy. However, his idea caught and enjoyed special support in Swiss linguistics. Twenty years later, he brought out a revised and expanded version of his essay: *Über Gegensinn und Gegenlaut in den klassischen, germanischen und slavischen Sprachen 1* (Frankfurt am Main: Moritz Diesterweg, 1905) (no more published). Outside the German speaking area, Abel's works do not seem to have aroused much interest. The main proponent of Abel's idea was Manfred Szadrowsky. Cerutti (see below) lists his works, but one of them should be mentioned here, too. Although it has some of the drawbacks that characterize Abel's pioneering article and later book, it

contains a wealth of examples not to be found anywhere else: Manfred Szadrow-sky, "Gegensinn im Schweizerdeutschen," *Zeitschrift für Deutsche Mundarten* 19 (1924), Nos. 1-2 (= *Festschrift Albert Bachmann zu seinem sechzigsten Geburtstage am 12. November 1923, gewidmet von Freunden und Schülern)*, pp. 11–84, with an index (pp. 83–84) that summarizes his examination of the opposites (benediction and curse, clean and dirty, birth and death, and so on). Another book on this subject (general discussion, a good bibliography, and *Gegensinn* examined from every point of view on the material of English) is Ursula Cerutti, *Sinn und Gegensinn im Englischen* (Winterthur: P. G. Keller, 1957). See also Wolfgang Meid, "Über konträre Bedeutung. Bemerkungen zum sogenannten 'Gegensinn'," *Studia Celtica* 14–15 (1979–1980): 193–199 (examples from Germanic and Celtic) and Edna Aphek and Yishai Tobin, "Semantic Polarity and the Origin of Language" in Walburga von Raffler-Engler, Jan Wind and Abraham Jonker, eds., *Studies in Language Origins*. Vol. 2. Amsterdam, Philadelphia: John Benjamins (1991): 263–84 (their material is mainly Hebrew). Freud discovered Abel's early work years after it was published. He noted that prohibition does not exist in dreams and connected this phenomenon with enantiosemy. See Sigmund Freud, "Über den Gegensinn der Worte. Referat über die gleichnamige Broschüre von Karl Abel 1884," *Jahrbuch für psychoanalytische und psychopathologische Forschungen* 2 (1910): 179–184.

8. Carl D. Buck, *A Dictionary of Selected Synonyms in the Principal Indo-European Languages* . . . (Chicago: The University of Chicago Press, 1949). Reprinted by the same publisher in 1988. At one time, a special term, *onomasiology*, was used for this type of research (the names of objects, actions, and properties in different dialects and languages), which flourished roughly between 1880 and 1920.

9. Works on the change of meaning are numerous. Heinz Kronasser's classic *Handbuch der Semasiologie. Kurze Einführung in die Geschichte, Problematik und Terminologie der Bedeutungslehre* (Heidelberg: Carl Winter, 1952) has not diminished in value since it was published. However, book-length studies on the change of meaning in English are few. The earliest of them is Richard C. Trench, *A Select Glossary of English Words Used Formerly in Senses Different from the Present* (London: John W. Parker and Son, 1859) (this is the second edition, perhaps the second printing; I was unable to find, let alone consult, the first). The edition still in use is by A. Smythe Palmer (the author of *Folk-Etymology* and several other popular books on English words) with his additional notes (London: Routledge & Son, New York: E. P. Dutton, 1900) (several reprints). *Zum Bedeutungswandel englischer Wörter* by Ernst Max Müller (Freiberg: Gerlach, 1908), is a glossary of the same type as Trench's, but the entries are considerably shorter. J. Copley (*Shift of Meaning* [London: Oxford University Press, 1961]) explains in the preface: "Under each entry I

have attempted to trace, wherever possible, the progression of meaning from Elizabethan to modern times." See also note 1, above. Those interested in the diachronic aspect of semantics will find a survey in Chapter 2 of Elizabeth C. Traugott and Richard B. Dashler's book, *Regularity in Semantic Change* (New York: Cambridge University Press, 2002) ("Prior and Current Work on Semantic Change").

10. Schuchardt's main forum was *Zeitschrift für romanische Philologie,* published in Germany. Thomas's critiques appeared in the French journal *Romania.* The idea of exceptionless sound laws was formulated by German language historians called *Junggrammatiker* (translated into English as *Neogrammarians*), and Schuchardt fought it from the start. But in his defense from Thomas and counterattacks by him and his supporters, the feeling that the opposing forces are "the German school," with its almost idealistic emphasis on meaning, against "the French school," with its "positivist" adherence to sound correspondences, is unmistakable. This episode in the history of etymology is well known. A contemporary, and himself an eminent scholar, Ernst Tappolet gave one of the best summaries of the event in his article "Phonetik und Semantik in der etymologischen Forschung," *Archiv für das Studium der neueren Sprachen und Literaturen* 115 (1905): 101–123 (see especially pp. 112–120).

Chapter Sixteen

1. Theodor Curti, *Die Entstehung der Sprache durch Nachahmung des Schalles* (Stuttgart: E. Schweizerbart [E. Koch], 1885), p. 13. The translation is mine.
2. Sir Richard Paget, *Human Speech: Some Observations, Experiments, and Conclusions as to the Nature, Purpose and Possible Improvement of Human Speech* (London: Routledge & Kegan Paul, 1930; reprinted by the same publisher in 1963), pp. 133–134.
3. Alexander Jóhannesson, *Some Remarks on the Origin of the N-Sound.* Fylgirit Árbókar Háskólans 1953–1954 (Reykjavík: H. F. Leiftur), pp. 4–5.
4. Alexander Jóhannesson, *Um frumtungu indógermana og frumheimkyni.* Fylgir Árbók Háskóla Íslands 1940–1941 (Reykjavík: Gutenberg, 1943).
5. The quotations appear on pp. 9–11 of his work cited in note 3. His other books and essays with the same content are *Uppruni mannlegs máls* (Reykjavík: Íslenzkt bókmenntafélag, 1960); *Origin of Language: Four Essays* (Reykjavík: H. F. Leiftur, 1949); *Gestural Origin of Language: Evidence from Six "Unrelated" Languages* (Reykjavík: H. F. Leiftur, 1952); *How did Homo Sapiens Express the Idea of Flat?* Fylgirit Árbókar Háskólans 1957–1958 (Reykjavík: H. F. Leiftur, 1958), and *The Third Stage in the Creation of Human Language* (Reykjavík: H. F. Leiftur, Oxford: B. H. Blackwell, 1963). (The "third stage" is gestural; all these books are variations on the same theme.)
6. *Human Speech . . . ,* as in note 2, p. 159.

7. C. Täuber, "Die Ursprache und ihre Entwicklung," *Globus* 97 (1910): 277–282.
8. C. Täuber, *Ortsnamen und Sprachwissenschaft, Ursprache und Begriffsent-wicklung* (Zürich: Verlag Art. Institut Orell Füssli, 1908).
9. "Die Ursprache . . . ," as in note 7, p. 281.
10. Some language historians try to combine sound symbolism and onomatopoeia with gestural theory. Here is a typical example from a book by Eduard Rossi, *Die Entstehung der Sprache und des menschlichen Geistes* (Munich, Basel: Ernst Reinhardt, 1962), p. 129. He does not refer to Paget or Jóhannesson and probably does not consider himself to be their follower, but some similarity between them is apparent: *to-, ta* (that): "The tongue moves through the mouth and shows the way to chewing and to the outside world in the same way"; *dhem-, dhema-* (to smoke; to steam): "breath imitates steam." Side by side with such pronouncements, we find the following: "The consonant *b* can be pronounced with different intensity. The air can therefore be emitted almost inaudibly, softly, in a gentle or strong puff, slowly or energetically. For that reason, the meanings of *b* vary considerably. It is articulated as an explosive sound in *Backe* (cheek) and *Ball* (ball); hence their meaning. By contrast, in *bar* (pure, utter, absolute), *beben* (to shake, tremble), *Bote* (messenger), and *Buße* (repentance), it is pronounced with a long *h* that gently trails off into silence, thus imparting an entirely different sense to all these words" (p. 128). (The translation is mine, and the English glosses have been added.) In the end, Rossi finds that sound and meaning are in perfect harmony in German words.
11. Jan N. Baudouin de Courtenay, *Vermenschlichung der Sprache*. Ein Aula-Vortrag, gehalten zu Dorpat am (19 Feb.) 2. März, 1892. Sammlung gemein-verständlicher wissenschaftlicher Vorträge. NF 8 (Hamburg: T. F. Richter, 1893). According to Baudouin de Courtenay, the fronting of sounds is only one of many features characterizing the "humanization" of language.
12. Callistus Augustus Count de Goddes-Liancourt and Frederick Pincott, *Primitive and Universal Laws of the Formation and Development of Language: A Rational and Inductive System Founded on the Natural Basis of Onomatops* (London: Wm. H. Allen, 1874), p. 94.
13. Ibidem, pp. 94 and 131.
14. Alexander Murray, *History of the European Languages* (Edinburgh: A. Constable, 1822).
15. D. P. Martynov, *Raskrytie tainy iazyka chelovecheskogo i oblichenie nesostoiatel'nosti uchenogo iazykoznaniia* (Moscow: M. G. Volchaninov, 1897).
16. From Roman Jakobson's note to Trubetzkoy's letter of November 6, 1924. *N. S. Trubetzkoy's Letters and Notes*. Prepared for publication by Roman Jakobson with the assistance of H. Baran, O. Ronen, and Martha Taylor (The Hague, Paris: Mouton), pp. 74–75, note 5.
17. Ibid.
18. Anton von Velics, *Über Ursprung und Urbedeutung der Wörter* (Budapest: Eigenthum des Autors, 1904).

19. Walter Whiter, *Etymologicon Universale* . . . 3 volumes (Cambridge: At the University Press for Richard Priestley, 1822–1825).

20. August Fick, *Wörterbuch der indogermanischen Grundsprache in ihrem Bestande vor der Völkertrennung. Ein sprachgeschichtlicher Versuch* (Göttingen: Vandenhoeck & Ruprecht, 1868).

21. August Fick, *Vergleichendes Wörterbuch der indogermanischen Sprachen. Ein sprachgeschichtlicher Versuch.* 3rd ed. (Göttingen: Vandenhoeck & Ruprecht, 1891–1909).

22. ἑπτά.

23. Alois Walde, *Vergleichendes Wörterbuch der indogermanischen Sprachen.* Julius Pokorny, ed. (Berlin: Walter de Gruyter, 1927–1932; reprint 1973).

24. Julius Pokorny, *Indogermanisches etymologisches Wörterbuch* (Bern and Munich: Francke, 1959).

25. Walter W. Skeat, *An Etymological Dictionary of the English Language* (Oxford: Clarendon Press, 1882), p. xxii.

26. Per Persson, *Studien zur Lehre von Wurzelerweiterung und Wurzelvariation* (Upsala Universitets Årsskrift 1891. Upsala: Akademiska bokhandeln, 1891).

27. See the reviews of Persson's book by Christian Bartholomae *(Wochenschrift für klassische Philologie* 9 [1892]: 395–397) and Antoine Meillet (*Revue critique d'histoire et de littérature* 56 (N.S. 33) [1892]: 483–485.

28. Per Persson, *Beiträge zur indogermanischen Wortforschung.* Skrifter utg. av Kungl. humanistiska vetenskaps-samfundet i Upsala, 12:1, 2 (Uppsala: K. W. Appelbergs boktryckeri, 1912).

29. The question about the role of enlargements is one of the most controversial in Indo-European etymology. Most researchers follow Persson and Walde-Pokorny. But I am not alone in my dissent. See the statements by eminent scholars, who, in the wake of Persson's earliest critics, voiced objections to his procedures, in my paper "The Changing Models of Etymology" in *Modelli recenti in linguistica. Atti del Convegno della Società Italiana di Glottologia, Macerata, 26–28 ottobre 2000.* Daniele Maggi and Diego Poli, eds. (Rome: Il Calamo, 2003), pp. 11–40 (discussion: pp. 19–28 and 39–40; the statements by Herman Lommel, E. J. Thomas, Manu Leumann, Jürgen Untermann, Bernhard Rosenkranz, and F. de Tollenaere, spanning the period 1915–1997: pp. 29–32).

30. Karl Jaberg, "Sinn und Unsinn, Klang und Rhythmus." In his *Sprachwissenschaftliche Forschungen und Erlebnisse. Neue Folge.* S. Heinimann, ed., Romanica Helvetica, 75 (Bern: Francke, 1965): 25, note 2, continued on p. 26.

Chapter Seventeen

1. Hans Aarsleff, "The Study and Use of Etymology in Leibnitz." In *Akten des Internationalen Leibnitz-Kongresses, Hannover, 14.–16. November 1966.* Vol.

3: *Erkenntnislehre, Logik, Sprachphilosophie, Editionsberichte.* Studia Leibnitiana Supplementa. 3 (Wiesbaden: Franz Steiner, 1969), p. 183. The article (pp. 173–189) is an excellent account of Leibnitz's etymological thinking in the context of his time.
2. ὅλος.
3. Gilles Ménage [a.k.a. Menagius], *Les origines de la langue françoise* (Paris: J. Annisson. 1650); 2nd ed.: *Dictionnaire étymologique ou les origins de la langue françoise* (Paris: Briasson; reprinted in 1750. A modern facsimile reprint Geneva: Slatkine Reprints, 1973).
4. See a brief assessment of Ménage's contribution to Romance philology in the article by Francis Bar, "La méthode étymologique de Ménage," *Cahiers de l'Association Internationale des Études Françaises* 11 (1959): 265–272.
5. On Leibnitz as an etymologist see Aarsleff's article, mentioned in note 1, John T. Waterman, "G. W. Leibniz: A Seventeenth-Century Etymologist." In *Linguistic and Literary Studies in Honor of Archibald A. Hill,* Vol. 1. Mohammad Ali Jazayery, Edgar C. Polomé, [and] Werner Winter, eds. (Lisse: Peter de Ridder, 1976), pp. 399–406, and L. Ness, *Gottfried Wilhelm Leibnitz als Sprachforscher und Etymologe.* Beilage zum Programm des Großherzoglichen Lyceums zu Heidelberg 1870 and 1871, Vol. 2, pp. 39–53 (Heidelberg: A. H. Avenarius, 1870 [vol. 1] and 1871 [vol. 2]). Each volume has its own pagination. The entire work runs to about one hundred pages and can still be recommended as a first introduction to the subject. Ness did not join the merry chorus of Ménage's denigrators but highlighted, though in passing, his achievements (vol. 1, pp. 12–13; vol. 2, p. 46). The most detailed recent works on Leibnitz's etymological views I have consulted are Renate E. Buerner, *G. W. Leibniz' Collectanea Etymologica. Ein Beitrag zur Geschichte der Etymologie* (Diss. University of Southern California, 1971, unpublished), and Sigrid von der Schulenburg, *Leibniz als Sprachforscher,* Veröffentlichungen des Leibniz-Archivs 4 (Frankfurt am Main: Klostermann, 1973).
6. Cornelius Kilianus, *Etymologicum teutonicæ linguæ....* (Antverpiæ: Ex Officina Plantiana, apud Joannem Meretrum; reprint Traiecti Batavorum: Apud Roelandum de Meyere, 1777. A modern reprint Amsterdam: Adolf M. Hakkert, 1972).
7. John Minsheu, *Ductor in Linguas . . . / Guide into Tongues.* London: Published by the author, 1617. Reprinted with *Vocabularium Hispanicolatinum. A Most Copious Spanish Dictionary.* Introduction by Jürgen Schäfer. Scholars' Facsimiles & Reprints 321. Delmar, New York, 1978. The second edition of *Ductor in Linguas...* (London: John Haviland) appeared in 1627.
8. Stephen Skinner, *Etymologicum Linguæ Anglicanæ. . . .* (Londini: Typis T. Roycroft . . ., 1671; reprint Los Angeles: Sherwin & Freutel, 1970).
9. Andreas Helvigius, *Originum Dictionum Germanicorum. . . .* (Hanoviæ: Impensis Conradi Eifridi, 1620). This dictionary has not been reprinted, and the extant copies of it are rare.

10. Anonymous, *Gazophylacium Anglicanum: Containing the Derivation of English Words.* . . . (London: Printed by E. H. and W. H., 1689; reprint Menston: The Scolar Press, 1969). English Linguistics 1500–1800. A Collection of Facsimile Reprints Selected and Edited by R. C. Alston, 166. *Gazophylacium* means "treasure trove."

11. William Somner, *Dictionarium Saxonico-Latino-Anglicum* . . . (Oxonii: Excudebat Gvliel. Hall pro Authore, 1659; reprint Menston, England: The Scolar Press, 1970). English Linguistics 1500–1800. A Collection of Facsimile Reprints Selected and Edited by R. C. Alston, 247.

12. Franciscus Junius, *Etymologicum Anglicanum.* . . . (Oxonii: E Theatro Sheldoniano, 1743; reprint Los Angeles: Sherwin & Freutel, 1970); George W. Lemon, *English Etymology; or, A Derivative Dictionary of the English Language: In Two Alphabets, Tracing the Etymology of those English Words, that are Derived I. From the Greek, and Latin Languages; II. From the Saxon, and other Northern Tongues.* The whole compiled from Vossius, Meric Casaubon, Spelman, Somner, Junius, Skinner, Verstegan, Ray, Nugent, Upton. Cleland, and other Etymologists (London: Printed for G. Robinson, 1783).—Not all the names in the subtitle belong to "etymologists," but all the philologists he mentioned said something about the history of words. In the present overview, one of them (in addition to those already familiar) should not be overlooked: Meric Casaubon, the author of *De Lingua Hebraica et De Lingua Saxonica* (Londini: Typis J. Flesher, 1650. No modern reprint).

13. Johann Wachter, *Glossarium Germanicum.* . . . (Lipsiæ: Apud Joh. Frid. Gleditschii B. Filium; reprint Hildesheim, NY: G. Olm, 1975).

14. Johan Ihre, *Glossarium Suiogothicum.* . . . (Upsaliæ: Typis Edmannianis).

15. For a long time his dictionary of Old English was the only updated source of information on this language (Somner, like Casaubon—see note 11—was published in 1650). Edward [Edvardvus] Lye, *Dictionarium Saxonico et Gothico-Latinum,* edited by Owen Manning (Londini: B. White, 1772).

16. Walter W. Skeat, *An Etymological Dictionary of the English Language* (Oxford: Clarendon Press, 1882; 2nd ed., 1884, 3rd ed, 1897; 4th ed., 1910; reprint 1963). Friedrich Kluge, *Etymologisches Wörterbuch der deutschen Sprache* (Straßburg: Karl J. Trübner, 1883). Numerous editions and reworkings, the latest (24th) to date by Elmar Seebold (Berlin, New York: Walter de Gruyter, 2003).

17. Hensleigh Wedgwood, *A Dictionary of English Etymology* (London: Trübner & Co., 1859–1865. 2nd ed., 1872; 3rd ed. 1888).

18. Here is the title of a typical article by Wedgwood out of 116 I have in my database: "On Words Admitting of Being Grouped around the Root *flap* or *flak,*" *Proceedings of the Philological Society* 6 (1852–1853): 143–152.

19. The same title as in note 17 (New York: Sheldon and Co.; Boston, MA: Gould and Lincoln, 1862).

20. London: Trübner, 1882.
21. Walter W. Skeat, *A Student's Pastime*... (Oxford: Clarendon Press, 1901), pp. xxxvi and xxxvii).
22. Eduard Mueller, *Etymologisches Wörterbuch der englischen Sprache* (Coethen: Paul Schettler, 1865–1867; 2nd ed., 1878).
23. Walter W. Skeat (as in note 21), p. xxxviii.
24. Alfred J. Wyatt in *The Cambridge Review, a Journal of University Life and Thought* 34 (1913–1914): 15, here quoted from Arthur Sherbo, "Walter William Skeat (1835–1912) in the Cambridge Review." *The Yearbook of Langland Studies* (Published by Colleagues Press in Association with The College of Arts and Letters, Michigan State University), 3 (1989): 111–112.
25. Everyone who has written about Skeat is heavily indebted to this introduction. See, for example, A. Schröer, "Walter William Skeat. 21. November 1835-6. Oktober 1912," *Englische Studien* 46 (1912–1913): 163–175. Schröer knew Skeat personally and tried to draw a verbal portrait of the deceased man. He also included two unpublished poems by Skeat—"A Life-time's Work" and "In Honorem F. J. F[urnivall] (A. D. 1900)"—and a poem "In memory of Walter William Skeat. . . ." by his daughter Bertha M. Skeat. Jo MacMurthy devoted an informative chapter to Skeat in her book *English Language, English Literature: The Creation of an Academic Discipline* (Hamden, CT: Archon Books, 1985), pp. 136–166. Skeat's inaugural lecture "On the Study of Anglo-Saxon," delivered in the Senate-house, Cambridge, on October 21, 1878, was published in *MacMillan's Magazine* 39 (1879): 304–313. He would celebrate his forty-fourth birthday in a month and had almost exactly thirty-four years to live (he died on October 6, 1912). Skeat was a dedicated student of English dialects. W. A. Craigie touches briefly on this side of his activities in the obituary "The Late Rev. Professor W. W. Skeat, Litt. D., LLD., D. C. L., Ph.D and the Late Henry Sweet, M.A., Ph. D, Vice-Presidents of the Society," *Transactions of the Yorkshire Dialect Society* 2, Part 14 (1913): 16–17. See also R. S., "The Roots of Language and Professor Skeat," *The Academy* 57 (1899): 63–64 (it reproduces Skeat's picture "From the Copyright Service of Portraits of Contributors to the 'Encyclopædia Britannica'," in the usual style of this collection: a scholar at his desk, quill in hand), and Anonymous, "Walter William Skeat" (an obituary: "Taken ill on 29 September Prof. Skeat passed in the night between Sunday and Monday last in his seventy-seventh year."), *Notes and Queries,* Series 11, vol. vi, pp. 299–300). One can see a variant of the same portrait in Eilert Ekwall's discussion of Skeat as a student of names ("Walter William Skeat [1835–1912]," *Onoma* 5 [1954]: 45–48.)
26. "*The Hawk* (1867) at Ringwood in Hampshire . . . was a monthly publication meant to run for one year only, and its circulation must have been small." Skeat contributed a poem and several prose pieces to it. See Bernard Jones, "William Barnes, the Philological Society up to 1873 and the *New English*

Dictionary." In *Speech Past and Present: Studies in English Dialectology in Memory of Ossi Ihalainen* (Frankfurt am Main: Peter Lang. Europäischer Verlag der Wissenschaften, 1996), p. 91.

27. Only some of them have been collected in *A Student's Pastime* and *Notes on English Etymology* (Oxford: Clarendon Press, 1901).
28. *A Student's Pastime,* as in note 21, p. lvi.
29. Laurence Urdang, "The (invariably) Right Reverend Walter W. Skeat," *Verbatim* 18, No. 1 (1991): 16.
30. Bernard Jones (as in note 26) makes this point (pp. 92 and 97) in discussing Skeat's late neglect of William Barnes. Barnes's main contribution to etymology is his book *TIW; or a View of the Roots and Stems of the English as a Teutonic Tongue* (London: John Russell Smith, 1862). Jones (p. 90) says: ". . . it does not follow that some of the speculative ideas of *TIW* were unworthy of serious thought by members of the [Philological] Society. It is likely that it was as far beyond them as Barnes's suggestions for the 'Language of the Stone Age'." This may be true, but it should be said in all fairness that Barnes's roots are mythic from beginning to end and are no more useful than Täuber's or Marr's. On the meaning of *TIW* see p. 176, above.
31. James A. H. Murray, "Cockney," *The Academy* 37 (1890): 320–321.
32. All three letters appeared in *Notes and Queries* for 1899 (9th series, vol. IV), on pp. 226, 310 (C. C. B.), and 274 (Murray).
33. *A Student's Pastime,* as in note 21, pp. xlviii –xlix.
34. Wyatt (see note 24) wrote in the obituary: "He was not a great original genius; he was a great popularizer (in the best sense) in a field of knowledge almost unexplored by his countrymen before." Also, the author of an unsigned obituary, in the same issue of *The Cambridge Review,* says: "Skeat's mind was not perhaps of a strictly brilliant and original type; but the kind of work which he chose for himself is one which is preeminently necessary and useful" (quoted by Sherbo on p. 113). Some others have been equally deferential but condescending.
35. The main ones are as follows: Ferdinand Holthausen, *Etymologisches Wörterbuch der englischen Sprache* (Leipzig: Bernard Tauchnitz, 1917. 2nd ed., 1927; 3rd ed., 1949) (extremely brief entries, often shorter than, for example, those in *Webster's Collegiate Dictionary*; of limited use, and only for a beginner who prefers to be introduced to English etymology in German); Ernest Weekley, *An Etymological Dictionary of Modern English* (London: John Murray, 1921; reprint New York: Dover, 1967), and *A Concise Etymological Dictionary of Modern English* (London: John Murray, 1924; reprint New York: E. P. Dutton, 1953); Joseph T. Shipley, *Dictionary of Word Origins.* The Philosophical Library, 3 (New York: Greenwood Press, 1945, 2nd ed., 1969) (a misleading ramble among English words); Eric Partridge, *Origins: A Short Etymological Dictionary of Modern English* (London: Routledge & Kegan

Paul, 1958. 2nd ed., 1966) (chaotic and uninformed); Ernst Klein, *A Comprehensive Etymological Dictionary of the English Language* (Amsterdam: Elsevier Publishing Company) (fine cover, excellent paper); Robert K. Barnhart, ed., *The Barnhart Dictionary of Etymology* (H. W. Wilson Company, 1988) (unoriginal); T. F. Hoad, ed., *The Concise Oxford Dictionary of English* (Oxford: Clarendon Press, 1988) (of the same type as Holthausen's and much more condensed than Skeat's "epitomes"); John Ayto, *Dictionary of Word Origins* (New York: Arcade Publishing. Little, Brown and Company, 1990; first American edition, 1991) (entries in the style of word histories); Robert K. Barnhart, ed., *The Barnhart Concise Dictionary of Etymology* (New York: HarperCollins, 1995). For more information see my article "An Annotated Survey of English Etymological Dictionaries and Glossaries," *Dictionaries* 19 (1998): 21–96. Titles containing the words *etymological dictionary* are often misnomers, because the books in question may turn out to be dictionaries with etymologies added. In this sense, almost all modern English dictionaries are "etymological." The baleful tradition of abusing the word *etymological* seems to have begun with Nathan Bailey (see note 4 to Chapter 1). The latest misnomer to date is *The Kenkyusha Dictionary of English Etymology* (Kenkyusha Limited, 1997) (a particularly misleading title).

36. *The Century Dictionary: An Encyclopedic Dictionary of the English Language.* William Dwight Whitney, ed. (New York: The Century Co., 1889–1911. Revised by Benjamin E. Smith, 1911). *The Universal Dictionary of the English Language.* Henry Cecil Wyld, ed. (London: Routledge & Kegan Paul, 1932).
37. Joseph Taylor, *Antiquitates Curiosæ: The Etymology of Many Remarkable & Old Sayings, Proverbs, and Singular Customs* (London: Printed for T. and J. Allman, 1818; reprint New York: S. Wood, 1820).
38. New York: E. P. Dutton, 1948, p. 9.
39. But even then a valuable anthology like *Etymologie.* Rüdiger Schmitt, ed. Wege der Forschung, 373 (Darmstadt: Wissenschaftliche Buchgesellschaft, 1977) (18 articles) could appear, though I doubt that its English counterpart would have found a publisher in the United States.
40. See a somewhat different appraisal of the field in Yakov Malkiel, *Etymology* (New York: Cambridge University Press, 1993), pp. 134–145.

Chapter Eighteen

1. N. N. Amosova, *Etimologicheskie osnovy slovarnogo sostava sovremennogo angliiskogo iazyka* (Moscow: Izdatel'stvo literatury na inostrannykh iazykakh, 1956).
2. Paul Bacquert, *L'étymologie anglaise* (Paris: Presses Universitaires de France, 1976) (the object of etymology, the history of English vowels and consonants,

the sources of English, a few word histories), and Jean-Jacques Blanchat, *L'étymologie anglaise* (Paris: Presses Universitaires de France, 1995) (in addition to the usual things, more is said about the history and methods of etymology). Although these books have the same title and are part of the same series, they are different in their approach to and treatment of the material, except that both are meant as introductory texts for students with an interest in English historical lexicology.

3. Alan S. C. Ross, *Etymology: With Especial Reference to English* (London: Deutsch, 1969) (learned; good examples, but in places unnecessarily complicated); William B. Lockwood, *An Informal Introduction to English Etymology* (Washington: Minerva Press, 1995) (the sources of English, interesting word histories; some of them—as is also the case with Ross—are based on the author's research); Gary Bevington, *Where Do Words Come From? An Introduction to Etymology* (Dubuque, IA: Kendall / Hunt, 1995). Bevington says: "When I began teaching introductory linguistics to undergraduates 25 years ago, I introduced each course (as I still do) by asking the students what they thought the course ought to be about. By far, the most common answer was the title of this book or a paraphrase thereof. . . . In beginning with etymology, I am able to show students that their natural curiosity about language is justified and that the questions they want to address are real and important" (p. v).

4. For example, James B. Greenough and George L. Kittredge, *Words and Their Ways in English Speech* (New York: Macmillan, 1901; reprint Boston: Beacon Press, 1962), and Vittore Pisani, *Lezioni sul lessico inglese* (Brescia: Paideia, 1968).

Index of English Words

Name Index

including personal, fictional, mythological, and place names and
the titles of books mentioned in the main text

Subject Index